The
Black Aesthetic

The
Black Aesthetic

edited by
ADDISON GAYLE, JR.

DOUBLEDAY & COMPANY, INC.
GARDEN CITY, NEW YORK 1971

IN MEMORIAM: FOR MY FATHER

*"Let the martial songs be written, let the dirges disappear.
Let a race of men now rise and take control."*

Margaret Walker

CONTENTS

Introduction xv

I THEORY

INTRODUCTION

A new note, discernible even to the most biased observer, was
sounded in the art of black people during the nineteen fifties
and sixties. "I will go on judging and elucidating novels and
plays and poetry by Negroes according to what general powers
I possess," writes Richard Gilman, "but the kind of Negro *writing*
I have been talking about, the act of creation of the self in
the face of the self's historic denial by our society, seems to me
to be at this point beyond my right to intrude."

Some critics, less amenable to conversion than Gilman, would
have us believe that only two elements separate the present-day
black artist from his forerunner. One such element is anger!
". . . Negro writers are demonstrating the responsibility of the
artist to the disciplines and traditions of art and literature . . . ,"
writes Herbert Hill; "simple protest and anger are not enough
and rhetoric will not be useful in masking the inadequacies of
literary craftsmanship." The other is black nationalism, which,
according to Robert Bone, "for all its militancy is politically
Utopian."

The element of black anger is neither new nor, as Herbert Hill
would have us believe, passé. The black artist in the American
society who creates without interjecting a note of anger is creat-

ing not as a black man, but as an American. For anger in black art is as old as the first utterances by black men on American soil:

> "If I had-a my way,
> I'd tear this building down
> Great God, then, if I had-a my way
> If I had-a my way, little children
> If I had-a my way,
> I'd tear this building down. . . ."

As old as Frances Ellen Watkins, who made one demand of her undertaker:

> "I ask no monument, proud and high
> To arrest the gaze of the passer-by,
> All that my yearning spirit craves
> Is bury me not in a land of slaves."

Nowhere does anger reach more intensive expression than in DuBois, who strikes a note that has found accord in the breast of contemporary black artists:

> "I hate them, oh!
> I hate them well,
> I hate them, Christ!
> As I hate hell!
> If I were God,
> I'd sound their knell
> This day."

Neither is black nationalism a new element in black life or black art. In 1836, ". . . some of the delegates [at the National Negro Convention]," writes Philip S. Foner, "were convinced that Canadian colonization was still the most urgent business at hand. Others felt that it was necessary to concentrate upon building a better social order in the United States. . . . One group doubted the efficacy of associating with any set of white abolitionists, and advocated restricting the convention to Negro membership. Another, convinced of the inability to achieve equality for Negroes in existing institutions, favored continuing the establishment of separate schools and churches for the Negro people." This sentiment reaches dramatic form in the fiction of Martin Delaney, *Blake, or the Huts of America* (1859); Sutton Griggs, *Imperium in Imperio* (1899); and DuBois, *Dark Princess* (1928).

Again, animosity against the inept, sterile critiques of American academicians—so prevalent in black critical writings today— is not new. As early as 1900, Pauline Hopkins realized that art was ". . . of great value to any people as a preserver of manners and customs—religious, political, and social. It is a record of growth and development from generation to generation. No one will do this for us; we must ourselves develop the men and women who will faithfully portray the inmost thoughts and feelings of the Negro with all the fire and romance which lie dormant in our history. . . ." Twenty-two years later, William Pickens was more direct: "It is not simply that the white story teller will not do full justice to the humanity of the black race; *he cannot.*" William Stanley Braithwaite, an American critic in every essential, quotes from an article in the *Independent Magazine* (1925): "The white writer seems to stand baffled before the enigma, and so he expends all his energies on dialect and in general on the Negro's minstrel characteristics. . . . We shall have to look to the Negro himself to go all the way. It is quite likely that no white man can do it. *It is reasonable to suppose that his white psychology will get in the way.*" (Italics mine)

Nevertheless, there is a discernible element in black art today that is new, and Hoyt W. Fuller has come closest to pointing it out: "The Negro revolt is as palpable in letters as it is in the streets." Change revolt to war, and the characteristics that distinguish the old art from the new are readily apparent. The serious black artist of today is at war with the American society

as few have been throughout American history. Too often, as
Richard Wright noted, the black (artists) ". . . entered the
court of American public opinion dressed in the knee pants of
servility, curtsying to show that the Negro was not inferior, that
he was human, and that he had a life comparable to other
people." They waged war not against the society but against the
societal laws and mores that barred *them* from equal membership. They were, in the main, anxious to become Americans, to
share in the fruits of the country's economic system and to
surrender their history and culture to a universal melting pot.
They were men of another era who believed in the American
dream more fervently than their white contemporaries. They
saw the nation as a land of innocence, young enough to hold
out promises of maturing into a nation of freedom, justice, and
equality. The days of innocence have passed. The child has
become the adult, and instead of improving with age, she has
grown increasingly worse. Yesterday America was evil personified in her youth; today she is evil personified in adulthood.

The dimensions of the black artist's war against the society
are highly visible. At the core of black art in the past was a
vendetta against the South. The black novel, from William Wells
Brown to Richard Wright, was concerned primarily with southern tyranny and injustice. Often the North escaped with no more
than a rap on the knuckles. "Northern white people," wrote
James Weldon Johnson in *The Autobiography of an Ex-Coloured
Man* (1912), "love the Negro in a sort of abstract way, as a
race; through a sense of justice, charity, and philanthropy, they
will liberally assist in his elevation. . . ."

With the exception of writers such as Dunbar and Chesnutt,
who viewed the black man's exodus from South to North as an
exchange of one hell for another, black writers spoke of the
North as the new Canaan, of northern whites as a different
breed of man from their southern counterparts. Is it any wonder
that black people, falling sway to increasing southern tyranny,
began, in 1917, the exodus that swelled the urban areas of
America in the sixties and seventies?

"I've seen them come dark/wondering/wide-eyed/dreaming/ out of Penn Station . . . ," writes Langston Hughes, "but the trains are late. The gates open/but there're bars/at each gate." The bars were erected by northern, not southern, whites. Black people had run away from white terrorism in Savannah in 1904 and Atlanta in 1906, only to experience white terrorism in Ohio in 1904, Illinois in 1908, and New York in 1935. The evenhanded treatment of blacks North and South made little imprint upon Negro leaders who, then as now, were more willing to combat injustices down south than up north.

The task of pointing out northern duplicity was left to the black artist, and no writer was more effective in this undertaking than Richard Wright. When Wright placed Bigger Thomas and Mr. Dalton in a northern setting and pointed up the fact that Bigger's condition resulted from Dalton's hypocrisy, he opened a Pandora's box of problems for white liberals and Negro leaders, neither of whom could bring themselves to share his vision. Dalton is a white liberal philanthropist who, although donating money to "Negro uplift organizations," owns the slums in which Bigger Thomas is forced to live. His control of the young black man is more despotic than that of the southern plantation owner over blacks in the South: for him, the weapons of control are economic, social, and political.

He is more sagacious and dishonest than his southern counterpart; he has discovered a way to "keep the nigger in his place" without such aids as signs and restrictive covenants. He has constructed a cosmology that allows him to pose as a humanitarian on the one hand, while he sets about defining the black man's limitations on the other. His most cherished symbol of the black man is Uncle Tom; and he remains enamored of Nigger Jim, the black everyboy toward whom he feels paternalistic. Like Theodore Gross, he is able to share with Joel Chandler Harris ". . . the fears, laughter, and anger of the Negro"; and he is equally convinced with Gross that Harris ". . . contributed the most popular Negro characters to American fiction—Uncle

Remus, Balaam, Ananias, and Mingo . . ."—characters whom
he, too, believes to be representative of the race.

Thomas Nelson Page, Thomas Dixon, and Hinton Helper
might create, for Southerners, the image of the black man as
". . . a degenerate, inferior, irresponsible, and bestial creature
'transformed by the exigency of war from a chattel to be bought
and sold into a possible beast to be feared and guarded.'" Dalton,
however, will not accept this image. Such portraits of black men
disturb his humanitarian (read sexual) ideal of the black man.
"In an effort to make Hell endurable," Robert Bone writes of
James Baldwin, "Baldwin attempts to spiritualize his sexual
rebellion. Subjectively, I have no doubt, he is convinced that he
has found God. Not the white God of his black father, but a
darker deity who dwells in the heart of carnal mystery. . . .
The stranger the sex partner, the better the orgasm, for it
violates a stronger taboo." Bone's inability to come to grips with
the sexual aspects of Baldwin's novels, reveals more about Bone
than it does about Baldwin.

At the least, it reveals a great deal about the Daltons of the
North. In order to protect the Marys of the earth (Dalton's
daughter in *Native Son*), they have defined the black man
in the most negative terms possible. To the northern mind, Nigger Jim and Uncle Tom are opposite ends of the same pole;
the young boy and the old man are both eunuchs, paternalistic
wards who, one step removed from the jungle, are capable
of limited, prescribed salvation. The inability of the Daltons to
see the black man as other than an impotent sexual force
accounts for much of the negative criticism by white writers
about black literature; it also accounts for the sexually impotent
black men who people the novels of William Styron and Norman Mailer.

The liberal ideology—both social and literary—of the northern
Daltons has become the primary target of the Afro-American
writer and critic. In the novels of John A. Williams, Sam Greenlee, Cecil Brown, and Ishmael Reed, the criticism of Don L. Lee,
Ron Wellburn, LeRoi Jones, and Hoyt Fuller, to name but a

few, the liberal shibboleths are called into question. The Daltons
are brought before the bar of black public opinion and revealed
for the modern-day plantation owners they are.

There is another, more important aspect to this war. The
black artist of the past worked with the white public in mind.
The guidelines by which he measured his production was its
acceptance or rejection by white people. To be damned by a
white critic and disavowed by a white public was reason enough
to damn the artist in the eyes of his own people. The invisible
censor, white power, hovered over him in the sanctuary of his
private room—whether at the piano or the typewriter—and, like
his black brothers, he debated about what he could say to the
world without bringing censure upon himself. The mannerisms
he had used to survive in the society outside, he now brought
to his art; and, to paraphrase Richard Wright, he was forced
to figure out how to sound each note and how to write down
each word.

The result was usually an artistic creation filled with half-
truths. His works were always seasoned with the proper amount
of anger—an anger that dared not reach the explosive level of
calling for total demolition of the American society—and condescension; condescension that meant he would assure his audience, at some point in the production, that he believed in the
principles of Americanism. To return to Richard Wright, he was
not ". . . ever expected to speak honestly about the problem.
[He had to] wrap it up in myth, legend, morality, folklore,
niceties, and plain lies."

Speaking honestly is a fundamental principle of today's black
artist. He has given up the futile practice of speaking to whites,
and has begun to speak to his brothers. Ofttimes, as in essays
in this anthology, he points up the wide disparity between the
pronouncements of liberal intellectuals and their actions. Yet
his purpose is not to convert the liberals (one does not waste
energy on the likes of Selden Rodman, Irving Howe, Theodore
Gross, Louis Simpson, Herbert Hill, or Robert Bone), but instead to point out to black people the true extent of the control

exercised upon them by the American society, in the hope that
a process of de-Americanization will occur in every black community in the nation.

The problem of the de-Americanization of black people lies
at the heart of the Black Aesthetic. "After the Egyptian and
Indian, the Greek and Roman, the Teuton and Mongolian," wrote
DuBois in 1903, "the Negro is a sort of seventh son, born with
a veil, and gifted with second sight in this American world—
a world which yields him no true self-consciousness, but only
lets him see himself through the revelation of the other world.
It is a peculiar sensation, this double consciousness, this sense
of always looking at one's self through the eyes of others, of
measuring one's soul by the tape of a world that looks on in
amused contempt and pity. One ever feels his twoness—an
American, a Negro; two souls, two thoughts, two unreconciled
strivings; two warring ideals in one dark body, whose dogged
strength alone keeps it from being torn asunder."

In 1961 the old master resolved the psychic tension in his own
breast by leaving the country that had rewarded his endeavors
with scorn and oppression. His denunciations of America and
his exodus back to the land of his forefathers provide an appropriate symbol of the black man who de-Americanized himself.

His act proclaimed to black men the world over that the
price for becoming an American was too high. It meant, at
the least, to desert one's heritage and culture; at the most, to
become part of all ". . . that has been instrumental in wanton
destruction of life, degradation of dignity, and contempt for the
human spirit." To be an American is to be opposed to humankind, against the dignity of the individual, and against the striving in man for compassion and tenderness: to be an American
is to lose one's humanity.

What else is one to make of My Lai, Vietnam? A black
soldier has been charged with joining his white compatriots in
the murder of innocent Vietnamese women and children. How
far has the Americanization of black men progressed when a
southern black man stands beside white men and shoots down,

not the enemies of his people, but the niggers of American construction?

To understand this incident and what must be done to correct it is to understand the Black Aesthetic. A critical methodology has no relevance to the black community unless it aids men in becoming better than they are. Such an element has been sorely lacking in the critical canons handed down from the academies by the Aristotelian Critics, the Practical Critics, the Formalistic Critics, and the New Critics. Each has this in common: it aims to evaluate the work of art in terms of *its* beauty and not in terms of the transformation from ugliness to beauty that the work of art demands from its audience.

The question for the black critic today is not how beautiful is a melody, a play, a poem, or a novel, but how much more beautiful has the poem, melody, play, or novel made the life of a single black man? How far has the work gone in transforming an American Negro into an African-American or black man? The Black Aesthetic, then, as conceived by this writer, is a corrective—a means of helping black people out of the polluted mainstream of Americanism, and offering logical, reasoned arguments as to why he should not desire to join the ranks of a Norman Mailer or a William Styron. To be an American writer is to be an American, and, for black people, there should no longer be honor attached to either position.

To paraphrase Saunders Redding, I have been enclothed with no authority to speak for others. Therefore, it is not my intention, in this introduction, to speak for the contributors to this anthology. Few of them may share my views; a great many may find them reprehensible. These are independent artists who demand the right to think for themselves and who, rightfully so, will resist the attempt by anyone—black or white—to articulate positions in their names.

Each has his own idea of the Black Aesthetic, of the function of the black artist in the American society and of the necessity for new and different critical approaches to the artistic endeavors of black artists. Few, I believe, would argue with my assertion that the black artist, due to his historical position in America at the present time, is engaged in a war with this nation that will determine the future of black art. Likewise, there are few among them—and here again this is only conjecture—who would disagree with the idea that unique experiences produce unique cultural artifacts, and that art is a product of such cultural experiences. To push this thesis to its logical conclusion, unique art derived from unique cultural experiences mandates unique critical tools for evaluation. Further than this, agreement need not go!

One final note: Less than a decade ago, anthologies on black writing were edited almost exclusively by whites. Today, there is a noticeable difference: the white academician edits an anthology and calls upon a black man to write the introduction. The editor then declares that his anthology "represents the best of black literature" or that he has chosen those works "which rank with the best in American artistic production."

This editor makes no such farcical and nonsensical claims. Represented in this anthology is not the best critical thought on the subject of the Black Aesthetic, but critical thought that is among the best. This anthology is not definitive and does not claim to be. The first of its kind to treat of this subject, it is meant as an incentive to young black critics to scan the pages of *The Black World* [*Negro Digest*], *Liberator Magazine, Soulbook, Journal of Negro Poetry, Amistad, Umbra,* and countless other black magazines, and anthologize the thousands of essays that no single anthology could possibly cover.

Many writers whose claim to recognition is equal to that of the other contributors and the editor have been left out of this anthology. This could not be helped. Perhaps it can be rectified. Instead of being content to write introduction for white editors, perhaps our serious black artists will edit anthologies themselves. If this is done, the present renaissance in black letters will escape the fate of its predecessor in the nineteen twenties, and endure. Then and only then will the revolution in black letters gain viability and continue right on!

I Theory

TOWARDS A BLACK AESTHETIC
Hoyt W. Fuller

The black revolt is as palpable in letters as it is in the streets, and if it has not yet made its impact upon the Literary Establishment, then the nature of the revolt itself is the reason. For the break between the revolutionary black writers and the "literary mainstream" is, perhaps of necessity, cleaner and more decisive than the noisier and more dramatic break between the black militants and traditional political and institutional structures. Just as black intellectuals have rejected the NAACP, on the one hand, and the two major political parties, on the other, and gone off in search of new and more effective means and methods of seizing power, so revolutionary black writers have turned their backs on the old "certainties" and struck out in new, if uncharted, directions. They have begun the journey toward a black aesthetic.

The road to that place—if it exists at all—cannot, by definition, lead through the literary mainstreams. Which is to say that few critics will look upon the new movement with sympathy, even if a number of publishers might be daring enough to publish the works which its adherents produce. The movement will be reviled as "racism-in-reverse," and its writers labeled "racists," opprobrious terms which are flung lightly at black people now

that the piper is being paid for all the long years of rejection
and abuse which black people have experienced at the hands
of white people—with few voices raised in objection.

Is this too harsh and sweeping a generalization? White people
might think so; black people will not; which is a way of stating
the problem and the prospect before us. Black people are being
called "violent" these days, as if violence is a new invention out
of the ghetto. But violence against the black minority is in-built
in the established American society. There is no need for the
white majority to take to the streets to clobber the blacks, although there certainly is *enough* of that; brutalization is inherent in all the customs and practices which bestow privileges
on the whites and relegate the blacks to the status of pariahs.

These are old and well-worn truths which hardly need repeat-
ing. What is new is the reaction to them. Rapidly now, black
people are turning onto that uncertain road, and they are doing
so with the approval of all kinds of fellow-travellers who
ordinarily are considered "safe" for the other side. In the fall
1967 issue of the *Journal of the National Medical Association*
(all-black), for example, Dr. Charles A. De Leon of Cleveland,
Ohio, explained why the new turn is necessary: "If young
Negroes are to avoid the unnecessary burden of self-hatred
(via identification with the aggressor) they will have to develop
a keen faculty for identifying, fractionating out, and rejecting
the absurdities of the conscious as well as the unconscious white
racism in American society from what is worthwhile in it."

Conscious and unconscious white racism is everywhere, infecting all the vital areas of national life. But the revolutionary
black writer, like the new breed of militant activist, has decided
that white racism will no longer exercise its insidious control over
his work. If the tag of "racist" is one the white critic will hang
on him in dismissing him, then he is more than willing to bear
that. He is not going to separate literature from life.

But just how widespread is white racism—conscious and unconscious—in the realm of letters? In a review of Gwendolyn
Brooks's *Selected Poems* in the old *New York Herald Tribune*

Book Week back in October 1963, poet Louis Simpson began by writing that the Chicago poet's book of poems "contains some lively pictures of Negro life," an ambiguous enough opener which did not necessarily suggest a literary putdown. But Mr. Simpson's next sentence dispelled all ambiguity. "I am not sure it is possible for a Negro to write well without making us aware he is a Negro," he wrote. "On the other hand, if being a Negro is the only subject, the writing is not important."

All the history of American race relations is contained in that appraisal, despite its disingenuousness. It is civilized, urbane, gentle and elegant; and it is arrogant, condescending, presumptuous and racist. To most white readers, no doubt, Mr. Simpson's words, if not his assessment, seemed eminently sensible; but it is all but impossible to imagine a black reader not reacting to the words with unalloyed fury.

Both black and white readers are likely to go to the core of Mr. Simpson's statement, which is: "if being a Negro is the only subject, the writing is not important." The white reader will, in all probability, find that clear and acceptable enough; indeed, he is used to hearing it. "Certainly," the argument might proceed, "to be important, writing must have *universal values, universal implications;* it cannot deal exclusively with Negro problems." The plain but unstated assumption being, of course, that there are no "universal values" and no "universal implications" in Negro life.

Mr. Simpson is a greatly respected American poet, a winner of the Pulitzer Prize for poetry, as is Miss Brooks, and it will be considered the depth of irresponsibility to accuse him of the viciousness of racism. He is probably the gentlest and most compassionate of men. Miss Brooks, who met Mr. Simpson at the University of California not many months after the review was published, reported that the gentleman was most kind and courteous to her. There is no reason to doubt it. The essential point here is not the presence of overt hostility; it is the absence of clarity of vision. The glass through which black life is viewed by white Americans is, inescapably (it is a matter of extent), befogged by the hot breath of history. True "objectivity" where race is concerned is as rare as a necklace of Hope diamonds.

In October 1967, a young man named Jonathan Kozol published a book called *Death at an Early Age*, which is an account of his experiences as a teacher in a predominantly Negro elementary school in Boston. Mr. Kozol broke with convention in his approach to teaching and incurred the displeasure of a great many people, including the vigilant policeman father of one of his few white pupils. The issue around which the young teacher's opponents seemed to rally was his use of a Langston Hughes poem in his classroom. Now the late Langston Hughes was a favorite target of some of the more aggressive right-wing pressure groups during his lifetime, but it remained for an official of the Boston School Committee to come to the heart of the argument against the poet. Explaining the opposition to the poem used by Mr. Kozol, the school official said that "no poem by any Negro author can be considered permissible if it involves suffering."

There is a direct connecting line between the school official's rejection of Negro poetry which deals with suffering and Mr. Simpson's facile dismissal of writing about Negroes "only." Negro life, which is characterized by suffering imposed by the maintenance of white privilege in America, must be denied validity and banished beyond the pale. The facts of Negro life accuse white people. In order to look at Negro life unflinchingly, the white viewer either must relegate it to the realm of the subhuman, thereby justifying an attitude of indifference, or else the white viewer must confront the imputation of guilt against him. And no man who considers himself humane wishes to admit complicity in crimes against the human spirit.

There is a myth abroad in American literary criticism that Negro writing has been favored by a "double standard" which judges it less stringently. The opposite is true. No one will seriously dispute that, on occasions, critics have been generous to Negro writers, for a variety of reasons; but there is no evidence that generosity has been the rule. Indeed, why should it be assumed that literary critics are more sympathetic to blacks than are other white people? During any year, hundreds of mediocre volumes of prose and poetry by white writers are published, little noted, and forgotten. At the same time, the few creative works by black writers are seized and dissected and, if not deemed of the "highest" literary quality, condemned as still more examples of the failure of black writers to scale the rare heights of literature. And the condemnation is especially strong for those black works which have not screened their themes of suffering, redemption and triumph behind frail façades of obscurity and conscious "universality."

Central to the problem of the irreconcilable conflict between the black writer and the white critic is the failure of recognition of a fundamental and obvious truth of American life—that the two races are residents of two separate and naturally antagonistic worlds. No manner of well-meaning rhetoric about "one country" and "one people," and even about the two races' long joint-occupancy of this troubled land, can obliterate the high, thick dividing walls which hate and history have erected—and maintain—between them. The breaking down of those barriers might be a goal, worthy or unworthy (depending on viewpoint), but the reality remains. The world of the black outsider, however much it approximates and parallels and imitates the world of the white insider, by its very nature is inheritor and generator of values and viewpoints which threaten the insiders. The outsiders' world, feeding on its own sources, fecundates and vibrates, stamping its progeny with its very special ethos, its insuperably logical bias.

The black writer, like the black artist generally, has wasted much time and talent denying a propensity every rule of human dignity demands that he possess, seeking an identity that can only do violence to his sense of self. Black Americans are, for all practical purposes, colonized in their native land, and it can be argued that those who would submit to subjection without struggle deserve to be enslaved. It is one thing to accept the guiding principles on which the American republic ostensibly was founded; it is quite another thing to accept the prevailing practices which violate those principles.

The rebellion in the streets is the black ghetto's response to the vast distance between the nation's principles and its practices. But that rebellion has roots which are deeper than most white people know; it is many-veined, and its blood has been sent pulsating to the very heart of black life. Across this country, young black men and women have been infected with a fever of affirmation. They are saying, "We are black and beautiful," and the ghetto is reacting with a liberating shock of realization which transcends mere chauvinism. They are rediscovering their heritage and their history, seeing it with newly focused eyes, struck with the wonder of that strength which has enabled them to endure and, in spirit, to defeat the power of prolonged and calculated oppression. After centuries of being told, in a million different ways, that they were not beautiful, and that whiteness of skin, straightness of hair, and aquilineness of features constituted the only measures of beauty, black people have revolted. The trend has not yet reached the point of avalanche, but the future can be clearly seen in the growing number of black people who are snapping off the shackles of imitation and are wearing their skin, their hair, and their features "natural" and with pride. In a poem called "Nittygritty," which is dedicated to poet LeRoi Jones, Joseph Bevans Bush put the new credo this way:

> . . . We all gonna come from behind
> those
> Wigs and start to stop using those
> Standards of beauty which can never
> Be a frame for our reference; wash
> That excess grease out of our hair,
> Come out of that bleach bag and get
> Into something meaningful to us as
> Nonwhite people—Black people . . .

If the poem lacks the resonances of William Shakespeare, that is intentional. The "great bard of Avon" has only limited relevance to the revolutionary spirit raging in the ghetto. Which is not to say that the black revolutionaries reject the "universal" statements inherent in Shakespeare's works; what they do reject, however, is the literary assumption that the style and language and the concerns of Shakespeare establish the appropriate limits and "frame of reference" for black poetry and people. This is above and beyond the doctrine of revolution to which so many of the brighter black intellectuals are committed, that philosophy articulated by the late Frantz Fanon which holds that, in the time of revolutionary struggle, the traditional Western liberal ideals are not merely irrelevant but they must be assiduously opposed. The young writers of the black ghetto have set out in search of a black aesthetic, a system of isolating and evaluating the artistic works of black people which reflect the special character and imperatives of black experience.

That was the meaning and intent of poet-playwright LeRoi Jones' aborted Black Arts Theater in Harlem in 1965, and it is the generative idea behind such later groups and institutions as Spirit House in Newark, the Black House in San Francisco, the New School of Afro-American Thought in Washington, D.C., the Institute for Black Studies in Los Angeles, Forum '66 in Detroit, and the Organization of Black American Culture in Chicago. It is a serious quest, and the black writers themselves are well aware of the possibility that what they seek is, after all, beyond codifying. They are fully aware of the dual nature of their heritage, and of the subtleties and complexities; but they are even more aware of the terrible reality of their outsideness, of their political and economic powerlessness, and of the desperate racial need for unity. And they have been convinced, over and over again, by the irrefutable facts of history and by the cold intransigence of the privileged white majority that the road to solidarity and strength leads inevitably through reclamation and indoctrination of black art and culture.

In Chicago, the Organization of Black American Culture has
moved boldly toward a definition of a black aesthetic. In the
writers' workshop sponsored by the group, the writers are deliberately striving to invest their work with the distinctive styles
and rhythms and colors of the ghetto, with those peculiar
qualities which, for example, characterize the music of a John
Coltrane or a Charlie Parker or a Ray Charles. Aiming toward
the publication of an anthology which will manifest this aesthetic, they have established criteria by which they measure
their own work and eliminate from consideration those poems,
short stories, plays, essays and sketches which do not adequately
reflect the black experience. What the sponsors of the workshop
most hope for in this delicate and dangerous experiment is the
emergence of new black critics who will be able to articulate
and expound the new aesthetic and eventually set in motion
the long overdue assault against the restrictive assumptions of
the white critics.

It is not that the writers of OBAC have nothing to start with.
That there exists already a mystique of blackness even some
white critics will agree. In the November 1967 issue of *Esquire*
magazine, for instance, George Frazier, a white writer who is
not in the least sympathetic with the likes of LeRoi Jones,
nevertheless did a commendable job of identifying elements of
the black mystique. Discussing "the Negro's immense style, a
style so seductive that it's little wonder that black men are, as
Shakespeare put it in *The Two Gentlemen of Verona*, 'pearls
in beauteous ladies' eyes,'" Mr. Frazier singled out the following examples;

"The formal daytime attire (black sack coats and striped
trousers) the Modern Jazz Quartet wore when appearing in
concert; the lazy amble with which Jimmy Brown used to return
to the huddle; the delight the late "Big Daddy" Lipscomb took
in making sideline tackles in full view of the crowd and the
way, after crushing a ball carrier to the ground, he would
chivalrously assist him to his feet; the constant cool of 'Satchel'
Paige; the chic of Bobby Short; the incomparable grace of John

Bubbles—things like that are style and they have nothing what-soever to do with ability (although the ability, God wot, is there, too). It is not that there are no white men with style, for there is Fred Astaire, for one, and Cary Grant, for another, but that there are so very, very few of them. Even in the dock, the black man has an air about him—Adam Clayton Powell, so blithe, so self-possessed, so casual, as contrasted with Tom Dodd, sanctimonious, whining, an absolute disgrace. What it is that made Miles Davis and Cassius Clay, Sugar Ray Robinson and Archie Moore and Ralph Ellison and Sammy Davis, Jr. seem so special was their style. . . .

"And then, of course, there is our speech.

"For what nuances, what plays of light and shade, what little sharpnesses our speech has are almost all of them, out of the black world—the talk of Negro musicians and whores and hoodlums and whatnot. 'Cool' and all the other words in common currency came out of the mouths of Negroes.

"'We love you madly,' said Duke Ellington, and now the phrase is almost a cliché. But it is a quality of the Negro's style—that he is forever creative, forever more stylish. There was a night when, as I stood with Duke Ellington outside the Hickory House, I looked up at the sky and said, 'I hope it's a good day tomorrow. I want to wake up early.'

"'Any day I wake up,' said Ellington, 'is a good day.'

"And that was style."

Well, yes. . . .

Black critics have the responsibility of approaching the works of black writers assuming these qualities to be present, and with the knowledge that white readers—and white critics—cannot be expected to recognize and to empathize with the subtleties and significance of black style and technique. They have the responsibility of rebutting the white critics and of putting things in the proper perspective. Within the past few years, for example, Chicago's white critics have given the backs of their hands to worthy works by black playwrights, part of their criticism directly attributable to their ignorance of the intricacies of black style and black life. Oscar Brown, Jr.'s rockingly soulful *Kicks and Company* was panned for many of the wrong reasons; and Douglas Turner Ward's two plays, *Day of Absence* and *Happy Ending*, were tolerated as labored and a bit tasteless. Both Brown and Ward had dealt satirically with race relations, and there were not many black people in the audiences who found themselves in agreement with the critics. It is the way things are—but not the way things will continue to be if the OBAC writers and those similarly concerned elsewhere in America have anything to say about it.

SOME REFLECTIONS ON THE BLACK AESTHETIC by LARRY NEAL

This outline below is a rough overview of some categories and elements that constituted a "Black Aesthetic" outlook. All of these categories need further elaboration, so I am working on a larger essay that will tie them all together.

1. RACE MEMORY (Africa, Middle Passage)

Rhythm as an expression of race memory; rhythm as a basic creative principle; rhythm as a existence, creative force as vector of existence. Swinging

formal manifestation
Samba, Calypso, Batucada, Cha-Cha, juba, gospel songs, jubilees, work song, spirituals.

Mythology
Spirit worship, Orishas, ancestors, African Gods. Syncretism/ catholic voodoo, macumba, Holy Ghost, Jesus as somebody you might know, like a personal diety. River spirits.

2. MIDDLE PASSAGE (Diaspora)

Race memory: terror, landlessness, claustrophobia: "America is a prison . . ." Malcolm X.

3. TRANSMUTATION AND SYNTHESIS

Funky Butt, Stomps, Jump Jim Crow, Buck n' Wing, Jigs, Snake, Grind, slow drag, jitterbug, twist, Watusi, fish, swim, boogaloo, etc. Dance to the *after* beat. Dance as race memory; transmitted through the collective folk consciousness.

formal manifestation
All aspects of Black dance styles in the New World. Pelvic. Dress and walk.

Neo-Mythology
Shamans: Preachers, poets, blues singers, musicians, mackdaddies, and politicians.

4. BLUES GOD/TONE AS MEANING AND MEMORY

Sound as racial memory, primeval. Life breath. Word is perceived as energy or force. Call and response Blues perceived as an emanation outside of man, but yet a manifestation of his being/reality. Same energy source as Gospel, field holler, but delineated in narrative song. The African voice transplanted. This God must be the meanest and the strongest. He survives and persists Once perceived as an evil force:

"... and I (Dude Botley) got to thinking about how many thousand of people (Buddy) Bolden had made happy and all of them women who used to idolize him 'Where are they now?' I say to myself. Then I hear Bolden's cornet. I look through the crack and there he is, relaxed back in the chair, blowing that silver cornet softly, just above a whisper, and I see he's got his hat over the bell of the horn. I put my ear close to the keyhole. I thought I heard Bolden play the blues before, and play hymns at funerals, but what he is playing now is real strange and

Neo-Mythology
Legba, Oshun,
Yemaya, Urzulie,
Soul Momma, Evil
women, Good loving
women, woman as primarily
need/man as doer. Blues
singer as poet and moral
judge; bad man Earth
centered, but directed
cosmologically. Folk poet,
philosopher, priest, priestess,
conjurer, preacher,
teacher, hustler, seer,
soothsayer . . .

BLUES GOD/TONE AS MEANING AND MEMORY (cont'd)

I listen carefully, because he's playing something that, for a while sounds like the blues, then like a hymn, I cannot make out the tune, but after awhile I catch on. He is mixing up the blues with the hymns. He plays the blues real sad and the hymn sadder than the blues and then the blues sadder than the hymn. That is the first time that I had ever heard hymns and blues cooked up together. A strange cold feeling comes over me; I get sort of scared because I know the Lord don't like that mixing the Devil's music with his music. . . . It sounded like a battle between the Good Lord and the Devil. Something tells me to listen and see who wins. If Bolden stops on the hymn, the Good Lord wins; if he stops on the blues, the Devil wins."

5 BLACK ARTS MOVEMENT/BLACK ART AESTHETIC

Feeling/contemporary and historical. Energy intensifies. Non-matrixed art forms: Coltrane, Ornette, Sun Ra. More concerned with the vibrations of the Word, than with the Word itself. Like signifying.

HISTORY AS UNITARY MYTH

Shango, Nat Turner, Denmark, Vesey, Brer' Rabbit, High John the Conqueror, Jack Johnson, Ray. Robinson, Signifying Monkey, Malcolm X, Adam Clayton Powell, Garvey, DuBois, Hon. Elijah Muhammed, Martin L. King, Rap Brown, Rev. Franklin,

HISTORY AS UNITARY MYTH (cont'd)

James Brown, Bessie Smith
Moms Mabley, King Pleasure,
Raeflt Johnson. Son House.
Louis Armstrong. . . .
Voodoo again/Ishmael Reed's
Hoodoo. Islamic suffis,
Third World's destiny.
The East as the Womb
and the Tomb. Fanon's
Third World, Bandung
Humanism. Revolution is the
operational mythology.
Symbol change. Expanded
metaphors as in the poetry
of Curtis Lyle and Stanley
Crouch; or L. Barrett's *Song
For MuMu*. . . Nigger styles and
masks such as Rinehart in the
Invisible Man. Style as in
James P. Johnson description
of stride pianists in the twenties.
Bobby Blue Bland wearing a dashiki
and a process. All of this links
up with the transmutation of
African styles and the revitalization
of these styles on the West.

5. BLACK ARTS MOVEMENT/BLACK ART AESTHETIC (cont'd)

The Black Nation as Poem. Ethical stance
as aesthetic. The synthesis of the above
presented outline. The integral unity of
culture, politics, and art. Spiritual.
Despises alienation in the European sense.
Art consciously committed; art addressed
primarily to Black and Third World people.
Black attempts to realize the world as
art by making Man more compatible to it
and it more compatible to Man. Styles
itself from nigger rhythms to cosmic
sensibility. Black love, conscious and
affirmed. Change.

NEGRO YOUTH SPEAKS
Alain Locke

The Younger Generation comes, bringing its gifts. They are the first fruits of the Negro Renaissance. Youth speaks, and the voice of the New Negro is heard. What stirs inarticulately in the masses is already vocal upon the lips of the talented few, and the future listens, however the present may shut its ears. Here we have Negro youth, with arresting visions and vibrant prophecies; forecasting in the mirror of art what we must see and recognize in the streets of reality tomorrow, foretelling in new notes and accents the maturing speech of full racial utterance.

Primarily, of course, it is youth that speaks in the voice of Negro youth, but the overtones are distinctive; Negro youth speaks out of an unique experience and with a particular representativeness. All classes of a people under social pressure are permeated with a common experience; they are emotionally welded as others cannot be. With them, even ordinary living has epic depth and lyric intensity, and this, their material handicap, is their spiritual advantage. So, in a day when art has run to classes, cliques and coteries, and life lacks more and more a vital common background, the Negro artist, out of the

depths of his group and personal experience, has to his hand
almost the conditions of a classical art.

Negro genius to-day relies upon the race-gift as a vast
spiritual endowment from which our best developments have
come and must come. Racial expression as a conscious motive,
it is true, is fading out of our latest art, but just as surely the
age of truer, finer group expression is coming in—for race
expression does not need to be deliberate to be vital. Indeed
at its best it never is. This was the case with our instinctive
and quite matchless folk-art, and begins to be the same again
as we approach cultural maturity in a phase of art that promises
now to be fully representative. The interval between has been
an awkward age, where from the anxious desire and attempt
to be representative much that was really unrepresentative has
come; we have lately had an art that was stiltedly self-conscious, and racially rhetorical rather than racially expressive.
Our poets have now stopped speaking for the Negro—they
speak as Negroes. Where formerly they spoke to others and
tried to interpret, they now speak to their own and try to express. They have stopped posing, being nearer the attainment
of poise.

The younger generation has thus achieved an objective attitude toward life. Race for them is but an idiom of experience,
a sort of added enriching adventure and discipline, giving
subtler overtones to life, making it more beautiful and interesting, even if more poignantly so. So experienced, it affords
a deepening rather than a narrowing of social vision. The
artistic problem of the Young Negro has not been so much
that of acquiring the outer mastery of form and technique
as that of achieving an inner mastery of mood and spirit.
That accomplished, there has come the happy release from
self-consciousness, rhetoric, bombast, and the hampering habit
of setting artistic values with primary regard for moral effect
—all those pathetic over-compensations of a group inferiority
complex which our social dilemmas inflicted upon several unhappy generations. Our poets no longer have the hard choice

between an over-assertive and an appealing attitude. By the
same effort they have shaken themselves free from the minstrel tradition and the fowling-nets of dialect, and through
acquiring ease and simplicity in serious expression, have carried
the folk-gift to the altitudes of art. There they seek and find
art's intrinsic values and satisfactions—and if America were deaf,
they would still sing.

But America listens—perhaps in curiosity at first; later, we
may be sure, in understanding. But—a moment of patience.
The generation now in the artistic vanguard inherits the fine
and dearly bought achievement of another generation of creative workmen who have been pioneers and path-breakers in
the cultural development and recognition of the Negro in the
arts. Though still in their prime, as veterans of a hard struggle, they must have the praise and gratitude that is due them.
We have had, in fiction, Chestnutt and Burghardt DuBois;
in drama DuBois again and Angelina Grimke; in poetry Dunbar, James Weldon Johnson, Fenton and Charles Bertram Johnson, Everett Hawkins, Lucien Watkins, Cotter, Jameson; and
in another file of poets, Miss Grimke, Anne Spencer, and
Georgia Douglas Johnson; in criticism and *belles lettres*, Braithwaite and Dr. DuBois; in painting, Tanner and Scott; in sculpture, Meta Warrick and May Jackson; in acting, Gilpin and
Robeson; in music, Burleigh. Nor must the fine collaboration of
white American artists be omitted; the work of Ridgely Torrence and Eugene O'Neill in drama, of Stribling, and Shands
and Clement Wood in fiction, all of which has helped in the
bringing of the materials of Negro life out of the shambles of
conventional polemics, cheap romance and journalism into the
domain of pure and unbiassed art. Then, rich in this legacy, but
richer still, I think, in their own endowment of talent, comes
the youngest generation of our Afro-American culture: in music
Diton, Dett, Grant Still, and Roland Hayes; in fiction, Jessie
Fauset, Walter White, Claude McKay (a forthcoming book);
in drama, Willis Richardson; in the field of the short story, Jean
Toomer, Eric Walrond, Rudolph Fisher; and finally a vivid gal-

axy of young Negro poets, McKay, Jean Toomer, Langston Hughes and Countée Cullen.

These constitute a new generation not because of years only, but because of a new aesthetic and a new philosophy of life. They have all swung above the horizon in the last three years, and we can say without disparagement of the past that in that short space of time they have gained collectively from publishers, editors, critics and the general public more recognition than has ever before come to Negro creative artists in an entire working lifetime. First novels of unquestioned distinction, first acceptances by premier journals whose pages are the ambition of veteran craftsmen, international acclaim, the conquest for us of new provinces of art, the development for the first time among us of literary coteries and channels for the contact of creative minds, and most important of all, a spiritual quickening and racial leavening such as no generation has yet felt and known. It has been their achievement also to bring the artistic advance of the Negro sharply into stepping alignment with contemporary artistic thought, mood and style. They are thoroughly modern, some of them ultra-modern, and Negro thoughts now wear the uniform of the age.

Through their work, these younger artists have declared for a lusty vigorous realism; the same that is molding contemporary American letters, but their achievement of it, as it has been doubly difficult, is doubly significant. The elder generation of Negro writers expressed itself in cautious moralism and guarded idealizations; the trammels of Puritanism were on its mind because the repressions of prejudice were heavy on its heart. They felt art must fight social battles and compensate social wrongs; "Be representative": put the better foot foremost, was the underlying mood. Just as with the Irish Renaissance, there were the riots and controversies over Synge's folk plays and other frank realisms of the younger school, so we are having and will have turbulent discussion and dissatisfaction with the stories, plays and poems of the younger Negro group. But writers like Rudolph Fisher, Zora Hurston, Jean Toomer,

Eric Walrond, Willis Richardson, and Langston Hughes take
their material objectively with detached artistic vision; they
have no thought of their racy folk types as typical of anything
but themselves or of their being taken or mistaken as racially
representative. Contrast Ellen Glasgow's *Barren Ground* with
Thomas Nelson Page, or Waldo Frank's *Holiday* with anything
of Mr. Cable's, and you will get the true clue for this contrast
between the younger and the elder generations of Negro literature; Realism in "crossing the Potomac" had also to cross the
color line. Indeed it was the other way round; the pioneer
writing of the fiction of the New South was the realistic fiction
of Negro life. Fortunately just at the time the younger generation was precipitating out, *Batouala* came to attention through
the award of the Prix Goncourt to René Maran, its author, in
1923. Though *Batouala* is not of the American Negro either
in substance or authorship, the influence of its daring realism
and Latin frankness was educative and emancipating. And so
not merely for modernity of style, but for vital originality of
substance, the young Negro writers dig deep into the racy
peasant undersoil of the race life. Jean Toomer writes:

> "Georgia opened me. And it may well be said that I re-
> ceived my initial impulse to an individual art from my experience
> there. For no other section of the country has so stirred me.
> There one finds soil, soil in the sense the Russians know it,
> —the soil every art and literature that is to live must be im-
> bedded in."

The newer motive, then, in being racial is to be so purely for
the sake of art. Nowhere is this more apparent, or more
justified than in the increasing tendency to evolve from the
racial substance something technically distinctive, something that
as an idiom of style may become a contribution to the general resources of art. In flavor of language, flow of phrase,
accent of rhythm in prose, verse and music, color and tone
of imagery, idiom and timbre of emotion and symbolism, it is

the ambition and promise of Negro artists to make a distinctive contribution. Much of this is already discernible. The interesting experiment of Weldon Johnson in *Creation: A Negro Sermon*, to transpose the dialect motive and carry it through in the idioms of imagery rather than the broken phonetics of speech, is a case in point. In music such transfusions of racial idioms with the modernistic styles of expression has already taken place; in the other arts it is just as possible and likely. Thus under the sophistications of modern style may be detected in almost all our artists a fresh distinctive note that the majority of them admit as the instinctive gift of the folk-spirit. Toomer gives a musical folk-lilt and a glamorous sensuous ecstasy to the style of the American prose modernists. McKay adds Aesop and peasant irony to the social novel and folk clarity and naïveté to lyric thought. Fisher adds the terseness and emotional raciness of Uncle Remus to the art of Maupassant and O. Henry. Walrond has a tropical color and almost volcanic gush that are unique even after more than a generation of exotic word painting by master artists. Langston Hughes has a distinctive fervency of color and rhythm, and a Biblical simplicity of speech that is colloquial in derivation, but full of artistry. Roland Hayes carries the rhapsodic gush and depth of folk-song to the old masters. Countée Cullen blends the simple with the sophisticated so originally as almost to put the vineyards themselves into his crystal goblets.

There is in all the marriage of a fresh emotional endowment with the finest niceties of art. Here for the enrichment of American and modern art, among our contemporaries, in a people who still have the ancient key, are some of the things we thought culture had forever lost. Art cannot disdain the gift of a natural irony, of a transfiguring imagination, of rhapsodic Biblical speech, of dynamic musical swing, of cosmic emotion such as only the gifted pagans knew, of a return to nature, not by way of the forced and worn formula of Romanticism, but through the closeness of an imagination that has never broken kinship with nature. Art must accept such gifts, and revaluate the giver.

Not all the new art is in the field of pure art values. There is poetry of sturdy social protest, and fiction of calm, dispassionate social analysis. But reason and realism have cured us of sentimentality: instead of the wail and appeal, there is challenge and indictment. Satire is just beneath the surface of our latest prose, and tonic irony has come into our poetic wells. These are good medicines for the common mind, for us they are necessary antidotes against social poison. Their influence means that at least for us the worst symptoms of the social distemper are passing. And so the social promise of our recent art is as great as the artistic. It has brought with it, first of all, that wholesome, welcome virtue of finding beauty in oneself; the younger generation can no longer be twitted as "cultural nondescripts" or accused of "being out of love with their own nativity." They have instinctive love and pride of race, and, spiritually compensating for the present lacks of America, ardent respect and love for Africa, the motherland. Gradually too, under some spiritualizing reaction, the brands and wounds of social persecution are becoming the proud stigmata of spiritual immunity and moral victory. Already enough progress has been made in this direction so that it is no longer true that the Negro mind is too engulfed in its own social dilemmas for control of the necessary perspective of art, or too depressed to attain the full horizons of self and social criticism. Indeed, by the evidence and promise of the cultured few, we are at last spiritually free, and offer through art an emancipating vision to America.

YOU TOUCH MY BLACK AESTHETIC
AND I'LL TOUCH YOURS
Julian Mayfield

In her poem *Soul*, Barbara Simmons says: "Tell me about soul/ Do I have it? Have you got it? Do you have it? Can you touch mine?/I'll touch yours." The sister is uncertain, and well she might be, for "soul" means so many things to so many people who are all so certain that they know what they are talking about that they may all be right, although their definitions contradict each other.

I feel much the same way about the term "Black Aesthetic." At the risk of sounding superstitious, I know deep down in my guts what it means, but so does every other writer who is grappling with this question, and some of them sound as silly to me as I must sound to them. This is not a cop-out, for like many another of our new terms, Black Aesthetic is easier to define in the negative. I know quite definitely what Black Esthetic is not.

It is *not*, as many people seem to think, a way of talking, a secret language invented by black people to confound the whites, or, as more-serious advocates of this theory would put it, a special language dredged up out of the black experience. I say it is not this, because anyone with proper application can learn it, but most blacks living the black experience do *not* speak it and can *not* understand it. The hippest guy I know is a young French Jew who insists that he is black. I met him in a barroom on the island of Ibiza, off the coast of Barcelona, a few years ago. He heard the proprieter call my name, and he turned a beaming smile on me, slapped my hand real hip fashion, and said: "Hey, Dad, I know who you are." Every other word out of his mouth was "motherfucker," "cat," "man," "brother," "sister," the whole bag. Raoul, as I shall call him, is a brilliant young man, gifted in several languages, and, I think, a sincere revolutionist. He seems to have read everything about black people that was ever written in French, English, Arabic, and Spanish, and, moreover, has a profounder grasp of what he has read than most blacks I know. Black musicians passing through Spain always greeted him like a brother, but as soon as I opened my mouth they put me down as a stone square. Once, when he was flying high after a lot of hashish and I thought I might catch him off guard, I asked him why he insisted on being black when anyone could see he was white. (It had nothing to do with the color of his skin or the texture of his tightly curled but definitely white hair—Adam Powell looks whiter but, damn it, for all his problems, he is black. There was just that indefinable something that Raoul didn't have.) He wove me a long, intricate tale of his background—a French or Arabic father and a black mother, or something like that—and so brilliantly was the tale conceived and executed that finally I gave up and admitted him to the race. For all I know, his story might have been true. If he wanted to be black that bad, then to hell with it.

I no longer believe that the gift of music has much to do with the Black Aesthetic either. I mean, it has something to do with it, but it is not a certain indicator. Yes, I know we blacks created the only original music the nation has, and yes, I know that Mahalia and Aretha and Dionne Warwick are the greatest, and so were Redding and Coltrane and, further back, the Duke and the Count, Billie Holiday, Ivie Anderson, and Bessie

Smith. The trouble with trying to make music a special preserve is that it offends my common sense. It is like grasping at extremely fragile straws. It belongs to whoever can dig it. Record it, and it's gone. Moreover, I confess that I am a musical glutton. I crave not only Yardbird, Bessie Smith, and Coltrane, but Segovia when he works with Bach, Khachaturian when his hundred instruments sweep over an entirely unknown world to me, and Carlos Gardel, the greatest popular singer who ever lived, whom I will not yield merely because he was an Argentinean.

Also, we might as well face it: there are some highly talented whites (singers, dancers, writers, etc.) who can put down any second-rate black who is shucking just because he happens to have the right complexion. In this period, I'm into the sounds of O. C. Smith. The other night while shaving I was sure I heard my man on television, and rushed out of the bathroom only to find that O. C. Smith was a white, blue-eyed boy named Tom Jones, who went on to do Otis Redding and James Brown. All you had to do was close your eyes and Tom Jones was black. *Working* musicians, who don't call themselves intellectuals, know this, and they will tell you, somewhat ruefully, that that is a bad white stud pushing drums behind Brubeck, and that Janis Joplin "sounds" black. My point here is not to deny our rich heritage in the arts—our music especially was wrenched up out of our experience in the hell of Western culture. But soul gut music alone does not a black man make, and it is a poor and shallow aesthetic indeed that is based on something that can so easily be borrowed by others.

Intelligence alone ought to reject the notion that the Black Aesthetic has anything to do with our supposed supersexuality. But here I am on dangerous ground, for this is a myth in which both blacks and whites believe with an unshakable faith as solid as the Rock of Ages. One supposes that the myth can do no harm as long as it helps us to groove in the night and achieve or produce the maximum number of orgasms, which is our national obsession. And let us not rob the poor, for in this land of faggotry the poorest black man has always been able to wake up in the morning with one pitiable certainty, and that was that his thing was larger than any white man's, and that he could manipulate it more skillfully and produce better results. White lynch mobs have always believed it, too, and they used to make a special point of slashing off a black man's penis and balls before they barbecued him. Even now, in a public toilet a white man will peep over into your stall to see if it is really true that yours is bigger than his.

Those of us who dare to attempt the act of creation must not be put off by the difficulty in finding an exact definition for the Black Aesthetic. We must not be distracted by that bewildering combination of forces the poet Margaret Walker described more than thirty years ago in her poem *For My People:*

> . . . Distressed and disturbed and deceived and
> devoured by money-hungry, glory-craving leeches,
> preyed on by facile force of state and fad and
> novelty, by false prophet and holy believer. . . .

For those who must create, there is a Black Aesthetic which cannot be stolen from us, and it rests on something much more substantial than hip talk, African dress, natural hair, and endless, fruitless discussions of "soul." It is in our racial memory, and the unshakable knowledge of who we are, where we have been, and, springing from this, where we are going. Where have we been? Up a hell of a long, hard road. It is what DuBois saw in 1903, in *The Souls of Black Folk:* "And there in the King's highway sat and sits a figure veiled and bowed, by which the traveller's footsteps hasten as they go. On the tainted air breeds fear. Three centuries' thought has been the raising and unveiling of that bowed human heart, and now behold a century new for the duty and the deed. The problem of the Twentieth Century is the problem of the color-line."

But each of us has his own images, for which we must not seek neat little definitions. For me the Black Aesthetic is in a photograph in the book *Harlem on My Mind* of two old black women, clinging to one another as they walk along the cold streets of New York City. Their faces, especially their eyes, are tired and worn, and their backs are bent, for they and their mothers before them have been working for centuries for nothing. It is in the remembered face of one of my grandmothers as she lay in her coffin in Rock Creek Baptist Church in the little South Carolina town where I was born. She washed clothes for one white family for fifty years! It is tired old men and women working, working, working, and then dying and leaving nothing because they hadn't earned anything. There is nothing beautiful about that. It is the bright hope on the faces of children sketched by the artist Tom Feelings, and the murdered hope one sees on the faces of these same children, now barely out of adolescence, as they are routinely shuffled off to prison careers, because everything else—school, parents, protest movement—has failed them. It's the drowsy, blinking addicts on the subway and the young winos sitting on the doorsteps waiting for the juice joints to open. But succeeding from all that, beautiful, relevant, and immediate, is a new breed of clean young black men who know they have been programmed by the white world and who reject the program.

The Black Aesthetic, if it is anything, is the search for a new program, because all the old programs spawned out of the Judaeo-Christian spirit have failed us. It is the search for a new spiritual quality, or the recapture of an old one, lost and buried deep in our African past. I rejected the Christian God a long time ago when I decided that whoever was responsible for the condition of this world could hardly be a friend of mine. I never found another god to worship, but this new breed does search for a deity, a new pattern of spiritual values, perhaps because they suspect that their passage through this life will be all too swift and they want it to have meaning. They wake up each morning knowing that no day is a good day to die, but that one day is as good as any other as long as they do not die alone. I cannot—will not—define my Black Aesthetic, nor will I allow it to be defined for me, but I know that somehow it revolves around this new breed of man and woman who have leaped out of the loins of all those slaves and semi-slaves, who survived so that we might survive. My Black Aesthetic is Bobby Seale, bound and gagged and straining at his leash in a Chicago courtroom. The liberal white world sees and records and reacts, and calls it "a travesty of American justice." But because we blacks remember and feel in our bones the wasted lives of those generations of old people dead and gone and dying still, we see more, and there is nothing mystical about it. We see that it is no travesty of American justice, that it is American justice unveiled, that Bobby Seale, black man, bound and gagged, is what American justice has been from the very beginning. My Black Aesthetic is the image of the beautiful Malcolm the last time I saw him in Africa, driven by his own recalled images, determined to return to what he knew was a certain early death because he must try to make a revolution in this white American hell-pit. He must try to wipe it clean, as it never was, for it was filthy from the very beginning.

(Considering the hundreds of thousands of people who have jumped on the Malcolm X bandwagon *since* he was killed, I suppose it is safe to say he had soul. It should be noted that neither in speech nor life-style did he affect any of the postures commonly associated with "soul" or the "Black Aesthetic." In that prison period when he was Big Red, the super-hip cat on the block, he acquired a great expertise in the handling of women, but as Malcolm X he never found his former sexual prowess anything of which to boast. As for language: "The first man I met in prison who made any positive impression upon me whatever was a fellow inmate, 'Bimbi.' . . . Bimbi put the aesthetic philosophy in a framework, so to speak. That ended my vicious cursing attacks. My approach sounded so weak along-

side his, and he never used a foul word." For the rest of his
life, Malcolm made a fantastically effective effort to master the
English language, not to become a precious little intellectual
and impress people with his learning—he was far bigger than
that—but to shape words into bullets that would strike home
at the center of his targets: American racism and the historic
weaknesses of black men which permit such racism to persist
without serious challenge. Grappling with problems of the Black
Aesthetic, I am struck by how often many of his most vociferous
post-assassination advocates seem to think the word "motherfucker" shouted at the top of the voice is a substitute for action
and clarity of thought.)

This is a great nation. It can absorb almost anything.

Suddenly, in the late fifties, when the nation is getting ac-
customed to Martin Luther King, Malcolm X and the Black
Muslims seem to burst forth with the shocking news that black
Americans do not, for some mysterious reason, like white
Americans. Liberal whites *and* Negroes are scared to death.
Malcolm says, "I'm telling it like it is," and he does. But within
a few months, the white boys on Madison Avenue "done took
Malcolm's phrase and gone," making it a household slogan with
which to sell soap ("Cold Power"), brassieres ("Lift Power"),
and gasoline ("Go Power"). The President of the United States
says, "We shall overcome," and a young black man raises the
cry of "Black Power," and hustlers shudder and say, "Not
'Black Power' but 'Green Power' and 'Black Capitalism,'" and
Dick Nixon, who would rather be President than right, responds,
"You Negro—excuse me—*black* hustling cats know where it's at.
Go 'head. Preach that bad rhetoric, and I'll throw some crumbs
your way."

My point is that superficial appurtenances such as music,
language, dress, and slogans, and other "Black Is Beautiful"
fads can so easily be chewed up, digested, and spat out by
this vigorous, if sick, society, that no aesthetic is safe within
its grinding teeth. White girls don Afro wigs and white boys sport
dashikis, and last night I saw Sammy Davis kiss not one but

two white women on television. But the business of revolution has nothing to do with Afros or dashikis or singing songs, beating drums, doing the bugaloo, or whatever the latest dance craze is. It has nothing to do with confronting liberal college professors who do not know one end of a pistol from another. It does have something to do with meeting armed, white construction workers and their cop supporters at city halls in Chicago and Philadelphia and getting it on and finding out just how tough we really are.

For those of us who read and write books and plays and poetry, the Black Aesthetic has to do with both love and killing, and learning to live, and *survive*, in a nation of killers, so that our children may breathe a purer and freer air.

The Black Aesthetic, for those trying to create today, is necessarily the business of making revolution, for we have tried everything else. Now, this the Tom Joneses and Janis Joplins cannot steal, and will not imitate. For deep in their guts they cannot feel what we have felt. Their eyes cannot see what our eyes have seen, and what the eyes of all those generations of dead and dying old black men and women saw, from slave ships to cotton fields to ghetto obsolescence; the crushing of manhood spirit in childhood, the destruction of what was pure and beautiful and godlike in ourselves before *we* could see it. "When" —Margaret Walker again—

"we discovered we were black and poor
    and small and different and nobody wondered
    and nobody understood."

Wiping it clean from the very beginning as though it never happened: that is enough to occupy the rest of our lives.

Let another generation deal with the niceties of beauty and art. This generation of black men and women has its work cut out for it.

BLACK CULTURAL NATIONALISM
Ron Karenga

Black art, like everything else in the black community, must respond positively to the reality of revolution.

It must become and remain a part of the revolutionary machinery that moves us to change quickly and creatively. We have always said, and continue to say, that the battle we are waging now is the battle for the minds of Black people, and that if we lose this battle, we cannot win the violent one. It becomes very important then, that art plays the role it should play in Black survival and not bog itself down in the meaningless madness of the Western world wasted. In order to avoid this madness, black artists and those who wish to be artists must accept the fact that what is needed is an aesthetic, a black aesthetic, that is a criteria for judging the validity and/or the beauty of a work of art.

Pursuing this further, we discover that all art can be judged on two levels—on the social level and on the artistic level. In terms of the artistic level, we will be brief in talking about this, because the artistic level involves a consideration of form and feeling, two things which obviously involve more technical consideration and terminology than we have space, time or will to develop adequately here. Let it be enough to say that the artistic consideration, although a necessary part, is not sufficient. What completes the picture is that social criteria for judging art. And it is this criteria that is the most important criteria. For all art must reflect and support the Black Revolution, and any art that does not discuss and contribute to the revolution is invalid, no matter how many lines and spaces are produced in proportion and symmetry and no matter how many sounds are boxed in or blown out and called music.

All we do and create, then, is based on tradition and reason, that is to say, on foundation and movement. For we begin to build on traditional foundation, but it is out of movement, that is experience, that we complete our creation. Tradition teaches us, Leopold Senghor tells us, that all African art has at least three characteristics: that is, it is functional, collective and committing or committed. Since this is traditionally valid, it stands to reason that we should attempt to use it as the foundation for a rational construction to meet our present day needs. And by no mere coincidence we find that the criteria is not only valid, but inspiring. That is why we say that all Black art, irregardless of any technical requirements, must have three basic characteristics which make it revolutionary. In brief, it must be functional, collective and committing. It must be functional, that is *useful*, as we cannot accept the false doctrine of "art for art's sake." For, in fact, there is no such thing as "art for art's sake." All art reflects the value system from which it comes. For if the artist created only for himself and not for others, he would lock himself up somewhere and paint or write or play just for himself. But he does not do that. On the contrary, he invites us over, even *insists* that we come to hear him or to see his work; in a word, he expresses a need for our evaluation and/or appreciation and our evaluation cannot be a favorable one if the work of art is not first functional, that is, useful.

So what, then, is the use of art—our art, Black art? Black art must expose the enemy, praise the people and support the revolution. It must be like LeRoi Jones' poems that are assassins' poems, poems that kill and shoot guns and "wrassle cops into alleys taking their weapons, leaving them dead with tongues pulled out and sent to Ireland." It must be functional like the poem of another revolutionary poet from "US," Clyde Halisi, who described the Master's words as "Sun Genies, dancing through the crowd snatching crosses and St. Christopher's from around niggers' necks and passing the white gapped legs in their minds to Simbas[1] to be disposed of."

Or, in terms of painting, we do not need pictures of oranges in a bowl or trees standing innocently in the midst of a waste-land. If we must paint oranges and trees, let our guerrillas be eating those oranges for strength and using those trees for cover. We need new images, and oranges in a bowl or fat white women smiling lewdly cannot be those images. All material is mute until the artist gives it a message, and that message must be a message of revolution. Then we have destroyed "art for art's sake," which is of no use anyhow, and have developed art for all our sake, art for Mose the miner, Sammy the shoeshine boy, T.C. the truck driver and K.P. the unwilling soldier.

In conclusion, the real function of art is to make revolution, using its own medium.

The second characteristic of Black art is that it must be collective. In a word, it must be from the people and must be returned to the people in a form more beautiful and colorful than it was in real life. For that is what art is: everyday life given more form and color. And in relationship to that, the Black artist can find no better subject than Black People themselves, and the Black artist who does not choose or develop this subject will find himself unproductive. For no one is any more than the context to which he owes his existence, and if an artist owes his existence to the Afroamerican context, then he also owes his art to that context and therefore must be held accountable to the people of that context. To say that art must

[1] Swahili for Young Lions, the Youth Movement in US Organization.

be collective, however, raises four questions. Number one, the question of popularization versus elevation; two, personality versus individuality; three, diversity in unity; and four, freedom *to* versus freedom *from*.

The question of popularization versus elevation is an old one; what it really seeks to do is to ask and to answer the question whether or not art should be lowered to the level of the people or the people raised to the level of art. Our contention is that if art is from the people, and for the people, there is no question of raising people to art or lowering art to the people, for they are one and the same thing. As we said previously—art is everyday life given more form and color. And what one seeks to do then is to use art as a means of educating the people, and being educated by them, so that it is a mutual exchange rather than a one-way communication. Art and people must develop at the same time and for the same reason. It must move with the masses and be moved by the masses.

For we should not demand that our people go to school to learn to appreciate art, but that an artist go to school formally or informally to learn new and better techniques of expressing his appreciation for the people and all they represent and his disdain for anything and everything that threatens or hinders their existence. Then and only then can both the artist and the people move forward with a positive pace rooted to the reality of revolution.

The second question raised is the question of personality versus individuality. Now this question is one of how much the emphasis on collective art destroys the individuality of the artist. We say that individualism is a luxury that we cannot afford, moreover, individualism is, in effect, non-existent. For since no one is any more than the context to which he owes his existence, he has no individuality, only personality. Individuality by definition is "me" in spite of everyone, and personality is "me" in relation to everyone. The one, a useless isolation and the other an important involvement. We have heard it even said that the individual is like an atom, that which can no longer be reduced, or the essence of humanity. However, aside from this being a rather strained analogy, it does not prove that a man who wants to be an individual can stand alone. For the atom itself is a part of a molecule and cannot exist without interdependence, and even then, it is at best a simple theoretical construction for the convenience of conversation. We say that there is no virtue in a false independence, but there is value in a real interdependence.

The third question raised with regard to collective art is an extension of the second one, and that is, does unity preclude diversity? Our answer to that is an emphatic, "NO," for there can be and is unity in diversity, even as there can be diversity in unity. What one seeks, however, is not a standardization of every move or creation, but a framework in which one can create and avoid the European gift of trial and error. One can seek the reality of the concept of diversity in unity or unity in diversity in listening to a Trippin ensemble.[2] In a Trippin ensemble the "leader" sets the pace and others come in, or go out, as it pleases them, but in the end they all come to a very dynamic and overwhelmingly harmonious conclusion. So it is with our dance—two partners dance together the same dance and yet they provide us with a demonstration of that which is unique in each of them. But that is not individuality—that is personality. For it is an expression of uniqueness, not isolation from, but in relation to, each other and the collective experience that they both have shared.

The last question is one of freedom *to* versus freedom *from*. This is really a political question, or social one, and is one that raises contradiction for the artist who rejects the social interpretation of art. However, when he demands freedom to do some-

[2] Trippin is our word for what white boys and others call jazz. In line with our obsession with self-determination which demands new definitions and nomenclature, we reject the word jazz, for jazz is taken from the white word, jazzy, i.e. sexy, because that is what he thought our music was. We call it Trippin because that is what we do when we play it or listen to it.

thing or freedom from the restriction that prohibits his doing something, he is asking for a socio-political right, and that, as we said, makes art social first and aesthetic second. Art does not exist in the abstract just like freedom does not exist in the abstract. It is not an independent living thing; it lives through us and through the meaning and message we give it. And an artist may have any freedom to do what he wishes as long as it does not take the freedom from the people to be protected from those images, words and sounds that are negative to their life and development. The people give us the freedom from isolation and alienation and random searching for subject matter and artists, in view of this, must not ask for freedom to deny this, but on the contrary must praise the people for this. In conclusion, the concept of collective art can ·best be expressed in the African proverb showing the interdependence of all by saying, "One hand washes the other."

The final thing that is characteristic of Black art is that it must be committing. It must commit us to revolution and change. It must commit us to a future that is ours. In a word, it must commit us to all that is US-yesterday, today and the sunrise of tomorrow. It must tell us like Halisi's poem, "Maulana and Word Magic," that we must give up the past or be found out and exposed, "as the notes of a new day come tripping through searching each one's heart for any traces of Peyton Place." It must commit us to the fact that the earth is ours and the fullness thereof. As LeRoi Jones says, "You can't steal nothing from the white man. He's already stole it, he owes you anything you want, even his life." So, "Black People take the shit you want, take their lives if need, but get what you want, what you need. Dance up and down the street, turn all the music up." This is commitment to the struggle, a commitment that includes the artist and the observer. We cannot let each other rest; there is so much to do, and we all know we have done so little. Art will revive us, inspire us, give us enough courage to face another disappointing day. It must not teach us resignation. For all our art must contribute to revolutionary change and if it does not, it is invalid.

Therefore, we say the blues are invalid; for they teach resignation, in a word acceptance of reality—and we have come to change reality. We will not submit to the resignation of our fathers who lost their money, their women, and their lives and sat around wondering "what did they do to be so black and blue." We will say again with Brother LeRoi, "We are lovers and the sons of lovers, and warriors and the sons of warriors." Therefore, we will love—and unwillingly though necessarily, make war, revolutionary war. We will not cry for those things that are gone, but find meaning in those things that remain with us. Perhaps people will object violently to the idea that the blues are invalid, but one should understand that they are not invalid historically. They will always represent a very beautiful, musical and psychological achievement of our people; but today they are not functional because they do not commit us to the struggle of today and tomorrow, but keep us in the past. And whatever we do, we cannot remain in the past, for we have too much at stake in the present. And we find our future much too much rewarding to be rejected.

Let our art remind us of our distaste for the enemy, our love for each other, and our commitment to the revolutionary struggle that will be fought with the rhythmic reality of a permanent revolution.

CULTURAL STRANGULATION:
BLACK LITERATURE AND THE WHITE AESTHETIC
Addison Gayle, Jr.

"This assumption that of all the hues of God, whiteness is inherently and obviously better than brownness or tan leads to curious acts. . . ."

W. E. B. DuBois

The expected opposition to the concept of a "Black Aesthetic" was not long in coming. In separate reviews of *Black Fire*, an anthology edited by LeRoi Jones and Larry Neal, critics from the Saturday Review and the New York Review of Books presented the expected rebuttal. Agreeing with Ralph Ellison that sociology and art are incompatible mates, these critics, nevertheless, invoked the cliches of the social ideology of the "we shall overcome" years in their attempt to steer Blacks from "the path of literary fantasy and folly."

Their major thesis is simple: There is no Black aesthetic because there is no white aesthetic. The Kerner Commission Report to the contrary, America is not two societies but one. Therefore, Americans of all races, colors and creeds share a common cultural heredity. This is to say that there is one predominant culture—the American culture—with tributary national and ethnic streams flowing into the larger river. Literature, the most important by-product of this cultural monolith, knows no parochial boundaries. To speak of a Black literature, a Black aesthetic, or a Black state, is to engage in racial chauvinism, separatist bias, and Black fantasy.

The question of a white aesthetic, however, is academic.

One has neither to talk about it nor define it. Most Americans, black and white, accept the existence of a "White Aesthetic" as naturally as they accept April 15th as the deadline for paying their income tax—with far less animosity towards the former than the latter. The white aesthetic, despite the academic critics, has always been with us: for long before Diotima pointed out the way to heavenly beauty to Socrates, the poets of biblical times were discussing beauty in terms of light and dark—the essential characteristics of a white and black aesthetic —and establishing the dichotomy of superior *vs.* inferior which would assume body and form in the 18th century. Therefore, more serious than a definition, is the problem of tracing the white aesthetic from its early origins and afterwards, outlining the various changes in the basic formula from culture to culture and from nation to nation. Such an undertaking would be more germane to a book than an essay; nevertheless, one may take a certain starting point and, using selective nations and cultures, make the critical point, while calling attention to the necessity of a more comprehensive study encompassing all of the nations and cultures of the world.

Let us propose Greece as the logical starting point, bearing in mind Will Durant's observation that "all of Western Civilization is but a footnote to Plato," and take Plato as the first writer to attempt a systematic aesthetic. Two documents by Plato, *The Symposium* and *The Republic,* reveal the twin components of Plato's aesthetic system.

In *The Symposium,* Plato divides the universe into spheres. In one sphere, the lower, one finds the forms of beauty; in the other, the higher, beauty, as Diotima tells Socrates, is absolute and supreme. In *The Republic,* Plato defines the poet as an imitator (a third-rate imitator—a point which modern critics have long since forgotten) who reflects the heavenly beauty in the earthly mirror. In other words, the poet recreates beauty as it exists in heaven; thus the poet, as Neo-Platonists from Aquinas to Coleridge have told us, is the custodian of beauty on earth.

However, Plato defines beauty only in ambiguous, mystical terms; leaving the problem of a more circumscribed, secular definition to philosophers, poets, and critics. During most of the history of the Western world, these aestheticians have been white; therefore, it is not surprising that, symbolically and literally, they have defined beauty in terms of whiteness. (An early contradiction to this tendency is the Marquis DeSade who inverted the symbols, making black beautiful, but demonic, and white pure, but sterile—the Marquis is considered by modern criticism to have been mentally deranged.)

The distinction between whiteness as beautiful (good) and blackness as ugly (evil) appears early in the literature of the middle ages—in the Morality Plays of England. Heavily influenced by both Platonism and Christianity, these plays set forth the distinctions which exist today. To be white was to be pure, good, universal, and beautiful; to be black was to be impure, evil, parochial, and ugly.

The characters and the plots of these plays followed this basic format. The villain is always evil, in most cases the devil; the protagonist, or hero, is always good, in most cases, angels or disciples. The plot then is simple; good (light) triumphs over the forces of evil (dark). As English literature became more sophisticated, the symbols were made to cover wider areas of the human and literary experience. To love was divine; to hate, evil. The fancied mistress of Petrarch was the purest of the pure; Grendel's mother, a creature from the "lower regions and marshes," is, like her son, a monster; the "bad" characters in Chaucer's *Canterbury Tales* tell dark stories; and the Satan of *Paradise Lost* must be vanquished by Gabriel, the angel of purity.

These ancients, as Swift might have called them, established their dichotomies as a result of the influences of Neo-Platonism and Christianity. Later, the symbols became internationalized. Robert Burton, in *The Anatomy of Melancholy*, writes of "dark despair" in the seventeenth century, and James Boswell describes melancholia, that state of mind common to intellectuals

of the 17th and 18th centuries, as a dark, dreaded affliction
which robbed men of their creative energies. This condition—
dark despair or melancholia—was later popularized in what is
referred to in English literature as its "dark period"—the period
of the Grave Yard School of poets and the Gothic novels.

The symbols thus far were largely applied to conditions,
although characters who symbolized evil influences were also
dark. In the early stages of English literature, these characters
were mythological and fictitious and not representative of people
of specific racial or ethnic groups. In the 18th century English
novel, however, the symbolism becomes ethnic and racial.

There were forerunners. As early as 1621, Shakespeare has
Iago refer to Othello as that "old Black ewe," attaching the
mystical sexual characteristic to blackness which would become
the motive for centuries of oppressive acts by white Americans.
In *The Tempest,* Shakespeare's last play, Caliban, though not
ostensibly black, is nevertheless a distant cousin of the colonial
Friday in Daniel Defoe's *Robinson Crusoe.*

Robinson Crusoe was published at a historically significant
time. In the year 1719, the English had all but completed their
colonization of Africa. The slave trade in America was on its
way to becoming a booming industry; in Africa, Black people
were enslaved mentally as well as physically by such strange
bedfellows as criminals, businessmen, and Christians. In the
social and political spheres, a rationale was needed, and help
came from the artist—in this case, the novelist—in the form of
Robinson Crusoe. In the novel, Defoe brings together both Christian and Platonic symbolism, sharpening the dichotomy between
light and dark on the one hand, while on the other establishing
a criterion for the inferiority of Black people as opposed to the
superiority of white.

One need only compare Crusoe with Friday to validate both
of these statements. Crusoe is majestic, wise, white and a
colonialist; Friday is savage, ignorant, black and a colonial.
Therefore, Crusoe, the colonialist, has a double task. On the

one hand he must transform the island (Africa—unproductive, barren, dead) into a little England (prosperous, life-giving, fertile), and he must recreate Friday in his own image, thus bringing him as close to being an Englishman as possible. At the end of the novel, Crusoe has accomplished both undertakings; the island is a replica of "mother England"; and Friday has been transformed into a white man, now capable of immigrating to the land of the gods.

From such mystical artifacts has the literature and criticism of the Western world sprung; and based upon such narrow prejudices as those of Defoe, the art of Black people throughout the world has been described as parochial and inferior. Friday was parochial and inferior until, having denounced his own culture, he assimilated another. Once this was done, symbolically, Friday underwent a change. To deal with him after the conversion was to deal with him in terms of a character who had been civilized and therefore had moved beyond racial parochialism.

However, Defoe was merely a hack novelist, not a thinker. It was left to shrewder minds than his to apply the rules of the white aesthetic to the practical areas of the Black literary and social worlds, and no shrewder minds were at work on this problem than those of writers and critics in America. In America, the rationale for both slavery and the inferiority of Black art and culture was supplied boldly, without the trappings of 18th century symbolism.

In 1867, in a book entitled *Nojoque: A Question for a Continent,* Hinton Helper provided the vehicle for the cultural and social symbols of inferiority under which Blacks have labored in this country. Helper intended, as he states frankly in his preface, "to write the negro out of America." In the headings of the two major chapters of the book, the whole symbolic apparatus of the white aesthetic handed down from Plato to America is graphically revealed: the heading of one chapter reads: "Black: A Thing of Ugliness, Disease"; another heading reads: "White: A Thing of Life, Health, and Beauty."

Under the first heading, Helper argues that the color black "has always been associated with sinister things such as mourning, the devil, the darkness of night." Under the second, "White has always been associated with the light of day, divine transfiguration, the beneficent moon and stars . . . the fair complexion of romantic ladies, the costumes of Romans and angels, and the white of the American flag so beautifully combined with blue and red without ever a touch of the black that has been for the flag of pirates."

Such is the American critical ethic based upon centuries of distortion of the Platonic ideal. By not adequately defining beauty, and implying at least that this was the job of the poet, Plato laid the foundation for the white aesthetic as defined by Daniel Defoe and Hinton Helper. However, the uses of that aesthetic to stifle and strangle the cultures of other nations is not to be attributed to Plato but, instead, to his hereditary brothers far from the Aegean. For Plato knew his poets. They were not, he surmised, a very trusting lot and, therefore, by adopting an ambiguous position on symbols, he limited their power in the realm of aesthetics. For Plato, there were two kinds of symbols: natural and proscriptive. Natural symbols corresponded to absolute beauty as created by God; proscriptive symbols, on the other hand, were symbols of beauty as proscribed by man, which is to say that certain symbols are said to mean such and such by man himself.

The irony of the trap in which the Black artist has found himself thoughout history is apparent. Those symbols which govern his life and art are proscriptive ones, set down by minds as diseased as Hinton Helper's. In other words, beauty has been in the eyes of an earthly beholder who has stipulated that beauty conforms to such and such a definition. To return to Friday, Defoe stipulated that civilized man was what Friday had to become, proscribed certain characteristics to the term "civilized," and presto, Friday, in order not to be regarded as a "savage under Western eyes," was forced to conform to this ideal. How well have the same stipulative definitions worked in the artistic sphere! Masterpieces are made at will by each new critic who argues that the subject of his doctoral dissertation is immortal. At one period of history, John Donne, according to the critic Samuel Johnson, is a second rate poet; at another period, according to the critic T. S. Eliot, he is one of the finest poets in the language. Dickens, argues Professor Ada Nisbet, is one of England's most representative novelists, while for F. R. Leavis, Dickens' work does not warrant him a place in *The Great Tradition.*

When Black literature is the subject, the verbiage reaches the height of the ridiculous. The good "Negro Novel," we are told by Robert Bone and Herbert Hill, is that novel in which the subject matter moves beyond the limitations of narrow parochialism. Form is the most important criterion of the work of art when Black literature is evaluated, whereas form, almost non-existent in Dostoyevsky's *Crime and Punishment,* and totally chaotic in Kafka's *The Trial,* must take second place to the supremacy of thought and message.

Richard Wright, says Theodore Gross, is not a major American novelist; while Ralph Ellison, on the strength of one novel, is. LeRoi Jones is not a major poet, Ed Bullins not a major playwright, Baldwin incapable of handling the novel form—all because white critics have said so.

Behind the symbol is the object or vehicle, and behind the vehicle is the definition. It is the definition with which we are concerned, for the extent of the cultural strangulation of Black literature by white critics has been the extent to which they have been allowed to define the terms in which the Black artist will deal with his own experience. The career of Paul Laurence Dunbar is the most striking example. Having internalized the definitions handed him by the American society, Dunbar would rather not have written about the Black experience at all, and three of his novels and most of his poetry support this argument. However, when forced to do so by his white liberal mentors, among them was the powerful critic,

William Dean Howells, Dunbar deals with Blacks in terms of
buffoonery, idiocy and comedy.

Like so many Black writers, past and present, Dunbar was
trapped by the definitions of other men, never capable of
realizing until near the end of his life, that those definitions
were not god-given, but man-given; and so circumscribed by
tradition and culture that they were irrelevant to an evaluation
of either his life or his art.

In a literary conflict involving Christianity, Zarathustra, Fried-
rich Nietzsche's iconoclast, calls for "a new table of the laws."
In similar iconoclastic fashion, the proponents of a Black Aesthetic, the idol smashers of America, call for a set of rules by
which Black literature and art is to be judged and evaluated.
For the historic practice of bowing to other men's gods and
definitions has produced a crisis of the highest magnitude,
and brought us, culturally, to the limits of racial armageddon.
The trend must be reversed.

The acceptance of the phrase "Black is Beautiful" is the first
step in the destruction of the old table of the laws and the
construction of new ones, for the phrase flies in the face of
the whole ethos of the white aesthetic. This step must be followed by serious scholarship and hard work; and Black critics
must dig beneath the phrase and unearth the treasure of beauty
lying deep in the untoured regions of the Black experience—
regions where others, due to historical conditioning and cultural
deprivation, cannot go.

BLACK ARTS: NOTEBOOK
John O'Neal

1. "Afro-American," etc., Is a Contradiction

It is extremely difficult to achieve clarity when the very condition of your being is tied to a basic contradiction. Because we have been in this place, America, and because unknown millions of us have been born, have lived, and have died here over the course of the past three and a half centuries, we have made an identity between ourselves and America. Yet it remains the same nation that sponsored the rape of Africa; that is now and always has been hostile to our presence here; the same that has exploited our labor, and our minds and culture—a nation that only in brief faltering moments has relented in a base attack on our very survival. Yet we still yield to such terms and names as Negro Americans, American Negroes, Afro-Americans, Black Americans, etc.

The concept of home and roots in America is the problem. People can only bring a nation out of mutual commitment to their common good. Here, we have simply been victims. Our concept must be a world concept, and we must see our roots as African. We are an African People.

2. The Decadence of Western Culture

We are simply not an American People. America exists as a contradiction to our People-hood. America is the historic mentor of the oppression of our People. America serves as the bulwark of colonial, neocolonial, and imperialistic forces that support and maintain the oppression of our People and other non-European Peoples in the world today.

In spite of all this, because of its affluence and because a certain fluidity is permitted within the American body politic, the siren's song the nation sings makes it intensely desirable for many to flirt with the certain death that waits in her rocky surf.

Some argue with considerable justification, and with even greater passion, that we live among a nation of devils who were born of devils. But the point, I think, is a simpler one: Western culture is simply decadent. It has lived past the point of the creativity of its values and continues only because of the accumulated momentum of its past, going blindly now on a course over which *persons* no longer have control. The machinery demands the perpetuation of itself quite apart from the intention or desire of the persons who operate and who are operated on by it.

For us, as a People, to try to find our Peopleness within the context of the American nation or the values of the West on which the nation is founded, would be like a chicken trying to find his chickenness in an oven. Why enjoin a struggle to become enmeshed in the very decadence that brings oppression on our People and to the majority of the Peoples of the world?

3. Seven Decades: the Coon Trap and How It Looks Now.

After the Egyptian and Indian, the Greek and Roman, Teuton and Mongolian, the Negro is a sort of seventh son born with a veil, and gifted with second sight in this American world—a world which yields him no true self-consciousness, but only lets him see himself through the revelation of the outer world. It is a peculiar sensation, this double consciousness, the sense of always looking at one's self through the eyes of others, of measuring one's soul by the tape of a world that looks on in amused contempt and pity. One ever feels his twoness—an American, a Negro, two souls, two thoughts, two unreconciled strivings; two warring ideals in one dark body, whose dogged strength alone keeps it from being torn asunder.

W. E. B. DuBois—*The Souls of Black Folk*
The coon trap:

> *I, Too*
>
> I, too, sing America
> I am the darker brother.
> They send me to eat in the kitchen
> when company comes,
> But I laugh
> And eat well
> And grow strong
> Tomorrow,
> I'll be at the table
> When company comes
> Nobody'll dare
> say to me
> "Eat in the Kitchen,"
> Then.
> Besides
> They'll see how beautiful I am
> and be ashamed—
> I, too, am America.

Langston Hughes (tch-tch-tch)—*I, Too* (published in numerous collections).

> *Poem for a Knee-grow*
>   (*I don't care to meet*)
> he was born here
> his forefathers died here
> fought here

worked here
their graves are here
in a marri ca
he's an a marri can
but are you really, brother,
chickens are born
in an oven sometimes but that don't make um
biscuits, nigger

Asoob Akibas, *Nkombo*, fall 1969.

DuBois cites the contradiction at the turn of the century, Hughes accepts the terms of the contradiction in the 40s, and Asoob (Renaldo Fernandez), a young poet from F.S.T.'s Blkartsouth in New Orleans, offers an avenue for thinking to its solution in 1969. We live in America, we have a presence here, but we are not an American people. Indeed, there is a considerable question about just who is American People, but whatever it is, it ain't us. We are an African People. We are not an American People.

America is our oven, but there are ways to survive in ovens, too. The oven's heat makes proper metal stronger.

4. Three Waters in Time and the Poet as Prophet.

I see three major lines of cultural development among contemporary humankind: European, Asian, and African. Each of these categories of peoples shows its own internal dynamic and has participated in various ways in relationships to Peoples in other cultural groups.

Think of a river going somewhere for the first time. The river's well established, but where it's going isn't—just that it's going. The river is humankind. Human consciousness is defined by ever-changing, ever-expanding limits of the river. The artists are the ones who move at the edge of that consciousness, moving out in front of the mainstream, showing the way for the river to go. If the artist's judgment is true, *and* the way he shows clear, then the mainstream of humankind will follow. When the mainstream of the people follow him, the artist is either thrust out again to forge ahead into unknown areas of human potential, or he is swallowed up and lost in the mainstream—no longer to create, but to go along.

If the artist's judgment is not true and is unclear, then he's left to dry up on the barren place he went to, while the mainstream of humankind rushes off in other directions—those ways illumined by clearer prophets. Sometimes the false way seems clearest and best to the mainstream, and it follows that way only to find an impenetrable passage, and the stream doubles back or turns around to find that the way the true prophet spoke of his work comes to life again when the river comes back the way once lost.

Think of three waters. The waters come from separate places but play close together, then farther on they mingle with the others; then, pulling apart again, each goes off to meet the other, then back and forth till they finally run together toward a place where they cannot go apart, yet cannot mix to make one stream without one or both backing up to come another way.

All waters find ultimate issue in a common source. The ultimate reunion in that source is the inevitable end of all striving. Nation is not divine; being is. The waters of being, not streams of nation.

The artist's job is to move at the edge of that stream not to hold a mirror up, but to see the way and show the basic how by going there and doing as much as he can without dying. If dying is a must for the vision to be, then dying must also be done, for the loss of the vision would make a worse death for the seer.

It is the job of the priest to find the wisdom in the artist's sight and to hold the people in common struggle toward that dream. It is for the scientist to find the means to take us there. And there are other tasks for others, but it is for the artist to see and show the way by being what he sees.

Dry and strange and lonely places keep the artist in constant danger, for the only protection is the Truth of his vision and his labor toward it. The only guarantee is that of death, if the vision or his labor is either false or incomplete.

Of the streams of humankind, we are from the family of Africa.

We live today on the threshold of a new era. Western culture has passed the point of it's own creativity and crashes on with malevolent splendor like a mighty river rolling into a boundless desert with vigor now, but toward certain extinction in the limitless arid wasteland, able only to consume the moisture rolling in.

Western culture, because of the concept of its own superiority, is doomed and damned. Damned because it is doomed and not doomed because it is damned, because each People begin with the defense of their own reality. Doomed because the technology that their concept of superiority stands on cannot defend them from the reaction of exploited Peoples unless they are willing to serve the cause of their own destruction also. Which is not altogether unlikely.

5. *Abstractivity*

Black people in America have a tendency toward *abstractivity* —the tendency to engage in abstract activity; the effort to do everything at once while accomplishing little that has to do with the projected goal; having only an abstract idea of the intended results of the activity to begin the activity with.

I know a cat who decided to open a print shop. He had, sometimes, fewer skills and less money, and not enough of either. Now, forty years later, he's still trying to open a print shop. He's got a few pieces of antiquated printing equipment; he has written an opera; he sells candy, notions, good-luck charms, dream books, birthday cards, and cigarettes, and somehow spends more money each month than he makes. In between times, he's a preacher. All the time, he's frustrated because of his abstractivity.

6. About Black

Black as a physical fact has little significance. Color, as a cultural, social, and political fact, is the most significant fact of our era. Black is important because it gives us ground from which to fight—a way to feel and think about ourselves and our own reality—a way to define.

7. On Power

Power is the ability to make decisions and implement them. Political power is ultimately dependent on the will (of the masses) of the people.

8. On Liberation Struggles and Revolution

A People's struggle for liberation must necessarily reach revolutionary proportions.

A People, that is, a group of people with similar cultures and common ancestry and history, may struggle for liberation from oppressive domination at the hands of a government imposed by an alien People who subject the oppressed People to the ends and terms of the alien People. Characteristic of colonialistic and imperialistic situations.

It's hard to think of revolution without thinking of it in Marxist terms. In the Marxist dictionary, "people" is used in a different fashion. Marxists speak of "the masses" of the people, as opposed to the ruling classes.

There is always a ruling group. Before liberation, after liberation—before revolution, after revolution.

Revolution is the process by which the masses of the people through their own action replace one ruling group and their system of government, with another ruling group and another system of government.

There may be revolution without liberation, but a People's

struggle for liberation must necessarily reach revolutionary proportions. A liberation struggle is therefore a revolutionary struggle.

Life magazine recently asked the question if revolution was possible in America. They said no. But the correct answer is yes; it is inevitable. Our struggle, however, the struggle of Black People, is properly a liberation struggle. America describes the context of, but does not and cannot define, the terms of that struggle. The world, with Africa as a base, defines our struggle. For we are an African People.

The first stage in any revolutionary struggle is the struggle for the minds of the (masses of the) People. The People seldom embrace struggle willingly, but accept it once the compelling necessity is clear. The recognition of the failure of reform within a system, the inability of a system to accommodate to the needs of the people, is the best way for Peoples' minds to be prepared for the revolutionary commitment. The failure of reform is the only way the masses of people in a more or less democratic society will come to the acceptance of the revolutionary imperative. If reform *can* produce the necessary changes, then revolution is not imperative.

It is necessary that the revolutionary alternatives expand at a rate equivalent to the rate of defections from the establishment. Increase in reformist activity therefore requires a proportionate increase in revolutionary activity. Increases in reformist and revolutionary activity will generate an increase in fascist reaction, and thereby increase the number of people with revolutionary inclinations, therefore increasing again the need for revolutionary activity.

The pressure on the establishment increases until it can no longer be tolerated, and concessions to reformists no longer make effective propaganda. The dialectic between reformist and revolutionist also requires the reformist to make greater demands, with which the establishment will eventually find no base for compromise. The only option left to the establishment at this point, then, is to embrace overt fascist repression—or capitulate to the revolutionary forces, which is of course impossible.

We grow close to the period of overt fascist repression by the United States.

Our work as Black artists is to help our People to recognize themselves and the inevitable demands of the struggle that lies ahead.

9. *The Abstract, the Concrete, and the Shadow of the Past*

Abstractions seem irrelevant in the face of concrete problems. Yet it's true that concretes are simply confounding if not placed in an orderly context; that is, within the context of an abstract idea that permits the arrangement of concretes into useful designs.

The Black Aesthetic! Forget the contradiction in language— I don't know another. Perhaps our/my struggle will show us/me that we/I must stop thinking in this language and learn to think in another one. But, right now, this is it!

Aesthetic: a philosophical term—the principles of art.
Black Aesthetic: the principles of Black Art.

But principles and systems must be discovered. They come after the fact as a result of reflection and observation. When we think, we think about something. What I think about Black Art can be stated very simply! With the exception of music, she lies a virgin bride. And the music has been raped! While we have stood by watching! We have to reclaim the music and give it all a place to grow and mean. We have just begun to recognize ourselves. Recognize Us—us-ness, the ourness of OURS, the peoplehood of Black. In this country and in the world since the beginning of the period of Western domination, we have failed to recognize and accept us as people. What Mr. Muhammad calls "knowledge of self and kind," we have been deprived of, for we have protested against our own existence as a People.

Principles and laws and rules, to be useful and effective, must be descriptive, not legislative. Dig it! Not what people must do, but what they do do. Tell me I must do, and by choice I may revolt. Tell me I do do, and I may simply recognize or deny the Truth.

The artists will create the art and the people will create the Artists; therefore, the People will create the art. Through the struggle of African Peoples, we will find a way for US to be. As the People and the life differ from the People and life of Western Peoples, then so will the Art Aesthetic differ.

The canons of Western art have only incidental significance for Us. The incidence of our circumstance in relation to the west. We cannot find our essence in the West, for we are not of the west. We come from different blood—from our roots will come our sustaining flow. From those roots only, can we relate positively to the West. We are an African People.

10. The Ignorant Tree *and the Shadow of the Past*

Val Ferdinand, a beautiful poet and a beautiful brother, recently reviewed Gordon Parks's *The Learning Tree* for *The Plain Truth*, a newspaper published by one of the Free Southern Theater workshops in New Orleans:

The Ignorant Tree
At first I thought *The Ignorant Tree* was a worse movie than *Slaves,* which was a waste of time and money, but I thought about it some more and now feel that *The Ignorant Tree* is perhaps one of the most truthful movies to hit the screen in a long time. The photography and direction have got to be some of the best work you are going to see in a long time. A lot of Parks's shots were so good that you just have to say, "Damn, that's a pretty sun." The direction and acting were so together that you forgot people were acting. As a producer, Parks did an even better job, because he somehow managed to find the

people who could play the parts he wanted them to play. There
can be little doubt but that the actor who played Newt right-
eously did his part, as did all of the supporting actors.

But damn, the script! My wife and I took a friend of ours
out for her birthday and we sat there groaning and moaning.
"That can't be a nigger"! "Who wrote this script"? etc. etc.
A little church scene near the beginning of the movie told the
whole story in a nutshell. As the actors were leaving, we spied
that it was an AME church. My wife said that they were kind
of quiet for a black church. . . .

I could go on at length about this picture, but I would prefer
that you go see it so that you can see for yourself how the
black upper class thinks and moves around in the society. Yeah,
Newt, you gon' make it! Be sure to check out how easily Newt
does things for money. Like the scene when he bargains up to
six bits with the white cop for the honor of diving to get the
body of a brother that the same cop has just shot in the back.
I mean, if you had just seen a pig blow away a brother in the
back (and the brother was only guilty of participating in an
integrated crap game . . .), if you had just seen this, do you
think that you would stand there and bargain with the same
cop about how much money you want to dive to find the
brother? Ah, man, I hope not. I hope we're past that. I hope
that none of us are just in it for the money. Things like fighting
our brothers in a circus ring for a few dollars. It makes you
sick. Yeah, brothers, go and see how a NEGRO views the world.

I agree with the substance of Ferdinand's critique, but it
seems to me that he missed the two most important points. It is
assumed that the purpose of the picture was to tell the story
of the coming of age of a Negro youth. No, I don't think that was
the point. It was first and foremost a demonstration film. Proof
of what Gordon Parks can do . . . in spite of . . . (being
Black). Dig it! Write a novel, write a screenplay, produce it,
direct it, write music, take pictures, and think, too. And do it
all good! See what-all a nigger (therefore niggers) can do! If
given a chance, even if you don't give them a chance they

take it, e.g., G.P., and get rich and be moral too, Man! And,
man, like that's *impossible*, but the nigger did it.

The second thing is that this is unfortunately the wrong
point. This is probably the biggest problem Negro artists have
faced in the past, and this shadow hides the present work
from so many—the white audience and consciousness. Sad, man,
sad sad sad sad. So in the end you're right. Why is it that
Niggers think they got to spend so much time trying to prove
(to whom?) that they're human. Because we don't know yet.

When Black Art happens, it is different.

Affirmation of the Black reality, not contradiction and denial.
Affirmation of Black potential, not trying to take black dreams
and paint them white till even we don't know the difference
any more. Black life is the model. Black life is a struggle for
unity and liberation of all African Peoples.

AFRO-AMERICAN LITERARY CRITICS:
AN INTRODUCTION
Darwin T. Turner

Each year, increasing numbers of American readers are becoming familiar with and often enthusiastic about black creative writers. White scholars, critics, and students fret anxiously about the probable date of Ellison's next novel. They debate the value of Gwendolyn Brooks's latest style. They choose sides to support or attack Eldridge Cleaver's repudiation of James Baldwin. Without hesitation, reasonably knowledgeable readers could rattle off names of black writers who have earned national attention and acclaim in various literary genres and fields. If, however, one wanted to silence the chatter, he would need merely to ask for the names of black literary critics; for, even in this decade of discovery of black culture, Afro-American critics remain blackly invisible. Few are known among the general reading public; and perhaps only one—Nathan Scott, Jr.—is judged to be both eminent and influential.

Even when their subject has been literature by Afro-American writers, black critics have failed to make America see them, to say nothing of reading or hearing their words. The best-known critics of Afro-American literature are white. White Vernon Loggins, author of *The Negro Author* (1931); Robert Bone, author of *The Negro Novel in America* (1952, 1965);

and Herbert Hill, editor of *Soon, One Morning* (1963) and
Anger and Beyond (1966), are better known than black Hugh
Gloster or Saunders Redding. The fact is ironic and regrettable, since black American critics can offer insights into the
language, styles, and meanings intended by black writers, insights frequently denied to those who have not shared the
experience of living as black people in the United States of
America.

The irony cannot be overemphasized. Many Americans today
read black writers with the hope of learning who black people
are, what they think, and what they propose to be. These
readers, however, seem not to comprehend that they will never
understand blacks as long as they seek such understanding
solely in judgments, evaluations, and interpretations made by
others who are equally distant from the black experience. The
individual who wishes to understand the literature of black
people must know the ablest interpreters of that literature.

Many superficial explanations for the apparent dearth of eminent black critics have been whispered at one time or another: Afro-Americans do not write well; or they cannot write
objectively about the work of other blacks; or they cannot
think abstractly and formulate critical theories. Since these
explanations are illogical and easily disproved, let us consider
some of the actual reasons before turning to a history of the
Afro-American critics themselves.

An established critic in a field is not necessarily the individual
who has written the best work on a particular subject; instead,
he is the individual who is most widely known for writing on
that subject. This one fact, more than any other, has segregated
black critics into the basement of the club of literary criticism:
the masses of literate Americans do not read the publications of
black critics and, consequently, do not know them.

Where does one look for a literary critic? He reads respected
newsstand periodicals: *The Saturday Review, The New York
Review of Books,* the New York *Times;* or, in years past,
Dial, The Atlantic, or *The Nation.* He looks in the nationally

known "little" magazines, such as *Poetry* or *The Kenyon Review*. He studies the anthologies of literary criticism, and he notes the names of editors of anthologies of literature. He scrutinizes the journals of the professional associations—*PMLA, American Literature, Shakespeare Quarterly*, for example. He attends lectures at the large universities and at the annual meetings of academic societies. In such arenas as these, one would expect to discover more literary critics than he could read or listen to in a lifetime.

But, except for rare individuals, the critics in these sources are white. Few anthologies include criticism by blacks: *The New Negro* (Alain Locke, 1925), *The Negro Caravan* (Sterling Brown *et al.*, 1941), *Soon, One Morning* (Herbert Hill, 1963), *Anger and Beyond* (Hill, 1966), *Images of the Negro in America* (Darwin T. Turner and Jean Bright, 1965), *Black Voices* (Abraham Chapman, 1968), *Images of the Negro in American Literature* (Seymour Gross and John Hardy, 1966), *Black Fire* (LeRoi Jones and Larry Neal, 1968), *Black Expression* (Addison Gayle, Jr., 1969), *Black American Literature: Essays* (Turner, 1969). Most of these anthologies have been published within the past five years; and, significantly, of the eight anthologies during that half decade, four have been edited by white men. Few blacks have been hired into the white world of professional journalism as critics or columnists (the William Stanley Braithwaites and Carl Rowans are rare), and few white readers have searched the back pages of black newspapers for critical reviews. In general, the blacks who are invited to review for nationally known periodicals are those who have distinguished themselves as creative writers rather than as critics. They are such men as Langston Hughes, Ralph Ellison, James Baldwin, and Arna Bontemps. Until recently, few black scholars were hired on the staffs of large universities even as visiting lecturers —the Hugh Glosters, Sterling Browns, and Alain Lockes of previous decades were conspicuous. From 1949 to 1965, no more than two or three black scholars read papers at the annual meeting of the Modern Language Association, and only a few more appeared on programs of the National Council of Teachers of English. In fact, as recently as 1939, black scholars felt that they had so little opportunity to present papers at the regional or national Modern Language Association meetings that they formed an organization for black teachers of language and literature—the College Language Association. In short, black critics have been denied opportunity to present their works in the most respected media—or at least they have not been encouraged to contribute.

These facts, however, do not entirely absolve blacks of the responsibility for failing to produce more critics. Afro-American professional journalism has failed to develop and promote a literary market. *Negro Digest*, now called *The Black World*, (1942–51, 1961 to date) has been the most enduring among the commercial magazines that devote significant space to literature, but the Johnson Publishing Company has not given the *Digest* support equal to that for *Ebony* and *Jet*. Black commercial publishers have alleged that they would waste money if they attempted to promote literary culture among the disinterested black masses. (One wonders how these publishers explain the fact that, with little advertising and limited distribution, Broadside Press has managed, in two years, to sell fifty-six thousand copies of the poetry of Don Lee.

Many white commercial publishers have similar reservations about the cultural interests of Americans, even though their potential market is eight times as large. Among whites, however, a substantial amount of literary criticism is published within the academic world. Here, too, black Americans have failed to promote literary scholarship as effectively as might be expected. Most major universities sponsor publishing companies, which promote the university's reputation within the academic community and simultaneously provide platforms for the university's scholars. In contrast, although many predominantly Negro colleges have offered courses and even majors in printing and in journalism, very few have attempted to publish anything more scholarly than a catalogue and a schedule of classes.

Even though any one of these colleges may complain that high costs and a limited market militate against establishing an individual publishing company, it seems feasible for several black colleges to pool their resources to form a combined press.

Equally significant is the failure of black institutions to promote journals. Relatively small white universities have sponsored journals that have gained respect; but, at black colleges, such journals—when attempted—have rarely endured for more than an issue or two: the *Journal of Negro Education* at Howard University, *Phylon* at Atlanta University, and the *Journal of Human Relations* at Central State College in Ohio are perhaps the most successful. And the College Language Association is the only professional association for blacks to give attention primarily to literature. Furthermore, no enduring journal has concentrated on the study and promotion of Afro-American contributions in the arts. *Phylon* probably has achieved more toward this end than any other journal, but *Phylon* has reflected the social-science orientation that might be expected from a periodical established by W. E. B. DuBois.

Finally, black scholars know how the fifteen-hour teaching schedule has buried research under mounds of freshman composition and how the small pay checks have driven potential critics into administrative positions merely to gain reasonable compensation for their drudgery.

After this pessimistic review of the problems of Afro-American literary critics, it may seem amazing that any have existed. And in limited space, I can do little more than name a few of the more prolific and to consider their practices briefly. I wish to give special attention to the Afro-American critics who have written about literature by blacks, and I shall include both literary historians and critics under the rubric of "critic." For convenience of discussion, I shall oversimplify by categorizing the historians and critics in six groups: (1) Afro-Americans who have become identified primarily with the "mainstream" of American criticism because of their research in the work of white authors; (2) black historians who have described literary achievements merely as a part of their broader study of Afro-American culture; (3) those individuals who have attracted attention because of their pronouncements about one particular black writer or one group of writers; (4) the creative writers, whose fame rests upon their own work rather than upon their criticism; (5) the academic critics, and (6) the new black critics, who argue for a Black Aesthetic. This survey is not definitive but suggestive: it is an introduction to a study that needs to be made.

i.

Some Afro-Americans have earned recognition primarily by writing about literature by whites. Probably the first such successful critic was William Stanley Braithwaite, a Bostonian black man of West Indian ancestry. A professional journalist, Braithwaite from 1913 to 1929 edited an annual anthology of magazine verse. In introductions to these volumes, Braithwaite directed attention to young white poets who had not yet been recognized by American critics. One should not look to Braithwaite for objective criticism, however. Generally, he assumed the role of a sociable master of ceremonies, introducing his protégés, rejoicing in their virtues, and abstaining from caustic condemnation. Although he published only one volume of criticism, *The Poetic Year,* a collection of essays about the poetry of 1916, he wrote a biography of the Brontë sisters, and he edited anthologies of Elizabethan, Georgian, and Restoration verse.

A second critic who published before World War I was Benjamin Brawley. Although his principal reputation today is based on his studies of black cultural history, Brawley, a professor at Morehouse College, Shaw University, and Howard University, also wrote *A Short History of English Literature,* designed for use in college classes. In taste, Brawley was a Victorian, in the conservative and genteel sense in which that term is understood. He preferred writers who wrote of beauty rather than squalor; and in his own biographical work he ignored those activities of his subjects that he could not commend. Although he must be mentioned at this point, Brawley will be considered more fully in a later section of this paper.

Some more-recent scholars have earned wider recognition for their publications about white authors than for their studies of blacks. For example, although Philip Butcher, a professor at Morgan State College, has written articles about young black novelists, he is better known for his two biographies of George Washington Cable, a nineteenth-century white novelist. Similarly, Esther Merle Jackson, recently a Fulbright professor at the University of Berlin and currently a professor at the University of Wisconsin, is better known as the author of a brilliant book-length study of Tennessee Williams than as a critic of black literature.

The contemporary black critic who is most firmly anchored in the mainstream is Nathan A. Scott, professor of theology at the University of Chicago, whose race is unknown to many of his ardent admirers. Scott occasionally has written about Afro-American literature, a field in which he is very knowledgeable. His best piece in black literary criticism is "The Dark and Haunted Tower of Richard Wright" (1964), one of the few articles commending Richard Wright as an existentialist. Nathan Scott's reputation, however, is based on such books as *Rehearsals of Discomposure* (1952) and *Modern Literature and the Religious Frontier* (1958), excellent works in which he examined philosophical and psychological dilemmas as they are revealed in the fiction of such writers as Kafka, Silone, Lawrence, and Eliot.

As was stated earlier, however, most of the attention in this paper will be focused on those black literary historians and critics who have been especially concerned with studies of black literature.

ii.

Criticism of black writers as a group is a relatively new venture. It was necessary, first, for black writers to produce a considerable body of literature and, second, for black and white critics to develop awareness that that work could be examined as literature rather than merely as sociology. As early as 1863, William Wells Brown included Phillis Wheatley among the black heroes whose lives he recorded in *The Black Man: His Antecedents, His Genius, and His Achievements*. Almost one half century later, Benjamin Brawley produced a pioneer work, *The Negro in Literature and Art* (1910). Like Brown, Brawley offered more biography than critical evaluation. Perceiving America's ignorance about black writers, Brawley chiefly assumed the responsibility of familiarizing readers with them; hence, he remained more historian than critic.

By the middle of the 1920s, the two requisite forces—an ample volume of work by black writers, and readers' respect for that work as literature—had coalesced. Therefore, most significant criticism of Afro-American literature dates from that time.

Prominent among the black scholars since 1925 who have earned reputations for knowledge of black literature, have been several whose major interests lay in other disciplines. The first of these was W. E. B. DuBois, who earned his doctorate from Harvard in history. Although he did not publish any books of criticism, DuBois, as the first editor of *The Crisis*, regularly commented on the work of black writers. Unfortunately, during the 1920s, one of the most exciting periods in the annals of Afro-American literature, DuBois proved incapable of shedding the ideals of an earlier generation. Like most black intellectuals of the last decade of the nineteenth century, DuBois sought to earn equality for black Americans by educating white Americans to awareness of their virtues and their sensitivity to oppression. A talented writer who judged creative literature to be a major vehicle for such education, DuBois was appalled by some black writers of the twenties who seemed to sully the black man's image by revealing the squalid aspects of Afro-American life and character.

Few men, if any, have had greater success than Alain Locke in familiarizing America with the culture of black people. Although he earned a doctorate from Harvard in philosophy, served for many years as chairman of the Philosophy Department at Howard University, and published studies in philosophy, Locke used his compendious knowledge and his aesthetic sensitivity to art, music, and literature as a basis for many articles and books about black culture. In 1925, he edited *The New Negro*, an anthology that is still respected as the best introduction to the temper and art of the early years of the Negro Awakening. He was the first to edit an anthology of Afro-American drama, *Plays of Negro Life* (1927). He edited one of the earliest critical anthologies of poetry, *Four Negro Poets* (1927). For more than twenty years, he annually reviewed literature of black Americans—first in *Opportunity*, then in *Phylon*. Like Braithwaite, he applauded more than he appraised; for his purpose was to record literary achievement and to encourage additional activity.

More recent historians of Afro-American literature are John Hope Franklin, Margaret Just Butcher, and Ernest Kaiser. In *From Slavery to Freedom* (1948, 1956), Franklin, professor of history at the University of Chicago, commented on Afro-American writers as part of the cultural history of black America. Margaret Butcher, a professor at Federal City College, included appraisals of literary works in *The Negro in American Culture* (1956), which she developed from notes and materials that Alain Locke had compiled. Ernest Kaiser, librarian at the Schomburg Collection in New York City, is best known as the author of brilliant essays on black scholarship in history. In addition, Kaiser, who is incredibly knowledgeable about literature by and about Afro-Americans, has written perceptively about current black writers. His work is frequently published in *Negro Digest* and in *Freedomways*, for which he regularly reviews recent books by and about blacks.

All these cultural historians have played important roles by familiarizing Americans with the names and works of black writers; but, because of their training and their purpose, they had no desire to provide for individual works or individual authors the kind of in-depth examination that is essential to literary criticism.

iii.

A few essayists have become known as critics chiefly because of their evaluation of one writer or one group. It may be unfair to place Harold Cruse in this category, for *The Crisis of the Negro Intellectual* (1967) is now judged on its own merits. Nevertheless, when the book was first published, the criticism Cruse had written for magazines was not known widely; consequently, his name was less familiar than were the names of black writers he attacked and black scholars whose critical theories he denounced. It is probable, therefore, that much of the early reaction to the book was stimulated by general interest in Cruse's assault on such writers as Lorraine Hansberry and John Killens. Similarly, the first international recognition of James Baldwin as a critic came in response to "Everybody's Protest Novel," which seemed to question the artistic competence of Richard Wright, who was then the most famed and respected among Afro-American novelists. As the wheel turns and attacker becomes the attacked, it is fashionable today to quote Eldridge Cleaver's denunciation of Baldwin in *Soul on Ice* (1968).

What is startling about these few instances is the apparent eagerness of the reading public to accept instantly the scathing pronouncements of an individual who had no previous reputation as a critic or who at least lacked a literary reputation comparable to that of the writer he rejected. The reason for this phenomenon, I believe, is that, despite fifty years of criticism of Afro-American literature, criteria for that criticism have not been established. Consequently, some readers judge literature by Afro-Americans according to its moral value, a few for its aesthetic value, most by its social value, and too many according to their responses to the personalities of the black authors. As long as this confusion continues, many readers, lacking confidence in their own ability to distinguish the worth-while black literature from the inept, echo the most recent voice they hear.

iv.

When a white publisher has wanted a black man to write about Afro-American literature, the publisher generally has turned to a famous creative writer. The reason is obvious. White publishers and readers have not been, and are not, familiar with the names and work of black scholars—the academic critics. Therefore, publishers have called upon the only blacks they have known—the famous writers.

Since all the best-known black writers and many of the less well-known have been asked or permitted to serve as historian, critic, or polemicist, only a minimal summary of their work is possible in a paper as brief as this.

In 1922, novelist and poet James Weldon Johnson edited an anthology, *The Book of American Negro Poetry* (revised in 1931), for which he wrote an excellent critical introduction to black poets. From 1926 to 1928, Countee Cullen, best-known Afro-American poet of his day, wrote randomly about literary topics in "The Black Tower," published monthly in *Opportunity*. In 1927, he, too, prepared an anthology of poetry, *Caroling Dusk*, for which he provided an introduction and headnotes. Both Johnson and Cullen, however, are suspect as critics. Like many other authors, they sometimes devised theory to defend their personal practices. Nevertheless, both gave more attention to aesthetic theory than was common among Afro-American critics.

During the twenties, novelist Wallace Thurman received frequent invitations to write articles about fiction. From the thirties until his death in the sixties, Langston Hughes probably received more requests to write about Afro-American authors than any other black writer prior to James Baldwin. Most often, Hughes described personalities rather than works, or he recited the problems of black writers. It is difficult to determine whether Hughes chose to restrict his writing in this manner, or, more probably, whether these were the subjects of prime interest to the soliciting editors. In the forties, Richard Wright was the one whom editors called for articles; and, when he chose, he produced as effectively in literary history as in fiction. One of the most perceptive analyses by an Afro-American writer is Wright's long essay on black poets, "The Literature of the Negro in the United States," published first in a French journal and later included in Wright's *White Man! Listen* (1957). In the essay, Wright describes the poets since Phillis Wheatley, and scrutinizes their relationships to American society.

The two best-known writer-critics are James Baldwin and Ralph Ellison, who come closer than any others to being the professional critics among black writers. A professional critic, as I use the term, is a man who earns his living primarily by writing about literature; for example, Brooks Atkinson, for years drama critic for the New York *Times,* or Edmund Wilson or George Jean Nathan. To survive, a professional critic normally must be associated with a newspaper or magazine; a free-lance critic risks starvation. (And, as I have said earlier, few blacks have been hired on the staffs of periodicals or dailies.) Nevertheless, Baldwin, in his early years in Paris, gambled at being a free-lance writer on literary subjects even before he became famous as a novelist. He included many of his better essays in *Notes of a Native Son* (1955) and *Nobody Knows My Name* (1961). Ralph Ellison also distinguished himself as a free-lance writer on literary and musical topics. Some of his more significant essays are included in his collection *Shadow and Act* (1964).

A writer-critic in great demand at the moment is Arna Bontemps, one of the last of the talented writers of the Harlem Renaissance. By preference and by invitation, Bontemps most frequently writes nostalgically and illuminatingly about the twenties and thirties. Although he has published many novels and anthologies, Bontemps has published no books of literary history, an oversight one hopes he will correct.

v.

The most significant group of black literary critics should be the academic critics, for these are the individuals trained to study and evaluate literature. They have the breadth of information to facilitate comparison of American writers with foreign ones and comparison of current writers with those of previous centuries. Unfortunately, because they have published most often for small printing houses or in professional journals (often those read by few whites), the academic critics are the least well-known of black critics.

The first major academic critic was Benjamin Brawley, whose early efforts were designed to promote appreciation rather than evaluation. For example, in his critical biography of Paul Laurence Dunbar (1936), Brawley deliberately ignored personal failings of the man, and minimized many of Dunbar's weaknesses as a writer. When the writers of the twenties appeared, Brawley, like DuBois, revealed himself unable to adapt to the tastes of a new generation: He continued to echo the precepts of Matthew Arnold. Complaining about what he believed to be the young writers' unnecessary interest in the ugliness of life, he argued that they lacked the high moral purpose essential to great literature. Perhaps the most accurate measure of Brawley's literary taste is the fact that he selected as Dunbar's best story a highly sentimental one in which a husband decides to remain with his wife because he is thrilled by the tenderness with which their newly born child clutches his hand.

Despite his deficiencies in criticism, Brawley was the first significant academic critic-historian of Afro-American literature. The next was Sterling Brown, younger than Brawley but his contemporary as a teacher at Howard University. Brown is the dean of black academic critics. No other black critic has inspired as much admiration and respect from his students and his successors in the field. In every stream of creative black literature, Sterling Brown is the source to which critics return. His first published critical books were *The Negro in American Fiction* (1937), a detailed examination of the Afro-American as a character, and *The Negro in Poetry and Drama* (1937). An almost unknown classic is his unpublished study of Afro-American drama, which he undertook as part of the Myrdal-Carnegie research project. Brown was the senior editor of *The Negro Caravan* (1941), the most comprehensive anthology of Afro-American letters that has been published. Unlike Brawley, Brown understood the need to evaluate the image of the black man as character and the achievement of the black man as writer. Brown has published no books since 1941, although he continued until recently to publish infrequent articles on folk tales, folklore, and folk speech. As a critic, Brown benefited from catholic taste and sensitivity, which enabled him to appreciate and applaud the realistic as well as the genteel, the folk as well as the sophisticated.

The best single volume of criticism by a black, I believe, is Saunders Redding's *To Make a Poet Black* (1939). A brilliant writer, the author of history, an autobiography, a novel, and a collection of essays, Redding, now a professor at Georgetown University, studied writers from Jupiter Hammon through those of the twenties. His insights are striking, and his style is admirable. This is a book to read; it is regrettable that Redding has not revised the book to bring it up to the present.

In the 1930s and 1940s, two other academic critics—Nick Ford and Hugh Gloster—published book-length studies of Afro-American literature. Ford examined twentieth-century fiction in *The Contemporary Negro Novel* (1936). Gloster's *Negro Voices in American Fiction* (1948)—the more detailed of the two—focuses on the Afro-American writers' depiction of the relationship of their black characters to the American scene. Gloster, however, was concerned more with sociological import than with aesthetic quality.

The forties and fifties spawned numerous Afro-American critics who published in *Phylon,* the *College Language Association Journal,* and other professional periodicals. Among the most productive of these were John Lash, Blyden Jackson, and Nick Ford. All three, at various times, prepared the annual review of Negro literature for *Phylon,* but also published frequently in other journals. All three concentrated on fiction. Criticism of poetry is surprisingly sparse during the period, and criticism of drama is almost non-existent.

A characteristic common to all these critics—and one that Harold Cruse denounces—is the tendency to evaluate literature by black writers according to the criteria established and approved for white American writers. In one sense, this standard is justifiable, for most of the black writers, in their effort to earn respect, initiated the styles supposedly approved. But this insistence encouraged excessively enthusiastic praise of writers working within tradition, and suspicion of the few who broke away from tradition.

vi.

For a decade, there was a hiatus in criticism by the academicians. Many of the black scholars drifted into administrative positions to secure financial rewards commensurate with their ability. Others abandoned Afro-American literature because they believed that black writers had finally become part of the mainstream of American literature. During this period—roughly, 1954 to 1965—significant social changes occurred. The Supreme Court desegregation decision of 1954 at first seemed to assure Afro-Americans the equality they had desired. Consequently, many black educators considered it deplorable and un-American to study Negro identity apart from American identity. However, by 1960, only six years later, it was evident that school integration had not produced the anticipated amalgamation. Meanwhile, intensifying insistence from black Americans persuaded blacks and whites to want to learn more about Afro-American culture and history.

This impulse has produced two developments. The first is the emergence of a new generation of academic critics and a return of many who had discontinued their studies about Afro-American literature: James Emanuel, W. Edward Farrison, Addison Gayle, Stephen Henderson, and George Kent are among the currently productive writers. Richard Long, Helen Johnson, and Richard

Barksdale are perfecting studies intended for publication. Of these, only Emanuel and Farrison have written books of criticism —Emanuel, a biography of Langston Hughes (1967), and Farrison, a biography of William Wells Brown (1969). Gayle, however, has published two anthologies of criticism by Afro-Americans—*Black Expression* (1969) and this volume on the Black Aesthetic and a collection of essays *The Black Situation* (1970).

The second development is perhaps more significant. A new group of black critics has developed. These reject the standards previously applied to works by Afro-Americans, and are demanding that that literature be judged according to an aesthetic grounded in Afro-American culture. Many of these new critics insist that, to have value, black literature must contribute to the revolutionary cause of black liberation, not merely in polemics against white oppression but also in reinterpretation of the black experience. All the new critics agree that the literature should not be judged good or bad according to its imitation of the styles and tastes of Europeans, but according to its presentation of the styles and traditions stemming from African and Afro-American culture. For example, they point out the foolishness of expecting iambic meter in work of a poet who moves instead to the rhythms of jazz or be-bop, and they argue that it is supercilious or even racist to complain that literature does not conform to the patterns and tastes of the white literary world if it does suit and meet the needs of black people.

None of these critics has yet produced a book; they were given platforms originally by Hoyt Fuller of *Negro Digest* and John Henrik Clarke of *Freedomways*. More recently, they have been publishing in newer magazines. The best-known are LeRoi Jones and Larry Neal, who coedited *Black Fire* (1968). Jones is known as a writer of the new literature; Neal has been more productive as an exponent of the theories of the new literature. Others of significance are Clarence Major, editor of *New Black Poetry* (1969); Carolyn Rodgers, whose "Black Poetry—Where It's At" (*Negro Digest*, 1969) is the best essay on the work of new black poets; Sarah Fabio; Cecil Brown, author of a recent novel, *The Life and Loves of Mr. Jive-Ass Nigger;* and Ed Bullins, the leading interpreter of current black theater.

It is important that these new critics are explaining theory rather than merely commenting on practice. Previously, as I have said, most Afro-American critics assumed that the desirable standards were necessarily those currently favored by the American literary establishment. This attitude inevitably restricted black writers to imitation rather than innovation: the "good" writer was expected to use the forms and styles that appealed to white readers. And he dared not aspire to the avant-garde, because he needed assurance that the style was approved. In a sense, then, he continued to permit himself to be defined by the white American. Today, however, black critics are postulating theories about what literature is or should be for black people, according to a Black Aesthetic, as was explained in a recent issue of *Negro Digest.*

The writings of these theorists and critics are not hammering at the consciousness of the American literary masses, because most new critics are not attempting to publish in the journals subscribed to predominantly by whites. Most are publishing in *Negro Digest, Journal of Black Poetry, Critique, The Black Scholar, Black Theater,* and other popular publications aimed at a black market. One who wishes to learn what the new black critics are doing and saying must read such journals as these.

At present, the major weakness of the Black Aesthetic critics are their tendencies to denigrate older black writers while lauding the newest. They are further handicapped by the necessity of devising theory prior to the creation of works. That is, Aristotle actually did little more than examine works he and other Greeks admired. He distinguished the elements these works shared. Then he stipulated that great literature must include such elements. Arnold, too, deduced his theories from literature already created. Many new black critics, however, are structuring theories while calling for writers to create the works that are needed to demonstrate the excellence of the theories.

It is not accidental, therefore, that most of the new critics are writers. And because their social theories are as revolutionary as their literary theories, few are permanently connected with the well-established academic institutions.

It is always dangerous to predict the future for any group of writers; nevertheless, a few guesses can be made about future directions of black critics. First, as increasing numbers of predominantly white institutions hire black instructors, and as additional money is given to black institutions, black scholars will find the time, the motivation, and the connections for publishing. This means that they will be producing increasing numbers of books about both white and black writers. As their publications increase, more black critics will become recognized and respected.

Second, as some of the present ferment subsides, the new black critics will look more closely at the current black writers. They will begin to evaluate more carefully on aesthetic bases, as Carolyn Rodgers is now doing. Perhaps by that time, or soon afterwards, they will have expanded American critical theory to a degree at which Americans can more fully appreciate poetry that depends on oral presentation and can appreciate drama that involves less physical action than has been the custom in the Anglo-American theatre. In short, the new black critics may develop theory that may become influential in the evaluation of all American literature.

I would like to conclude on this note of optimism. But I cannot. The chances are great that unless America changes drastically within the next few years, most American readers will continue to look at literature through the eyes of the white critics rather than the black. Full awareness of black critics will develop only when publishers make greater effort to look beyond the prestige colleges for authors of scholarly books, and when the literary public learns to look beyond the prestige journals for literary scholarship. And full appreciation of the criticism of Afro-American literature will develop only when all readers perceive that a thorough knowledge and understanding of the Afro-American experience, culture, and literary history is a prerequisite for an individual who wishes to be a critic of that literature.

II Music

INTRODUCTION TO BLACK AESTHETICS IN MUSIC
Jimmy Stewart

Usually when a serious examination of the cultural products of a people is undertaken, there is always the tacit assumption, on the part of the person who is doing the writing and on the part of those who read it, that the ingredients that go into the production of those products are the integral results of their particular cultural communality. This is presupposed by writers and readers alike when they deal with, in this particular case, the aesthetics of music. This has been, in most of the kinds of writings we've been accustomed to, the reason for the culpability we attribute to whites in their handling of materials pertaining to our culture—particularly those writings, mostly by whites, that deal with the aesthetics of the music of Black people in this country. The assumption is, of course, that the music of Black people in this country, aside from certain unavoidable ethnic considerations, can be defined in the same terms and by the same requirements as those that define the music produced by them (whites). Consequently, in most of the works available pertaining to the aesthetics of our music, the terms of their inquiries bear this general assumption.

But the fact of the matter is that such a case has never existed in this country. There have always been two musical

traditions: the musical tradition or aesthetic of white people in
the West, and the musical tradition of Black people in this
country. Even though there has been considerable borrowing
between the two cultures, the two distinctive aesthetic traditions
have always existed. And it has been this cultural tradition or
aesthetic that has determined the values in the music in each
case and that has determined everything in the terms of the
respective musics, e.g., the way the musical instruments were
utilized, and the over-all philosophy of music. In relation to this,
the fact that aesthetics as a formal concern involving the material
and mechanics of creation is fundamentally a reflective occupa-
tion, and the fact that, generally speaking, musicians as a group
are not generally concerned with the philosophical or theoretical
problems of how they make music, may account in part for the
present state of affairs we find in the West in general—that
those who were concerned about such matters, the musicologists
and historians, were in every case *procureurs* of the traditions
of their own particular cultural history, and in and by its terms
they established the basis for the critical standards for the music
or musics they became "authorities" of. Even in the face of the
fact that actually, in this country, the cultural condition required
a recognition of two distinct cultural matrices, the obstacles
that this recognition, by implication, introduced into their aesthetic formulations presented no apparent obstacles to them
(whites), since the critical system was theirs entirely, and not
one, as a formal criticism, of our own making. The incongruity
of this situation as a condition of a disjunct cultural situation
has been exacerbated at this present moment to the point that
our present necessity for a sequestered body of critical thought
is not even debatable.

Hitherto, the literature concerning the aesthetics of our music
has abounded with all sorts of white cultural paternalism in
judgments regarding the music produced. It could not have
been otherwise, since most of the people who provided the
critical material were white, and generally the attitudes they
have shared, and still do for that matter, are that the concep-

tions of culture in their context is applicable to us and to those products of our culture as well. This applies to all the intellectual assumptions whites bring to bear in their critical evaluations in the West in general, and in this country in particular. The situation here is all the more deplorable for the fact that it is the judgments of whites that are being foisted on Black people— a situation not only extremely reprehensible to us in its disgusting avoidance of acknowledging the requirements of our specific cultural frame, but a situation further compounded by being one wherein the requirements are those aesthetic values we find in what the critic produces in his or her role as the agent of a particular cultural tradition. For in America there has never existed a common cultural interest and heritage in the sense in which cultural interest and heritages exist in other countries. This, though the idolum of a national culture is promulgated in the aesthetic writings produced by the compradors of the white national aesthetic, may account for the reason why, until now, nobody among them, the majority of whom are white, have been able to deliver an adequate theory of aesthetic value concerning what we have produced. This is due in a great part to the long historical consequence of the way slavery was practiced in this country, and the ensuing consequence of the slaves' introduction into the domus of the enslaving society. The exclusive belief by whites, and those blacks who share it, that black people in this country constitute a culturally lost minority stems from this history. In addition, the terms that were used by whites to define culture, specifically in the case where culture is defined as the accumulation of discernible artifacts of a people, which in turn was construed to mean that any form "culture" took, i.e., discernible artifacts such as sculpture, pottery, garment designs, and so on, contributed greatly to this notion by whites that Black people in this country possessed no culture. And since they had ruthlessly seen to it that no formal representation of the culture of those Black people brought to the West (neither in the form of artifacts or language or religious worship) was retained in their new slave

situation in the new world, then the logical conclusion by terms
of their definition of culture enabled them to add insult to
injury by saying that the Black people in this country are a
culturally lost people in the West.

But, as a matter of fact and to the contrary, culture in
our sense transcends those kinds of objectifications of our experiences, by being manifestly cultural in terms of their movement *with* existence, instead of as an ossification of existence
that happens when an object of art is produced. African philosophy and metaphysics have always been animated by a total
vision of life; so we, as legatees of that vision of the world,
have manifested that index of our culture in the only approxi-
mation we could: in our music. This is observable in a formal
sense in the music we have produced in the West, but more
significantly in that music's inner dynamic. In the inner workings
of our music has been the ideal paradigm of our understanding
of the creative process as a movement *with* existence.

This means, then, that the concern of aesthetic being, in our
sense, is to accompany reality, to "move with it," so to speak,
and not against it, which all, yes *all*, the white cultural art forms
do. The art of the white culture is, in that sense, against life
and art. This is why none of the world's non-white peoples have
ever evolved museums. This is why black people in the West
never had to wait for a phonograph record or a book to
accomplish the transmission of our cultural values. Art, in our
sense, must be understood as the accomplishment of creating,
the operation of creating. What results therefrom is merely the
momentary residue of that operation—a perishable object and
nothing more, and anything else you might imbue it with
(which the white aesthetic purports to do) is nothing else but
mummification. The point is—and this is the crux of our two
opposing conceptions of being—that the imperishability of creation is not in what is created, is not in the art product, is not
in the *thing* as it exists as an object, but in the procedure of its
becoming what it is. The opposite view of this, the view that
European aesthetics developed, has been responsible for the

cul de sac that workers in that tradition have encountered in this century. They have been forced to reappraise their aesthetics to such an extent that they have decided, as for example, Pollack did, to posit their aesthetic, on the "action" aspect in its production, even though the fundamental material nature of painting qua painting is its fixity, as it has always been, and not its motion. Picasso, for another, presumed to resolve the ubiquitous dilemma of the same aesthetic by expropriating certain visible aspects of the traditional African wood carvings he discovered in Parisian *objet d'art* shops around the turn of this century, and applying them to his exhausted tradition.

To give you an idea of what he had to do to achieve what he did, consider that he had to negate entirely the most cherished characteristic of Western painting: the property of perspective. Or to choose another example of Black aesthetics in relationship to physical matter and durability in the tactile properties of aesthetic products, we might look at the state of certain pieces of art as physical articles, which in the case of music can only refer to notations on paper. In the sense that music has no property as physical matter, in the sense in which a painting does or a building, it comes as close as we know to being in existence in a sense in which none of the other forms of art are. Even though those forms that utilize words possess this property, as well as the dance to an elaborate degree, they nonetheless lack the simultaneity one encounters in the musical experience.

Our music in the Afro-Christian era was largely vocal and therefore amenable to pitch-ordering—a situation that was altered considerably when we began to handle musical instruments. The employment of instruments, with the attendant problems of sound production, meant that a regulation was introduced into our aural framework, where previously the antiphonal features in our singing, which didn't have to come through an attachment, could have been varied at will. The fact that the instruments could not accommodate the microtonal variants that were peculiar to our singing meant that adjustments had to

be made, which, put another way, meant simply that when
those Black brothers got hold of those instruments, the instruments didn't come with free lessons and all, like you get at
Wurlitzer. And the whites didn't much care how or what we
did with them. It was a matter of being left to our own
resources to determine how the music was going to be produced
on those instruments. This, and the fact that none of the
instruments we used were invented by us, meant that we had
to impose on borrowed instruments an aesthetic convention that
we obviously possessed even before we acquired them. This is
significant. It indicates that a Black aesthetic existed, and that
this aesthetic has always governed what we have produced.
However, let us go back to an examination of the nature of our
religious worship, then. In the pre-Christian slave period, all
the Blacks that were brought to this country brought their gods
with them, which meant that if a Black man was brought here
and he was from the Dagomba people, the god he brought he
called Wuni. If he was from the Fo people, he called his god
Mawu. If he was from the Kikuyu people, he called his god
Ngai. What I'm getting to is that, even aside from the vicious
practices of the slavers to eradicate any form of a formal religious
worship among us, there never existed in our situation a dominant tribal metaphysical frame such as existed in Haiti, for
example. So when a form of worship arose among Black people
in this country, that form of worship comprised a synthesis of all
the ingredients of those various forms of our previous African
worships we retained in the New World. These were spiritual
things, not physical artifacts. The orishas were in those early
churches. The gods were in our voices, and when we left those
churches and went out into the world, those gods went with us.
They went with us out into those fields, in our work songs and
blues. And so, by the time we got to King Oliver, the gods that
had been in the churches had to be where gods always really
are—in the world, among people. When those Black men began
to handle those instruments, they were directly in contact with
their gods. They were fully in contact with power. An instrument

focuses and situates your function, whether you are driving a
car or a lathe, or playing a saxophone. You could sing anywhere,
whenever you pleased. You could sing while you worked, which
was just what we were doing during those early vocal periods
of our music. But a musical instrument entailed preparation
and a concentration of function. You couldn't do anything else
while you were doing that. Here, you might say, as a formal
category of our aesthetics Jazz began, but only in the sense
that a distinction was established. Because the fact of the matter
is that the kind of arbitrary compartmentalizing we invariably
do when we try to intelligently talk about our music doesn't
exist at all. For example, the collective improvisation that Ornette
Coleman introduced into our music in the sixties was employed
in the Oliver and Armstrong period, all the way back to our
early churches, back to forms in Africa, yet conspicuously absent
in the BeBop development of the forties. Yet the repeated
cadences, or "fours," which typified the music of the BeBop
phase relate directly to the call and response that is still
a definite practice in certain of our Baptist churches today. In
addition to these examples of an aesthetic continuum's existing,
the only parting comment I wish to make on its nature before
we move to the social aspects that must be taken into account
is that the state of our aesthetics before the acquisition of
musical instruments might be said to resemble a compost of
diverse Black spiritual factors. But the inevitable secularization
that followed in the wake of the Civil War, and the constraints
of segregation which held at bay the physical distention of
Black people, could not stay the ideas, the ideologies, that the
black musician freely appropriated from the white society. This
culminated in the monstrous display of an aesthetic individualism
(an antiquated white Renaissance concept) during the Bop
movement, which in the forties was a white aesthetic counterpart
to the theory of laissez faire, and corresponded to a capitalistic
philosophy more rampant in its economics then than ever before.
It was during this period that the words "genius" and "artist"
came to signify the approbative status of aesthetic stature that

most Black musicians were pursuing then and that was being
bestowed on them by white critics.

We find, from the hindsights of historical perspective, that
the situation I mentioned as pertaining to the attitudes and
values of the proponents of our music during the forties and
fifties didn't just suddenly occur, but was in truth the logical
consequence of the bourgeois impedimenta that were always
a part of the music. The contention was that what occurred
then—the quest for white approval—was adumbrated in the
creole ethics that accompanied the development of the music
from its New Orleans days to then. Even though this white
approval was sought, in many ways, obvious and/or subtle, it
nonetheless characterized our Black artists under the various
regimes. For example, in the 1800s, within the limited confines
of the Negro community in New Orleans, the Black people were
moving toward two definite societies: the society of the café-
au-lait creole members of the community, and that of the Blacks.
The expressed social philosophy of this creole class was the
eventual assimilation of their members into the white society—
something they achieved partially in a genetic sense, and toward
which end they were attempting by other means to go, politically
and socially. But the white society halted this movement by
closing all access the creoles had into the dominant white social
stream. This foreclosure on the plans of this class to eventually
assimilate into the great American schema forced them to reappraise and utilize their resources within the segregated limits
of the negro community. This meant that the skills, and equally
significant values, were brought into the larger Black portion
of the community. And as the century ground on into the
twentieth with the war (World War One), Black soldiers went
to Europe, the home of white values in the West, and, back in
America, were exposed in the twenties to the egalitarianism of
the white aesthetes and the white upper middle class that
brought blacks and whites into closer proximity than they had
ever shared previously. In perspective it seems no surprise that
the black artist of the forties and fifties was a ready prey for

the aesthetic ideological traps the whites had laid for him. And as we reach for an understanding of what was going on, in terms of the development of our music, we get a more coherent view of its development in terms of those social components that determined the attitudes the men had concerning themselves and toward what they produced, than what theretofore was available to us in accounts by whites. The astounding fact of the matter is that though there were inchoate rumblings of perceiving ourselves as a "national" entity in this country in the thoughts and writings of such men as Martin Delaney and Blyden, the factors in support of Negroes conceiving of themselves as merely a disenfranchised minority in the national American system torpedoed that notion, and our energies were expended, instead of seeking full equality, legally and socially. Consequently, these same "nationalistic" imperatives, expressed as they were in the political realm and reflected in our aesthetic philosophy, were in the same fashion ignored in the integrationist process of casting our music as a "cultural contribution" to the music of the white national culture of America. Lacking a "national" frame of cultural reference, thus actually lacking a bourgeoisie which in that context could supply and support an aesthetic—as an ideology—we took the aesthetic ideology of the white national culture. This understanding of our aesthetics historically shows, without a doubt, that the music of the sixties represents an absolute break with the past in this sense.

But before we get to the national basis of our aesthetic ideology, let us consider some of the factors in the past that, retrospectively, indicated the necessity of consciously moving our music ahead ideologically. These factors in the past have been the relationship of the music to function, to our social functions. And in that assessment, the form of our instrumentation then was governed by the function the music served in our social framework. The early bands were usually sextets, consisting principally of a lead horn, usually a cornet; a clarinet, which supplied obbligatos, runs, and various other ornamental figurations to the lead voice; and a trombone, which behaved as a sort of melodic bass, often "counter" moving melodically or utilizing "slide" devices and fills whenever the other voices or parts were stationary. In addition to these, the rhythm section then comprised drums, guitar, and bass. There were variations to this arrangement, but basically this was the instrumental composition of the early bands. Occasionally the tuba was used instead of the bass, particularly during the marching affairs, at lodge functions, and to and from the cemeteries. Understandably the piano was not used on those occasions. The piano, significantly, occupied a niche all by itself in those early days. The very nature of its stationary weight would have made it an awkward addition to the bands during those affairs, which were very mobile. The smaller instruments were more suitable. As the music became more sedentary, at least in the form of its presentation at dances, at homes, and in bars, the piano figured more prominently in the make-up of the band. However, prior to that, the piano had been the major source of music in the bawdyhouses that proliferated in New Orleans during the "sporting house" period, e.g., the whore-house period in Storyville, when the piano was usually played unaccompanied. The player supplied his own rhythmic and harmonic background. To achieve this, he made use of all the musical adornments that we now accept as standard to the type of playing associated with that period: mordants, turns, appoggiaturas, and clever chordal manipulations. But when the piano was added to the other instrumental combinations as a supportive voice, that elaborate and ornate conception of piano playing had to be altered as a contributing musical voice. From the role of establishing the harmonic frame for the compositions that were played, the piano progressed, or retrogressed, depending on how you interpret the importance of the instrument, to that of a more skeletal form of piano style in the form of playing we've come to know as "comping." By saying "progressed" or "retrogressed," as I did above, I chose to view the role of this instrument, the progression of this instrument, from a period of elaborate expression to a diminution of its function and importance in the music of the sixties. This seems to be due to its being the most "European" of the instruments utilized in the instrumentation of our music; the pitches' being unalterably fixed meant that it was the only instrument impervious to the pitch variations that were possible on the other instruments, which were and still are so essential to the production of our music. It was the most "white" instrument in our groups. So the music of the sixties was the force of our aesthetics, which obliged us to discard the piano. We could no longer pay obeisance to the Western tempered harmonic system in the form of the harmonic demands this instrument imposed on the music.

Changes in the manner and make-up of the aesthetic product reflect the changes in the relationships of the product to its social activities, its place, and its function. It is finally in this sense, in the sense of the changing relationships of the music, in this case, to the departments of social activities, that a coherent understanding of Black aesthetics emerges. The music that accompanied the parades and the dances, the music played in the bawdyhouses, and the music played in the bars situated our art as a function in our communities, and as an art it had also a function as entertainment. But as we've seen, that finally had to end. For in the Bop movement of the forties, a rift was becoming apparent between the music and its function in the Black community. That wedge expressed (aside from the immediate espousals on the part of some of our Black artists on the primacy of the seriousness of what they were doing) a deeper development that meant they were examining their aesthetic in its relationship to the economic and political factors that determined its being. So when Mingus and Max Roach addressed themselves to the forms of cultural imperialism that the white proprietors and entrepreneurs practiced, it was apparent, without a doubt, that the days of producing our music within the context of those former departments of social activities were at an end. And the music that ushered forth would no longer be compatible to those departments, e.g., the bars and the entire popular music field. It meant that our music, which was in essence the music from Ornette Coleman to the present, would no longer be applied to these departments of the white American social organization. Which gives us every indication that our music, in terms of form and content, has now become more and more expressive of our own distinctive theory of art. And this theory is by implication posited in a "nationalistic" context of culture. Which, after all, all cultural theories are. Within this frame, and only by this frame, can a valid definition of aesthetics in the context of our culture be arrived at. The necessity for a sequestered body of critical thought is part of moving our music toward the future, where the music we will supply will be applied to the departments we will create in that world.

I hope that in reading the essays that will accompany this introduction in this section on Black aesthetics in music, the reader will keep in mind that the requirements of a totally new vision of aesthetic reality will require that some of the *continuants* of the past, as they pertained to certain aspects of the production of our music, must be severed, and that, perhaps to the lament of some, many of the requirements of the past cannot be taken intact into the future. It is in this one aspect that the music of the sixties is crucially different from the music that went before it, in that in one fundamental sense the requirements of all our musics prior to the sixties developed out of a definite system of protocol, i.e., there was a well-defined procedure for qualification as a musician that required that the neophyte musician serve a required period of apprenticeship by studying the acknowledged masters, which he did usually by listening to records, then the arduous practicing or "shedding" where he perniciously attempted to emulate his teacher, and then finally putting all of it to the test by applying it with others in the act of making music, which meant working with combos and bands of various sizes and so forth. Concomitantly, a serious form of competitiveness was nurtured that stimulated creativity, in most cases of the kind that Basie nurtured in the bands he had that included Chuck Berry and

Hershel Evans at the same time, and Hershel and Lester Young
at another. Norman Ganz produced a situation of this sort in his
Jazz at the Philharmonic packaging, by staging Howard McGee
with Roy Eldridge (if my memory serves me correctly), Illinois
Jacquet with Prez, Gene Ammons with Sonny Stitt, and Bird
with Willie Smith, and numerous other couplings I'm sure the
reader can recall, which I haven't mentioned. This was a fundamental practice that was traditionally expressive of our culture.
Our poets practiced it in our traditional African societies, where
poets engaged each other in contests of improvisational verse-
making. One that immediately comes to mind is such a contest
the Swahili poets used to participate in, called *kufumbana*,
in which two poets try to "trip the other up" by composing
two lines of a verse, which the other must complete by two
lines in the same meter and rhyme. But in addition to this,
the fact that each line had to have sixteen syllables with a
caesura, which is a pause denoting the rhythmic division in
a line of verse, should give you an idea of the skill that
was required. This is what went on in our "jam sessions"
in our music in this country, and this is a feature of the
way our music was produced then, and what I called a "con-
tinuant" in that context. Values of aesthetic status were bound
to be created that had nothing at all to do with what the
whites were talking about when they spoke about our musical
giants. And those values were concomitant with customs of
aesthetic succession in very much the way I've described above.
This is what all our muscians, in the context of that development of our music we know by the name of Jazz, were required
to pass through. From the days that Louis served his apprenticeship in the band of King Oliver, to the time when Coleman
Hawkins had to assert his aesthetic supremacy over all the
tenor saxophonists that remained in America while he sojourned
in Europe, which he did on his return. This is told in an
apocryphal story of how Ben Webster baited the "Hawk" by
tauntingly inviting him to bring his horn with him the next
time he came to the club Ben was currently playing in, and

how the "Hawk" continued to return to the club to hear Webster play but never brought his instrument and how Ben got somebody to take the Hawk's tenor from his apartment and bring it to the club, thus forcing Ben and Coleman to "get one on." These practices were adhered to. The music literally proliferates with tales such as this one. Even the John Coltrane/Sonny Rollins encounter, and the self-imposed retirement of Sonny from the music scene after that encounter, gave credence to those arguments that Trane and Sonny had indeed participated in a contest of saxophone playing and Sonny had lost and that a new voice in tenor playing was on the scene. And Bird—most conclusively Bird—complied with this form of aesthetic succession by literally demolishing every existing practitioner of the music extant in his day. Thus he asserted his supremacy by the terms of the requirement of the art in that way in which the music we made came to be. But in terms of what I've described, the music of the sixties represents a cleavage with the past in this essential and fundamental sense, in that Ornette and those who are considered as forerunners of the new Black music did not "earn" their leadership status in any of the ways by which leadership was "earned" in our music previously, from New Orleans to the present. And what can be stated as "revolutionary" involves more than technical innovation. It involves the temerity of these men to suggest that all the assumptions or at least some of the basic and most fundamental ones, which I've recounted above, had to be discarded. This is at the essential core of what has happened in the new revolutionary Black music. This connects to the ideological position of Black music in the sense that the ego-ridden individualism of our music in all the antecedent periods of its development is superannuated at this time in our history. Thus the entire context of the music that John Coltrane produced in conjunction with Pharaoh Sanders was a conjunction and relationship one could have hardly conceptualized between Gene Ammons and Sonny Stitt, for example, since Sonny and Gene's association was governed in a definite sense by the procedures of aesthetic behavior that I am sure they would agree was customary in terms of how things were always done in "jazz." It would be safe to assume that such assumptions applied in the case of the collaborating functions of John and Pharaoh, or Milford Graves and Don Pullins, or Sun Ra's entire orchestral constituency. A. B. Spellman has presented an adequate explanation of the ideological basis of the new music in his essay "Revolution in Sound," which appeared in the August 1969 issue of *Ebony* magazine. His statement in that article that "these black art-conscious musicians do not constitute a vanguard in the political sense" may qualify as a correct assessment of the state of the musicians and the language they use, since the language is not vanguardist in a political sense, which is the case here, but we must be careful, however, not to overlook the revolutionary political implications in terms of the inner dynamic of the new Black music. What I mean is that the rhetoric does not have to be explicitly political, but it may be implicit in practice, which I've tried to bring to your attention in relating as I did how the music of the sixties differs fundamentally from the music of our past. In this sense, the music is certainly consistent with nationalist-revolutionary tenets, even if Sun Ra is speaking of space spheres. When Leon Thomas sings "The Creator Has a Master Plan," there is something explicitly political in that.

In practice, in the social sense and consequently in the economic sense, the musicians are in a very critical relationship to the departments of the existing state of the art-and-entertainment dispensation industry in this country. Insofar as these departments have always been in the control of whites, the implicit indicators of the new music are forcing the new-music practitioners and their products into an untenable relationship between themselves what they produce, and their function in the art-and-entertainment apparatus in the general white American society. And if the white musical industry has made it appear that the proponents of the music of the forties and the fifties have secured a hard-fought-for position in their system of things, then the regrettable consequence portends an aesthetic advocacy as deliberately iconoclastic in terms of those continuants of our own past as those Black aesthetics pose vis-à-vis the white cultural hegemony.

OF THE SORROW SONGS
W. E. B. DuBois

I walk through the churchyard
   To lay this body down;
I know moon-rise, I know star-rise;
I walk in the moonlight, I walk in the starlight;
I'll lie in the grave and stretch out my arms,
I'll go to judgment in the evening of the day,
And my soul and thy soul shall meet that day,
   When I lay this body down.

NEGRO SONG.

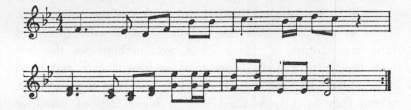

They that walked in darkness sang songs in the olden days—
Sorrow Songs—for they were weary at heart. And so before each
thought that I have written in this book I have set a phrase, a
haunting echo of these weird old songs in which the soul of the
black slave spoke to men. Ever since I was a child these songs
have stirred me strangely. They came out of the South unknown
to me, one by one, and yet at once I knew them as of me
and of mine. Then in after years when I came to Nashville
I saw the great temple builded of these songs towering over

the pale city. To me Jubilee Hall seemed ever made of the songs themselves, and its bricks were red with the blood and dust of toil. Out of them rose for me morning, noon, and night, bursts of wonderful melody, full of the voices of my brothers and sisters, full of the voices of the past.

Little of beauty has America given the world save the rude grandeur God himself stamped on her bosom; the human spirit in this new world has expressed itself in vigor and ingenuity rather than in beauty. And so by fateful chance the Negro folk-song—the rhythmic cry of the slave—stands to-day not simply as the sole American music, but as the most beautiful expression of human experience born this side the seas. It has been neglected, it has been, and is, half despised, and above all it has been persistently mistaken and misunderstood; but notwithstanding, it still remains as the singular spiritual heritage of the nation and the greatest gift of the Negro people.

Away back in the thirties the melody of these slave songs stirred the nation, but the songs were soon half forgotten. Some, like "Near the lake where drooped the willow," passed into current airs and their source was forgotten; others were caricatured on the "minstrel" stage and their memory died away. Then in war-time came the singular Port Royal experiment after the capture of Hilton Head, and perhaps for the first time the North met the Southern slave face to face and heart to heart with no third witness. The Sea Islands of the Carolinas, where they met, were filled with a black folk of primitive type, touched and moulded less by the world about them than any others outside the Black Belt. Their appearance was uncouth, their language funny, but their hearts were human and their singing stirred men with a mighty power. Thomas Wentworth Higginson hastened to tell of these songs, and Miss McKim and others urged upon the world their rare beauty. But the world listened only half credulously until the Fisk Jubilee Singers sang the slave songs so deeply into the world's heart that it can never wholly forget them again.

There was once a blacksmith's son born at Cadiz, New York, who in the changes of time taught school in Ohio and helped defend Cincinnati from Kirby Smith. Then he fought at Chancellorsville and Gettysburg and finally served in the Freedman's Bureau at Nashville. Here he formed a Sunday-school class of black children in 1866, and sang with them and taught them to sing. And then they taught him to sing, and when once the glory of the Jubilee songs passed into the soul of George L. White, he knew his life-work was to let those Negroes sing to the world as they had sung to him. So in 1871 the pilgrimage of the Fisk Jubilee Singers began. North to Cincinnati they rode,—four half-clothed black boys and five girl-women,—led by a man with a cause and a purpose. They stopped at Wilberforce, the oldest of Negro schools, where a black bishop heard them. Then they went, fighting cold and starvation, shut out of hotels, and cheerfully sneered at, ever northward; and ever the magic of their song kept thrilling hearts, until a burst of applause in the Congregational Council at Oberlin revealed them to the world. They came to New York and Henry Ward Beecher dared to welcome them, even though the metropolitan dailies sneered at his "Nigger Minstrels." So their songs conquered till they sang across the land and across the sea, before Queen and Kaiser, in Scotland and Ireland, Holland and Switzerland. Seven years they sang, and brought back a hundred and fifty thousand dollars to found Fisk University.

Since their day they have been imitated—sometimes well, by the singers of Hampton and Atlanta, sometimes ill, by straggling quartettes. Caricature has sought again to spoil the quaint beauty of the music, and has filled the air with many debased melodies which vulgar ears scarce know from the real. But the true Negro folk-song still lives in the hearts of those who have heard them truly sung and in the hearts of the Negro people.

What are these songs, and what do they mean? I know little of music and can say nothing in technical phrase, but I know

something of men, and knowing them, I know that these songs
are the articulate message of the slave to the world. They tell
us in these eager days that life was joyous to the black slave,
careless and happy. I can easily believe this of some, of many.
But not all the past South, though it rose from the dead, can
gainsay the heart-touching witness of these songs. They are the
music of an unhappy people, of the children of disappointment;
they tell of death and suffering and unvoiced longing toward
a truer world, of misty wanderings and hidden ways.

The songs are indeed the siftings of centuries; the music is
far more ancient than the words, and in it we can trace here
and there signs of development. My grandfather's grandmother
was seized by an evil Dutch trader two centuries ago; and
coming to the valleys of the Hudson and Housatonic, black,
little, and lithe, she shivered and shrank in the harsh north
winds, looked longingly at the hills, and often crooned a
heathen melody to the child between her knees, thus:

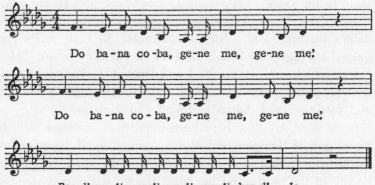

Do ba - na co - ba, ge - ne me, ge - ne me!

Do   ba - na co - ba, ge - ne   me, ge - ne me!

Ben d'. nu - li, nu - li, nu - li, nu - li, ben d'   le.

The child sang it to his children and they to their children's
children, and so two hundred years it has traveled down to
us and we sing it to our children, knowing as little as our
fathers what its words may mean, but knowing well the meaning
of its music.

This was primitive African music; it may be seen in larger form in the strange chant which heralds "The Coming of John":

> *You may bury me in the East,*
> *You may bury me in the West,*
> *But I'll hear the trumpet sound in that morning,*

—the voice of exile.

Ten master songs, more or less, one may pluck from this forest of melody—songs of undoubted Negro origin and wide popular currency, and songs peculiarly characteristic of the slave. One of these I have just mentioned. Another whose strains begin this book is "Nobody knows the trouble I've seen." When, struck with a sudden poverty, the United States refused to fulfill its promises of land to the freedmen, a brigadier-general went down to the Sea Islands to carry the news. An old woman on the outskirts of the throng began singing this song; all the mass joined with her, swaying. And the soldier wept.

The third song is the cradle-song of death which all men know,—"Swing low, sweet chariot,"—whose bars begin the life story of "Alexander Crummell." Then there is the song of many waters, "Roll, Jordan, roll," a mighty chorus with minor cadences. There were many songs of the fugitive like that which opens "The Wings of Atlanta," and the more familiar "Been A-Listening." The seventh is the song of the End and the Beginning—"My Lord, what a mourning! when the stars begin to fall"; a strain of this is placed before "The Dawn of Freedom." The song of groping—"My way's cloudy"—begins "The Meaning of Progress"; the ninth is the song of this chapter—"Wrestlin' Jacob, the day is a-breaking," a pæan of hopeful strife. The last master song is the song of songs—"Steal away,"—sprung from "The Faith of the Fathers."

There are many others of the Negro folk-songs as striking and characteristic as these, as, for instance, the three strains in the third, eighth, and ninth chapters; and others I am sure could easily make a selection on more scientific principles. There are,

too, songs that seem to be a step removed from the more
primitive types: there is the maze-like medley, "Bright sparkles,"
one phrase of which heads "The Black Belt"; the Easter carol,
"Dust, dust and ashes"; the dirge, "My mother's took her flight
and gone home"; and that burst of melody hovering over "The
Passing of the First-Born"—"I hope my mother will be there in
that beautiful world on high."

These represent a third step in the development of the slave
song, of which "You may bury me in the East" is the first,
and songs like "March on" (chapter six) and "Steal away" are
the second. The first is African music, the second Afro-American,
while the third is a blending of Negro music with the music
heard in the foster land. The result is still distinctively Negro
and the method of blending original, but the elements are both
Negro and Caucasian. One might go further and find a fourth
step in this development, where the songs of white America
have been distinctively influenced by the slave songs or have
incorporated whole phrases of Negro melody, as "Swanee River"
and "Old Black Joe." Side by side, too, with the growth has
gone the debasements and imitations—the Negro "minstrel"
songs, many of the "gospel" hymns, and some of the contemporary "coon" songs,—a mass of music in which the novice
may easily lose himself and never find the real Negro melodies.

In these songs, I have said, the slave spoke to the world. Such
a message is naturally veiled and half articulate. Words and
music have lost each other and new and cant phrases of a
dimly understood theology have displaced the older sentiment.
Once in a while we catch a strange word of an unknown
tongue, as the "Mighty Myo," which figures as a river of death;
more often slight words or mere doggerel are joined to music of
singular sweetness. Purely secular songs are few in number,
partly because many of them were turned into hymns by a
change of words, partly because the frolics were seldom heard
by the stranger, and the music less often caught. Of nearly
all the songs, however, the music is distinctly sorrowful. The
ten master songs I have mentioned tell in word and music of

trouble and exile, of strife and hiding; they grope toward some unseen power and sigh for rest in the End.

The words that are left to us are not without interest, and, cleared of evident dross, they conceal much of real poetry and meaning beneath conventional theology and unmeaning rhapsody. Like all primitive folk, the slave stood near to Nature's heart. Life was a "rough and rolling sea" like the brown Atlantic of the Sea Islands; the "Wilderness" was the home of God, and the "lonesome valley" led to the way of life. "Winter'll soon be over," was the picture of life and death to a tropical imagination. The sudden wild thunder-storms of the South awed and impressed the Negroes—at times the rumbling seemed to them "mournful," at times imperious:

> *My Lord calls me,*
> *He calls me by the thunder,*
> *The trumpet sounds it in my soul.*

The monotonous toil and exposure is painted in many words. One sees the ploughmen in the hot, moist furrow, singing:

> *Dere's no rain to wet you,*
> *Dere's no sun to burn you,*
> *Oh, push along, believer,*
> *I want to go home.*

The bowed and bent old man cries, with thrice-repeated wail:

> *O Lord, keep me from sinking down,*

and he rebukes the devil of doubt who can whisper:

> *Jesus is dead and God's gone away.*

Yet the soul-hunger is there, the restlessness of the savage, the wail of the wanderer, and the plaint is put in one little phrase:

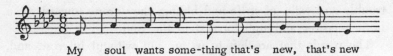

My soul wants some-thing that's new, that's new

Over the inner thoughts of the slaves and their relations one
with another the shadow of fear ever hung, so that we get but
glimpses here and there, and also with them, eloquent omissions
and silences. Mother and child are sung, but seldom father;
fugitive and weary wanderer call for pity and affection, but
there is little of wooing and wedding; the rocks and the mountains are well known, but home is unknown. Strange blending
of love and helplessness signs through the refrain:

> *Yonder's my ole mudder,*
> *Been waggin' at de hill so long;*
> *'Bout time she cross over,*
> *Git home bime-by.*

Elsewhere comes the cry of the "motherless" and the "Farewell,
farewell, my only child."

Love-songs are scarce and fall into two categories—the frivolous
and light, and the sad. Of deep successful love there is ominous
silence, and in one of the oldest of these songs there is a depth
of history and meaning:

Poor Ro - sy, poor— gal; Poor Ro - sy,

poor— gal; Ro - sy break my poor heart,

Heav'n shall-a-be my home.

A black woman said of the song, "It can't be sung without a full heart and a troubled sperrit." The same voice sings here that sings in the German folk-song:

Jetz Geh i' an's brunele, trink' aber net.

Of death the Negro showed little fear, but talked of it familiarly and even fondly as simply a crossing of the waters, perhaps —who knows?—back to his ancient forests again. Later days transfigured his fatalism, and amid the dust and dirt the toiler sang:

> *Dust, dust and ashes, fly over my grave,*
> *But the Lord shall bear my spirit home.*

The things evidently borrowed from the surrounding world undergo characteristic change when they enter the mouth of the slave. Especially is this true of Bible phrases. "Weep, O captive daughter of Zion," is quaintly turned into "Zion, weep-a-low," and the wheels of Ezekiel are turned every way in the mystic dreaming of the slave, till he says:

> *There's a little wheel a-turnin' in-a-my heart.*

As in olden time, the words of these hymns were improvised by some leading minstrel of the religious band. The circumstances of the gathering, however, the rhythm of the songs, and the limitations of allowable thought, confined the poetry for the most part to single or double lines, and they seldom were expanded to quatrains or longer tales, although there are some few examples of sustained efforts, chiefly paraphrases of the Bible. Three short series of verses have always attracted me,—the one that heads this chapter, of one line of which Thomas Wentworth Higginson has fittingly said, "Never, it seems to me, since man first lived and suffered was his infinite longing for peace uttered more plaintively." The second and third are descriptions of the Last Judgment,—the one a late improvisation, with some traces of outside influence:

> *Oh, the stars in the elements are falling,*
> *And the moon drips away into blood,*
> *And the ransomed of the Lord are returning unto God,*
> *Blessed be the name of the Lord.*

And the other earlier and homelier picture from the low coast lands:

> *Michael, haul the boat ashore,*
> *Then you'll hear the horn they blow,*
> *Then you'll hear the trumpet sound,*
> *Trumpet sound the world around,*
> *Trumpet sound for rich and poor,*
> *Trumpet sound the Jubilee,*
> *Trumpet sound for you and me.*

Through all the sorrow of the Sorrow Songs there breathes a hope—a faith in the ultimate justice of things. The minor cadences of despair change often to triumph and calm confidence. Sometimes it is faith in life, sometimes a faith in death, sometimes assurance of boundless justice in some fair world beyond. But whichever it is, the meaning is always clear: that sometime, somewhere, men will judge men by their souls and not by their skins. Is such a hope justified? Do the Sorrow Songs sing true?

The silently growing assumption of this age is that the probation of races is past, and that the backward races of to-day are of proven inefficiency and not worth the saving. Such an assumption is the arrogance of peoples irreverent toward Time and ignorant of the deeds of men. A thousand years ago such an assumption, easily possible, would have made it difficult for the Teuton to prove his right to life. Two thousand years ago such dogmatism, readily welcome, would have scouted the idea of blond races ever leading civilization. So woefully unorganized is sociological knowledge that the meaning of progress, the meaning of "swift" and "slow" in human doing, and the limits of human perfectibility, are veiled, unanswered sphinxes on the shores of science. Why should Æschylus have sung two thousand years before Shakespeare was born? Why has civilization flourished in Europe, and flickered, flamed, and died in Africa? So long as the world stands meekly dumb before such questions, shall this nation proclaim its ignorance and unhallowed prejudices by denying freedom of opportunity to those who brought the Sorrow Songs to the Seats of the Mighty?

Your country? How came it yours? Before the Pilgrims landed we were here. Here we have brought our three gifts and mingled them with yours: a gift of story and song—soft, stirring melody in an ill-harmonized and unmelodious land; the gift of sweat and brawn to beat back the wilderness, conquer the soil, and lay the foundations of this vast economic empire two hundred years earlier than your weak hands could have done it; the third, a gift of the Spirit. Around us the history of the land has centred for thrice a hundred years; out of the nation's heart we have called all that was best to throttle and subdue all that was worst; fire and blood, prayer and sacrifice, have billowed over this people, and they have found peace only in the altars of the God of Right. Nor has our gift of the Spirit been merely passive. Actively we have woven ourselves with the very warp and woof of this nation—we fought their battles, shared their sorrow, mingled our blood with theirs, and generation after generation have pleaded with a headstrong, careless people to despise not Justice, Mercy, and Truth, lest the nation be smitten with a curse. Our song, our toil, our cheer, and warning have been given to this nation in blood-brotherhood. Are not these gifts worth the giving? Is not this work and striving? Would America have been America without her Negro people?

Even so is the hope that sang in the songs of my fathers well sung. If somewhere in this whirl and chaos of things there dwells Eternal Good, pitiful yet masterful, then anon in His

good time America shall rend the Veil and the prisoned shall
go free. Free, free as the sunshine trickling down the morning
into these high windows of mine, free as yonder fresh young
voices welling up to me from the caverns of brick and mortar
below—swelling with song, instinct with life, tremulous treble
and darkening bass. My children, my little children, are singing
to the sunshine, and thus they sing:

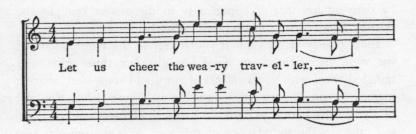

long   the   heav - en - ly   way.

And the traveller girds himself, and sets his face toward the Morning, and goes his way.

JAZZ AT HOME
J. A. *Rogers*

Jazz is a marvel of paradox: too fundamentally human, at least as modern humanity goes, to be typically racial, too international to be characteristically national, too much abroad in the world to have a special home. And yet jazz in spite of it all is one part American and three parts American Negro, and was originally the nobody's child of the levee and the city slum. Transplanted exotic—a rather hardy one, we admit—of the mundane world capitals, sport of the sophisticated, it is really at home in its humble native soil wherever the modern unsophisticated Negro feels happy and sings and dances to his mood. It follows that jazz is more at home in Harlem than in Paris, though from the look and sound of certain quarters of Paris one would hardly think so. It is just the epidemic contagiousness of jazz that makes it, like the measles, sweep the block. But somebody had to have it first: that was the Negro.

What after all is this taking new thing, that, condemned in certain quarters, enthusiastically welcomed in others, has nonchalantly gone on until it ranks with the movie and the dollar as a foremost exponent of modern Americanism? Jazz isn't music merely, it is a spirit that can express itself in almost anything. The true spirit of jazz is a joyous revolt from convention, custom, authority, boredom, even sorrow—from everything that would confine the soul of man and hinder its riding free on the air. The Negroes who invented it called their songs the "Blues," and they weren't capable of satire or deception. Jazz was their explosive attempt to cast off the blues and be happy, carefree happy, even in the midst of sordidness and sorrow. And that is why it has been such a balm for modern ennui, and has become a safety valve for modern machine-ridden and convention-bound society. It is the revolt of the emotions against repression.

The story is told of the clever group of "Jazz-specialists" who, originating dear knows in what scattered places, had found themselves and the frills of the art in New York and had been drawn to the gay Bohemias of Paris. In a little cabaret of Montmartre they had just "entertained" into the wee small hours fascinated society and royalty; and, of course, had been paid royally for it. Then, the entertainment over and the guests away, the "entertainers" entertained themselves with their very best, which is always impromptu, for the sheer joy of it. That is jazz.

In its elementals, jazz has always existed. It is in the Indian war-dance, the Highland fling, the Irish jig, the Cossack dance, the Spanish fandango, the Brazilian *maxixe*, the dance of the whirling dervish, the hula hula of the South Seas, the *danse du vêntre* of the Orient, the *carmagnole* of the French Revolution, the strains of Gypsy music, and the ragtime of the Negro. Jazz proper, however, is something more than all these. It is a release of all the suppressed emotions at once, a blowing off of the lid, as it were. It is hilarity expressing itself through pandemonium; musical fireworks.

The direct predecessor of jazz is ragtime. That both are atavistically African there is little doubt, but to what extent it is difficult to determine. In its barbaric rhythm and exuberance there is something of the bamboula, a wild, abandoned dance of the West African and the Haitian Negro, so stirringly described by the anonymous author of *Untrodden Fields of Anthropology*, or of the *ganza* ceremony so brilliantly depicted in Maran's *Batouala*. But jazz time is faster and more complex than African music. With its cowbells, auto horns, calliopes, rattles, dinner gongs, kitchen utensils, cymbals, screams, crashes, clankings and monotonous rhythm it bears all the marks of a nerve-strung, strident, mechanized civilization. It is a thing of the jungles—modern man-made jungles.

The earliest jazz-makers were the itinerant piano players who would wander up and down the Mississippi from saloon to saloon, from dive to dive. Seated at the piano with a carefree air that a king might envy, their box-back coats flowing over the stool, their Stetsons pulled well over their eyes, and cigars at an angle of forty-five degrees, they would "whip the ivories" to marvellous chords and hidden racy, joyous meanings, evoking the intense delight of their hearers who would smother them at the close with huzzas and whiskey. Often wholly illiterate, these humble troubadours knowing nothing of written music or composition, but with minds like cameras, would listen to the rude improvisations of the dock laborers and the railroad gangs and reproduce them, reflecting perfectly the sentiments and the longings of these humble folk. The improvised bands at Negro dances in the South, or the little boys with their harmonicas and jews'-harps, each one putting his own individuality into the air, played also no inconsiderable part in its evolution. "Poverty," says J. A. Jackson of the *Billboard*, "compelled improvised instruments. Bones, tambourines, make-shift string instruments, tin can and hollow wood effects, all now utilized as musical novelties, were among early Negroes the product of necessity. When these were not available 'patting juba' prevailed. Present-day 'Charleston' is but a variation of this. Its early expression was the 'patting' for the buck dance."

The origin of the present jazz craze is interesting. More cities claim its birthplace than claimed Homer dead. New Orleans, San Francisco, Memphis, Chicago, all assert the honor is theirs. Jazz, as it is to-day, seems to have come into being this way, however: W. C. Handy, a Negro, having digested the airs of the itinerant musicians referred to, evolved the first classic, *Memphis Blues.* Then came Jasbo Brown, a reckless musician of a Negro cabaret in Chicago, who played this and other blues, blowing his own extravagant moods and risqué interpretations into them, while hilarious with gin. To give further meanings to his veiled allusions he would make the trombone "talk" by putting a derby hat and later a tin can at its mouth. The delighted patrons would shout, "More, Jasbo. More, Jas, more." And so the name originated.

As to the jazz dance itself: at this time Shelton Brooks, a Negro comedian, invented a new "strut," called "Walkin' the Dog." Jasbo's anarchic airs found in this strut a soul mate. Then as a result of their union came "The Texas Tommy," the highest point of brilliant, acrobatic execution and nifty foot-work so far evolved in jazz dancing. The latest of these dances is the "Charleston," which has brought something really new to the dance step. The "Charleston" calls for activity of the whole body. One characteristic is a fantastic fling of the legs from the hip downwards. The dance ends in what is known as the "camel-walk"—in reality a gorilla-like shamble—and finishes with a peculiar hop like that of the Indian war dance. Imagine one suffering from a fit of rhythmic ague and you have the effect precisely.

The cleverest "Charleston" dancers perhaps are urchins of five and six who may be seen any time on the streets of Harlem, keeping time with their hands, and surrounded by admiring crowds. But put it on a well-set stage, danced by a bobbed-hair chorus, and you have an effect that reminds you of the abandon of the Furies. And so Broadway studies Harlem. Not all of the visitors of the twenty or more well-attended cabarets of Harlem are idle pleasure seekers or underworld devotees. Many are serious artists, actors and producers seeking something new, some suggestion to be taken, too often in pallid imitation, to Broadway's lights and stars.

This makes it difficult to say whether jazz is more characteristic of the Negro or of contemporary America. As was shown, it is of Negro origin plus the influence of the American environment. It is Negro-American. Jazz proper, however, is in idiom—rhythmic, musical and pantomimic—thoroughly American Negro; it is his spiritual picture on that lighter comedy side, just as the spirituals are the picture on the tragedy side. The two are poles apart, but the former is by no means to be despised and it is just as characteristically the product of the peculiar and unique experience of the Negro in this country. The African Negro hasn't it, and the Caucasian never could have invented it. Once achieved, it is common property, and jazz has absorbed the national spirit, that tremendous spirit of go, the nervousness, lack of conventionality and boisterous good-nature characteristic of the American, white or black, as compared with the more rigid formal natures of the Englishman or German.

But there still remains something elusive about jazz that few, if any of the white artists, have been able to capture. The Negro is admittedly its best expositor. That elusive something, for lack of a better name, I'll call Negro rhythm. The average Negro, particularly of the lower classes, puts rhythm into whatever he does, whether it be shining shoes or carrying a basket on the head to market as the Jamaican women do. Some years ago while wandering in Cincinnati I happened upon a Negro revival meeting at its height. The majority present were women, a goodly few of whom were white. Under the influence of the "spirit" the sisters would come forward and strut—much of jazz enters where it would be least expected. The Negro women had the perfect jazz abandon, while the white ones moved lamely and woodenly. This same lack of spontaneity is evident to a degree in the cultivated and inhibited Negro.

In its playing technique, jazz is similarly original and spontaneous. The performance of the Negro musicians is much imitated, but seldom equalled. Lieutenant Europe, leader of the famous band of the "Fifteenth New York Regiment," said that the bandmaster of the Garde Republicaine, amazed at his jazz effects, could not believe without demonstration that his band had not used special instruments. Jazz has a virtuoso technique all its own: its best performers, singers and players, lift it far above the level of mere "trick" or mechanical effects. Abbie Mitchell, Ethel Waters, and Florence Mills; the Blues singers, Clara, Mamie, and Bessie Smith; Eubie Blake, the pianist; "Buddy" Gilmore, the drummer, and "Bill" Robinson, the pantomimic dancer—to mention merely an illustrative few—are inimitable artists, with an inventive, improvising skill that defies imitation. And those who know their work most intimately trace its uniqueness without exception to the folk-roots of their artistry.

Musically jazz has a great future. It is rapidly being sublimated. In the more famous jazz orchestras like those of Will Marion Cook, Paul Whiteman, Sissle and Blake, Sam Stewart, Fletcher Henderson, Vincent Lopez and the Clef Club units, there are none of the vulgarities and crudities of the lowly origin or the only too prevalent cheap imitations. The pioneer work in the artistic development of jazz was done by Negro artists; it was the lead of the so-called "syncopated orchestras" of Tyers and Will Marion Cook, the former playing for the Castles of dancing fame, and the latter touring as a concertizing orchestra in the great American centers and abroad. Because of the difficulties of financial backing, these expert combinations have had to yield ground to white orchestras of the type of the Paul Whiteman and Vincent Lopez, organizations that are now demonstrating the finer possibilities of jazz music. "Jazz," says Serge Koussevitzy, the new conductor of the Boston Symphony, "is an important contribution to modern musical literature. It has an epochal significance—it is not superficial, it is fundamental. Jazz comes from the soil, where all music has its beginning." And Leopold Stokowski says more extendedly of it:

"Jazz has come to stay because it is an expression of the times, of the breathless, energetic, superactive times in which we are living, it is useless to fight against it. Already its new vigor, its new vitality is beginning to manifest itself. . . . America's contribution to the music of the past will have the same re-vivifying effect as the injection of new, and in the larger sense, vulgar blood into dying aristocracy. Music will then be vulgarized in the best sense of the word, and enter more and more into the daily lives of people. . . . The Negro musicians of America are playing a great part in this change. They have an open mind, and unbiassed outlook. They are not hampered by conventions or traditions, and with their new ideas, their constant experiment, they are causing new blood to flow in the veins of music. The jazz players make their instruments do entirely new things, things finished musicians are taught to avoid. They are pathfinders into new realms."

And thus it has come about that serious modernistic music and musicians, most notably and avowedly in the work of the French modernists Auric, Satie and Darius Milhaud, have become the confessed debtors of American Negro jazz. With the same nonchalance and impudence with which it left the levee and the dive to stride like an upstart conqueror, almost overnight, into the grand salon, jazz now begins its conquest of musical Parnassus.

Whatever the ultimate result of the attempt to raise jazz from the mob-level upon which it originated, its true home is still its original cradle, the none too respectable cabaret. And here we have the seamy side to the story. Here we have some of the charm of Bohemia, but much more of the demoralization of vice. Its rash spirit is in Grey's popular song, *Runnin' Wild:*

> Runnin' wild; lost control
> Runnin' wild; mighty bold,
> Feelin' gay and reckless too
> Carefree all the time; never blue
> Always goin' I don't know where
> Always showin' that I don't care
> Don' love nobody, it ain't worth while
> All alone; runnin' wild.

Jazz reached the height of its vogue at a time when minds were reacting from the horrors and strain of war. Humanity welcomed it because in its fresh joyousness men found a temporary forgetfulness, infinitely less harmful than drugs or alcohol. It is partly for some such reasons that it dominates the amusement life of America to-day. No one can sensibly condone its excesses or minimize its social danger if uncontrolled; all culture is built upon inhibitions and control. But it is doubtful whether the "jazz-hounds" of high and low estate would use their time to better advantage. In all probability their tastes would find some equally morbid, mischievous vent. Jazz, it is needless to say, will remain a recreation for the industrious and a dissipater of energy for the frivolous, a tonic for the strong and a poison for the weak.

Yet in spite of its present vices and vulgarizations, its sex informalities, its morally anarchic spirit, jazz has a popular mission to perform. Joy, after all, has a physical basis. Those who laugh and dance and sing are better off even in their vices than those who do not. Moreover, jazz with its mocking disregard for formality is a leveller and makes for democracy. The jazz spirit, being primitive, demands more frankness and sincerity. Just as it already has done in art and music, so eventually in human relations and social manners, it will no doubt have the effect of putting more reality in life by taking some of the needless artificiality out. . . . Naturalness finds the artificial in conduct ridiculous. "Cervantes smiled Spain's chivalry away," said Byron. And so this new spirit of joy and spontaneity may itself play the rôle of reformer. Where at present it vulgarizes, with more wholesome growth in the future, it may on the contrary truly democratize. At all events, jazz is rejuvenation, a recharging of the batteries of civilization with primitive new vigor. It has come to stay, and they are wise, who instead of protesting against it, try to lift and divert it into nobler channels.

THE CHANGING SAME
(R&B AND NEW BLACK MUSIC)
LeRoi Jones

The blues impulse transferred . . . containing a race, and its expression. *Primal* (mixtures . . . transfers and imitations). Through its many changes, it remained the exact replication of The Black Man In The West.

An expression of the culture at its most un-self- (therefore showing the larger consciousness of a *one self,* immune to bullshit) conscious. The direct expression of a place . . . jazz seeks another place as it weakens, a middle-class place. Except the consciously separate from those aspirations. Hence the so-called avant-garde or new music, the new Black Music, is separate because it seeks to be equally separate, equally unself-conscious . . . meaning more conscious of the real weights of existence as the straightest R&B. There are simply more temptations for the middle-class Negro because he can make believe in America more, cop out easier, become whiter and slighter with less trouble, than most R&B people. Simply because he is closer to begin with.

Jazz, too often, becomes a music of special, not necessarily emotional, occasion. But R&B now, with the same help from white America in its exploitation of energy for profit, the same as if it was a gold mine, strings that music out along a similar weakening line. Beginning with their own vacuous "understanding" of what Black music is, or how it acts upon you, they believe, from the Beatles on down, that it is about white life.

The Blues, its "kinds" and diversity, its identifying parent styles. The phenomenon of jazz is another way of specifying cultural influences. The jazz that is most European, popular or avant, or the jazz that is Blackest, still makes reference to a central body of cultural experience. The impulse, the force that pushes you to sing . . . all up in there . . . is one thing . . . what it produces is another. It can be expressive of the entire force, or make it the occasion of some special pleading. Or it is all equal . . . we simply identify the part of the world in which we are most responsive. It is all there. We are exact (even in our lies). The elements that turn our singing into direction reflections of our selves are heavy and palpable as weather.

We are moved and directed by our total response to the possibility of all effects.

We are bodies responding differently, a (total) force, like against you. You react to push it, re-create it, resist it. It is the opposite pressure producing (in this case) the sound, the music.

The City Blues tradition is called that by me only to recognize different elements active in its creation. The slick city people we become after the exodus, the unleashing of an energy into the Northern urban situation. Wholesale.

The line we could trace, as musical "tradition," is what we as a people dig and pass on, as best we can. The call and response form of Africa (lead and chorus) has never left us, as a mode of (musical) expression. It has come down both as vocal and instrumental form.

The rhythm quartet of the last thirty years is a very obvious continuation of Black vocal tradition, and a condensation in the form from the larger tribal singing units . . . through the form of the large religious choirs (chorus) which were initially *dancers and singers,* of religious and/or ritual purpose.

Indeed, to go back in any historical (or emotional) line of ascent in Black music leads us inevitably to religion, i.e., spirit worship. This phenomenon is always at the root in Black art, the worship of spirit—or at least the summoning of or by such force. As even the music itself was that, a reflection of, or the no thing itself.

The slave ship destroyed a great many formal art traditions of the Black man. The white man enforced such cultural rape. A "cultureless" people is a people without a memory. No history. This is the best state for slaves; to be objects, just like the rest of massa's possessions.

The breakdown of Black cultural tradition meant finally the destruction of most formal art and social tradition. Including the breakdown of the Black pre-American religious forms. Forcibly so. Christianity replaced African religions as the outlet for spirit worship. And Christian forms were traded, consciously and unconsciously, for their own. Christian forms were emphasized under threat of death. What resulted were Afro-Christian forms. These are forms which persist today.

The stripping away, gradual erosion, of the pure African form as means of expression by Black people, and the gradual embracing of mixed Afro-Christian, Afro-American forms is an initial reference to the cultural philosophy of Black People, Black Art.

Another such reference, or such stripping, is an American phenomenon, i.e., it is something that affected all of America, in fact the entire West. This, of course, is the loss of religiosity in the West, in general.

Black Music is African in origin, African-American in its totality, and its various forms (especially the vocal) show just how the African impulses were redistributed in its expression, and the expression itself became Christianized and post-Christianized.

Even today a great many of the best known R&B groups, quartets, etc., have church backgrounds, and the music itself is as churchified as it has ever been . . . in varying degrees of its complete emotional identification with the Black African-American culture (Sam and Dave, etc. at one end . . . Dionne Warwick in the middle . . . Leslie Uggams, the other end . . . and fading).

The church continues, but not the devotion (at no level of its existence is it as large, though in the poorest, most abstractly altruistic levels of churchgoing, the emotion is the devotion, and the God, the God of that feeling and movement, remains as powerful though "redistributed" somewhat).

But the kind of church Black people belonged to usually connected them with the society as a whole . . . identified them, their aspirations, their culture: because the church was one of the few places complete fullness of expression by the Black was not constantly censored by the white man. Even the asking of freedom, though in terms veiled with the biblical references of "The Jews," went down in church.

It was only those arts and cultural practices that were less obviously capable of "alien" social statement that could survive during slavery. (And even today in contemporary America, it is much the same . . . though instead of out and out murder there are hardly more merciful ways of limiting Black protest or simple statement . . . in the arts just as in any other aspect of American life.)

Blues (Lyric) its song quality is, it seems, the deepest expression of memory. Experience re/feeling. It is the racial memory. It is the "abstract" design of racial character that is evident, would be evident, in creation carrying the force of that racial memory.

Just as the God spoken about in the Black songs is not the same one in the white songs. Though the words might look the same. (They are not even pronounced alike.) But it is a different quality of energy they summon. It is the simple tone of varying evolution by which we distinguish the races. The peoples. The body is directly figured in it. "The life of the organs."

But evolution is not merely physical: yet if you can understand what the physical alludes to, is reflect of, then it will be understood that each process in "life" is duplicated at all levels.

The Blues (impulse) lyric (song) is even descriptive of a plane of evolution, a direction . . . coming and going . . . through whatever worlds. Environment, as the social workers say . . . but Total Environment (including at all levels, the spiritual).

Identification is Sound Identification is Sight Identification is Touch, Feeling, Smell, Movement. (For instance, I can tell, even in the shadows, halfway across the field, whether it is a white man or Black man running. Though Whitney Young would like to see us all run the same.)

For instance, a white man could box like Muhammad Ali, only *after* seeing Muhammad Ali box. He could not initiate that style. It is no description, it *is* the culture. (AD 1966)

The Spirituals . . . The Camp Meeting Songs at backwoods churches . . . or Slave Songs talking about deliverance.

The God the slaves worshipped (for the most part, except maybe the "pure white" God of the toms) had to be willing to free them, somehow, someway . . . one sweet day.

The God, the perfection of what the spiritual delivery and world are said to be, is what the worshippers sang. That perfect Black land. The land changed with the God in charge. The churches the slaves and freedmen went to identified these Gods, and their will in heaven, as well as earth.

The closer the church was to Africa, the Blacker the God. (The Blacker the spirit.) The closer to the will (and meaning) of the West, the whiter the God, the whiter the spirit worshipped. The whiter the worshippers. This is still so. And the hard Black core of America is African.

From the different churches, the different Gods, the different versions of Earth. The different weights and "classic" versions of reality. And the different singing. Different expressions (of a whole). A whole people . . . a nation, in captivity.

Rhythm and Blues is part of "the national genius," of the Black man, of the Black nation. It is the direct, no monkey business expression of urban and rural (in its various stylistic variations) Black America.

The hard, driving shouting of James Brown identifies a place and image in America. A people and an energy, harnessed and not harnessed by America. JB is straight out, open, and speaking from the most deeply religious people on this continent.

The energy is harnessed because what JB does has to go down in a system governed by "aliens," and he will probably never become, say, as wealthy, etc., that is he will never reap the *material* benefits that several bunches of white folks will, from his own efforts. But the will of the expression transcends the physical-mental "material," finally alien system-world it has to go through to allow any "benefits" in it. Because the will of the expression is spiritual, and as such it must transcend its mineral, vegetable, animal, environment.

Form and content are both mutually expressive of the whole. And they are both equally expressive . . . each have an identifying motif and function. In Black music, both identify place and direction. We want different contents and different forms because we have different feelings. We are different peoples.

James Brown's form and content identify an entire group of people in America. However these may be transmuted and reused, reappear in other areas, in other musics for different purposes in the society, the initial energy and image are about a specific grouping of people, Black People.

Music makes an image. What image? What environment (in that word's most extended meaning, i.e., total, external and internal, environment)? I mean there is a world powered by that image. The world James Brown's images power is the lowest placement (the most alien) in the white American social order. Therefore, it is the Blackest and potentially the strongest.

It is not simply "the strongest" because of the transmutation and harnessing I spoke of earlier. This is social, but it is total. The world is a total. (And in this sense, the total function of "free music" can be understood. See, especially, H. Dumas' story in *Negro Digest* "Will the Circle Be Unbroken?" and understand the implications of music as an autonomous *judge* of civilizations, etc. Wow!)

By image, I mean that music (art for that matter . . . or any thing else if analyzed) summons and describes where its energies were gotten. The blinking lights and shiny heads, or the gray concrete and endless dreams. But the description is of a total environment. The content speaks of this environment, as does the form.

The "whitened" Negro and white man want a different content from the people James Brown "describes." They are different peoples. The softness and so-called "well being" of the white man's environment is described in his music (art) . . . in all expressions of his self. All people's are.

If you play James Brown (say, "Money Won't Change You . . . but time will take you out") in a bank, the total environment is changed. Not only the sardonic comment of the lyrics, but the total emotional placement of the rhythm, instrumentation and sound. An energy is released in the bank, a summoning of images that take the bank, and everybody in it, on a trip. That is, they visit another place. A place where Black People live.

But dig, not only is it a place where Black People live, it is a place, in the spiritual precincts of its emotional telling, where Black People move in almost absolute openness and strength. (For instance, what is a white person who walks into a James Brown or Sam and Dave song? How would he function? What would be the social metaphor for his existence in that world? What would he be doing?)

This is as true, finally, with the John Coltrane world or the Sun-Ra world. In the Albert Ayler world, or Ornette Coleman world, you would say, "well, they might just be playing away furiously at some stringed instrument." You understand?

In the Leslie Uggams world? They would be marrying a

half-white singer and directing the show . . . maybe even whispering lyrics and stuff from the wings. You understand? *The song and the people is the same.*

The reaction to any expression moves the deepest part of the psyche and makes its identifications throughout. The middle-class Negro wants a different content (image) from James Brown, because he has come from a different place, and wants a different thing (he thinks). The something you want to hear is the thing you already are or move toward.

We feel, Where is the expression going? What will it lead to? What does it characterize? What does it make us feel like? What is its image? Jazz content, of course, is as pregnant.

The implications of content.

The form content of much of what is called New Thing or Avant-Garde or New Music differs (or seems to differ) from Rhythm and Blues, R&B oriented jazz, or what the cat on the block digs. (And here I'm talking about what is essentially *Black Music.* Although, to be sure, too often the "unswinging-ness" of much of the "new" is because of its association, derivation and even straight-out imitation of certain aspects of contemporary European and white Euro-American music . . . whether they are making believe they are Bach or Webern.) Avant-garde, finally, is a bad term because it also means a lot of quacks and quackers, too.

But the significant difference is, again, direction, intent, sense of identification . . . "kind" of consciousness. And that's what it's about; consciousness. What are you *with* (the word Con-With/Scio-Know). The "new" musicians are self-conscious. Just as the boppers were. Extremely conscious of self. They are more conscious of a total self (or *want* to be) than the R&B people who, for the most part, are all-expression. Emotional expression. Many times self-consciousness turns out to be just what it is as a common figure of speech. It produces world-weariness, cynicism, corniness. Even in the name of Art. Or what have you . . . social uplift, "Now we can play good as white folks," or "I went to Juilliard, and this piece exhibits a Bach-like contrapuntal line," and so forth right on out to lunch.

But at its best and most expressive, the New Black Music is expression, and expression of reflection as well. What is presented is a consciously proposed learning experience. (See "The New Wave.") It is no wonder that many of the new Black musicians are or say they want to be "Spiritual Men" (Some of the boppers embraced Islam), or else they are interested in the Wisdom Religion itself, i.e., the rise to spirit. It is expanding the consciousness of the given that they are interested in, not merely expressing what is already there, or alluded to. They are interested in the *unknown*. The mystical.

But it is interpretation. The Miracles are spiritual. They sing (and sing about) feeling. Their content is about feeling . . . the form is to make feeling, etc. The self-conscious (reflective, long-form, New Thing, bop, etc.) Art Musicians cultivate consciousness that wants more feeling, to rise . . . up a scale one measures with one's life. It is about thought, but thought can kill it. Life is complex in the same simplicity.

R&B is about emotion, issues purely out of emotion. New Black Music is also about emotion, but from a different place, and, finally, towards a different end. What these musicians feel is a more complete existence. That is, the digging of everything. What the wisdom religion preaches.

(But the actual New Black Music will be a larger expression. It will include the pretension of The New Music, as actuality, as summoner of Black Spirit, the evolved music of the then evolved people.)

The differences between rhythm and blues and the so-called new music or art jazz, the different places, are artificial, or they are merely indicative of the different placements of spirit. (Even "purely" social, like what the musicians want, etc.)

For instance, use of Indian music, old spirituals, even heavily rhythmic blues licks (and soon electronic devices) by new music musicians point toward the final close in the spectrum of the sound that will come. A really new, really all inclusive music. The whole people.

Any analysis of the content of R&B, the lyrics, or the total musical will and direction, will give a placement in contrast to analysis of new jazz content. (Even to the analysis of the implied vocalism of the new music: what are its intent and direction, what place it makes, etc., are concerned.) Again even the purely social, as analyzing reference, will give the sense of difference, what directions, what needs are present in the performers, and then, why the music naturally flows out of this.

The songs of R&B, for instance, what are they about? What are the people, for the most part, singing about? Their lives. That's what the New Musicians are playing about, and the projection of forms for those lives. (And I think any analysis will immediately show, as I pointed out in *Blues People,* that the songs, the music, changed, as the people did.) Mainly, I think the songs are about what is known as "love," requited and un. But the most popular songs are always a little sad, in tune with the temper of the people's lives. The extremes. Wild Joy—Deep Hurt.

The songs about unrequited, incompleted, obstructed, etc., love probably outnumber the others very easily. Thinking very quickly of just the songs that come readily to my mind, generally current, and favorites of mine (and on that other *top ten,* which is, you bet, the indication of where the minds, the people, are). "Walk On By" "Where Did Our Love Go?" "What Becomes of the Broken Hearted?" "The Tracks of My Tears," high poetry in the final character of their delivery . . . but to a very large extent, the songs are about love affairs which do not, did not, come off. For God knows how many reasons. Infidelity, not enough dough, incredibly "secret" reasons where the loved and the lover or the lovers are already separated and longing one for the other, according to who's singing, male or female. And all more precise and specific than the Moynihan Report, e.g., listen to Jr. Walker's "Road Runner." And this missed love that runs through these songs is exactly reflect of what is the term of love and loving in the Black world of America Twentieth Century.

The miss-understanding, nay, gap . . . abyss, that separates Black man and Black woman is always, over and over, again and again, told about and cried about. And it's old, in this country, to us. "Come back baby, Baby, please don't go . . . Cause the way I love you, Baby, you will never know . . . So come back, Baby, let's talk it over . . . one more time." A blues which bees older than Ray Charles or Lightnin' Hopkins, for that matter. "I got to laugh to keep from cryin," which The Miracles make, "I got to dance to keep from cryin," is not only a song but the culture itself. It is finally the same cry, the same people. You really got a hold on me. As old as our breath here.

But there are many songs about love triumphant. "I feel good . . . I got you . . . Hey!" the score, the together self, at one and in love and swinging, flying God-like. But a differently realized life-triumph than in the older more formally religious songs. The Jordans, the Promised Lands, now be cars and women-flesh, and especially dough. (Like, *power.*) There are many many songs about Money, e.g., Barrett Deems "Money," J.B.'s "I Got Money . . . now all I need is love," among so many others. But the songs are dealing with the everyday, and how to get through it and to the other side (or maybe not) which for the most part still bees that world, but on top of it, power full, and beauty full.

The older religiosity falls away from the music, but the deepest feel of spirit worship always remains, as the music's emotional patterns continue to make reference to. The new jazz people are usually much more self-consciously concerned about "God" than the R&B folks. But most of the R&B people were *really* in the church at one time, and sang there first, only to drift or rush away later.

Even the poorest, Blackest, Black people drifted away from the church. Away from a church, usually corrupted, Europeanized, or both, that could no longer provide for their complete

vision of what this world ought to be, or the next. The refuge
the church had provided during the early days of the Black
man's captivity in America, when it was really the one place
he could completely unleash his emotions and hear words of
encouragement for his life here on earth. Now the world had
opened up, and the church had not. But the emotionalism the
church contained, and the spirit it signified, would always demand the animating life of the Black man, and as Frazier says,
"The masses of Negroes may increasingly criticize their church
and their ministers, but they cannot escape from their heritage.
They may develop a more secular outlook on life and complain
that the church and the ministers are not sufficiently concerned
with the problems of the Negro race, yet they find in their
religious heritage an opportunity to satisfy their deepest emotional yearnings." (*The Negro Church in America*, E. Franklin
Frazier, Shocken, 1963, p. 73.)

It was the more emotional Blacker churches that the blues
people were members of, rather than the usually whiter, more
middle-class churches the jazz people went to. The church, as I
said, carries directly over into the secular music, which is really
not secular at all. It's an old cliché that if you just change the
lyrics of the spirituals they are R&B songs. That's true by and
large, though there are more brazen, even whiter, strings and
echo effects the blues people use that most of the spiritual
and gospel people don't use. But that's changed and changing,
too, and in the straight city jamup gospel, echo chambers,
strings, electric guitars, all are in evidence, and Jesus is jamup
contemporary, with a process and silk suit too, my man.

But the gospel singers have always had a more direct connection with the blues than the other religious singers. In
fact, gospel singing is a city blues phenomenon, and Professor
Thomas Dorsey, who is generally credited with popularizing
the gospel form back in Chicago in the late twenties and
thirties was once a blues singer-piano player named Georgia
Tom, and even worked with Ma Rainey. (He was last known
to be arranging for Mahalia Jackson, who with Ray Charles at
another much more legitimate and powerful level, were the

popularizers of Black church sound in "popular" music during
the 50's.) But then so many of them, from G.T., and even before
that to J.B., have all come that way.

The meeting of the practical God (i.e., of the existent
American idiom) and the mystical (abstract) God is also the
meeting of the tones, of the moods, of the knowledge, the different musics and the emergence of the new music, the really
new music, the all-inclusive whole. The emergence also of the
new people, the Black people conscious of all their strength, in
a unified portrait of strength, beauty and contemplation.

The new music began by calling itself "free," and this is
social and is in direct commentary on the scene it appears in.
Once free, it is spiritual. But it is soulful before, after, any time,
anyway. And the spiritual and free and soulful must mingle
with the practical, as practical, as existent, anywhere.

The R&B people left the practical God behind to slide into
the slicker scene, where the dough was, and the swift folks
congregated. The new jazz people never had that practical
God, as practical, and seek the mystical God both emotionally
and intellectually.

John Coltrane, Albert Ayler, Sun Ra, Pharaoh Sanders, come
to mind immediately as God-seekers. In the name of energy
sometimes, as with Ayler and drummer Sunny Murray. Since
God is, indeed, energy. To play strong forever would be the
cry and the worshipful purpose of life.

The titles of Trane's tunes, "A Love Supreme," "Meditations,"
"Ascension," imply a strong religious will, conscious of the re-
ligious evolution the pure mind seeks. The music is a way into
God. The absolute open expression of everything.

Albert Ayler uses the older practical religion as key and
description of his own quest. *Spirits. Ghosts. Spiritual Unity,
Angels,* etc. And his music shows a graphic connection with
an older sense of the self. The music sounds like old timey
religious tunes and some kind of spiritual march music, or
probably the combination as a religious marching song if you
can get to that. (New crusades, so to speak. A recent interview
article, with Albert Ayler and his brother, trumpet player Donald

Ayler, was titled "The Truth Is Marching In," and this is an excellent metaphor of where Albert and his brother Donald want to move.)

Albert's music, which he characterizes as "spiritual," has much in common with older Black-American religious forms. An openness that characterizes the "shouts" and "hollers." But having the instruments shout and holler, say a saxophone, which was made by a German, and played, as white folks call it, "legitimately" sounds like dead Lily Pons at a funeral, is changed by Ayler, or by members of any Sanctified or Holy Roller church (the blacker churches) into howling spirit summoner tied around the "mad" Black man's neck. The Daddy Grace band on 125th Street and 8th Avenue in Harlem, in the Grace Temple, is a brass band, with somewhat the same instrumentation as a European brass choir, but at the lips of Daddy's summoners, the band is "free" and makes sounds to tear down the walls of anywhere. The instruments shout and holler just like the folks. It is their lives being projected then, and they are different from the lives Telemann, or Vivaldi sought to reanimate with their music.

But James Brown still shouts, and he is as secular as the old shouters, and the new ones. With the instruments, however, many people would like them to be more securely European oriented, playing notes of the European tempered scale. While the Eastern Colored peoples' music demands, at least, that many many half, quarter, etc. tones be sounded, implied, hummed, slurred, that the whole sound of a life get in . . . no matter the "precision" the Europeans claim with their "reasonable" scale which will get only the sounds of an order and reason that patently deny most colored peoples the right to exist. To play their music is to be them and to act out their lives, as if you were them. There is then, a whole world of most intimacy and most expression, which is yours, colored man, but which you will lose playing melancholy baby in B-flat, or the *Emperor Concerto*, for that matter. Music lessons of a dying people.

THE BLACK AESTHETIC IMPERATIVE
Ron Wellburn

Any attempt to define or illustrate an aesthetic for contemporary African-American music must proceed from the basis that the music, like the lives and life-styles of its creators, is at a stage more crucial than is obvious. If we speak of the "development" of a music, that term, like "evolution," ought to be understood as having had an involuntary impetus. It is the politics of culture in the United States that is responsible for the character of black music. Black music has been the vanguard reflection of black feeling and the continuous repository of black consciousness. It has a symbiotic relationship to black poetry, drama, and fiction, and also painting, sculpture, and dance forms. Black music culture in America has attempted to maintain manifestations of its African heritage amidst continual harassments against religious expression. Black culture cannot be separated from economic and political considerations; nor can black music be separated from its related creative/expressive forms. For the 1970s and beyond, the success of political, economic, and educational thrusts by the black community will depend on both an aesthetic that black artists formulate and the extent to which we are able to control our culture, and specifically our music, from theft and exploitation by aliens. It is imperative for black artists today to become concerned about the politics of this society, which draws its lifeblood from black culture. We must recognize that the music created by young whites is, like that of their forebears, a musical subculture; the musical culture is ours and we must learn to protect it. In this essay, I am to be particularly concerned about contemporary American classical music; for want of a better descriptive, I will refer to it as "jazz." However, what has been happening in American music culture and aesthetics will necessitate brief comments on soul and rock music. The latter form is included because of the threat it has become to jazz and its survival; this is the first time that jazz has been so strategically undermined by a music strictly in the popular idiom. What has been described as the "evolution of jazz" or of the blues is really the black musician's continual response to cultural subterfuge by "white jazz." The late-sixties rock movement is testimony to the endurance of black music, as well as to our careless watch over it; rock music reflects the spiritual, creative, and sociological weaknesses of white America; and finally, it is a profound indication that the racial impasse in this country is coming to a head. If for no other reason, this is why we must endeavor to hold our grip on our music at this time, while we prepare an aesthetic consciousness that will keep the music in our hands for the future. The consciousness found in black poetry during the sixties has caught up to the music. Our music is the foremost expressive quality of our being; black music describes and celebrates life through black people. The degree to which we shape our music and *protect* it will dictate the full range and extent of our survival in the United States.

Black people in the Americas must be understood as an Eastern people whose African homeland is only a part of the Afro-Asian world. It is helpful to contrast Eastern and Western cultural values and distinguish their most essential differences.

In terms of the "evolutionary aesthetic progress" of a music or a literature, Eastern culture is more stable than that of Europe. Because traditional values in a culture tend to be immediate in their disposal to the Eastern man, culture does not change its aesthetic conception rapidly, if indeed at all. On the other hand, the nature of fluctuation in European cultural genres reflects instabilities in European social and spiritual values. Western man has understood fluctuation as mere chaos, and each so-called level of aesthetic development was an attempt to restore order to the universe in those terms. The Western aesthetic sense fosters the notion of conquering the universe, not blending with it as you are, as one finds in the Eastern world.

The instabilities of the Western world have evolutionized its aesthetic values into obsolescence and decay. Black music in the Americas has been victimized by its proximity and accessibility to this European idea of "aesthetic development," hence the jazz-is-dead argument by white critics and some musicians. The fact that black music has changed in its various ways over a seventy-year period is not because it has been searching for any aesthetic ideal based on Plato's *Republic;* the changes have been caused by economic, social, and spiritual pressures. Soul music of the mid-sixties, and jazz since 1960, were attempts to keep the music of black people in the black idiom. It can be said accurately that these changes have occurred in a paradoxical manner. In jazz it was the mystical sensibility within Ornette Coleman and Cecil Taylor and Sun Ra that caused them to create a music in 1957 that unwittingly on their part was to become an expression of black nationalism by 1963. It must be understood that the music did not take this position on its own; because of its inherent essentials, it did not need to; it was forced to become harmonically, melodically, rhythmically, and spontaneously liberated from restricting European musical structures. Since improvisation is not the basis of European music, the new music withdrew from Europe spiritually and psychologically, thus forcing the white listener further outside his level of comprehension.

Any changes that occur in Afro-American music during the 1970's will be forced changes that will be brought about by the harassment of an Afro-Asian people in anti-cultural white America, and the spiritual, sociopolitical, and economic positions these people will be forced to take.

It is difficult to discuss aesthetics and aesthetic changes in black music through a particular decade. The roots of the musical consciousness of the sixties were planted in the mid-fifties, and to a large degree had matured by 1960. But whatever constitutes a Black Aesthetic has and will rest on the musician. The black musician is ahead of everyone in the expression of true black sensibility. For him, negritude or soul or blackness has never been a matter for soapbox articulation. The musician has not expressed his self through the power of speech or an African wardrobe. More than any other kind of black artist, the musician creates his own and his people's soul essence, his own negritude. He can also do more damage to the oppressor's image of himself than heavily armed urban guerrillas. All the entities of a Black Aesthetic have long been in existence, but they have been seldom recognized. Black musicians do not really *think about* the aesthetic; they simply project it. Soul is a manner of dancing, walking, speaking, interpreting life as we see and know it. In *The Negro and His Music* (1936), Alain Locke advocated we ". . . become musical by nurture and not rest content with being musical by nature." We should all, then, re-establish ourselves as musicians: every black American can at least become a drummer or learn to play on a simple reed flute, just as every black person can dance.

Besides a life-style reference, black music and the Black Aesthetic will need a spiritual reference. So far, we have had an Africanized Christian conception of the spirit world that in its European form is limiting. Hence, many musicians have turned to Islam, and others have gone farther east to Buddhism.

Whatever other Eastern religion besides Christianity is leaned to heavily in the coming years will be the result of a forced stance, just like the character of the music and the life-style. The argument for Islam is strong today, but those who have gone farther east have incorporated a panreligiosity into their conception of the universe. Black people in America have more in common spiritually with the spirit world of the Asian continent than with European Christianity. The presence of "exotic" instruments and musical flavorings is, in the hands of black musicians, a serious attempt to assimilate into the Black Aesthetic non-Western elements, without assimilating the present idiom into something that will not relate to the Afro-American experience. The Afro-American is really no stranger to any music or any religion, because of his heritage in mysticism. But the Afro-Asian world is somewhat of a stranger to the scientific emphasis of Europe; science and technology replaced mysticism, and the rest of the world is now forced to hold on to its mysticism while learning to use these European achievements in a meaningful manner.

The progress of the Black Aesthetic in jazz styles has reflected the motion of the spirit, and the images that the spirit manages to project. It is too easy to say that it has moved toward Africa; it is more accurate to say that it has moved into the heart and soul of the universe, meaning into the people that it reflects. It is a curious and almost unexplainable phenomenon that two approaches to a Black Aesthetic in jazz commenced simultaneously. In the years to come, it will be clearer to us why one managed to survive and the other was killed, or perhaps went underground. Somewhere along the line, a Black Aesthetic must emerge having the ingredients of both the jazz forms and an energy boost from the popular soul form.

Percussionist Art Blakey has made several trips to Africa since the mid-forties. When he returned in 1955, he literaly brought in a drum fever, which served as the primary impetus to the black musician's reaction to the West Coast "cool," a predominantly white jazz musicians' thing that had sucked its blood

from Lester Young and Miles Davis back in 1949. Within the
next three years after Blakey's return, he recorded several albums using African percussion, while Olatunji and Guy Warren
got more exposure by performing in the same idiom. The music
was a fiery, relentless, and yet subtle display of African passion
and beauty that could be rhythmically overpowering.

Meanwhile, the jazz mainstream took on a harder sound,
rhythmically similar to bop but harmonically richer. In 1957,
Horace Silver started his own group and composed a number
of jazz pieces that have become famous. "Juicy Lucy," "Cookin'
at the Continental," "Señor Blues," and others mingled big-city
jazz blues with an urban image of soulful blues and "funk" in
the tenor-trumpet lines, while Silver's own brand of piano mixed
these with Cape Verdian creole elements.

Another pianist, Bobby Timmons, the son of a Philadelphia
preacher, joined Blakey's Jazz Messengers around this time and
composed the memorable "Moanin'" and "Dat Dere." The brand
of funk Blakey's group projects has the big-city sound; his and
Silver's (his former employee) are very similar, and both have
left an indelible stamp on Blue Note records. But Timmons,
especially through those two compositions, injected the camp-
meeting and gospel sound into the Blakey group. The sensibility for grits and gravy invoked in the music assumed a rural
instead of an urban frame of reference. Melodically, Timmons
is deep in the rural existence and rural memory of the black
American; his compositions are reminiscent of the levee hollers,
work and chain-gang songs, and the country blues.

For bassist Charles Mingus, the rule was "better git it in your
soul." Mingus made a strong impression on the texture of the
music before 1960. His *Blues and Roots* (Atlantic) album ex-
plores a wide range of soul/down-home impressions from
"Wednesday Night Prayer Meeting" to the "Cryin' Blues" to
"Tensions."

Ray Charles emerged into the jazz vocalist spotlight, and his
band, perhaps the first of the contemporary soul bands, also

left a great impression under the direction of Hank Crawford and the soloing of David "Fathead" Newman.

The final big push for this back-to-the-roots idiom began in September 1959, when Bobby Timmons joined Cannonball Adderley and his brother Nat. Timmons' "Dis Here" catapulted Cannonball into the success he continues to enjoy. Timmons' presence and his originality were perfect for this group; he shared a folk-gospel-soil reference with both Adderleys and with bassist Sam Jones, all natives of Florida. There was a warmth and closeness in their music not to be found in its urban counterpart. Like Jean Toomer's *Cane*, it evoked a nostalgia for the South in people not even born there—a racial memory. The music re-enforced images and memories of "the country."

Besides the Adderleys' rural frame of reference, a feeling of wide-open spaces and land happens to be the basic characteristic of the "southwestern tenor saxophone sound," a sharp, piercing timbre strong in the high register, which has been around in R&B bands in the Texas-Arkansas area and reached jazz prominence by 1961. Booker Ervin, Don Wilkerson, "Fathead," and James Clay projected this blues-drenched brand of soul. Significantly, Ornette Coleman hails from Texas, and Pharaoh Sanders from Arkansas, and the sound and feeling of the region, with all of its sweeping grandeur, is in their playing styles.

Although there were numerous others involved, these were the most important taste makers of the soul/funk movement from 1957–62. Nearly all black musicians joined it in one way or another. With the proficiency of Jimmy Smith and Wes Montgomery, the organ and guitar received their greatest exposure in the serious jazz mode. However, in the mostly all-white jazz critical establishment, whites worried about the exclusiveness of soul music (fewer whites were in the movement than were in the "avant garde" at its strongest). They warned about the future of jazz, that the music would drift into commercialism, etc. *Downbeat* and *Metronome* magazines from 1959–63 were at the peak of this frustrating turn of events. When tenor-organ-guitar combinations became popular, the critics called for "art." Integration was a dominant social theme at this time. Jazz, the music of the American-American, had become too black and exclusive. One morning in the spring of 1962, we all woke up to the fresh, clean sound of "Desafinado," and the white sycophant establishment applauded the resurgence of Stan Getz. Bossa nova, or rather, a watered-down version of the original, proved to be the successful antidote. The bossa nova interjection was not a musical movement, but it served its purpose: it killed off the down-home, earthy musical dominance of black music; it was popular long enough to let whites straighten themselves out psychologically. Also, bossa nova rapidly attained the commercialism jazz critics had warned about with soul jazz.

The music now known as "soul music" actually gathered momentum around the time that the soul/funk jazz movement was being killed off. It did make certain changes in the R&B idiom: the use of 6/4 rhythm on slow love ballads, along with the replacement of drumsticks by brushes; an emphasis on the beat amidst other, richer percussive subtleties; a choral and less staccato vocal background; the replacement of the tenor saxophone with the heavier baritone model; and with the song writing of Smokey Robinson and the team of Holland, Dozier, and Holland, a richer melodic framework, reminiscent of the church and the jazz blues. Black vocal groups are noted for their ability to "chirp," but with Aretha Franklin and James Brown, the preference ranges from urgent singing to the pure shout. Any black shouter throughout the history of black song in America handles the most African sensibility in American life.

The James Brown band's saxophone section deserves special attention. It is the most deadly and earthy music section in the history of American music. The riffs on "Cold Sweat" or "Lickin' Stick" evoke racial memory. The voices that are the reed section give it its wicked and its spiritual essence (in black music, one and the same). Drums, Fender bass, and rhythm guitar are approached by black musicians as spiritual/melodic voices. Timbre and sensibility come closer to Wolof traditional orchestras of xylophones, lyres, and drums. The James Brown band represents the quintessence of an African-directed movement in black music expression from the popular idiom, and it has influenced many of the latest dance styles. In this combination of music and the body, the wedding of impulses, we find soul in its most expressive and resilient terms. Black poets will waste their words if they do not give articulation to the spirit of the dance motion.

The new music started in three geographic areas: New York's Lower East Side, Chicago, and Los Angeles. The respective personalities involved were Cecil Taylor, Sun Ra, and Ornette Coleman. The socio-aesthetic reasons for the impetus of this evolution in black music are not as simply aligned as those under which bebop sprang. In 1941, Diz and Monk "began to work out some complex variations on chords . . . and we used them at night to scare the no-talent guys." Given the presence of white musicians at Minton's, they must have comprised a majority of the "no-talent guys" *for a strictly black musical idiom.* Diz and Monk and their cohorts were restructuring the European-derived elements of their music. It was Monk, the high priest, who insures the meaning of what Diz alluded to: ". . . we're going to create something that they can't steal because they can't play it." (e.g., *Hear Me Talkin' to Ya,* pp. 337–41) That statement by a man who doesn't do much talking sums up the changing Black Aesthetic in jazz history.

Bebop promised new musical freedom. The new music, which the critics called everything from "free jazz" to "anti-jazz," marked a complete break with chordal music restrictions. As the music grew, it was evident that it was an insurrection against European musical bondage. But at its inception there was no real conscious spirit of rebellion; in a sense, it just happened; yet, social and music history will prove that these innovators were great men in the vanguard of a great age; they possessed profound spiritual qualities and dynamic creative energy; their deep sensibilities permitted them to interpret the restless sixties five years in advance. They have been unusual men because their souls are large; their souls defy limitations on their own expressiveness, on labels for what they are doing, and on their musical tastes. Out of their sensibilities, and the sensibilities they have inspired since 1957, a new aesthetic for black music was founded on *feeling:* black music was to give spontaneous expression to black feeling. The function of the total sensibility preceded form in importance. Self/spirit became the focal point, individually and collectively. White critics drew irrelevant parallels with the spiritually alienated music of the serial composers. In form, timbre, and spontaneity, the new black music was moving from European rigidity, and though many whites have screamed "black nationalism!" none have quite figured out what is happening.

Sun Ra must be recognized as a forerunner in composition and improvisational format. He nurtured an organization of strong musicians who have been with him on and off since the mid-fifties. The earliest Sun Ra records have so many thematic centers and variations that either side of a recording seems longer than it actually is. The band's orchestration was flexible enough for many ensemble passages that did not require repetition. Meanwhile, a sun-conscious mysticism developed, with its earthly reference as Egypt and its otherworldly reference as outer space. By the mid-sixties, his Solar Arkestra had become liberated from traditional composition and become more spontaneously conceived and executed. Sun Ra is the first contemporary composer of black music of a symphonic quality. Upon improvisational liberation, the total Arkestra could take the music where it wanted it to go. Bill Dixon and John Coltrane have tried this format. The form may be symphonic, but the effect is hardly European. Sun Ra prefers to work with densities of sound, appropriate for his soul-space reference. He has developed a myth-science, and his outer-space consciousness should not be taken lightly; he is ahead of the space age, is a part of an energy unit, the sun, and with piano or amplified piano, vibes, or marimbas or organ, his universe-consciousness has made a lasting imprint on black music.

In the Greenwich Village enclaves, pianist Cecil Taylor created a version of the New Music that was not the experimentation his critics perceived. Taylor is an exceptionally gifted and well-schooled musician and an outstanding composer/arranger. He once described jazz as ". . . the imposition of black feeling on an Aryan culture," which might best describe what he, particularly, is doing. One can hear Bartók and Stravinsky in his work, but only because his articulation is so rapid. In the late fifties, everything he did seemed to come out in a minor key. *Looking Ahead* (Contemporary) is probably his easiest-obtainable record of the few made before 1960 (*Coltrane Time*, on United Artists, was originally Taylor's record in 1958). *The World of Cecil Taylor* (1960) on the invaluable but now defunct Candid label, presents Taylor in a relaxed setting doing his thing. His linear development is best recognized here, and there are few real chord structures to inhibit him. With drummer Sunny Murray and altoist Jimmy Lyons, he recorded two albums in Copenhagen in 1963 that illustrate a high level of group improvisation and co-ordinated energy. Many New Music bands have followed this format of group playing, which was the way jazz started out. *Unit Structures* (1966) and *Conquistador* (1967) again show us Cecil Taylor the skilled composer/arranger. The best example of his energetic style can be heard on "Communications ♯11" (the *Jazz Composer's Orchestra*), where he thrashes, swirls, and dances, snarls and ice-skates his percussive ideas with overpowering strength. It is this energy that distinguishes Cecil Taylor's music from any European classicism. The piano becomes the orchestra it can be, and on this record Taylor engulfs the arrangement of Viennese-born Mike Mantler. Taylor is quite melodic in his approach; the machine-gun effect of his articulation contains two or three musical ideas operating simultaneously.

Ornette Coleman was kicked out of a black blues band in Texas for teaching another musician bebop. After settling in

Los Angeles, he began working out compositional and improvisational alterations for his own pleasure; he soon attracted attention. When in 1959 he and trumpeter Don Cherry played the old Five Spot in New York, it was his irreverence, sincerity, and humor that made it clear that Cecil Taylor was not by himself, and that something was afoot in jazz. Coleman disorganized all established concepts of *perfect* harmony, pitch, and rhythmic senses. Charlie Parker brought harmonic improvising to its peak; Coleman merely broke it down again and reestablished it in terms that were spontaneous. Don Heckman spent months deciphering this music for *Downbeat*. Critics finally realized that Coleman was not observing the restrictions of the twelve- or sixteen-bar blues or even the thirty-two-bar aaba form; his conception is closer to folk blues and wide-open (Texas) jazz playing. He starts any particular idea wherever he chooses, wherever he feels it, and the ideas often overlap choruses; he does not observe the conventional chorus break. Despite all the excitement, Ornette Coleman, as altoist, trumpeter, violinist, or composer, is a very old-fashioned musician. He is closer to bebop than altoists Byard Lancaster or Sonny Simmons; or the late Eric Dolphy, who was able to achieve a sarcastic vocal quality on both alto sax and bass clarinet.

Ornette Coleman has influenced Archie Shepp's street-blues sarcasm and blatant come-on in rapping. But most of these qualities are pure Shepp. His musical references delve into urban folklore and personalities. Archie Shepp has been accused of vaudeville by critics who have no conception of the movement toward music plus something else occurring in the black community.

Cecil Taylor's music has fire and energy-consuming impulses (in that sense it is electric!). Coleman is perhaps "free-bop," and Sun Ra pulls away from earth bondage. The evolvement of John Coltrane's music envisioned earth man re-establishing his relationship with the universe in spiritual terms, not necessarily going out to it in the physical sense. Since most of the non-white world is concerned about earth aliens and not space aliens, and about full stomachs, the music of the mystic Ohnedaruth is of great significance.

Coltrane had turned heads his way in 1955 with Miles Davis and in 1957 with Monk. His obbligatic sense was metamorphosized on his Prestige recordings: it was compressed horizontally and extended vertically, so that by the time he recorded *Giant Steps* (Atlantic) in 1959, the "sheets of sound" technique was a fact, and the entire language of black music was irrevocably changed. Up to 1961, Trane was concerned with time and harmonics, the bases of European music; he destroyed their European conception for all time. He first used the soprano sax on *My Favorite Things* (1961), and as he was becoming deeply interested in the relationship between man and God, his music involved more space and melody. Melodic improvisation, extended over long periods of time, as in Asia, became his forte. By 1965, he expressed a panreligious reference for the music, which actually defies attempts to place him solely in Islam; the quality and meaning of the music, and its power, place its impetus somewhere in the Himalayas. Coltrane's music was distinctly Afro-Asian; while it got its vitality from the African world, East and West, its deepest spiritual qualities were East Indian. McCoy Tyner, Jimmy Garrison, and Elvin Jones brought the group's music closer to Ravi Shankar and Bismillah Khan in its use of the long form of hypnotic creativity. Tyner was lyric personified. His 3/4 or 6/8 accompaniments voiced in fourths were unlike anything heard before in Western music. One imagines him building cities. He has a lyric urgency that is strongly African. Elvin Jones liberated Coltrane and countless other black musicians from the traditional 4/4 bebop rhythms. Max Roach developed 3/4, but in the Coltrane band Jones gave it spiritual dimensions. He is not as heavy-handed as he seems; his style is a fusion of African elements and Indian sensibility. As he affirmed the liberation of impulses, he set the stage for Coltrane's need for more drummers.

In the work of Sunny Murray and Rashid Ali can be heard

the spreading effect of multiple impulses, which appears to be as far away from the beat of soul music as anything can be. Bassists and drummers, often more of one or the other or both in any group, re-evaluated the roles of their instruments. The idea of the rhythm section gave way to the "energy unit," which meant that bass and drums became soloists in a collective performance. Mingus influenced the new bassists, and blacks Henry Grimes and Richard Davis emerged with indestructible foundation for rhythm. Louis Worrell and Jimmy Garrison influenced the polymetric percussion work that seems to be no rhythm and several rhythms at the same time. Besides Murray and Ali with freer impulses, and Ed Blackwell and Elvin Jones who were, then, aligned with set rhythmic variations, Andrew Cyrille and Milford Graves fall somewhere in the middle, but to the impulsive side of center. Rhythmically, a performing group seemed to float, then suddenly lurched, and jet-streamed or changed direction, carried by its own internal rhythm; the frame of reference was inner-directed, with bass and drums together having the pulse of breathing and body motion.

Coltrane hoped to enlarge his group to the size of the *Ascension* format (seven horns, piano, drums and two basses). Like the drum, the horn is a voice, and the late Dolphy used his reed instruments to that effect. He developed long-phrased passages of vocal ecstacy, and went as far as he could with his excursions. He needed a horn, a voice, a being of "deep spiritual reservoir" to continue in this musical search for God and gods where he had to leave off; he found an extension of his projection in Pharaoh Sanders. Pharaoh's articulation in the extreme high registers of the tenor sax is not only astounding, but for many, unbearable. He is no screeching Junior Walker, nor does he use the propulsion and creaking-door effect of Albert Ayler. There is melody in his high register and long phrases; and there is blood, scars, hope, and the compassion to love and to be. Pharaoh Sanders represents the ultimate spiritual projection thus far. He and John Coltrane reached into the heart of the universe through the hearts of the people.

With percussion instruments, Coltrane was helpful in removing congas and bongos from an infectious rhythmic taste in soul/funk groups and restoring their African intentions. He performed with these drums often from 1965 on. Big Black, whose long performances are closest to Trane's in their conception, is a conga man. African percussion and reed instruments have been coming into jazz since bebop, but many other kinds are coming in now. Ed Blockwell and Nat Bettis are adept with rhythm logs. Thumb pianos and lyres are also coming in. Maracas and tambourines never really left black music in the Americas. Rufus Harley works gallantly with the difficult bagpipe, a North African instrument that got into Scotland by visits. Yusef Lateef long ago used Arabic and East Asian reed flutes; we can expect more of these, and flutes from Yugoslavia and Greece that are of Arab origin. Milford Graves has recorded with the tabla, and Giuseppi Logan and others play well the various oboes from Pakistan. Whether Far Eastern instruments such as the Japanese koto come into the New Music in the black community, remains to be seen. Jazz/ New Music can conceivably develop into a Third World music consciousness, and its strongest references could come in from the Afro-Arab sector. The music of the Afro-Asian world as a whole is one large musical culture that is harmonically, melodically, and rhythmically closer to the African-American sensibility than non-Gypsy-flavored European folk ballads and hymns. Our Black Aesthetic has been in the Afro-Asian world for centuries, waiting for us to use it and protect it.

In *The Negro and His Music,* Alain Locke recognized the importance of music for the salvation of the black American. "One of the handicaps of Negro music today," he said, "is that it is too popular." Even during the depression, black music and musicians were being exploited as commodities. Jazz has evolved as its practitioners were throwing off the leeches. Locke felt that we needed ". . . a class of well-trained musicians who know and love the folk music and are able to develop it into great classical music, and a class of trained music lovers who will support by appreciation the best in the Negro's musical heritage and not allow it to be prostituted. . . ." In America's game of musical beds, black music is now the reluctant prostitute of rock music in its various forms—stolen musics derived from R&B. Ameer Baraka (LeRoi Jones) has mentioned in *Black Music* that the names that rock groups give themselves fit their idea of the black people they are imitating. One better, it is indicative of just how unhuman they must be. The people, or forces, practicing this music have no conception of a mystical universe, and hence no conception of their drums and guitars as voices embodying spirits. They do not even approach music spiritually. The music that is being imitated is lost in the amplifiers; sound, not subtlety, is needed. Alfons Dauer, a European, noted perceptively that the European's rhythmic conception is based on hearing, while the African's conception of rhythm is based on motion. White rock is sustained by props that, if removed, would destroy the music and probably its listeners. Blow out Con Edison during simultaneous rock and soul music concerts, and see who suffers the most.

Rock attempts to imitate the city blues of the forties and fifties. Paul Butterfield worships Muddy Waters, who has never had so much money in his life. In fact, a black fathers/white sons syndrome is developing. A Chess label album cover pictures a black God giving the life-touch, à la Michaelangelo, to a white neo-Greek hippie in shades. This is part of the Euro-American scheme. The black music impetus is only to be recognized as sire to the white world; a kind of wooden-Indian or buffalo-nickel wish. A vampirish situation indeed!

Other features of rock music should be pointed out so that they will not creep into the Black Aesthetic. The Euro-American lives in a psychological and real world where mysticism has been replaced by science and technology; hence, he doesn't know how to use his inventions constructively for peaceful purposes. Rock music has some falsely attractive elements that show no relationship at all to any Afro-Asian music of the past. Rock musicians are in no orisha line. But they are in a technological lineage extending through John Cage, Stockhausen, Edgard Varèse, all the way back to Marconi and the wireless. White rock is a technology, not a real music. It is an affectation, not a felt experience. It is parasitic, not symbiotic, to black culture and life-styles. It has a quasi-aesthetic. Ralph Nader's Raiders are worried that American (white) youth will do damage to their nervous systems with this musico-technology; at least he and Ameer Baraka would agree that the white race might die out.

African-Americans should continue to move as far away from this madness as humanly possible, spiritually, psychologically, and in the immediate physical sense at least. We cannot afford to allow our music to remain a surrogate for white American psychosexual illusions. A time is coming when we will have to develop a music that will have the same strong relationship to our mystical nature and conception of the universe as religious songs of the nineteenth century and our daily life in Africa's past; a religious music will evolve that we won't be ashamed to dance to, as we continue our motion for survival and liberation. If this music is stolen and imitated, we will understand it as stealing our religion and abusing it. We should then respond accordingly. Black music should not be allowed to become popular outside the black community, which means that the black community must support the music, as Alain Locke begged almost forty years ago. We must become more concerned about *protecting* black music and culture than in merely *defending* it; defending is a gesture, a reaction after the goods have been swiped, something we could do via public masturbation when we hear the newest minstrels doing their thing. *Protection restricts harassment from without.*

Alain Locke and Ameer Baraka, thirty years apart, agreed that the art and folk forms of black music must be fused into a vital and superior product. Locke said: "We must distinguish between a superficial jazz that is superficially Negroid and a deeper jazz that is characteristically Negro." Much can still be developed from Afro-Cuban and Afro-Caribbean idioms. Mix these with James Brown's soul, subtle or obvious African drum and dance patterns, and Indian spontaneous and long composition, and you might have something like Pharaoh Sanders and Leon Thomas' "The Creator Has a Master Plan." Black music in the 1970s must incorporate a world of non-white musics if black people in America hold the key to the world's survival. All kinds of percussion instruments can be used (and you *can* do the popcorn to the merengue). Saxophones and other horns, or even pianos, do not necessarily have to be amplified as Miles Davis prefers now. Afro-Asian music has done without it for centuries, but if it must be done it must be done wisely. It was inevitable with the guitar and the organ; but the varitone gimmick for saxophone muddles the feeling and sound. Electronic music can make the black man blind from the sight of money and the white man rich on his deathbed, laughing absurdly at having fooled the niggers this last go-round. Black musicians should re-evaluate the technological intrusions now threatening our music; times may come when that technology will be useless. Our music is our key to survival.

REFLECTIONS ON THE EVOLUTION
OF POST-WAR JAZZ
Leslie B. Rout, Jr.

I
The Time of the Boppers
1945–50

When Jesus Christ began preaching his gospel to the world, the Bible informs us that the local sages could not believe "anything good" could have come out of a hicktown like Nazareth. According to George W. Pierce, a renowned student of insect life, the most *avant-garde* cacophony being produced will not be heard tonight in some Harlem loft. Nay friends, the most "far out" combo will be blowing improvised solos around the summer world in your local field or hedge! Put another way, did you ever pay attention while the grasshopper, click beetle, cicada, and katydid bantered back and forth? Not until I spent a night in the Paraguayan Chaco being serenaded by thousands of such insects, did Pierce's argument take on the aura of credibility.

Jazz buffs and historians might listen to such stories respectfully, then confidently reply that they could top such paradoxical tales. For example, they might relate how the initial step in the development of post-World War II jazz styles occurred in 1939, by accident, in an obscure Harlem chili house. The blackman upon whom this supernatural flash was bestowed was Charles Christopher Parker, Jr., better known to all his legions as "Yardbird" or "Bird." Parker had become bored with the hackneyed chords employed by most of his contemporaries, and was seeking something new. One night in December, while playing the song "Cherokee" with guitarist Biddy Fleet, Parker discovered that by running higher intervals of a chord as a melody line and backing these with appropriately related chord changes, he could play what he had been hearing. As Parker put it, "I came alive." Skeptics, please note that the red peppers and beans in close proximity were probably in no way responsible.

While the "Bird" unquestionably dominated the 1940–60 generation of jazz performers, he was not the only originator of the post-war jazz movement. As early as 1938–39, Swing, the pre-eminent jazz style of the pre-War era, had nearly exhausted its inventive potential. Youth and the listening public were still entranced with the likes of Glenn Miller, Benny Goodman, and Artie Shaw, but young jazzmen found those same offerings increasingly *jejune*. In 1940, a Harlem jazz club, Minton's Playhouse, became the headquarters of a clique of young musicians who were hoping to create a new musical language. Along with Parker, the Minton's experimenters of 1940–41 (notably John Birks "Dizzy" Gillespie, trumpet; Kenny Clark, drums; Thelonious Monk, Mary Lou Williams, pianists; and Charles Christian, guitar) evolved the basis of the jazz style eventually called "re-bop," "be-bop," and inevitable perhaps, "bop." One observer of the Minton's scene, when asked about the origins of be-bop, provided a reply that was simplicity in itself; "Bird was responsible for the actual playing of it, and Dizzy (Gillespie) put (*i.e.*, wrote) it down."

Whimsy aside, the perfecting of the new jazz style took time, and no one party was totally responsible. The innovators had to make a living while polishing and perfecting their creation; in candid terms, this meant playing in aggregations that performed the "old" jazz. Fortunately, such band leaders as Earl

Hines and Billy Eckstine (1942–45) allowed their orchestras
to become musical laboratories. By the time "Dizzy" Gillespie
formed the first bop combo in 1944 most of the rough edges
had been rounded off, and the sponsors of a revolutionary
new style were ready to test it on an unsuspecting public. Before the war ended, the center for bop had moved from Harlem
to mid-town Manhattan. The new jazz had begun making
converts, East, North, West, and South. Even staid Europe
soon had a significant number of disciples.

Chiefly because of his gregarious personality, "Dizzy" Gillespie was elected premier bopper by the communications
media, and the trumpet star formed a large ensemble in 1946.
This was to be until June, 1950, the paramount orchestra dedicated to the preservation and promulgation of bop. In 1947,
Woodrow Wilson ("Woody") Herman formed another such
ensemble; by 1949, even Benny Goodman had one leg up
on the bop band wagon. In addition to these orchestras, at
least a dozen top flight combos, including that led by Charlie
Parker, made their appearance upon the national scene. Proponents of Swing and Dixieland took a dim view of mush-
rooming "boperations," but they were powerless to halt the
changes taking place.

Unfortunately, the election of King be-bop by critics, musicians
and certain jazz fanatics in no way indicated that the public
concurred. The new jazz was difficult to dance to, full of
"weird" notes and unexpected intervals; these features alone
suggested troublesome days ahead. The press and radio concentrated their attentions on the sartorial eccentricities favored
by bop musicians (that is, their berets, horn-rimmed glasses
and lepard-skin jackets). To some observers, the eccentricities
became the essence of the music. Such persons might support
the latest fad for a year or two, but then what? These un-
certainties were multiplied by the fact that any musician with
a beret or horn-rimmed glasses now became a "bop" musician.
Youngsters who could hardly blow their horns, but who could
sprout a goatee and shout "cool, my man," loudly proclaimed

both their devotion and expertise. The result was increasing confusion in the public mind as to what bop was, and who were its most credible exponents.

Though Gillespie maintained his position as the high priest of bop, the major financial attraction of the 1946–50 period was the orchestra of Stanley Newcomb Kenton. Fronting a 19–20 piece outfit and dubbing his repertoire "Progressive Jazz," Kenton's brassy, intensely controversial crew became the first jazz orchestra to earn $1,000,000 in a twelve-month period (1948). While the musical efforts of the band rarely fell into the generally accepted bop framework, such Kenton soloists as Art Pepper (alto sax), Ray Wetzel (trumpet), Bob Cooper (tenor sax), and Eddie Bert (trombone) bopped freely whenever awarded solo opportunities.

The year 1949 marked the beginning of the end of the bop era. Its collapse gave the entire jazz world a bad case of indigestion. In November, 1949, Charlie Barnet, who had formed a bop orchestra earlier in the year, announced, "We're running in the red, so there's no percentage in going on." The following month, Woody Herman also threw in the sponge. He was joined by Charlie Ventura, whose combo had been elected the outstanding small jazz group in the 1949 *Metronome* magazine annual poll. One musician who had never believed bop to have been more than a corpse was Doc Evans, a Dixieland trumpeter since time immemorial. In December, 1949, with Evans playing a dixie-style dirge, "concerned" students at the University of Minnesota gave "old-man be-bop" an officious funeral. Disbanding his orchestra in July, 1950, even Dizzy Gillespie announced that bop had reached the end of the trail.

Bop ceased to exist as a style of jazz totally distinct from other styles, but the majority of jazz soloists continued to perform in the tradition of Charlie Parker and Dizzy Gillespie. Bop's harmonic and chromatic ideas gradually became accepted parts of American popular music; only the name really died. Woodrow Wilson Herman summed it up most succinctly. When asked in 1955 whether bop was dead, he replied: "No . . . the funny and sad thing is today you can play the same music that was damned in 1947 and 1948 and get away with it completely." Repetition of sounds apparently works wonders on the public ear. It is now 1969. The next time you come home after listening to live jazz, put a stack of Charlie Parker records on your hi-fi set and listen: many of today's jazzmen are still "getting away with it."

II
The Socio-Economic Origins
of the Be-Bop Revolution

While America today is at least dimly aware of the pre-eminent role of the Afro-American in both the origin and development of jazz prior to World War II, the blackman had rarely been the recipient of the profits which theoretically should have come his way. The problem, in part, lay in the belief of popular music's overlords (*i.e.*, booking agencies, record companies, owners of major nightclubs) back in the 1920's that the white public would never accept musical innovations unless the supposed innovator was also white. While this assumption was probably valid at the time, its socio-economic ramifications were catastrophic. Witness the case of the late Fletcher Henderson. As early as 1928, this bandleader had worked out the basis of the jazz style later known as Swing. By the early 30's he had assembled an outstanding aggregation—but it was still a black orchestra. A compromise of sorts resulted: Benny Goodman became "King of Swing"—everywhere except in Harlem and other urban ghettos—and Fletcher Henderson became his chief arranger.

White bands led by Artie Shaw, Tommy Dorsey, Glenn Miller, and Bunny Berrigan soon joined Goodman as members of the Swing hierarchy. Black powerhouse battalions led by Count Basie, Chick Webb and Jimmy Lunceford came into existence, played better jazz, but earned less than half as much as their white counterparts. In all fairness, it must be noted that Goodman and Shaw demonstrated their belief that racial bars in jazz should not be tolerated by hiring black musicians despite strong opposition. Curiously enough, such attitudes probably increased black discontent, because from the latter's point of view, acceptance into white orchestras demonstrated how badly black swingsters were needed! Why then be satisfied with a few crumbs while "Whitey" took the cake?

What was obvious was that improvement in the blackman's socio-economic status in jazz necessitated some kind of musical turnover. The time was ripe in 1940–41, because Swing had then passed its inventive peak. It should not be surprising therefore that a major purpose of the previously mentioned "Minton's" clique was the creation of a jazz form that whites could not play! Ideally, this would insure for black jazzmen the recognition they craved, plus a lion's share of profits, any skeptic could have pointed out that the new jazz would be financed largely by white customers. Some of these would be musicians, and most certainly they would eventually be able to reproduce what they heard. Furthermore, since the black innovators would employ Western tools (i.e., saxophones, chords, traditional notation) to express themselves, it was only a question of time before the whites at least partially caught on. Black hopes of maintaining a monopoly on their creation were ultimately fanciful, but conditions tended to change after World War II. As has been previously noted, from the onset of the be-bop era, Dizzy Gillespie was accepted as be-bop's pre-eminent figure. For the first time, a jazz style would have a blackman as its publicly acknowledged leader. Young partisans of all races slavishly copied Gillespie's affectations, as well as the social and physical habits of other famous boppers.

It was the social-psychological outlook of the boppers that was most unnerving. The music had seemingly sprung from nowhere, and insinuated itself into the public consciousness following a war which had caused a maximum amount of social dislocation. The young post-war boppers (and the hosts of non-playing bop adherents) began by rejecting all past jazz forms; bop was the only jazz. Sometimes audiences in clubs proved hostile or apathetic to the music. Obviously, thought the young bop musician, pearls have been cast before swine. Never did it occur to him that his fumbling imitation of Parker or Gillespie might further postpone the public's acceptance of the new jazz. The boppers reacted by adopting a patronizing attitude toward paying patrons, not announcing tunes and generally performing as if the feelings of the audience were not important. Many of these practices have since become traditional.

Dixieland had been good time music, nice to get drunk to. Swing had been music largely for dancers. With the bop era, jazz musicians became more conscious of their role as "artists." In practice this meant that they often acted like *prima donnas.* Charlie Parker, Dexter Gordon and other greats were predictably late for club and recording dates, often not showing up at all. Young jazzmen took their cues accordingly. Time considerations were unimportant, and those who objected to the bopper's cavalier attitude on the subject were obviously "square." Laws were for the common folk, not for boppers who could easily dispense with the assistance of the Establishment. Idealistically, the new jazz would help black jazzmen establish themselves as artists rather than as musical comedians. In a sense, it was an attempt by both black and white jazzmen to destroy the things they hated—Tin Pan Alley, unscrupulous agents and bookers, band leaders who could not play and, indirectly, middle class society. Indeed, the be-bop panorama was all of these things—plus an apparent acceptance of "horse" (*i.e.*, heroin) as a necessity for existence.

It is undeniable that musicians had been heroin users prior to 1945, but a frightful number of bop's leading figures were hopeless addicts. To both young bopper and fan, if the heroes were hooked, a ride on the "horse" was for them, too. Only since a growing number of youths have become users of psychedelic and other drugs has it become possible for many to realize how heavily the nuances of fad, curiosity, or the weight of social pressure can weigh on immature minds. Some misguided souls thought that, through heroin, peaks of performance could be reached which nonusers could never hope to arrive at. Others became addicted because this was a means of rebelling against family and/or society. Some died, some ruined their health and a few men broke the habit; but only the "pusher" (*i.e.,* drug supplier) rejoiced on his way to the bank.

And so the word "bop" temporarily at least faded into disuse. "Modern Jazz" was a better descriptive monicker, and it did not evoke visions of hopped-up musicians sneering at customers or collapsing on the bandstand. Artistically, be-bop had been a smashing success. Cashwise, however, it had laid an egg. Musical entrepreneurs subsequently looked elsewhere for commercially exploitable presentations. New crooners, vocal quartets and Glenn Miller-styled dance bands provided entertainment for the masses during most of the 1950's. Unfortunately, the bop era marked the parting of the ways between jazz and the public. After 1949–50, modern jazz was a creation loved by the hip—beautiful when well performed, but appreciated by only a few.

III
The New Thing—1959

In 1959 with one LP released and one other completed, Ornette Coleman came to New York. He huffed and puffed and the house of be-bop began crumbling at the edges. With his white plastic saxophone, dark-hued Mr. Coleman blew up a storm that is still raging. Cometh now "free jazz," what its advocates term the "new thing," but what was really the first new jazz form since the development of be-bop. As usual, there were impassioned statements pro and con with numerous musicians and jazz critics playing an equivocal role. Many had been wrong about bop in 1945–46 and nobody wanted to look foolish this time. Coleman has since become a major influence, affecting in some fashion the playing style of countless numbers.

Coleman's music has been described as raw, shrill, beautiful, repulsive, provocative, but rarely boring and always extremely personal. Some listeners respond wildly in support of Coleman, while others walked out of clubs five minutes after he started playing.

As in the development of bop, while Coleman was the man whose break with convention was most pronounced, such little known pianists as Cecil Taylor and Sun-Ra and saxophonists John Coltrane and Sonny Rollins, had been edging away from conformity for some time. In keeping with previous jazz developments, the music of Ornette Coleman made its greatest impact on the young practitioners of the jazz art. There were other significant influences on jazz performers also. The 1960's have been years of burgeoning racial tension, and numerous young performers (chiefly New York-based) began touting free jazz as a music of revolt. Most of these free-blowers were Afro-Americans, some of them were highly articulate, and they interpreted the jazz they played to be a condemnation of this society. Critics such as LeRoi Jones spoke of free jazz as "black music" and emphatically insisted that whites could not play it. The impression usually given by this new *avant garde,* white or black, was that they were sick of the capitalist world, the nightclub circuit—and also people who did not sing paeans of praise about their latest musical efforts. It remains to be seen what the firebrands of today will be saying or playing a decade from now, especially if they taste success in some fashion.

Considering the stylistic changes of the last two decades, one might assume that the socio-economic *milieu* in which jazzmen carry on their activities has changed radically. Nothing could be further from the truth. A couple of examples should readily demonstrate this contention. A most menacing development since the end of World War II has been the oversupply of good jazz performers. Admittedly, the introduction of the jazz LP has allowed more musicians to be heard and has created a means whereby many musicians can eke out a reasonable livelihood. At the same time, the number of large jazz ensembles has not made any significant increase during the last 20 years and the number of jazz clubs has obviously decreased. One notes, for example, that as of the fall of 1967 there did not exist on the South Side of Chicago a single club that booked nationally established jazz talent on a consistent basis! In reality then, despite the theoretical improbability of there being too many talented jazzmen, the jazz world cannot put an unlimited number of saxophonists, percussionists, trumpeters, and pianists to work. Taking the cue, many gifted jazzmen have entered other fields, because they could not find sufficient work in the jazz musical jungle.

Note also that there remains no means of comprehensively regulating hours, working conditions, or entrance into the field. One realizes that the jazz artist is not a steelworker, and that in a comparatively free society, the jazz artist cannot be forced to accept a great deal of regimentation. On the other hand, I have known many jazzmen who do not pay social security and because of the nature of their work cannot get many forms of insurance. Freedom is one thing, degradation another.

The fact is that jazzmen have almost no control over the business end of their vocation. Few of them can determine which of the records they make will be released, or even what club engagements they will play. Such problems as poor acoustics, out-of-tune pianos, domineering club-owners, and unfavorable relations with the communications media have long been topics of serious concern for jazzmen, but little has been done to remedy these grievances. Disgracefully, jazz, perhaps America's only art form, had to wait until 1968 before an individual jazzman, Ornette Coleman, received a Guggenheim Foundation fellowship. Bear in mind that classical musicians and composers have been happily drawing similar kinds of stipends for years.

Jazzmen have blamed nearly everyone for these and other similar situations, but the problem is really theirs. It is unlikely that conditions will improve significantly until jazz performers have taken it upon themselves to organize on a much more sophisticated level than they have done in the past. It is an open secret that some musicians, both black and white, selected the jazz world as their center of operations particularly because they viewed it as being one free from what they believed to be excessive social and cultural restrictions. This craving for individualism has resulted in the creation of an unofficial hierarchical system whereby a handful of artists walk off with the profits, and the mass of the others have difficulty working even six months out of the year.

Since 1945–46, jazz has evolved into an extremely self-conscious art music. It tends to manifest an inherent effervescence, but it can no longer masquerade as being either the music of the young or of the masses. Despite the number of long-playing records being turned out, or the apparent prosperity of a Miles Davis or a Cannonball Adderley, the lack of places where the music can be heard and the decreasing number of traveling aggregations means that the field is not prospering. What is to be done?

Probably a majority of those who consider themselves jazz musicians are black. An overwhelming majority of those considered giants in the field have been Afro-Americans. If jazz is to thrive, that race which nursed it, rehearsed it, and first paraded it across the American stream of consciousness will have to do something, as they have the most to lose.

The halycon days are over. Tightly-knit associations of jazz artists, allied on either a regional or local basis and led predominantly by black Americans, must gain significant control over the production, cost, and presentation of their art, or face the perpetuation of the intolerable conditions so often criticized. There is no doubt that such a task proves more difficult than putting together a new jazz style, but just as necessary. Doc Evans and friends, as you may recall, thought that they had buried be-bop. The next funeral may be for lady jazz—and she is, we hope, much too vital to pass away.

A COMPARATIVE ANALYSIS OF THE AFRICAN AND
THE WESTERN AESTHETICS
Ortiz M. Walton

The art of improvisation first found expression in Africa. This can be seen as a natural development in a culture that encouraged free expression of emotion through art. The accent culturally and aesthetically was on spontaneity. Spontaneity in turn means to express feelings as they occur, hence improvisation becomes instrumental toward the attainment of spontaneity. The melodies used in African music were considered merely a starting point for elaborating and developing melody through improvisation. It is highly probable that improvisation first began through the use of various vocal devices such as trills, glissandos, vibrato, and falsetto. These were all devices to alter the melody, or to add to it, and can thus be considered to be rudimentary forms of improvisation. Although trills, etc., were used in the West, particularly during the Baroque period, these were always written or notated. In Africa, notation was not used, the music being passed down through memory. Therefore, these European devices cannot be said to be improvisation.

Western music became highly rationalized with the Greeks.

There are, for example, many references in Aristotle concerning music theory. The seeds were sown then that would ultimately lead to the process of rationalization of music. This process as applied to Western institutions has been discussed at length by the sociologist Max Weber. The latter correlated this phenomenon with the rise of capitalism in the West. But as we can see, the process had already taken place with the Greek theorists, insofar as music was concerned.

The Greeks attempted to catch the magic of music, to discover its essence. They attempted to analyze music into certain modes or scales, each of which had its own psychological quality. The latter were termed ethoi. This was the beginning of a system of notation in the West, which has been added onto in the following centuries, casting Western music into a rigid, unalterable, fixed phenomenon. The Church, during the medieval period, also encouraged the invention of notational devices. One might add that this was also to a great extent an attempt to inculcate Church doctrine, which was contained in the chants and hymns. If only one set of notes could be selected and if all variations melodically were precluded, then the content could easily be controlled. Music has always been a potent force and has occasionally been used to subvert. Ecclesiastical heretics could more easily be weeded out by their non-conformity to ecclesiastical canons. Prior to this arrangement, during the early medieval period, a notational device had been worked out called neumes, but these only indicated a rise or fall in pitch, but not how much rise or fall. Thus the element of predictability, though on its way, was not then fully established. The final element or variable to be controlled was pitch variation. For even though bound by the fixed notational system, the pitch of these various notes was a variable, and the ratios of vibrations between the notes changed from octave to octave. Bach completed the process of rationalizing the scale by tempering it. One octave was artificially made to resemble another. G♭, which was formerly different in pitch from F♯, was now made to sound identical to it, although this process was the result of making the various intervals out of tune. Now the diatonic scale took over from the non-tempered Church modes and added an additional element of rationalization and predictability to the music of the West.

Consequences for the West

European instrument makers reflected this tendency toward rationalization by expressing the same tendency in a new technology of tempered instruments. Much of the music of the medieval period had been vocal. The instruments that were used were either of the viol type suited to a style of playing called continuo, or of the valveless wind type. The viols were non-fretted and resembled African string instruments. They were non-tempered and could either play a single note over and over again, ostinato style, or as a figured bass, which was a prearranged series of notes outlining the chords from which a written melody would be played.

Valveless horns resembling their African prototypes, and keyless woodwind instruments, were replaced by the highly rationalized and mechanical keys and valves. It is difficult to comprehend these developments in the West except as a passion for the rational. Certainly the technical ability of players on the non-tempered and non-mechanized instruments was considerable, since many of the concertos and sonatas written for such non-tempered instruments were difficult even for the new instruments. The order of the auditory world had now been transformed into a visual mechanical and predictive phenomenon. Now all a player had to do was look at the music and put the finger a certain place and out would come the sound that had been conceived long before in somebody's head. Instruments now differed only insofar as the particular maker had more or less expertise in the mass production of uniform instruments. The standard pitch was also conceived of during this process, and now the A had a vibration of 440 per second, as opposed to the much lower and slower-vibrating A of the Baroque and pre-Baroque periods. This made the entire tempered scale have a different timbre. The quality now became more shrill and less capable of subtle variation.

Perhaps it was because of the intrinsic freedom inherent in improvisation that it held on until the time of Beethoven. Up to this time, composers and performers were synonymous, and public performances usually included some, if not all, improvisation. Bach and Mozart often took part in contests testing improvisatory skills. But these men were also vassals to a lord or rich family who paid them for their efforts. However, the music-publishing business was on the rise and sought a direct profit from musical enterprises, especially musical composition. Music publishing, ironically, freed the Western musician from the lowly position of servant that Haydn and others occupied, only to enslave them in the tradition of written composition and the wiles of capitalistic commercial endeavors.

The culminating achievement toward complete rationalization of music was the invention of the symphony orchestra. Here specialization reached its peak, for every man had a specific sheet of music to play, the same way each time. No melodic, harmonic, or rhythmic deviations were to be allowed, and an assembly-line-type operation was set into motion by a foreman, the conductor. Each player, like an assembly-line worker, was expected to contribute his share to the final product. The symphony orchestra is furthermore organized along lines of maximal efficiency, with a division into sections, and a further hierarchy of section foremen or leaders and sidemen. A large clock usually adorns the rehearsal hall, and orchestra members are expected to be neat and punctual. In accordance with union rules, members are given a ten-minute coffee break, during which they may discuss their grievances. As in a factory, there is the professional manager who collects the money and pays people according to their relative efficiency and position on the hierarchy. There is none of the romantic conception of musicians playing their instruments in lonely churchyards in southern France, like Casals. Nor is there the freedom that is associated with an artist like Picasso, casually throwing paint on walls to discover new color combinations. Instead, there is the awesome impression of gravity, of men having an important mission to accomplish. Gray morning coats and knee-length tails are worn, and the facial expressions, rather than reflecting the ecstasy of creation, are severe and strained. Each note is indicated not only as to exact pitch, but in terms of loudness, intensity, duration, and even the feeling state that is intended by the composer. One note may thus have four or five signs concerning how it is to be played.

As on the assembly line, if one gets behind or plays the wrong rhythms or notes, the whole line comes to a stop. To avoid this occurrence, this foreman or conductor is obliged to rehearse the same music time after time, year after year. The workers, when fed up, will occasionally discreetly sabotage the music during a concert. This throws the foreman or conductor off, and he must apply his technical know-how to return to the normal functioning of the machine.

The consumer, or concertgoer, like his counterpart in the world of commerce, has been made into a passive recipient of various sounds. He either accepts the product or rejects it, but never is he allowed to add his own creativity to it. His response to the music comes in box-office receipts, not in his active participation, as is the case in African music. Composers' names are like any other trade-mark—signifying the quality of the merchandise. Some of these names or trade-marks are brand names, such as Mozart or Beethoven; they command respect and are used in polite company. So even though one has heard Beethoven's Symphony Number 5 for the hundredth time, he still keeps listening to it, claiming falsely that he hears something new every time. His participation is limited to applause after the finale or occasional coughing during the sections played loud enough to cover the sound. It is highly amusing to hear the coughing of those who are not familiar with the score. They begin the tension-releasing coughing in the *mezzo forte* passages, but it suddenly becomes noticeable when the music becomes softer. In such a situation, the "listener" becomes embarrassed and ceases the now-epidemic coughing at once, which makes it apparent that the problem is not of medical origin. It would be considered absolute madness to dance or pop the fingers during a symphony or opera performance. When an occasional listener attempts to whistle softly or hum the melody line, he is immediately the object of menacing stares.

It will become apparent soon that my lengthy discussion of Western musical values and concepts is germane to our discussion of African music, since it is only via a comparative analysis that the full import of both the European and the non-European musical systems can be explicated. In Africa, none of the afore-mentioned musical "innovations" took place, and it is from Africa that the basic concepts of Black music emerged. The cries, falsettos, slurs, and trills found their way directly to Black music during the slave era. The tendency for instruments to act as imitations of the human voice is also a direct African carry-over. Contrasted with the music-for-the-elite philosophy prevalent in the West, African music retained its functional and collective characteristics. The element of improvisation was developed rather than abandoned, and it found its way into Black music in this country. Similarly, the unifying element of audience participation was also retained. These foregoing statements are in direct opposition to self-styled ethnomusicologists who hold that Black music is of European origin or that it is a completely new music. Again, the peculiar savage circumstances of America *did* go to shape the music in a different manner from most contemporary African music, at least superficially so. But a close listening to Hugh Masekela, who is from the sister to the United States, South Africa, will reveal a close similarity between South African Black music and that of the United States. In both, one can find the same mingling of joy touched with a melancholy pathos. In both, one can find the element of social protest. When Masekela sings of the oppression in the diamond mines, it is very similar to songs about the ghetto that have become so popular in this country. Another outstanding difference between Western and African music is the latter's use of syncopation. In European music, syncopation was not the natural by-product of its structure, as was the case in Africa. The accented off-beats that characterize syncopation had to be developed as a product of the "rest." The "rest" was not invented until the twelfth century. Until this time, free rhythm was employed, with the neumes not denoting the duration of a note. At this time, the rhythm, which consisted of groups of syllables and of neumes, was unmeasured: it was like the prose rhythm of the Psalms and other poetry in the Bible. Since most of these literary pieces are of an even, measured quality, and since the music composed during this period was often in unison, with very little harmony, it can be assumed that the music was also non-syncopated. The music of Palestrina and Monteverdi bears this out. In Africa, on the other hand, syncopation was a necessary and vital part of the musical structure. It was built right into the music and the languages that the music reflected. No such connection between language and music existed in Europe, with the exception of the influence of the vowel-oriented Italian language. But this influence was limited in practical application to vocal music. African language, however, not only contains a generous proportion of vowels, but is based upon a system of tonality and accents, which allows for the possibility of music that could be interpreted as language, with the additional possibility of incorporating lingual rhythms into music vis-à-vis the talking drums. African writing can thus be achieved through the subtle use of music.

In the case of the West, mathematics had to be used to achieve what for the Africans was a natural phenomenon. In comparing the two general cultures, Lévi-Strauss comments:

"The rise of handwriting always stands in an immediate relation with the establishment of cities and empires, the organization of men into a political system, and the formation of classes and castes." The Africans, however, did not need an alphabet to convey information; instead, they developed the drum language, which could imitate the spoken language. This constitutes in essence a form of writing minus the disadvantages of Western-style alphabetic writing. Jahn explains the difficulty in applying the Latin alphabet to African languages: When the alphabet was introduced to Africa, ". . . it was necessary to utilize accents in order to make it possible to write the language in letters at all. Thus, for example, the Yoruba language has three different pitches: high, middle, and low. A word like ǫkǫ (the cedilla is necessary to distinguish the open from the closed o) has a different meaning for each different pitch. Alphabetical script therefore distinguishes the high pitch by the accent ó, the low by the accent ò, the middle tone remains unmarked, and the intermediate pitches as in oko—canoe. What expense, what trouble, how many auxiliary marks, are necessary in order even to write a name such as Láyíko Oròkúlábèbèjà." He goes on to state that pitch is in fact more important in many African languages than either vowels or consonants: "The dun-dun, the most well-known of the African talking drums, is capable of not only representing the tones but also all of the modulations." The talking drum does not use a kind of Morse system, as imagined by most non-Africans. The drum language is the immediate and natural reproduction of speech; it is a script intelligible to every trained person, only it is directed not to the eye but to the ear. The young European learns in school to connect optical phonetic signs with their meanings, and, similarly, the young African had formerly to learn the art of understanding the acoustical phonetic signs of the drums.

Africans therefore acquired at an early age the principles of music, since it was such an intrinsic part of the language education. Perhaps this goes a long way to explain the seminal influence exerted by African music, and also why African music is participated in by such a large group, making a collective art form.

Since the inculcation of Western languages and methods of education, the drum script has all but been lost. The official drummers, who once were chosen carefully for their work and considered sacred, were discouraged from practicing their art. Much of the history of Africa had been retained in this manner, despite the Western contention that Africa lacked a history. Even so, the basic texture, rhythms, and linguistic influences were preserved both in African and Afro-American music.

Antiphony, and the Origin of Improvisation

Whenever a musical phrase, sung or played by a soloist, is afterward repeated or answered by an instrumental or vocal chorus or group, antiphony takes place. It is referred to commonly as call-response or question-answer, form. Much of African music is of this nature, owing to the cultural demand for collective, participatory music. The chorus could, because of antiphony, be unfamiliar with the melody and yet be able to sing it. The soloist could vary his stanzas easily and also change the melody from time to time. The more skilled the performer, the more adept he was in the art of improvisation. Instrumental antiphony was of a similar nature, with the master drummer setting the beat and pattern, followed by answer-like figures from the chorus of drummers. The master drummer would also employ deviations in the various rhythmic patterns, and gradually improvisational abilities increased. Without improvisation, there cannot be freedom of expression or spontaneity, and without these, music would be worthless to African culture, which is in unity with the arts.*

* The five varieties of antiphony developed in African music are: instrument-instrument, instrument-voice, instrument-chorus, solo voice-chorus, vocal solo-instrument.

The Origin of Polyphony

Like antiphony, polyphony** can be traced to African origin. When two or more independent musical phrases are played at the same time, polyphony occurs. This form was first practiced by African drummers, playing many rhythmic patterns, each independent of the other and yet played to fit into the general musical or over-all pattern. When one drummer plays in one meter, and another in another, polyphony is the inevitable result. The intricacy of African polphony is obscured by the masterful techniques and ease with which it is accomplished. It is still not clear just how and under what circumstances slaves were brought to America. In the tricknological history books, usually the story goes that African chiefs sold other Africans, who were already enslaved to the white slave merchants. But there are also suggestions here and there that force might have been employed in the process. Thus Thomas Pettigrew writes that wars had to be fought in order to get slaves. Unfortunately, he does not go further to explicate the matter, nor does he reveal his sources. It is certainly within the realm of probability that a people who did not hesitate to use force and violence against America's original inhabitants would not abhor its use in the acquisition of those who were earmarked to build America—African slaves. Perhaps black scholars will begin to research this important area and substantiate this hypothesis.

African slaves undoubtedly came from all parts of the continent, including Egypt and parts of East Africa. They were shipped not only to the United States, but to all sections of the West Indies and Latin America. In the latter cases, African musical and cultural survivals are at first glance more pronounced, since most of these countries were under the influence

** The three forms of polyphony are: multi-rhythmic, multi-melodic, and multi-rhythm-multi-melody simultaneously.

of the Catholic Church, which was more tolerant to the African gods than the largely Protestant slaveholding group in the United States. They have also been able to avoid the effects of technology and commercialism that have plagued musicians of African descent here. Almost all the names given to Latin American dances are names of African religious dances. These include the rhumba, samba, mambo, etc. The following illustration of an Afro-Cuban orchestra reveals many instruments of African origin, including claves, guerro, conga drums, timbale, marimba, bongos, etc. In some of these countries, such as Brazil, Cuba, and Haiti, African religions such as Voodoo are practiced. Voodoo in fact is the religion most practiced by Haitians, from Papa Doc Duvalier to the average citizen. Duvalier is a Voodoo priest as well as a medical doctor. The music of these countries did not develop therefore in quite the same way as that of the African people in the United States. Slavery conditions in this country were much harsher than those in the Indies and Latin America. And of course, here, unlike the other slave sectors, was a concerted effort to remove all traces of African culture from language to music. But the black man in America was, despite these attempts, able to hold on to the essential elements of African music, which even find expression in today's contemporary Black music. Black culture, of which Black music is a reflection, has also retained much that is African. This can be seen immediately in the highly expressive artistic styles of Black poets, painters, and musicians. Our language is not English, or at least many of the words we use are not English. Our life-styles are also subject to African influence, as well as our personal philosophies, which are inclined toward an ability to be deeply sympathetic to the plights of others, and to feel deeply, whether it be in joy or grief. All over the United States today, Voodoo is still practiced, despite earlier attempts to ban it. Voodoo is a way of life that permeates every phase of life, unlike Western religion, which is separate from a secular life. As both a religion and a philosophy, Voodoo remained in the United States and was manifest in both Black religious music and the blues. Specific Africanisms were also introduced early in America. These included the expressive use of the voice, the instrumental imitation of the human voice, songs about animals and songs of a parable nature, vocal devices such as falsetto, trills, glissando, bends, slurs, and melisma. African-like instruments were invented when the materials were available—instruments such as bones (claves), washbucket bass, kazoo (merliton) and various drums (especially in Louisiana). Of course, the slavemaster didn't buy expensive instruments for his slaves, who were considered mere property, nor was the slave allowed to bring over his own. For this reason, slave music was primarily vocal. After the Civil War, relatively inexpensive instruments became available as war surplus, left over from the regimental bands. Now blacks also had an income, if but a meager one, to buy the desired instruments, making it possible to redevelop an instrumental music.

III Poetry

THE NEGRO ARTIST AND THE
RACIAL MOUNTAIN
Langston Hughes

One of the most promising of the young Negro poets said
to me once, "I want to be a poet—not a Negro poet," meaning,
I believe, "I want to write like a white poet"; meaning subconsciously "I would like to be a white poet"; meaning behind
that, "I would like to be white." And I was sorry the young man
said that, for no great poet has ever been afraid of being
himself. And I doubted then that, with his desire to run away
spiritually from his race, this boy would ever be a great poet.
But this is the mountain standing in the way of any true
Negro art in America—this urge within the race toward whiteness, the desire to pour racial individuality into the mold of
American standardization, and to be as little Negro and as
much American as possible.

But let us look at the immediate background of this young
poet. His family is of what I suppose one would call the
Negro middle class: people who are by no means rich yet
never uncomfortable nor hungry—smug, contented, respectable
folk, members of the Baptist church. The father goes to work
every morning. He is a chief steward at a large white club.
The mother sometimes does fancy sewing or supervises parties
for the rich families of the town. The children go to a mixed

school. In the home they read white papers and magazines. And the mother often says "Don't be like niggers" when the children are bad. A frequent phrase from the father is, "Look how well a white man does things." And so the word white comes to be unconsciously a symbol of all the virtues. It holds for the children beauty, morality, and money. The whisper of "I want to be white" runs silently through their minds. This young poet's home is, I believe, a fairly typical home of the colored middle class. One sees immediately how difficult it would be for an artist born in such a home to interest himself in interpreting the beauty of his own people. He is never taught to see that beauty. He is taught rather not to see it, or if he does, to be ashamed of it when it is not according to Caucasian patterns.

For racial culture the home of a self-styled "high-class" Negro has nothing better to offer. Instead there will perhaps be more aping of things white than in a less cultured or less wealthy home. The father is perhaps a doctor, lawyer, landowner, or politician. The mother may be a social worker, or a teacher, or she may do nothing and have a maid. Father is often dark but he has usually married the lightest woman he could find. The family attend a fashionable church where few really colored faces are to be found. And they themselves draw a color line. In the North they go to white theaters and white movies. And in the South they have at least two cars and a house "like white folks." Nordic manners, Nordic faces, Nordic hair, Nordic art (if any), and an Episcopal heaven. A very high mountain indeed for the would-be racial artist to climb in order to discover himself and his people.

But then there are the low-down folks, the so-called common element, and they are the majority—may the Lord be praised! The people who have their nip of gin on Saturday nights and are not too important to themselves or the community, or too well fed, or too learned to watch the lazy world go round. They live on Seventh Street in Washington or State Street in Chicago and they do not particularly care whether they are like white folks or anybody else. Their joy runs, bang! into ecstasy. Their religion soars to a shout. Work maybe a little today, rest a little tomorrow. Play awhile. Sing awhile. O, let's dance! These common people are not afraid of spirituals, as for a long time their more intellectual brethren were, and jazz is their child. They furnish a wealth of colorful, distinctive material for any artist because they still hold their own individuality in the face of American standardizations. And perhaps these common people will give to the world its truly great Negro artist, the one who is not afraid to be himself. Whereas the better-class Negro would tell the artist what to do, the people at least let him alone when he does appear. And they are not ashamed of him—if they know he exists at all. And they accept what beauty is their own without question.

Certainly there is, for the American Negro artist who can escape the restrictions the more advanced among his own group would put upon him, a great field of unused material ready for his art. Without going outside his race, and even among the better classes with their "white" culture and conscious American manners, but still Negro enough to be different, there is sufficient matter to furnish a black artist with a lifetime of creative work. And when he chooses to touch on the relations between Negroes and whites in this country with their innumerable overtones and undertones, surely, and especially for literature and the drama, there is an inexhaustible supply of themes at hand. To these the Negro artist can give his racial individuality, his heritage of rhythm and warmth, and his incongruous humor that so often, as in the Blues, becomes ironic laughter mixed with tears. But let us look again at the mountain.

A prominent Negro clubwoman in Philadelphia paid eleven dollars to hear Raquel Meller sing Andalusian popular songs. But she told me a few weeks before she would not think of going to hear "that woman," Clara Smith, a great black artist, sing Negro folksongs. And many an upper-class Negro church, even now, would not dream of employing a spiritual in its services. The drab melodies in white folks' hymnbooks are much to be preferred. "We want to worship the Lord correctly and quietly. We don't believe in 'shouting.' Let's be dull like the Nordics," they say, in effect.

The road for the serious black artist, then, who would produce a racial art is most certainly rocky and the mountain is high. Until recently he received almost no encouragement for his work from either white or colored people. The fine novels of Chesnutt go out of print with neither race noticing their passing. The quaint charm and humor of Dunbar's dialect verse brought to him, in his day, largely the same kind of encouragement one would give a sideshow freak (A colored man writing poetry! How odd!) or a clown (How amusing!).

The present vogue in things Negro, although it may do as much harm as good for the budding colored artist, has at least done this: it has brought him forcibly to the attention of his own people among whom for so long, unless the other race had noticed him beforehand, he was a prophet with little honor. I understand that Charles Gilpin acted for years in Negro theaters without any special acclaim from his own, but when Broadway gave him eight curtain calls, Negroes, too, began to beat a tin pan in his honor. I know a young colored writer, a manual worker by day, who had been writing well for the colored magazines for some years, but it was not until he recently broke into the white publications and his first book was accepted by a prominent New York publisher that the "best" Negroes in his city took the trouble to discover that he lived there. Then almost immediately they decided to give a grand dinner for him. But the society ladies were careful to whisper to his mother that perhaps she'd better not come. They were not sure she would have an evening gown.

The Negro artist works against an undertow of sharp criticism and misunderstanding from his own group and unintentional bribes from the whites. "Oh, be respectable, write about nice people, show how good we are," say the Negroes. "Be stereotyped, don't go too far, don't shatter our illusions about you, don't amuse us too seriously. We will pay you," say the whites. Both would have told Jean Toomer not to write *Cane*. The colored people did not praise it. The white people did not buy it. Most of the colored people who did read *Cane* hate it. They are afraid of it. Although the critics gave it good reviews the public remained indifferent. Yet (excepting the work of Du-Bois) *Cane* contains the finest prose written by a Negro in America. And like the singing of Robeson, it is truly racial.

But in spite of the Nordicized Negro intelligentsia and the desires of some white editors we have an honest American Negro literature already with us. Now I await the rise of the Negro theater. Our folk music, having achieved world-wide fame, offers itself to the genius of the great individual American Negro composer who is to come. And within the next decade I expect to see the work of a growing school of colored artists who paint and model the beauty of dark faces and create with new technique the expression of their own soul-world. And the Negro dancers who will dance like flame and the singers who will continue to carry our songs to all who listen—they will be with us in even greater numbers tomorrow.

Most of my own poems are racial in theme and treatment, derived from the life I know. In many of them I try to grasp and hold some of the meanings and rhythms of jazz. I am as sincere as I know how to be in these poems and yet after every reading I answer questions like these from my own people: Do you think Negroes should always write about Negroes? I wish you wouldn't read some of your poems to white folks. How do you find anything interesting in a place like a cabaret? Why do you write about black people? You aren't black. What makes you do so many jazz poems?

But jazz to me is one of the inherent expressions of Negro life in America: the eternal tom-tom beating in the Negro soul —the tom-tom of revolt against weariness in a white world, a world of subway trains, and work, work, work; the tom-tom of joy and laughter, and pain swallowed in a smile. Yet the

Philadelphia clubwoman is ashamed to say that her race created it and she does not like me to write about it. The old subconscious "white is best" runs through her mind. Years of study under white teachers, a lifetime of white books, pictures, and papers, and white manners, morals, and Puritan standards made her dislike the spirituals. And now she turns up her nose at jazz and all its manifestations—likewise almost everything else distinctly racial. She doesn't care for the Winold Reiss portraits of Negroes because they are "too Negro." She does not want a true picture of herself from anybody. She wants the artist to flatter her, to make the white world believe that all Negroes are as smug and as near white in soul as she wants to be. But, to my mind, it is the duty of the younger Negro artist, if he accepts any duties at all from outsiders, to change through the force of his art that old whispering "I want to be white," hidden in the aspirations of his people, to "Why should I want to be white? I am a Negro—and beautiful!"

So I am ashamed for the black poet who says, "I want to be a poet, not a Negro poet," as though his own racial world were not as interesting as any other world. I am ashamed, too, for the colored artist who runs from the painting of Negro faces to the painting of sunsets after the manner of the academicians because he fears the strange un-whiteness of his own features. An artist must be free to choose what he does, certainly, but he must also never be afraid to do what he might choose.

Let the blare of Negro jazz bands and the bellowing voice of Bessie Smith singing Blues penetrate the closed ears of the colored near-intellectuals until they listen and perhaps understand. Let Paul Robeson singing "Water Boy," and Rudolph Fisher writing about the streets of Harlem, and Jean Toomer holding the heart of Georgia in his hands, and Aaron Douglas drawing strange black fantasies cause the smug Negro middle class to turn from their white, respectable, ordinary books and papers to catch a glimmer of their own beauty. We younger Negro artists who create now intend to express our individual dark-skinned selves without fear or shame. If white people are pleased we are glad. If they are not, it doesn't matter. We know we are beautiful. And ugly too. The tom-tom cries and the tom-tom laughs. If colored people are pleased we are glad. If they are not, their displeasure doesn't matter either. We build our temples for tomorrow, strong as we know how, and we stand on top of the mountain, free within ourselves.

TRIPPING WITH BLACK WRITING
Sarah Webster Fabio

The move toward liberation from slave to serf to self, for Black folk, has meant a long, arduous trip. The history of this development, which we might call "The Black Experience," has been chronicled in the annals of Black Literature. Always the movement has had to be bilateral—that is, both external and internal; language has played an important part in communicating the experience from within and without. And while Blacks have had to define and validate Black reality, they, concurrently, have had to protest and protect themselves from exploitation and dehumanization. They had to not only devise ways of speaking in tongues so that "the man" could not always understand everything, but also had to speak out of both sides of their mouths—hurrahing Black; badmouthing White.

Original hoodoo, badmouthing the man, forerunners of the "Stomp Me, O Lord" slave accounts and protests Black-perspective accounts of what was really going down with the wind, start with Lucy Terry, digging the scene of an Indian Massacre, 1746:

> And had not her petticoats stopt her
> The awful creatures had not cotched her
> And tommyhawked her on the head
> And left her on the ground for dead.

Or Jupiter Hammon on *An Evening Thought, Salvation by Christ, with Penitential Cries,"* turning hearts and souls away from an unbearable reality to spiritualism:

> Lord turn our dark benighted Souls;
> Give us a true Motion,
> And let the Hearts of all the World,
> Make Christ their Salvation.

Early turnings; trying to turn these bedeviled mothers around, shame them in their human trafficking; these wrenchings of conscience from those short on conscience but long on bread and black gold—earliest forms of Black power. Image-making from early days from pure spirit and communion with nature. Nation-building from the ground. Loss of king-of-the-jungle images, lion-and-panther form. Beaten to the ground; gagged and shackled, but singing free:

> Keep a-inching along
> like a poor inch worm
> JESUS IS COMING BY AND BY.

Or George Moses Horton transcending that hell-bound scene in *On Liberty and Slavery*, rapping on "the man," calling on the ancestors' spirit world:

> Say unto foul oppression, Cease:
> Ye tyrants rage no more,
> And let the joyful trump of peace,
> Now bid the vassal soar.

> Soar on the pinions of that dove
> Which long has cooed for thee,
> And breathed her notes from Afric's grove,
> The Sound of liberty. . . .

And with *The Life of Olanudah Equiano or Gustavus Vassa, The African, Written by Himself,* the beginning of the Black gift to American Mainstream Literature, a new genre—the slave narrative. "For-real" world literature. Gustavus Vassa running it down how he was run across the world, making giant steps, building civilization. Born in Benin, slaved in Virginia and Pennsylvania, farmed-out on a Caribbean plantation, working out as an abolitionist in England—as a self-made man. Bootstrap pulling; defying laws of gravity and gravitation. Gaming for self, and bootstrap-yanking for brother boots.

Getting that soul together in times of dehumanization and desecration of the souls of Black men. *Life and Times,* Frederick Douglass, a put-down as early as 1845; altogether in 1881. Whipping it to the original outhouse ruler of the "Harry Sam" vintage, Abe Lincoln; running down such a heavy game that runaway slave turns presidential adviser and Consul General to Haiti. Shades of Papa Doc! Wearing two faces. Seer. Invoking spirits, calling for an exorcism of the spirit and body of racism manifested by *Dred Scott* decision and the act of nullifying the Fourteenth Amendment in 1883. Instances of bad Supreme Court decisions which made him cry out:

> But when a deed is done for slavery, caste, and oppression and a blow is struck at human progress, whether so intended or not, the heart of humanity sickens in sorrow and writhes in pain. It makes us feel as if some one were stamping upon the graves of our mothers, or desecrating our sacred temples. Only base men and oppressors can rejoice in a triumph of injustice over the weak and defenseless, for weakness ought itself to protect from assaults of pride, prejudice, and power. . . .
> (pp. 541–47)

No man can put a chain about the ankle of his fellow-man, without at last finding the other end of it about his own neck.

The lesson of all the ages upon this point is, that a wrong done to one man is a wrong done to all men. It may not be felt at the moment, and the evil may be long delayed, but so sure as there is a moral government of the universe, so sure will the harvest of evil come.

Stomp us, O Lord! Getting into the power of speaking in tongues. W. E. B. DuBois. *The Souls of Black Folk*. Those of the double consciousness, born with veils over their eyes . . . From *Darkwater*, "A Litany at Atlanta, Done at Atlanta, in the Day of Death, 1906":

. . . Wherefore do we pray? Is not the God of the fathers dead? Have not seers seen in Heaven's halls Thine hearsed and lifeless form stark amidst the black and rolling smoke of sin, where all along bow bitter forms of endless dead? . . .
Thou art still the God of our black fathers, and in Thy soul's soul sit some soft darkenings of the evening, some shadowings of the velvet night.

Stomp us, O Lord! James Weldon Johnson raising *God's Trombones*, giving a new folk "Creation," rhapsodizing about Africa's prodigal son's return home. Setting the beat of marching feet on the road to victory in "Lift Every Voice and Sing":

. . . Stony the road we trod,
   Bitter the chastening rod,
   Felt in the days when hope unborn had died;
   Yet with a steady beat,
   Have not our weary feet
   Come to the place for which our fathers sighed?

Speaking in tongues. Uncle Julius, in "The Goophered Grapevine," describes one of Sycorax's daughters, Aun' Peggy, who has goophered, cunju'd, bewitched the scuppernon' vineyard:

She sa'ntered 'roun' mongs' de vimes, en tuk a leaf fum dis one, en a grape-hull fum dat one, en a grape-seed fum annuder one; en den a little twig fum here, en a little pinch er dirt fum dere,—en put it all in a big black bottle, wid a snake's toof en a speckle' hen's gall en some ha'rs fum a black cat's tail, en den fill' de bottle wid scuppernon' wine.

Speaking in tongues and running his games. Charles Chesnutt. And Paul Laurence Dunbar running it down how "We wear the Mask/That grins and lies." An African orientation . . .

Alain Locke—that necessary critic for *The New Negro;* a special critic for a special time. Harlem Renaissance. Fathering Negritude. Giving the possibility of showing forth a triumph of spirit and mind. A decolonized mind shining through colonial language. Locke sees Caliban's early move:

. . . Then eventually came the time when the hectic rhetoric and dogged moralism had to fall back in sheer exhaustion on the original basis of cultural supply. Through Dunbar,—part of whose poetry, nevertheless, reflects the last stand of this rhetorical advance, Negro poetry came penitently back to the folk-tradition, and humbled itself to dialect for fresh spiritual food and raiment.

William Stanley Braithwaite, who gave America the possibility of an American poetry, speaks of Dunbar as closing one age in Black poetry and beginning another. Check out the Sesqui-Centennial Edition of *Braithwaite's Anthology of Magazine Verse for 1926, Yearbook of American Poetry.* Black poetry—a main tributary of mainstream American poetry. A Black man willing to bring an indigenous, non-derivative poetry into being. He got lost in the shuffle after 1929. But he'd done his thing. Sterling Brown, one of the most capable writers using Black form chronicling the literary movement in *Negro Caravan.* Sterling Brown in his *Negro Poetry and Drama* said this:

"Dialect, or the speech of the people, is capable of expressing whatever the people are. And the folk Negro is a great deal more than a buffoon or a plaintive minstrel. Poets more intent upon learning the ways of the folk, their speech, and their character, that is to say better poets, could have smashed the mold. But first they would have had to believe in what they were doing. And this was difficult in a period of conciliation and middle class striving for recognition and respectability."

Early there was a self-consciousness and a mold which a deriding white America put on Black folk speech. This meant that many feigned representing folk speech, according to Brown, by:

"A few pat phrases, a few stock situations and characteristics, some misspelling: these were the chief things necessary. The wit and beauty possible to folk speech, the folk-shrewdness, the humanity, the stoicism of these people they seldom say."

The Harlem Renaissance period closed the credibility gap between the Black man, his articulation of his experience, and his selfhood. Zora Neal Hurston, anthropologist, throwing light on language. Open the way for today's freedom-wigged freaks. Stone-cold, bad-blood revolutionaries. Escapees from prisons of Anglo rhetoric. Frontiersmen in the lumbering netherlands of Black language. Medicine men schooled in witchcraft, black magic, the voodoo of words. Immortalized, subterranean, out-of-this-world travelers. Dutchmen. LeRois. LeRoi Joneses. Quick-change sleight-of-hand magicians. Dons. Don Lees. Changing. "Change your enemy change your change change change your enemy change change . . . change your mind nigger." Killens. Killens' chilluns. On their jobs. Taking care of business. "De-niggerizing the world." Voodoo cowboys. Loop Garoo Kids. Riding loose—cool ones—into the whirlwind of change; who, as they gallop into town, have a "posse of spells phone in sick."

Ishmaels. Ishmael Reeds. Yeah. Yellow Back Radio Done Show Good Broke-Down. Up against the wall, Prospero.

Calibans all. Exploding Prospero's premises with extraordinary, for-real, supernatural departures. Trips. More benevolent despotism, spelled Tyranny. Any way you look at it. And his gift of language—his "prison in which Caliban's achievements will be realized and restricted"—is a boomerang. New-breed Blacks, those desperadoes who "Take the Money and Run," leave "the man" behind bound and bankrupt; marooned on a barren island of derivative Anglo-Saxon, European-like culture. Walled in by the "law and order" of his own restrictive rhetoric. And those newly free? They are on their jobs making jujus, working their mojos, peeping Chuck's hold cards. Understanding the real meaning of his excessive articulation of so much nonsense. Seers and sages. Reporters such as Eldridge Cleaver sending back messages about the "technologically gifted moon men": "I heard what he said; he said 'oink.'" LeRoi Jones-created criminals intent on robbing the family of its jewels in *Home on the Range*. Mystified, momentarily, with the father's talk; "Crillilly bagfest. Gobble Gobble. Gobble." But understand their task is to give these robots the gift of soul, of language of the real world. Once more, Mr. Tooful: "I was born in Kansas City in 1920. My father was the vice-president of a fertilizer company. Before that we were phantoms. . . ." Which explains all that shit. Packaged under the brand name of "Standard English," mainstream American literature. Or Sister Carolyn Rodgers taking a look at the spineless, flat imitation in "Portrait of a White Nigger"! who "talks like/a biscuit that will/not rise . . . got a jelly mind/and shimmy thighs"; whose purpose in life is reduced to an endless search trying "to find the MAGIC that/will/PRESTO"/Black/off/ . . ."

No mere children of nature these. They are indeed, Sycorax-the-Sorceress' offspring. With magic potions to tame the beasts of nature. With so many thumping, twangling instruments giving the beat. Informing William Melvin Kelley and his likes that he moves to the rhythms of *A Different Drummer*. Dere's Us'ns and dere's *Dem*. Magic knowledge. Source of power found rooted in the residue of a wellspring of aged and ageless African native culture—soul. Spooky Stuff. Sins of the father's revisited! Great balls of fire!! Brother, brush off your Br'er Rabbit's foot. Shine up your John-The-Conqueror root. Whip up your own brand gris-gris. It's Voodoo time again.

LeRoi Jones, dramatizing the dilemma. Don Lee, chronicling the changes. Ishmael Reed, S-p-e-l-l-i-n-g it out. Nikki Giovanni, recording "Records": "a negro needs to kill/something/trying to record/that this country must be/destroyed/if we are to live/ must be destroyed if we are to live/must be destroyed if we are to live." Jimmy Garret, bucking the whitewashed system. White power—the same which done got his mama—challenged to a duel. By a deathly game of dozens, in the one-act *And We Own the Night*. Cracker-walled prisons of rhetoric crumbled before the double-whammied eyes of crumb-snatching blues logic, Semple-fied by Langston Hughes, passed on as sacrament to Stanley Crouch and Dante. Stone walls of martial law and bad conditions failing to imprison the spirit of Blacks. Etheridge Knight, breaking through in *Cell Song*, answering the call to "take/your words and scrape/the sky, shake rain/on the desert, sprinkle/salt on the tail/of a girl . . ." And Sonia Sanchez preparing for *Homecoming*: "Leaving behind me/all those hide and /seek faces . . . I have learned it/ain't like they say/in the newspapers." Soul talk for soul folk. *Boss Soul*, by Sarah Fabio: ". . . gut bucket, gospel spiritual, jazz/touching cords of Feeling any live person/has to tune into or turn on to that/special deepdown/inside you thing."

New Day. Dawn. Light of Broken Night. Night breaks. Night trippers. Check out the Bad, Bold scene of the Mojo workers. Dig the star-crossed bones uncovered by Ishmael Reed in *15 Nigromancers From Now*. If you dare. Any day or night—or

séance in between—get on down to what's really there. Clean-
picked bones. The skulls of ones who talked too much. Get to
that. Another necessary trip: *Amistad,* with Charles Harris
and John Williams piloting.

Black writers, finding themselves up a tree with "the man's"
rhetoric and aesthetic, which hangs them up, lynching their
black visions, cut it loose. All the way—swinging free. Flying
home. Wings flapping, raucously, in the breeze. So many un-
natural demands from the establishment, the tradition, beamed
into a subject people from a hostile, alien culture, shined off as
irrelevant, self-defeating. Needing to respond as integral beings
not having to compromise integrity. Bringing black perspective,
black aesthetic, black rhetoric, black language to add authentic-
ity to the felt reality. Knowing America has no rhetoric matching its racist reality; no reality matching its "universal" and
"democratic" idealistic state of existence. Knowing the simple-
minded, fascist, pseudo-Europeanized mandate of "universality"
to be a funky issue in any aesthetic consideration. A hustle
to make walleyed, white-eyed America the all-seeing Cyclops
of our age.

Giving the finger to blind justice. Peeping the loosened blind-
fold. Peeping her peeping; favoring the apples of her eye—
rotten though they may be. Playing the game of dozens with
her. Combating her status-quo games. Knowing the truth about
this society. One that devaluates the lives of a people for the
duration of its existence. One that dehumanizes them for fun
and profit. A mere matter of pragmatism and utilitarianism.
Knowing that society to be guilty of: emasculating manhood;
deflowering womanhood; exploiting spirit and soul; blinding
vision; binding motion; dulling sensitivity; gagging speech.

Black Writing—repressed, suppressed, ignored, denounced.
Black writers having rained upon them not respect, riches,
rewards, but disrespect, discouragement, non-recognition, de-
culturation, assimilation, isolation, starvation, expatriation, de-
rangement, criminal indictment. LeRoi Jones's case but a recent
and flagrant example of a system's way of dealing with creative,

liberated black minds. The same brutal white backlash that cut the cord of David Walker's life after his writing of his "Appeal" in the early nineteenth century still tears at the flesh of articulate Blacks of the recent past and the present—men such as Malcolm X, Martin Luther King, Eldridge Cleaver, Bobby Seale.

No turning back, though. This is the day of Biggers and ghosts of Biggers. Black writers—most of them poets plus—have always been barometers, even when America kept bell jars on them. Have always been/still are/will be. Always traveling with ears to the ground; attuned to the drumbeats of the age. Check out the Harlem Renaissance poets, such as Langston Hughes, Claude McKay, Sterling Brown. Check out the post depression poets of the thirties, including Richard Wright. Check out Margaret Walker's words to her people in the early forties. Check out the poets in *Beyond the Blues,* a time when Black poetry was so far underground it had to travel to England for publication. Check out Black poets publishing with Broadside Press, Third World Press, Success Press. Check out Black periodicals—*Journal of Black Poetry, Black Dialogue, Negro Digest, Liberator.*

Take the A-Train to Black liberation. Black writing of the seventies will be the Sweet Chariots of our time: swinging low/ swinging high/swinging free. Communicant. Continuum. Change. Consummation.

BLACKNESS CAN: A QUEST FOR AESTHETICS
James A. Emanuel

(I will be as black as blackness can, The blacker the mantle the mightier the man . . .
—W. E. B. *DuBois*, The Song of the Smoke)

Writing in 1925 his now famous essay about the bold black artist who was then being crowned "the New Negro," Alain Locke recorded the following prediction:

> With this renewed self-respect and self-dependence, the life of the Negro community is bound to enter a new dynamic phase, the buoyancy from within compensating for whatever pressure there may be of conditions from without. The migrant masses, shifting from countryside to city, hurdle several generations of experience at a leap, but more important, the same thing happens spiritually in the life-attitudes and self-expression of the Young Negro, in his poetry, his art, his education, and his new outlook, with the additional advantage, of course, of the poise and greater certainty of knowing what it is all about. From this comes the promise and warrant of a new leadership.

But "the New Negro" slowly died. In the 1930s, the Depression emaciated him. In the 1940s, global warfare drained the energies and diverted the attitudes vital to his recovery. In the 1950s, fitful surges toward racial integration deluded him into believing that the question of his death had become less relevant. When the 1960s began, his grandchildren waved him a respectful but apprehensive farewell from their fiery buses and grim lunch counters in the South. On the verge of the 1970s, they threw away his clothes, his hair, and his name. They emerged as the Young Blacks, fevered by the past and determined to make non-negotiable demands upon the future.

The Young Blacks' fire has spread to some of their more spirited elders, including authors and critics. This conflagration, certain to sweep literary black America in the 1970s with harrowing choices, is implicitly foretold in the passage quoted above. Locke must have known that, in this drama of the 1920s (now restaged more than a decade after his death by what he called "the three norns [Fates] who have traditionally presided over the Negro problem"), relatively few actors could transform their lines into living philosophy. In no country can masses of people "hurdle several generations of experience with a leap" without a staggering casualty list. Nor can the best-educated and the most artistically gifted of a race—including those blessed with the "certainty of knowing what it is all about"—survive the accompanying concentrated doses of racial philosophy without proportionate losses.

Although almost half a century separates these two periods of upheaval in black America, the phenomena are instructively similar. In the 1920s, one kind of "New Negro" followed the trail of wartime migrants from the South—a countrified working-man whose mind expanded among the new freedoms and new hazards of the North. He has been comparable, in the late 1960s, to the black urban slum dweller whose awareness of sit-ins and street demonstrations has quickened him with new visions of working-class power. The literary, artistic "New Negro" of the 1920s, on the other hand, suddenly found himself attractive to white authors, white publishers, and white party-givers. He can be likened to three categories of black people today: (1) the black college student whose matriculation has been solicited, or whose elective courses have suddenly included Black Studies, at universities reacting to the current swell of racial pride; (2) the black actor, entertainer, or model whose multiplying image on television and in other public media has nourished both him and his people; and (3) the black author or critic who has received writing and editing contracts from highly reputable publishing firms that have traditionally ignored him.

One significant national difference, however, marks these periods and their dominant attitudes. The loud, joyous relief from war that characterized the Jazz Age seems frivolous today when viewed from the menacing gloom of our demoralizing war abroad and our iconoclastic ruin at home. At the fulcrum of this half-century-long span sits the black American, more aware of his nascent power than of his historic leverage. America's contrasting national attitudes of confidence and joy versus cynicism and despair represent the dichotomy that has been steadily controlled and internally balanced by this black man and his ancestors for two hundred and fifty years. Facing the 1970s with a consequent subconscious poise, he must also look backward to the leap that his forebears often could not take, one that he can hardly take now. In the 1920s it was the leap described by Locke as the jump "from medieval America to modern." Today it is the leap from the physical underside to the spiritual and ideological peak of national life, from suffering as the hindmost, to thinking and acting as the foremost, of Americans.

Precariously balanced, then, at the center of American life, the black man feels the tremors of directional forces, sensing for the first time the magnitude of his own motive power. A prescient boldness of imagination opens to him a view of himself as the democratic spokesman for his country, the body and soul of its final possibilities. But the logic behind this revolutionary self-image, requiring support from his fellow citizens, black and white, cannot of itself move him to fulfill his destiny. White America has shown that it cannot be trusted to respond wisely and humanely to any massive expression of black America's consciousness of long abuse, even when that expression is restrained in nature and is demonstrably linked

with moral urgencies in our international impasse. The assassination of Reverend Martin Luther King, Jr., symbolized the
death of the black man's naïve Christianized faith. But black
people are far from being united in their acceptance of their
fated role as examplars of the new American. The perceptual
leap from a centuries-old environment of despisal and scorn
to one of globally recognized leadership and heroism would
be extremely difficult even if it were being encouraged. But
ignorance, duplicity, and organized opposition on the part of
both white and black Americans are formidable impediments
to the required reversal of self-image.

The area of black people's activity in which this revaluation
and leadership should most authentically occur is that in which
critical intelligence as an instrument and racial responsibility as
a principle are most irrevocably joined. Educational and
journalistic institutions seem best indicated by these considerations. If rigorous concern for truth and for its means of historical
development and preservation are to be more important in the
1970s than commercialized rapport with the average black buyer
of newspapers and magazines, then schools and colleges will
remain the primary battleground for what Locke correctly emphasized in the 1920s: "the mind of the Negro." Further,
since the truth of human experience is concentrated and preserved best through literary art, it is mainly the black author
and his public interpreter, the critic, who will inspire their
race toward its destiny.

These public thinkers, veritably forced to respond creatively
and critically to the evolving spirit of black America, have
become self-conscious to an unprecedented degree. The spotlight of social responsibility, which in times of crises searches
out elevated positions before it can fix upon individuals with
elevated principles, has illuminated the customarily private work-
rooms of black literary men, regardless of their competence.
America faces an exciting decade in which the Young Blacks
will throng the air with animated poetry and prose. Their
intensities, mirrored in the daily lives of their growing audience,

will often be emulated by their elder contemporaries who find it either useful or pleasing to express racial passions long subdued by accommodation and despair. The nature of literature itself, then, appears to be changing for black authors and their followers. It seems to be more social, more programmatic, more therapeutic. There is some resultant confusion of posture with performance, of theme with permanent merit. Yet it is undeniable that, to black men as American citizens, erect literary postures and libertarian themes are symbolically and materially of singular importance.

In order to identify the basic issues involved, and to estimate the magnitude of their probable impact upon black America of the 1970s, one needs a sampling from the record of the growing controversy. More than a year of commentary, as found in the pages of *Negro Digest* alone from September 1968 through November 1969, adequately outlines this crucial impasse in our literary tradition. The main issues are centralized conveniently in the tentatively accepted phrase around which the disputation swells: "the black aesthetic."

If the term itself is appropriate, the theory involved should emphasize beauty, artfulness, and good taste—in short, "aesthetic" qualities. The black aesthetic, as a formally accepted set of literary principles, has not quite yet been born. The 1970s, should that decade indeed witness such a birth, might well dawn upon new notions of functional beauty, subordinating such skills as authentic rhyme and phonetic subtleties to the celebration of American blackness as the crest of the human spirit. As of October 1969, according to the editor of *Negro Digest* (Hoyt W. Fuller), two poets from Chicago's Organization of Black American Culture, which Fuller helped to establish in 1967, were "setting up preliminary criteria for the evaluation of black poetry." This action by two young black writers, Rhonda Davis and Carolyn Rodgers, responds to some of the needs of their fellow authors, whom Fuller describes in *The New York Times Book Review* of October 19, 1969, as "stripping themselves of the creative chains with which the literary Establishment

bound them for so long." Whether or not such criteria can sub-
stantially influence a still-evolving poetic tradition remains to
be seen.

It might be useful to consider why a *black* aesthetic is
needed, just as one might wonder, rhetorically, about the validity
of *black* studies and *black* universities. Black Man Thinking,
however, quickly disposes of these objections—which are usually
made by *white* America—when he reflects that the nation itself
has always insisted upon the overwhelming significance of blackness. Therefore, to view any subject deliberately through a
black man's eyes is to accept a traditionally American emphasis.
And to use such an approach for the purpose of deep intellectual exploration, designed to benefit one's race rather than
to disparage it, is to turn deficit into profit—an admirable success
in any free society.

The need for a black aesthetic, in the opinion of the popular
young poet Don L. Lee, derives from the fact that "black
people see nothing in the same frame of reference as white
people."[1] The absolutism of this statement, mitigated by the
presently fluid definition of "black," is representative of the
hardening attitudes that are feeding irreversible currents into the
flow of literary ideas. This concept of a unique "black" perception is differently set forth by Cecil Brown, who declares:
"Every Negro baby in America is born . . . into a world of
white values, and if he is to survive that world, he has to
achieve blackness" (12–68:48). Assuming these statements of
Lee and Brown to be complementary, one sees the lifelong
tension in black people's minds as their struggle to will into
being an environment of salutary blackness to counteract hostilities and debasements projected by white society. A black
aesthetic could ease that struggle by making it wholly conscious and public among culturally alert citizens, and by serving

[1] September/October 1968 number of *Negro Digest*, page 31. Future references to essays in *Negro Digest* will be simplified in the text; this one
would read 9/10–68:31.

as a standard by which the success of the transformation could be measured.

This need for a black aesthetic has been argued, not only on the basis of the black man's psyche, but also on the basis of institutionalized racism. The South African poet and essayist William Keorapetse Kgositsile points out that young writers "come out of Western institutions of higher learning strongly convinced that the university in the West is an extension of racism," because of which "the Black poet's sensitivity explodes" (9/10-68:41). The Church, which has recently suffered from the disaffection of Young Blacks, has been scored as an institution that encourages racism. Carolyn F. Gerald, in her thoughtful examination of the role of cultural images in the revilement and belittling of black people, reminds us that "white images are implanted at the core of black life, the most obvious example being that of the Church, where God is white" (1-69:46). Universities as well as churches are subsumed by Don L. Lee in what he sees as "a decadent culture that has systematically, over the centuries, debased and dehumanized us with the fury and passion of an unfeeling computer" (3-69:52). And poet Lee can be allowed to make his point through self-contradiction, in attacking the part of his society that thrives malignantly on that very fallacy.

A black aesthetic must develop, authors are saying with mounting emphasis, because of racism in the literary establishment. Black writers object vigorously to the domination of white publishers, white editors, and white critics over the public acceptance and interpretation of their works. Relating this onerous situation to the distortions fostered by our schools and colleges, Hoyt W. Fuller accuses the establishment: "Generations of black students have gone out into the world as professionals believing that the white view of black literature is the valid view" (3-69:83). The editor of *Negro Digest* continues by expressing bitter resentment of the establishment's belief that "only white writers have the 'objectivity' toward race which is necessary to produce *art* when the subject matter is race."

Naming earlier a few of the offending publications, Lee strength-
ens Fuller's protest by declaring his glad anticipation of the
day when *"no* white boys in the pages of *The Nation,* the
New Republic, Saturday Review, New York *Times,* etc., will
direct or affect our efforts" (9/10–68:32).

The seriousness and possible ramifications of these strictures
against the privileged eminence of white critics and editors
should not be underestimated. As of November 1969, black
subterranean rumblings had risen and spread with sufficient
heat to threaten the birth of a new scholarly journal, to be
devoted to black literature and culture, because of allegations
of racism in its tentative organization and in its self-opinions.
The same month, a national academic convention, echoing the
October disruptions of the Montreal international conference of
the African Studies Association, fell into a predicament prophetic
of the 1970s. It faced potential black-and-white polarization
stemming from preconvention hostilities over the elevated role
of the white critic of black literature.

American literature might never record, with regard to black
literature, any thoughtful consensus among its stellar critics,
for they have generally failed to give that literature the respect
of serious examination. Thoughtless statements by such men as
Richard Gilman and Louis Simpson—to name just two white
critics who have been justifiably censured since the fall of 1968
in the pages of *Negro Digest*—remain representative targets.
Editor Fuller keeps alive the memory of Gilman, then theater
editor of *Newsweek,* declaring from his platform seat at the
Negro Writers Conference at the New School for Social Research
in 1965 that black writers, being incomplete men, could not yet
perform as good playwrights. Similarly unforgetful on behalf
of his fellow writers, Fuller recalls (also in his November 1968
number) Louis Simpson's judgment that "being a Negro" is
"not important" as poetic matter. The added reminder that
Simpson and Gilman softened their detractions, In *Harper's*
and in the *New Republic,* respectively, because "now it is not
politically expedient" to publish such viewpoints, erodes the

flimsy position of careless or shallow white critics. As for the silent white giants of the academy, their unforgivable long neglect has rather suddenly changed the challenging terrain of black literature into a no man's land into which only the most spirited of them will dare to venture and hold their ground.

White critics are simply not wanted, not only by many of the Young Blacks, but also by some of their older, more charitable contemporaries. Young playwrights at the Pan-African Cultural Festival in Algiers in July 1969 proclaimed their artistic freedom: negatively, they said "to hell with the Richard Gilmans of this world"; positively, they foresaw a new functional style developing directly from honestly racial substance. Some young poets think of white critics as "subhumans" trying to define and direct their efforts. Addison Gayle, Jr., briefly tracing the racial dichotomy in criticism from Plato through the medieval morality play, *Robinson Crusoe*, Hinton Helper, and on to the twentieth century, argues, "the extent of the cultural strangulation of Black literature by white critics has been the extent to which they have been allowed to define the terms in which the Black artist will deal with his own experience" (7–69:38).

White critics exacerbate this unfortunate situation by continuing their "strangulation," often through arbitrary disparagement of generations of black authors. For example, in *The New York Times Book Review* (Children's Books) of November 19, 1969, Selden Rodman records his disrespect for the creations of outstanding black writers, saying:

> . . . until recently there hasn't been any Afro-American verse that was more than just that—verse. When I was editing anthologies in 1938, and again in 1946, I remember going through the complete works of Countee Cullen, Claude McKay, Langston Hughes, and the others, hoping desperately to find a *poem,* and falling back reluctantly on the spirituals and blues (page 7).

Rodman characterizes the objects of his disfavor as "black verse-smiths" and laments the publication of their poetry (in this instance, in Walter Lowenfel's *The Writing on the Wall* (1969) as "a disservice to poetry, and perhaps in the long run to the black cause itself." One easily understands why so many black writers are "hoping desperately" that negligent judgments so "undeep and unabiding"—to borrow a phrase from poet Gwendolyn Brooks—will be swiftly demoted from the rank of legitimate criticism. It should be literary suicide for any critic, white or black, to demean so effortlessly Cullen's *Heritage,* McKay's *The White House,* Hughes's *Mulatto,* and the best poems of the numberless black authors lumped together in bold denigration as "the others."

Whiter villains, almost ghostlike in anonymity but massively real in power, are those many white publishers whose racist predilections drive them, in dispensing black-vogue editing and writing contracts, toward overriding preferences for white experts. The trade publishers among them, serving an over-the-counter morality fleshed out at the cash register, and disposed, as businessmen, to manufacture whatever salable commodity they cannot find at hand, produce bastard white critics upon their printing presses and cry up their wares through scores of white book reviewers. Although this system pays unavoidable homage, through book contracts, to the few conventionally competent white critics now active, it thrives upon privileged mediocrity. When black authors are allowed to profit from the black vogue, trade publishers either use more-highly selective criteria in granting contracts, or otherwise alter their standards —the end result being invariably the exclusion of too many able black authors and critics. Sometimes these trade publishers, turning semipolitical, enforce the exclusions through the sinister practice of blacklisting. Sometimes they are enforced through publishers' arbitrary rejection of black critics' offers to write books designed to explore the black literary tradition in depth.

Consideration of racism in publishing leads inevitably to serious doubts about the integrity, or at least the literary assumptions, of American university presses. Among the many books published from May 1 to July 31, 1969, by the sixty-six presses listed in *Scholarly Books in America* (October 1969)—a list covering seventy-two pages—only two books are concerned with black literature. They are William Edward Farrison's *William Wells Brown: Author and Reformer* (The University of Chicago Press) and Mercer Cook and Stephen E. Henderson's *The Militant Black Writer in Africa and the United States* (The University of Wisconsin Press). At least three factors should have combined before the dynamic 1970s to thrust the university presses into the forefront as publishers of studies of black literature: their commitment to thorough and objective scholarship; their closeness to the nationwide reservoir of professional critics, black and white; and their degree of immunity from the narrowness of popular taste and from some of the debasements of commercialism. The fact that the university presses have been sluggish for so long in a discipline so promising in intellectual discoveries and so rewarding to the democratic conscience indicates that they have collectively judged black literature to be unworthy of prolonged investigation. Thus outfaced by the most significant cultural challenge of the twentieth century, university presses are uniquely culpable in the light of their professional eminence and idealistic stance. The indictment of trade publishers and of university presses is compounded by the existence of documented proof of the racism and actual dishonesty of editors-in-chief and of directors in their communications with black authors.

The ignorance about black literature, combined with the duplicity and hostility in much of the white literary establishment, then, throws upon black America the burden of discovering and preserving its literary culture. It avails little to argue that the black publishing industry should expand and help multiply books in the racial tradition. The slow expansion of scholarly publication is foreseeable in the purposes of the recently established Negro Universities Press in Connecticut, for its 1969 catalogue declares, "Books on and about the Negro and the Black Experience are of *special* concern to the Press." Future developments in black and black-front publishing, whenever they are merely mercenary responses to the demands of the growing black audience now extrapolated, might not rise far above mechanical exploitation. Black America's cultural dilemma now is the eternal problem of the artist: the problem of material, purpose, and method. To the black artist serving as the culture hero of his race, his material is the unsorted mass of what is being called the black experience; his purpose is to memorialize in beauty and in truth the essence of that heritage. His method, if he is faithful to himself as a man and as an artist, must be sanctioned in his own being whenever it cannot be purely individual. It must—to enlist the language that closes Robert Hayden's poem *Frederick Douglass*—convey his personal gift to "lives grown out of his life, the lives/fleshing his dream of the beautiful, needful thing."

The notion of a black aesthetic does not seem conspiratorial or inflammatory within the circle of brother artists when its three components are first examined. Surely black writers have much "black experience"; they should desire to understand it, to make it beautiful, and to transmit that mature sense of life to others. Surely they cannot seriously object to proposals on style, on the means of enlivening with form the truth beneath the affectionate shibboleth "Black is beautiful." But black artists, color aside, belong to an obstinate fraternity traditionally individualistic, mainly because so much of their sensitive being is in their creative works. Anyone touching those works unfeelingly, either with Philistine dullness or with presumptuous dogma, incurs estrangement; and should he remain to make an institution of his error, he invites animosity, if not rebellion. Insensitivity will not likely be the blunder of framers of the black aesthetic, for they are, for the most part, literary artists themselves. But racial passion and belated zeal in striking back at the iron face of prejudice might harden into a dogmatic insistence that all black writers concentrate on punitive exclusion of whites and on recuperative embraces of blacks. Such a program would offer much emotional solace to those in direst need of it, but it would sour the free-running sympathies of a number of creative artists. Trouble looms, then, in the universal personality of the artist as the man most likely to ignore all voices but his own.

In order to estimate further the controversial as well as the uncontested voices now defining tentatively the black aesthetic, one can return to sampling the *Negro Digest*. Fifteen months of commentary in that popular journal does not reveal the entire range of opinion now in ferment, but it does define the general outlines of energetic thought that are mounting the offensive. The positive commentary, as distinguished from the illogical "get Whitey" mood that nerves much of the attack already represented by quotations, centers upon the following topics: the identification of black poets, the function of black poets, the nature of black American experience, the poetic techniques, the qualifications of black critics, the critical terminology, and the black critics' pitfalls.

Some stumbling is discernible in the first step of the black aesthetic, for the creed of its formulators is being composed for a somewhat nebulous advance guard. In her essay "Who Speaks Negro? What Is Black?" (9/10–68), Sarah Webster Fabio, after stating that a black writer could be "Negro in the use of the standard English language" (page 33), answers her titular questions thus:

Negro is a psychological, sociological, and economical fabrication to justify the *status quo* in America. Nigger is the tension created by a black man's attempt to accommodate himself to become a Negro in order to survive in a racist country. Black is the selfhood and soul of anyone with one drop of black blood, in America, who does not deny himself. . . . America wants Negroes and niggers but not black people (page 34).

To Don L. Lee, writing for the same number, a Negro is a similarly abstract lie: ". . . a filthy invention, which didn't come into existence until about 1620"; his next sentence refers to a Negro as an "imitation white" forsaking his "true experience," which is "the Black Experience" (page 27).

"Negro" and "black" are scarcely more denotative for modern usage when Carolyn F. Gerald, in her already mentioned essay, reminds us, ". . . the word *black* is a translation from the Portuguese slave term *negro,* gone into the English language as Negro" (page 46). Her reminder sanctions the Young Blacks' current distaste for the slavery-time connotations of "Negro." Her subsequent sentences refer to the social brotherhood in "black" as a powerful attributive in the fight against what poet Claude McKay has called "the potent poison" of Negrophobia. She writes:

> But black is also the generalized term which we use to symbolize unity of origin, whether we are called Anglophobe, Francophobe, coloured, mulatto, West Indian or American Negro by the white image-makers. *Black* is the highly imagistic term we use . . . to destroy the myth based on the complex of images which polarize black and white.

The faltering toward racial identity and unity—not in the mind of any one of these three writers, but in the projected synthesis that any creed presupposes—reveals itself here. The polarization mentioned by Carolyn F. Gerald is presented as the black man's dug-in acceptance of the battlefield historically marked out by whites. It assumes no subpolarization among the despised along an axis terminated by the blackest, on the one hand, and the least black, or the most nearly white, on the other. But, whereas this polarization leaves each writer in the group free to call himself either Negro or black with impunity, the statements of Sarah Webster Fabio and Don L. Lee imply impatience, at the minimum, toward the writer who does not correctly label himself with a racial tag. The utter seriousness and honesty of their comments, however, lead one to suppose that they would permit a writer's "black" works to belie his "Negro" label, whether it be mistakenly applied by himself or by another.

(Lee's poem *Gwendolyn Brooks,* as a matter of fact, supports the supposition in his case.)

Humorously awkward blunders, shrewd deceptions, and severe critical injustices would be unavoidable if authors and critics took these labels nervously to heart. A Negro sentence (one written in standard English) could turn black with a down-home fillip at the end. A Negro critic attempting to evaluate a black poet's skill in using a Negro sonnet to praise so black an experience as relishing a dish of "chitlins" might be disqualified on various aesthetic grounds. It would be deplorable—and impossible, one hopes—that writers should become guiltily introspective in a color-me-black syndrome, and that critics should become luggers of motley game-bags rather than become windows to a "selfhood and soul" not stricken with the pathologies of American color-consciousness.

But color has been unshakably real in America; and the function of black poets, as envisioned in these sampled essays, takes practical cognizance of that fact. The profound morality at the core of the black aesthetic is evident in remarks made by Kgositsile and Lee. The former, in his previously mentioned essay, describes the function of black poetry as the "restoration of human and humane values for the salvation of man" (page 41). Black poetry, asserts the latter, must "show those who control the world how to live" (9/10–68:28). "We must move that white boy toward righteousness," Lee continues, "show him what a human being *is,* and can be" (page 29). He specifies that the purpose of black poets (who "will be examples of their poems" [page 28]) is no less than the redefinition of man. Such confident insistence from a black African and from a black American that their tradition be recognized as central to the redemption of mankind should not be underestimated.

Further, the direct connection between universal benefit and black American need is implied in the anticipated ministerial role of authors of the 1970s. Sociology professor Gerald A. McWorter, in his essay in the March 1969 number, advises black authors to be "models of peace and understanding" for their

race (page 90). Don L. Lee, thinking like both Whitman and
Yeats, writes in the same number:

> Black art, as is African art, is perishable. . . . Like, a poem is
> written not to be read and put aside but to actually become a part
> of the giver and receiver; to perform some function, to move the
> emotions, to become a part of the dance, or to simply make one
> act. Whereas the work itself is perishable, the *style* and *spirit* of
> the creation is maintained and is used to produce new works (page
> 78).

These two essays, one by an academician and one by a poet—
neither restricting his activities to the single category—hint at a
conceivable personalism in the black aesthetic. Historical duality in black men's consciousnesses, inseparable from such personalism, is likewise observable. For example, the second half
of McWorter's partly quoted sentence reads, " . . . but when
necessary, we must fire the earth and fill the air with bullets."
One might wonder, then, about complexities and poetic dualities
in Lee as a black "giver and receiver" of racial ideas. It seems
fair that the query subside temporarily in the following work
by Marvin X, entitled "Don L. Lee Is a Poem" (9–69:59):

> Don L. Lee
> Is a poem
>
> When he walks
> When he talks
>   is a poem.
>
> Don don't smoke pot
> He always loaded
>   on his poems
>
> Don L. Lee
> Is a poem
>
> A good poem.

Black authors, as advocates of social morality through either their persons or their works, are outgrowing their tendency to argue their humanity before the court of white opinion. The African concept of *negritude*, mentioned briefly by Kgositsile and explored in more detail by Richard A. Long (5–69), began and developed in ways meaningful to framers of the black aesthetic. During the Harlem Awakening of the 1920s, a lasting black American literary creed might have been born; but the requisite wary thoughtfulness and stern impulse to hoard and consolidate against a time of disaster were too infrequent. Langston Hughes laid the full groundwork by penetrating what he called his black "soul world" to an unprecedented and still unsurpassed degree; and his African themes combined with those of Claude McKay to forecast *negritude* beyond the Atlantic. Had a black aesthetic been formulated in the 1920s, it would probably have been free of individual restrictions and racial recriminations—echoing the very exuberance and geniality that made the Jazz Age incompatible with hardening creeds.

While hard times and "Hoover blankets" were chilling black Americans in the 1930s, the African cultural leaders were nurturing their distillation from the Harlem Awakening: its literary celebration of vital parts of their common ancestral heritage. In the 1940s, *negritude*, coalescing around shared black African realities rather than against apartheid-level white hostilities, was as self-justifying as the concept of brotherhood. In the 1950s, institutionalized in both a journal and a formal society, *negritude* was able to beam rays of influence back toward black America. But in America in the 1960s, the non-violent black youth, who had to pass through the valley of the angry "white backlash" into a morass of public espionage, private harassment, and racist assassination, grew inevitably into a new breed of men.

Now casting off faster than they are putting on—and thus outdistancing a black leadership unaccustomed to revolutionary philosophical change—they are returning to the primal nudity of man born defenseless in a monstrous environment. While the clothing industry obediently manufactures the symbols of their alienation and while merchants stack up overpriced "picks" for their Afros, their purity of predicament remains metaphorically uncorrupted. That is, their union in fundamental spirit with their elders, authors included, is acknowledged in the black community's uncomplicated, uncompromised reading of native brotherhood in the image of the clenched fist. Phenomenal reality dictates that that image close out more than it close in. It is precisely this enforced inbreeding of beleaguered minds (literary ones included), emotionalized by desperation, that restrains the Americanization of *negritude* while denying the relevance of white opinion.

The function of black authors, then, according to most of the recent essays in *Negro Digest,* should be to build psychological peace within the black community while carrying on psychological war across the color line. Carolyn F. Gerald's essay insists that black writers "are involved in a black-white war over the control of image. For to manipulate an image is to control a peoplehood" (page 45). After carefully defending her thesis, she advocates "reverse symbolism as the tool for projecting our own image upon the universe" (page 47). Her counterpunching "mythmaker," scientifically aware of his reshaping of a reality "deep beyond the threshold of reason" (page 43), compares to Cecil Brown's wished-for supplier of a "positive protest that creates as it eliminates, . . . deals with the opposition's ugliness by concentrating on its own beauty" (page 46). Other essayists also use the word "peoplehood" and urge aggressive promotion of racial virtues in black people.

The selected commentators on the black aesthetic are understandably silent on the details of stylistic technique expected from authors. Their vision, however, is interdisciplinary in breadth. Don L. Lee predicts, "Black poems will complement the art of Tom Feelings and Omar Lama; will be read to the music of Coltrane and Sun Ra" (9/10–68:30). Ameer Baraka (LeRoi Jones) is less cryptic than he seems when he prophesies about forthcoming style: "How is a description of Who"; and

"The forms will run and sing and thump and make war too"
(9–69:5, 6). "Carry yr book with you," he adds, in a bit of moral-
izing complementary to that of Professor McWorter and Don L.
Lee.

LeRoi Jones's fleshly book to be carried is the black experience to be celebrated. Black authors can write in that book,
implies Hoyt W. Fuller in his afore-mentioned review of *The
Militant Black Writer*, "through a conscious plunging into the
bosom of their blackness—a saturation of the total self in the
life-loving, life-sustaining fountain of Soul." Their easiest, or
first, subject, one speculates, will be the physical merits of the
race. Essayist Earl Ofari recalls a nineteenth-century black
orator's praise of ". . . the fine tough muscular system, the
beautiful rich color, the full broad features, and the gracefully
frizzled hair of the Negro (8–69:21). In the same number, the
young photographer Chester Higgins, Jr., emphasizes that he
values in his race ". . . the reality of poverty, of beauty, of
gentleness, of warmth, and of blackness" (page 42).

Black experience, one might automatically assume, is known
to every black author. Henry James was pondering a similar assumption when he had May Bartram stick John Marcher with
the following sentences in *The Beast in the Jungle:* "You take
your 'feelings' for granted. You were to suffer your fate. That
was not necessarily to know it." This disparity between an experience and knowledge of that experience is the longest bridge
that an artist must cross. Don L. Lee, by burying in a preposi-
tional phrase his picture of the black poet ". . . studying his
own poetry and the poetry of other black poets" (9/10–68:28),
misses the Jamesian emphasis while touching the crucial point.
In order to transform his own sufferings—or joys—as a black man
into usable knowledge for his readers, the author must first absorb and order his experiences in his mind. Only then can he
create feelingly and coherently the combination of fact and
meaning that black audiences require for the re-exploration of
their lives. A cultural community of widely separated black
authors studying one another's best works systematically would

represent a dynamic interchange of the spirit—corrective and
instructive and increasingly beautiful in its recorded expression.

The black experience to be explored, although it yields its
essence with difficulty and only to the sensitive participant,
has vivid facets handily available to the literary craftsman. Don
L. Lee, in the last-quoted essay, enumerates a few of the concrete images: ". . . sleeping in subways, being bitten by rats,
six people living in a kitchenette" (page 27). No aesthetic could
justifiably claim that such images are racially exclusive, although
black Americans could establish priority with regard to the last
two. Cecil Brown, typical of other essayists in his being wary
of such a fallacy, declares, "A black writer can write about
anything, . . . literally, and what he has to say will still be said
by a black man" (page 48). Such a statement, unarguable and
not significant in itself, does keep alive the possibility that the
black aesthetic will not falter on repressive provincialism.

Somewhere between style and content belong the special
language and symbols that, to black authors, might be either
the substance of experience or the technique by which that
experience is brought to the printed page. Sarah Webster Fabio
floods the reader's imagination with this challenging description of language arts within the race:

> Black language is direct, creative, intelligent communication
> between black people based on a shared reality, awareness, under-
> standing which generates interaction; it . . . places premium on
> imagistic renderings and concretizations of abstractions, poetic
> usages . . . , idiosyncrasies—those individualized stylistic nuances
> (such as violation of structured syntax)—which nevertheless hit
> "home" and evoke truth; it is an idiom of integrated insight,
> a knowledge emanating from a juxtaposition of feeling and fact
> . . . (pages 34–35).

The description is carefully and perceptively written. It contains implicit suggestions for new techniques, especially in poetry, as well as bases for new critical terminology that must keep
pace with those evolutions in technique. One of the most useful

functions of the black aesthetic will be the fostering of such originality as this passage foresees, and the quick recognition of it when it appears.

Some of the objective literary symbols of the 1970s are already evident. At the first Pan-African Cultural Festival, in Algiers, black Americans varied in their attitudes toward what Hoyt W. Fuller calls ". . . those symbols of African poverty—sandals and *dashikis*" (10–69:77). Fuller's description of them moving among—and sometimes wearing—Nehru suits, Mao shirts, *boubous, jellabas,* and *agbabas* implies literary value in such colorful and racially symbolic images. Clearly, Don L. Lee's observation that the "images and symbols that are used will come out of the poet's immediate surroundings" (9/10–68:27) must be modified or interpreted to take into consideration the foreign travel and residence of many black authors. When pondering the means of that reversal of symbolism discussed by Carolyn F. Gerald as an absolute necessity, one notices the inherent reversal in favorable literary juxtapositions of non-Western with Western articles of apparel.

The task of listing credentials for the black critic is approached only obliquely. The essayists' usual failure to distinguish between black author and black critic is either an oversight or an implication that imaginative creation and reflective evaluation can, in their opinion, temporarily be exercised by the same faculties. The urgency of the differentiation will depend upon the quality of critical writing in the immediate future. Not to be postponed, however, is the black critic's establishment of his own psychological equilibrium, if it is menaced by what Hoyt W. Fuller observed in Algiers. Black men who ". . . want most to be 'American,'" he comments, "are terribly threatened by *dashikis*"; for, unlike Nehru suits, "*dashikis* thrust upon them images they cannot yet accept" (10–69:77). Fuller's concluding statement in the same paragraph is more broadly challenging to critics:

But, as usual, neither the white press nor its sycophants, the black integrationists, have much understanding of the black-consciousness movement. The spiritual identification with Africa and the Third World has little directly to do with literal emulation of African clothing and customs; it has more to do with a rejection of things Western. . . .

Three points that follow reflection upon Fuller's remarks seem worthy of the strict attention of black literary critics and framers of the black aesthetic. First, the critic must be able to accept sympathetically and without distortion all images—within the living culture and within the record of that culture, regardless of whether he can personally wear them comfortably upon his body. Second, the critic who is a "black integrationist" must somehow avoid sycophancy and must somehow understand the "black-consciousness movement"—the former achievement undeniably requiring courage and independence, the latter requiring suffering the blows of honest memory and present awareness. Third, Fuller's choice of the words "emulation" and "rejection" catch the Americanized black man in a posture of reaching-beyond and turning-from. In the realm of ideas, which is the critic's special province, it is his highest duty to aid his constituency in *surpassing* African customs and in turning *toward* that new Afro-American blackness-of-being that the African Kgositsile would call "the salvation of man" and that the American Lee would style the best evidence of "what a human being *is,* and can be."

One hopes that black critics, newly assessing their qualifications, will not be discouraged to the point of resignation by Professor McWorter's prescribed training for literary competition:

If one thinks Black, one must live Black, dress Black, sleep Black, look Black, speak Black, love Black, move Black, vacation Black, write Black, study Black, eat Black, conference Black, work Black, read Black, go to Black movies, lectures, hospitals, businesses, schools, churches, countries, restaurants, communities, and . . . "get ourselves together" . . . (page 89).

For black writers, such activity would indeed constitute Hoyt W. Fuller's recommended "plunging into the bosom of their blackness," a total immersion that is only theoretically possible in an economy dominated by white people. Yet, should a conventionally educated critic attempt that plunge, he would undoubtedly emerge more sensitive to the full weight of black consciousness, more able to use it as an enriching corrective to the illusions that have been staple in American culture.

The black critic, smarting from the pains of self-appraisal, must anticipate the necessity of either mastering or rejecting a stream of new critical terminology. In poetry, for example, the language of such Establishment luminaries as Richards, Empson, Brooks, and Wimsatt seems bewilderingly useless before the onslaught of young Carolyn M. Rodgers' attempt ". . . to place all Black poetry in several broad categories, all of which have variations on the main form" (9–69:7). Her ten main categories are the following: signifying, teachin/rappin, coversoff, spaced, bein, love, shoutin, jazz, du-wah, and pyramid. Among her twenty-three subdivisions, four apply to the category of coversoff: rundown, hipto, digup, and coatpull. After quoting from two relevant poems, she explains, "These poets hip you to something, pull the covers off of something, or run it down to you, or ask you to just dig it—your coat is being pulled" (9–69:9).

To dismiss this terminology as lively waywardness for the "do-now" opening of the seventies would be unresponsive to its merits. Variations on what Miss Rodgers calls coatpull have been done by Langston Hughes; mindblower, by LeRoi Jones; badmouth, by Claude McKay—just to name a few that come easily to mind. Hughes's volume *Ask Your Mama*, which has awaited knowledgeable extensive criticism since 1961, contains examples of all ten categories. The engaging terminology emphasizes content, but the challenge is the implicit call for stylistic innovators of impressive talent. Rappin is only complaining, and riffin is only rhythm, if made tame by a mediocre poet.

A few of the pitfalls that gape before the black critic and

author alike have been mentioned in these essays in *Negro Digest*. Addison Gayle's final paragraph makes a vital point:

> The acceptance of the phrase "Black Is Beautiful" . . . must be followed by serious scholarship and hard work; and Black critics must dig beneath the phrase and unearth the treasure of beauty lying deep in the untoured regions of the Black experience . . . (pages 38–39).

"Serious scholarship" includes acquiring a historical perspective that takes just account of time, place, and individual circumstance in the past. Destruction of the past is rarely a necessary prelude to building for the future. It is, for example, of the utmost importance, for the sake of critical integrity and historical justice, that such a titanic figure as Richard Wright be not brought low in our esteem on other than the most formidable evidence. Cecil M. Brown argues thus: "For Wright, it was his damnation to be born black, and his will to achieve whiteness— *i.e.*, to pull himself up to the literary standards of white America" (page 48). Brown tries harder to reverse Wright's image in the following passage:

> To reject Wright's art is not to reject protest; it is to reject negative protest, . . . the white man's concept of protest, which is that of a raging, ferocious, uncool, demoralized black boy banging on the immaculate door of White Society, begging, not so much for political justice as for his own identity, . . . consuming himself, so that in the final analysis, his destiny is at the mercy of the White Man (page 46).

It is true that a race demanding public recognition of its heroes should not erect false ones. But no aesthetic is justified in destroying past heroes merely to make way for new contenders. With regard to Brown's first statement, one should bear in mind that the black man's supposed self-hatred exists primarily in the white man's self-protective interpretation of the black American's psyche. Applying an observation of Carolyn F.

Gerald, one might conclude that the assumed self-hatred is merely ". . . the reverse side of [the white man's] positive projection of himself" (page 45). Further, "to achieve whiteness" literally is but a doltish fantasy uncongenial to Wright's mind. And to equate literary ambition, in a man of independent judgment, with any version of such an illusory desire seriously weakens the charge and glorifies whiteness far beyond its meager deserts.

Brown's second statement, urging the rejection of Wright's art as "negative protest," exemplifies the kind of proud but hasty thinking that might hinder the balanced growth of the black aesthetic. The statement grants an unearned validity to "the white man's concept of protest"—which is imbedded in the Establishment's incomplete analyses of Wright's works—by flinging the stone of that shallow concept against the armor of a heroic black writer. The black critic must accept, as his first principle, that no literary art can be fairly judged without a minute examination of its context. Richard Wright's literary art remains to be discovered in its fullness (as was implied by the essay "Fever and Feeling: Notes on the Imagery in *Native Son*," my contribution to the same special Richard Wright number). If the "ferocious, uncool, demoralized black boy" scored in the passage is a Bigger Thomas "begging . . . for his own identity," one should reconsider the means by which the doomed young man finds it within his own black experience, together with the will to surpass the dubious humanitarianism beneath "the mercy of the White Man."

The value of black America's literary past—which is the vital question raised by Brown's passages—must be critically estimated and carefully preserved. This action demands thorough research into the autobiographical and biographical record, as well as research into closely allied primary materials. Pursuing the example at hand, if a "begging" Richard Wright should by chance be imagined behind a door-banging, pleading Bigger Thomas, one should postpone judgment until supportive evidence from Wright's correspondence has been documented. In the meantime, one might weigh, in Wright's favor, the biographical record of the expatriate's courageous speech at the American Church in Paris—specifying individuals, dates, and places related to American espionage directed against black men abroad—shortly before his death.

Black America's past literary tradition will not depend for its survival upon the racial attitudes of its leading authors. The literary attitudes of the foremost black critics of the 1970s, however, combined with their literary competence, will lastingly affect twentieth-century opinions. It is imperative that the black aesthetic encourage such professional training as will enable critics to validate or enhance their interpretations of black authors' works, whenever appropriate, through references to other literatures. Again enlisting the example of Wright, one hopes that a black critic would think of comparing the final scenes of *Native Son* with those of Camus's *The Stranger*, published two years later. He might well argue, after such a comparison, that Bigger finally emerges just as independent of "the mercy of the White Man" as Meursault is free of the guillotine-backed judgment of the court. The murders committed by Bigger and Meursault lead them to a self-knowledge and a self-justification impossible to men on their knees before a hostile or indifferent society.

The pitfall pertinent to these references to *Native Son* is not that the black aesthetic might fail to encourage a potential critic's piling up university credits, but that it might overemphasize the visibly black as the most acceptable stimulus to mental engagement. The social and cultural equivalent of this literary danger is conveyed in poet Nikki Giovanni's warning: "As a group, we appear to be vying with each other for the title Brother and Sister Black. That will not get us our freedom" (6–69:34). This connection between cultural labels and the freedom of an entire race might not seem so tenuously drawn when one recalls three or four southern white writers born in the middle of the nineteenth century. Led by Thomas Nelson Page in the creation of what is now called the plantation tradition (which pictured black men either as simple-minded, clownish, picturesque slaves or as miserable, confused freedmen after emancipation), these few men helped to insure the political suppression of the black race during their generation.

The black and white labels already prepared for the 1970s are cause for reflection. Don L. Lee's afore-mentioned castigation of Negroes as "imitation whites," and Hoyt W. Fuller's reference to "simulated whiteness" (in his book review) as the outdated goal of blacks aspiring to manhood, should be absorbed into the black aesthetic only after some interpretative consensus. It would be grossly unfair to our black heritage to label "white," and therefore objectionable, *all* the components of the cultural and literary tradition of the Establishment, as if the profoundest minds and best spirits among our black forebears had had nothing to do with the formation and sanction of parts of that tradition. (Neither Fuller nor Lee would be inclined to transfer credit from black men to those very whites who have fraudulently invested it for so long.) Being blindly black is preferable to being blindly white, in the same way that becoming redemptively brave excels remaining stubbornly secure; but neither attitude befits men whose ultimate mission is the salvation of a group larger than their own.

Framers of the black aesthetic will not be blind. The symposium in the November 1969 number of *Negro Digest* reveals enough realism and sharp observation among the seventeen contributors to strengthen this hope. The two topics of the essays ("The Measure and Meaning of the Sixties" and "What Lies Ahead for Black Americans?") supply the title of the thirty-seven-page symposium, which recovers some of the already sampled attitudes of Richard A. Long, Don L. Lee, Gerald McWorter, Carolyn F. Gerald, and Cecil M. Brown. Significantly, the difference that an average of ten months of reflection has made in those attitudes is typically one of refinement or elaboration indicative of clear and steady attention to racial and national developments. Black, observes Long, ". . . is ugly when a leader of one of the baddest bands of blacks sips tea with a few woolly-headed whites at a white university and tells them that the students of the Black college across town are *all* Uncle Toms" (page 4). Lee points to a dangerous crevice in the rock of black solidarity: "The new class division, one group of negroes saying that other negroes are not relevant, and blacks saying that Afro-Americans are not relevant, and vice versa" (page 13).

Similarly widening a former emphasis, McWorter exhorts his "righteous warriors" as follows: "We must commit ourselves to the task of constructing a new world, a world of men not beasts, a world where love is what time it is and people have evolved beyond hate" (page 21). Carolyn F. Gerald, turning from persuasive psychologizing about the literary image to pointed instruction in the recent history of the black literary journal, reports usable findings:

. . . the fiction or poetry of survival is rendered through imagery, through symbols, through experimentation with different rhythms, with different syntactical forms, with a different vocabulary, through the indirectness of its statement about our condition (page 24).

And Brown, correctly seeing counterrevolution in television programing, writes, ". . . the moment protest is introduced into the media it ceases being protest and becomes 'the news,' 'a new TV show about spooks, etc.'" (page 35). Little can be done about the ponderable distance that art places between man and his experience; and Brown would not likely argue for the cessation of the news of protest. He then complains with understandable foreboding, however, about a practice that makes black America unsure of itself: "The latest technique is to have blacks on television, yes, but to have them putting each other down, on screen."

The seventeen authors of the symposium, as a group, focus upon ten general topics. (Since their essays are easily accessible, only a negligible failure to credit them individually should

ensue if one forces upon them a "black togetherness" in order
to present actual trends of thought among black writers.) With
regard to general racial goals, they say nothing that overleaps
the essayists who preceded them, although such a concept as
a "post-American future" (McWorter, page 21) shows their
advanced position. Concerning the black orientation of mind
that is to secure these goals, they wish it to be revolutionary
but righteous; they recognize obstacles to the spread of black
consciousness—mainly pretense and intolerance among those who
wear its mantle sweepingly, as well as the dragging Americanisms
of the loyal and the fearful.

Blackness as sentiment without substance, as pride without
program, is inadequate for the November essayists. They insist
upon the necessary knowledge, ideology, and leadership. Richard A. Long, for example, cannot abide an ignorance of history.
John A. Williams believes that the ". . . major task of black
art is to delineate the political and social situation" of today,
lest everyone perish (page 5). And John Henrik Clarke, wondering if black America is equipped for nation building, cau-
tions: "We are, collectively, black and beautiful, but does this
fact help us to know what makes an airplane fly or how to
cure a stomach ache?" (page 10)

Suggesting few details for the missing ideology, and concerned about the missing leadership that could best advance
one—as well as about the institutional tardiness in fostering
black leadership—the essayists show their ambivalence toward
America. Under the watchful eyes of black children, according
to hopeful admonitions, each of their elders must morally res-
urrect himself "from the American graveyard." Local urgencies
will produce, A. B. Spellman envisions, a new breed of leader,
"one with little national charisma but with a functional local
constituency" (page 22). Spellman's cynical prophecy about
Black Studies bodies them forth as "a monster in the 1970s";
he foresees white colleges in particular "turning out hundreds
of black-talking *bourgies* with Ph.D.s in Malcolm X and John
Coltrane" (page 22). Edward Vaughn, with the bitterness

naturally proceeding from firsthand engagement with demoralizing facts, records his knowledge of "Black Studies programs
turning into agencies for spying on Black people" (pages 29–30).

Yet, these latest essayists do not doubt that black literature
itself will flourish; they seem able to imagine the black writer,
center stage, "doing his own thing" despite signals in the wings,
hissing and apple-munching in the pit, and policemen in the
aisles. Further, they imagine black literature absorbing all the
traditional means (mythology, ritual, symbols, and innovative
language) as it "reorganizes itself, serving the cause of blackness" before continuing into new artistic realms. The approximately thirty revolutionary black journals referred to by Carolyn
F. Gerald have, since their recent establishment, provided out-
lets for the energies that—having temporarily been forced to
"forsake civil rights and integration"—will burst upon the 1970s
more purposefully.

Although black publishers and black bookstore owners receive
some praise in the November symposium, white publishers are
either scorned or waved into nonentity. Taking black authors'
manuscripts, says Joe Goncalves, they change them for white
people's consumption and arrange book distribution to suit a
white public. Their corruptive touch is the imprint of the
American majority, to Vaughn and Spellman, each of whom
uses the phrase "a waste of time" in rejecting cooperation with
whites "for anything" (Vaughn), "in any way, shape, or form"
(Spellman). Cecil M. Brown's blast at hypocrisy in television
complements such views. The 1960s, ending with an accumulation of reneges and turnabouts, are reduced by John Henrik
Clarke to ". . . that decade of the black man's beautiful
dreaming before awakening to a new reality. . . . that each
generation must take and secure [freedom] with its own hands"
(pages 33–34).

This November symposium crystallizes some literary trends
and indicates the large terrain through which the black aesthetic
must cut new pathways. The black aesthetic, having at least a
name, consequently has a past. "For it is through our names,"

writes Ralph Ellison in "Hidden Name and Complex Fate,"
"that we first place ourselves in the world." The Scottish poet
and critic Edwin Muir records similarly in *The Animals:* "For
with names the world was called/Out of the empty air,/With
names was built and walled,/Line and circle and square. . . ."
The creative task of calling forth the black American world
of fact and spirit was undertaken in the eighteenth century in
poetry and non-fiction; in the nineteenth century, in fiction
and drama. The critical task of naming and placing, undertaken
before World War I by Benjamin Brawley and William Stanley
Braithwaite, has been evolving slowly into a tradition that, in
the 1970s, offers a reciprocal challenge to the framers of the
black aesthetic.

Those who accept the responsibility of charting a course
for black authors and critics, bearing in mind that such activity
is anathema to many of its assumed beneficiaries, must look
backward as well as forward. In their close inspection of roads
already traveled, they should buttress their aesthetic by references to earlier harbingers of the techniques, themes, and
matter recommended for the 1970s. The reversal of imagery
advocated by Carolyn F. Gerald, for example, is discernible
in the sixth and seventh stanzas of DuBois' nineteenth-century
poem *The Song of the Smoke,* in which blackness is joyful,
just, powerful, and divine—and in which hell is white. And
Countee Cullen's well-known poem *Heritage,* which vigorously
and logically proceeds to "fashion dark gods" in its final stanza,
and chips away at the foundation of what the essayist plainly
describes as "the Church, where God is white." Don L. Lee's
concept of a functional black poem that should "become a
part of the giver and receiver" is exemplified in Calvin C.
Hernton's poem *The Distant Drum,* in which both poet and
reader are made to agree that a poem can become their common
fist "Beating against your ear." Hernton's style approximates
the use of "word bullets," one of Carolyn M. Rodgers' new
terms (a style named "homicidal art" in my essay in the an-

thology *Black Expression* and typified in Claude McKay's poem *The White House*).

This fifteen-month span of essays in *Negro Digest*, then, touches upon such crucial concerns of the black aesthetic as definition, function, materials, technique, training, and evaluation. The essayists as a group do not look to the past for guidance; and in some matters, such as the use of "black" and "Negro" (which was intermittently argued, along with substitute terms, in the black press between 1899 and 1930), this failure to indicate historical precedent seems a disadvantage. Their forward-looking stance, however, yields the profit of a stimulating insistence that the hour has struck for a unified leap into black America's distinguished future.

The immediate issue is the question of the racial integrity and the intellectual breadth of the molders of the black aesthetic. That question is phrased with precision and modernity—and with a shade of not-to-be-missed pathos—in the following opening and close of Sonia Sanchez's poem *blk/rhetoric* (9–69:64):

> who's gonna make all
> that beautiful blk/rhetoric
> mean something.
> . . . .
> like. this. is an S.O.S.
> me. calling. . . .
>   calling. . . .
>   some/one.
> pleasereplysoon.

THE BLACK AESTHETIC
IN THE THIRTIES, FORTIES, AND FIFTIES
Dudley Randall

Every poet is molded by his age, by the great events or Great Event that took place during his impressionable years. In the thirties it was the Great Depression and the Spanish Civil War. In the forties it was World War II. In the fifties it was McCarthyism, the Korean War, and the beginning of the Freedom movement with the Supreme Court school-desegregation decision of 1954.

Some poets, such as Langston Hughes and Arna Bontemps, lived from the Negro Renaissance through the post-Renaissance period into the period of the Black Aesthetic and black power of the sixties. Others, like Gwendolyn Brooks and Robert Hayden, published their first books in the forties and are still creating. I shall describe these later poets only as they wrote in the middle period between the Renaissance and the Black Aesthetic, as their further development does not come within the scope of this essay.

During this middle period, and previously during the Harlem Renaissance, there was no such concept as a black aesthetic. Negro writers wanted to be accepted into the mainstream of American literature. The closest thing to a black aesthetic was

Langston Hughes's declaration in "The Negro Artist and the Racial Mountain" (1926). He wrote:

> One of the most promising of the young Negro poets said to me once, "I want to be a poet—not a Negro poet," meaning, I believe, "I want to write like a white poet"; meaning subconsciously, "I would like to be a white poet"; meaning behind that, "I would like to be white." And I was sorry the young man said that, for no great poet has ever been afraid of being himself. And I doubted then that, with his desire to run away spiritually from his race, this boy would ever be a great poet. But this is the mountain standing in the way of any true Negro art in America—this urge within the race toward whiteness, the desire to pour racial individuality into the mold of American standardization, and to be as little Negro and as much American as possible.

Hughes went on to state:

> . . . But, to my mind, it is the duty of the younger Negro artist, if he accepts any duty at all from outsiders, to change through the force of his art that old whispering "I want to be white," hidden in the aspirations of his people, to "Why should I want to be white? I am a Negro—and beautiful!"

This is as close to the Black Aesthetic cry of "I'm black, and beautiful!" as it is possible to come.
Hughes continued:

> So I am ashamed for the black poet who says, "I want to be a poet, not a Negro poet," as though his own racial world were not as interesting as any other world.

Hughes concluded with the oft-quoted declaration:

> We younger Negro artists who create now intend to express our individual dark-skinned selves without fear or shame. If white people are pleased, we are glad. If they are not, it doesn't matter. We know we are beautiful. And ugly too. The tom-tom

cries and the tom-tom laughs. If colored people are pleased we are glad. If they are not, their displeasure doesn't matter either. We build our temples for tomorrow, strong as we know how, and we stand on top of the mountain, free within ourselves.

This sounds much like the Black Aesthetic credo, but there are significant points of difference. For instance, Hughes uses the word Negro. Some Negro ideologues have forbidden Negroes to call Negroes Negroes. Hughes stresses individualism ("express our individual dark-skinned selves"). In the Black Aesthetic, individualism is frowned upon. Feedback from black people, or the mandates of self-appointed literary commissars, is supposed to guide the poet. But Hughes says, "If colored people are pleased we are glad. If they are not, their displeasure doesn't matter either." (Another expression of individualism.) Hughes says, "We know we are beautiful. And ugly too." In the Black Aesthetic, Negroes are always beautiful.

In my own opinion, this feedback usually comes from the most vocal group, ideologues or politicians, who are eager to use the persuasiveness of literature to seize or consolidate power for themselves. Politicians such as Stalin or Khrushchev have a certain low cunning, but they cannot grasp the complexity or paradoxes of life and literature, and they try to impose their own simple-mindedness and conformity upon them.

The Great Event of the 1920s was the Depression. In contrast to the affluent 1960s, poverty was everywhere. Millionaires as well as poor people lost everything. Everyone was in this catastrophe together. Eyes were turned toward Russia and communism, and the Communists were active in organizing rent strikes, labor unions, and campaigns for relief. Federal Writers' Projects were started, where black and white authors worked together. Even if black writers did not join the Communist Party, as did Richard Wright, they were sympathetic toward it and its policy of non-discrimination. Black writers did not give up their struggle for Negro rights, but regarded it as part of the struggle for the rights of man everywhere. A

popular union organizing slogan was, "Black and white, unite
and fight."

Robert Hayden wrote his *Speech*, in which he urged black
and white workers to cooperate:

> I have seen the hand
> Holding the blowtorch
> To the dark, anguish-twisted body;
> I have seen the hand
> Giving the high-sign
> To fire on the white pickets;
> And it was the same hand,
> Brothers, listen to me,
> It was the same hand.

The horizons of poets were widened beyond their own Negro
struggle to include world events. In his first book, *Heart-Shape
in the Dust*, Hayden wrote of youths dying in the Spanish
Civil War, in *Spring Campaign:*

> She wears a gas mask, fair Corinna does,
> And thinks of spring's first air raid while
> seeking spring's first rose.

In the same book (1940), he foretold the death of Adolf
Hitler, in *Prophecy:*

> He fell with his mouth
> Crushing into the cold earth
> And lay unharming at last
> Under the falling leaves and the fog. . . .
>
> They returned to the ruined city
> And began to build again.

Hayden's second book, *A Ballad of Remembrance*, was not
published until 1962, but in the meantime there were the
brochures *The Lion and the Archer* (with Myron O'Higgins,

1948) and *Figure of Time* (1955), published in his own
"Counterpoise Series." The surrealistic *A Ballad of Remembrance* is chilling with its whirling, glittering images and
rhythms and its feeling of nightmare and irrationality. It cap-
tures the black experience, but filtered through the poet's sensitive subjectivity:

> Accommodate, muttered the Zulu king, throned
> like a copper toad in a glaucous poison jewel.
> Love, chimed the saints and the angels and the
>   mermaids.
> Hate, shrieked the gumetal priestess
> from her spiked bellcollar curved like a
>   fleur-de-lys!
>
> As well have a talon as a finger, a muzzle
> as a mouth. As well have a hollow as a heart.
> And she pinwheeled away in coruscations
> of laughter, scattering those others before her.

In *Middle Passage* and *Runagate Runagate*, Hayden incor-
porates all the innovations of the experimental poets of the
1920s: varied and expressive rhythms; anti-poetic materials such
as quotations from handbills, legal documents, ships' logs; scraps
of poetry, hymns, spirituals; fusing all these together to make
two exciting narratives of the beginning and of the escape
from slavery.

Gwendolyn Brooks, in *A Street in Broneville* (1945), wrote
of the black people on the South Side of Chicago, but world
events widened her vision to include also sonnets of black men
at war. In her Pulitzer prize-winning *Annie Allen* (1949), she
uses many poetic forms with easy mastery, from ballads to
crisp sonnets:

> What shall I give my children? who are poor,
> Who are adjudged the leastwise of the land,
> Who are my sweetest lepers, who demand
> No velvet and no velvety velour. . . .

In the tight, seven-lined trochaic stanzas of *The Anniad*, she deftly balances narrative, images, and rhythm:

> Leads her to a lonely room
>
> Which she makes a chapel of.
> Where she genuflects to love.
> All the prayerbooks in her eyes
> Open soft as sacrifice
> Or the dolour of a dove.
> Tender candles ray by ray
> Warm and gratify the gray.

Like Tolson and Hayden, she has the long poem firmly in control.

Langston Hughes continued to write of black urban folk, but now he abandoned the glamour of night clubs and of a Harlem pandering to white seekers of thrills. He wrote of the maids, porters, and laborers of Harlem instead of the dancers, singers, and "lean-headed jazzers" of the cabarets. His series on "Madame Alberta K. Washington" presents with humor a strong-minded Negro domestic worker.

He still wrote on racial themes, but he wrote within the context of democracy for all. The Negro struggle was a part of the world-wide struggle for freedom. This universality is expressed in *I Dream a World:*

> A world I dream where black or white,
> Whatever race you be,
> Will share the bounties of the earth
> And every man is free. . . .

In his poems, instances of injustice are ironically juxtaposed with the American Dream or with American ideals, as in his poem *Freedom Train*. An unsolvable dilemma is presented in his *Merry-Go-Round*, where a Negro child asks in frustration, where is the back of the merry-go-round, as black people always have to sit at the back.

The very title of M. B. Tolson's book *Rendezvous with America* (1944) suggests a widening of the poet's interest. He writes from the point of view of the Negro, but he has expanding sympathy with other ethnic groups, shown in his title poem.

> A blind man said,
> "Look at the kikes,"
> And I saw
> Rosenwald sowing the seeds of culture in the Black Belt. . . .
>
> A blind man said,
> "Look at the Chinks,"
> And I saw
> Lin Yutang crying the World Charter in the white man's
> wilderness. . . .

In this book, Tolson uses a wide variety of poetic forms, from rhymed quatrains and sonnets to long poems written in varying measures. He shows his architectonic power in building long poems that do not bore the reader, foreshadowing his mastery of longer forms in *Libretto to the Republic of Liberia* and *Harlem Gallery*. His sonnets are dramatic—compressing narrative, characterization, theme, and dramatic tension into fourteen lines. Perhaps his most successful sonnet is *Incident at Versailles*, with its succinct characterization of Clemenceau, Lloyd George, and Wilson, and its implicit prophecy of all the future disasters that were to spring from the racism of these world leaders. In general, the language of the poems is vigorous, although it is sometimes marred by clichés and archaic syntax.

In 1953 he published *Libretto for the Republic of Liberia*, a long poem commissioned for the centennial of the African nation, which earned him the title of Poet Laureate of Liberia.

The preface was written by Allen Tate, and appeared also in *Poetry* magazine, with an excerpt from the book.

In his preface, Tate said that Tolson had for the first time incorporated the modern poetic language into a poem written by a Negro. In this poem, Tolson used all the devices dear to the New Criticism: recondite allusions, scraps of foreign languages, African proverbs, symbolism, objective correlatives. Many parts of the poem are obscure, not through some private symbolism of the author, but because of the unusual words, foreign phrases, and learned allusions. If the reader has a well-stored mind, or is willing to use dictionaries, encyclopedias, atlases, and other reference books, the poem should present no great difficulty. Reading this poem is like reading other learned poets, such as Milton and T. S. Eliot.

The history of the poem is interesting. Tolson sent the manuscript to Tate, who returned it. Then Tolson rewrote the poem according to the tenets of the New Criticism. The irony is that, about this time, the New Criticism was declining, and the Beat poets, with their looser, freer, more emotional language and form, were coming into popularity. In any case, the learned allusive language is not the spontaneous speech of the Negro people.

Hayden, Brooks, and Tolson can be grouped together as poets conscious of technique, who were familiar with and learned from the modern experimental masters such as Hart Crane, Eliot, Pound, and Yeats, and not from minor poets such as Housman or Edna St. Vincent Millay, or traditional poets such as Keats, all of whom influenced Countee Cullen.

They were conscious of their Negro race, but they regarded it in the wider context of a world-wide depression and a world-wide war against fascism. Their world view was wider and more inclusive than that of the Renaissance poets.

Other poets, perhaps not more conscious of race, but in whose work race occupies a more central position, were Sterling Brown, Margaret Walker, and Frank Marshall Davis.

Sterling Brown was in the same age group as the Renaissance

poets, but his sole collection of poetry, *Southern Road,* was published in 1932. In this book, the influence of Negro folk poetry, of spirituals, blues, and ballads, is evident. Like Langston Hughes, he brings the blues stanza into formal verse. He has the unusual and valuable quality of humor, which permeates his ballads of Slim Greer, a picaresque adventurer. There are ballads of John Henry and of the chain gang, and poems of sharecroppers and southern rural life. These are poems of Negro life written out of black experience grounded in folk poetry which he intensifies with his art.

Margaret Walker, born in Jackson, Mississippi, is also influenced by Negro folk poetry. In her only volume of poetry, *For My People,* published in 1942 in the Yale University Series of Younger Poets, there are ballads of rural southern folk, of the witch Molly Means, of "Bad-man Stagolee" and "Big John Henry."

Unlike Brown, however, whose poems not in the folk tradition and folk forms were apt to be personal and subjective, Walker used the classical sonnet form (sometimes without rhyme) to write about Negroes. The sonnet about miners and sharecroppers titled *Childhood,* and the one titled *The Struggle Staggers Us* are outstanding in this series.

> Ours is a struggle from a too-warm bed;
> too cluttered with a patience full of sleep.
> Out of this blackness we must struggle forth;
> from want of bread, of pride, of dignity.

More experimental than Brown, and probably influenced by Carl Sandburg, she wrote some poems in long free-verse paragraphs like those of Fenton Johnson. The most famous of these is the title poem, *For My People.* This poem gains its force not by tropes—turns of language or thought—or logical development of a theme, but by the sheer overpowering accumulation of a mass of details delivered in rhythmical parallel phrases.

We Have Been Believers is another powerful poem in a similar form and on a racial theme.

Race is central also in Frank Marshall Davis' books *Black Man's Verse, I Am the American Negro,* and *47th Street.*

A Chicago poet, he is inspired not by traditional Negro folk poetry, as are Brown and Walker, but by the teeming black life of a northern metropolis. His free verse shows the influence of Sandburg and Masters. In *Giles Johnson Ph.D.* and *Robert Whitmore,* he satirizes the pretensions of the black bourgeoisie. In the labor-organizing thirties, he wrote of share-croppers and labor unions. His poetry is black-centered, without the focus on wider horizons found in the poetry of Hayden and Tolson.

Fenton Johnson was another poet who wrote in free verse influenced by Carl Sandburg. His earlier poetry was romantic, conventional, and traditional. In his later poetry he adopted the long free-verse line-strophe of Sandburg, and wrote poems expressing his disillusionment with America. Although marred by clichés and conventional expressions such as "fallen woman," they are new and different in their mood of frustration and despair.

These poets exemplify the trends of the thirties, forties, and fifties. There was a world depression, and a world war. In their outlook, black poets saw race as one problem among the world problems of poverty and fascism, and appealed to all men of good will to help solve the problem. As for their style, they no longer considered it sufficient to pour new wine of content into old bottles of form, but absorbed the techniques of the experimental poets Hart Crane, Pound, and Eliot. In this group were Tolson, Hayden, and Brooks. Another group—Brown, Walker, Davis, and Fenton Johnson—were influenced in varying degrees by Negro folk poetry and by Sandburg and Masters. Race was central in their poetry. Langston Hughes, growing beyond the Renaissance attraction to the more superficial and merely picturesque aspects of Negro life, wrote of its more serious aspects in the speech of the urban working man and in blues and jazz cadences.

There was no consciously formulated Black Aesthetic. Black poets considered themselves as part of American literature, although most of them were excluded from textbooks, anthologies, and, to a great extent, from magazines. It remains to be seen whether, in our time, the Black Aesthetic will stimulate superior poetry. The proof will have to be in the poems produced.

However, I will not hedge in caution, but will be imprudent enough to weigh the historical facts, note the trends, and make a prediction.

In the forties, black poets absorbed the innovations of white poets. In future years, they will not only absorb them, but will transcend them, and create their own innovations. Both Don Lee and Ameer Baraka are well-read, but they and poets like them will not only absorb what they're read, but, using their heritage of folk poetry and black music, will build something new upon that. In short, they'll do their own thing. They will not depend upon white publishers, white audiences, or white critics, as there are black publishers, black critics, and an increasing black audience. Robert Hayden and Gwendolyn Brooks are mature and at the height of their powers, and are capable of change and growth. There are many younger poets not yet even published in book form. All that I can foresee is a poetry of increasing power and richness, which will make a glorious contribution to the world.

TOWARD A DEFINITION:
BLACK POETRY OF THE SIXTIES (AFTER LEROI JONES)
Don L. Lee

We are going to talk about black art forms and movements. Those black artists that are active and hip would gladly agree, I'm sure, that black music is our most advanced form of black art. The reasons for this are innumerable, but basically that, regardless of outward conditions during slavery, postslavery, etc., black music was able to endure and grow as A) a communicative language, B) a sustaining spiritual force, C) an entertaining outlet, C) a creative extension of our African selves, D) one of the few mediums of expression that was open and virtually free of interferences.

Very few people understand the music of John Coltrane; his early critics and some of his fellow musicians called him crazy. Clifford Brown and Charlie Parker were giants in their time, but they stayed broke (penniless). Thelonius Monk transformed and enlarged the sounds of the piano, but he is still not taught in our institutions of higher learning. What this gets down to is that to understand the aesthetic of black art or that which is uniquely black, we must start with the art form that was least distorted and was not molded into that which is referred to as a pure product of European-American culture.

In reading LeRoi Jones's critique in *Black Music*, we come

to understand that there are two distinct levels on which the aesthetic works: gut-emotion level, which must predominate, and a technical level, which must not be *too* obvious but must seem (and in fact be) natural and real. Jones goes on to say: "The white musicians' commitment to jazz, the *ultimate concern,* proposed that the sub-cultural attitudes that reduced the music as a profound expression of human feelings, could be *learned* and need not be passed on as a secret blood rite. And Negro is essentially the expression of an attitude, or a collection of attitudes, about the world, and only secondarily an attitude about the way music is made."

As a collection of attitudes about the world, the aesthetic moves toward a semblance of a definition if we can understand the sensibility of the persons we are trying to reach. Especially since we are to deal with black poetry of the sixties, we must understand that which went down before the decade of the sixties. Also, poetry as most of us understand it, *is* rather an exclusive art form written and preferred by the intellectually astute. That is to say, the poetry on the written page very seldom found its way into the home or neighborhood of the common black man, i.e., poetry in my home was almost as strange as money.

The one subject that wasn't taught, but was consciously learned in our early educational experiences was that writing of any kind was something that black people *just didn't do.* Today it's popular to refer back to the Harlem Renaissance of the twenties as a successful "Negro" literary movement in black letters. That statement is only partially true; actually, the arts or black arts as we now know them were alive and active only at a very superficial, elitest level, being mainly patronized by the uptown whites, e.g., Carl Van Vechten, Max Eastman, DuBose Heyward, etc. Whereas, black people in Harlem hardly knew that anything of a literary movement was in process, let alone took part in it. Langston Hughes clarifies this in his autobiography, *The Big Sea.* He states: "The ordinary Negroes hadn't heard of the Negro Renaissance." Which is to imply that because of its restrictions, the black literary movement of the twenties forecast its own death. Out of the many writers who took part, only a few are still widely read today: Langston Hughes, Sterling A. Brown, Arna Bontemps, and Claude McKay.

Sensibility: awareness, consciousness, fineness of feeling. Actually, what it gets down to is, that which shaped our sensibilities shaped us. What was it? Why are some of us Negroes, some blacks, and some don't know what we are? Most of us have been shaped by the same consciousness: a white nationalist consciousness called Americanism that's really a refined, or unrefined, depending on your viewpoint, weak version of the European sensibility. Whereas, black people in this country are products of a dual culture: the duality is that of being formally educated as a "European-American" and informally schooled as a black man, i.e., public schools or private schools in the A.M. and street schools and home schools in the P.M.

The black sensibility is not new. The only thing new about blackness today is the magnitude in which it has been generated and the amount of people it has reached. You see, there has always been a visible portion of the "Negro people" that were black, but then they were dismissed as being *crazy.*

Aesthetic: "The branch of philosophy dealing with the beautiful, chiefly with respect to theories of its essential character, tests by which it may be judged, and its relation to the human mind; also, the branch of psychology treating of the sensations and emotions evoked by the fine arts and belles-lettres." (Webster's)

A Black Aesthetic would, in effect, encompass much of the definition above, but in the context of Western culture is and becomes a serious and profound variation on a loose theme. Harold Cruse, in his *Crisis of the Negro Intellectual,* gives a view of the prevailing school of criticism: "The impact of the Negro presence on American art forms has been tremendous, and also historically conditioned; but this fact the American psyche is loath to admit in its established critical school of thought. As Americans, white people in America are also Westerners, and American white values are shaped by Western cultural values. Americans possess no critical standards for the cultural arts that have not been derived from the European experience. On the other hand, the basic ingredients for native (non-European) American originality in art forms derive from American Negroes, who came to America from a non-Western background. We need only point to American music to prove the point. Thus in American art a peculiar kind of cultural duality exists, which is an ideological reflection of the basic attitudes of blacks and whites toward each other."

Black poetry of the sixties is not too different from black poetry of the forties and fifties; there has always existed in the verse a certain amount of blackness. But in the sixties the black arts emerged as never before: e.g., music, theater (black drama), art (painting, sculpture), film, prose (novel, essay), and poetry. The new and powerful voices of the sixties came to light mainly because of the temper of the times; it accented the human-rights struggle of black people in the world. Also, television played a very important role in projecting blackness in the early sixties—mainly in a gross misunderstanding, over-representing it as something new and queer. The men of the moment were: John Coltrane, LeRoi Jones, Cecil Taylor, James Baldwin, Charles White, Marion Brown, Ornette Coleman, Don Cherry, John A. Williams, Lerone Dennett, Mari Evans, William Melvin Kelley, John O. Killens, Grachun Manour III, Thelonius Monk, Sunny Murray, Ed Bullins, Ronald Milner, Calvin C. Hernton, Larry Neal, Dudley Randall, James Brown, A. B. B. Spellman, Lew Alcindor, Hoyt Fuller, Conrad Kent Rivers, Archie Shepp, Sun Ra, Pharaoh Sanders, Gwendolyn Brooks, Malcolm X, Frantz Fanon, Martin Luther King, and we can go on for days.

Black art of the sixties, on the national scene, started with the advent of LeRoi Jones (Ameer Baraka) and the black theater. We in the Midwest felt the pressures from both the west and the east coasts. In the vanguard in terms of publishing black writing was *Negro Digest* under the extraordinary editorship of Hoyt Fuller, and a new quarterly came into existence in the mid-sixties, *The Journal of Black Poetry*, edited by quietly patient Joe Goncalves. Other publications that regularly published black poets were: *Soul Book, Black Dialogue, Liberator*, and *Black Expression*. New presses to emerge in the sixties that concentrated on poetry books were led by Broadside Press of Detroit, Michigan, under the editorship of Dudley Randall (a nationally known poet himself), Jihad Press of Newark, Free Black Press of Chicago, Black Dialogue Press of New York by way of California. The Journal of Black Poetry Press of California, and the Third World Press of Chicago. Broadside Press has been by far the most successful and productive.

The Poetry: The language of the new writers seems to move in one direction; that is to say that the poets of the sixties are actually defining and legitimizing their own communicative medium. We will see that the language as a whole is not formal or proper Anglo-Saxon English. It carries its own syntax, which is not conventional, and by Western standards could be referred to as non-communicative, obscene, profane, or vulgar. In short, it's the language of the street, charged so as to heighten the sensitivity level of the reader. We find that this concentration on language is not unique to black poets of the sixties. James Weldon Johnson, in his *American Negro Poetry*, talks about two poets of another generation that were experimenters and innovators in language: "Langston Hughes and Sterling A. Brown do use a dialect, but it is not the dialect of the comic minstrel tradition; it is the common, racy, living, authentic speech of the Negro in certain phases of real life." So we find that language is constant only as man is.

The decade of the sixties, especially that of the mid-sixties, brought to us a new consciousness, a perception that has come to be known as a *black consciousness*. Embodied in most of the poetry of the sixties, we find at least a semblance of this sensibility. Along with the new awareness, we get a form that on the surface speaks of newness (actually, most of the forms and styles used by the newer poets may be as confusing as some

of the new black music forms.) In effect, the form that is
used may be a starting point for determining and categorizing
the Black Aesthetic. Some of the common occurrences, we find
in the black poets of the sixties are:

1. polyrhythmic, uneven, short, and explosive lines
2. intensity; depth, yet simplicity; spirituality, yet flexibility
3. irony; humor; signifying
4. sarcasm—a new comedy
5. direction; positive movement; teaching, nation-building
6. subject matter—concrete; reflects a collective and personal life-
   style.
7. music: the unique use of vowels and consonants with the
   developed rap demands that the poetry be real, and read out
   loud.

All that's mentioned above, and more, can be seen much
more clearly in some of the poetry. First, exclusion is automatic
in a critique of this kind; I've purposely restricted myself to
the poets who have published widely and in most cases have
published several books. These writers look upon themselves as
black men or black women first, then as poets. Thus, understanding their responsibility to themselves and to their community is a priority in no uncertain terms. Ron Wellburn said
of the new poets: "No poets in America serve in such a priestly
capacity as do black poets. Priests, musicians, deacons, chanters,
poets—all bear the song and its power as their unfailing weapon."

Mari Evans moves beyond the self-reliant assertion of the
natural fact in her poem *I Am a Black Woman*—not just a
woman. Mari in this poem creates an identity, a personality, a
role that is not newly black, but generically and historically
black: "Look on me and be renewed." One may contrast her
with Stephanie in her book *Moving Deep*, in which Stephanie
characterizes herself as woman, a lover—simply; or with West
Indian poets who prior to 1939 made a point of being "universal," which was to be not specifically black. Indeed, Mari is
universal here in exploring the natural arena of the role of the

woman in human society. Her historical identity is created through allusions to Nat Turner and "Anzio"—all caught in a historical timelessness. She was/is always there. The naturalness and the biological origins of herself are poignant, yet stoically strong:

> "I saw my mate leap screaming to the sea
> and I/with these hands/cupped the lifebreath
> from my issue in the canebrake."

A kind of mystical yet hard strength reminiscent of Jean Toomer's women in *Cane*. The woman herein recreated is not fragmented, hysterical, doesn't have sexual problems with her mate, doesn't feel caught up in a "liberated womanhood" complex/bag—which is to say she is not out to define herself (that is, from the position of weakness, as "the others" do) and thus will not be looked upon as an aberration of the twentieth-century white woman.

Margaret Danner is a poet of African descent. Africa is throughout her poetry. If a true test for a black poem is whether you can tell the author's color, we find that Sister Danner's poem *And Through the Caribbean Sea* is an interesting example, because she does not mention the word black in the poem. But there is no doubt as to who she is. The colors are not literally black, but still black:

> We, like shades that were first conjured up
> by an African witch-doctor's ire,
> (indigo for the drum and the smoke of night,
>
> tangerine for the dancing smudged fire)
> have been forced to exist in a huge kaleidoscope world.
> We've been shifting with time and sifting through
> space,
>
> at each whimsical turn of the hands that have thrown
> the Kaleidoscope, until any pattern or place
> or shade is our own. . . .

The bright arrangement of red and tangerine is very black, whether here, in the West Indies, or in Africa. Also, the poem is very subtle. She begins her poem with an inclusive "we," which means she acknowledges that she herself is a part of the kaleidoscopic arrangement; and then with subtle simile immediately establishes the link, tells who "we" are, which is the same as saying where we came from. All her references are African—indigo, drum, dancing, tangerine, African mask! Those references or allusions that are not African are meant to indicate a loss of identity: Louis Quinze Frame, Rococo, etc.

Eugene Perkins and Ebon emerged in the late sixties as two of the stronger men poets. Perkins becomes a poet because he's a man of his time and place: America, Chicago, Now. In *Black Patches*, from his book *Black Is Beautiful*, the colors are copper and ebony. Black Chicago is recreated into an analytical photograph. A white social worker might make references to Woodlawn and Robert Taylor Homes, but would hardly see them for what they are:

> The Congo Villages stand unclaimed under the
> shadows of grotesque tenements
> and the towering concrete
> of welfare prisons. . . .

Critics would call his references metaphors, but politically they are profound and well-stated truisms. It is Fanon and Nkrumah; it's Lumumba, DuBois, and Stokely, all squeezed and purified in four simple lines. He knows the beauty of the life-style, but also its weaknesses:

> A carnival strip in an ebony jungle
> Still clinging to a tradition
> of self styled hustlers
> Jewish economy
> and street corner preachers

A distinct few white people even allude to the "black patches" of this continent, but because they think they're liberal (and are in reality stupid), they can't creatively criticize as Perkins does. With this in mind, we realize how much of a poet Brother Perkins is when he cops the lid off white boy's façade:

> hide marijuana cigarettes
> between the pages of "Black Boy"
> and "The Rise and Fall of the Third Reich"

Ebon also lends his interpretation to that which he considers black. Anyone who has ever heard Ebon read can still hear and see the deep voice bounding out like a black barker at a secret blood rite, as in *Legacy: In Memory of Trane*, from his book *Revolution:*

> Juba-Lover
> bringing tales of
> Coaldust gods
> wrapped in sound.
> striving to journey home.
> beyond the light
> into darkness . . .
> into Truth
> his voice a glistening Nommo
> speechless now, hushed by
> milky smiles
> and snow June hate.
> leaving songs of praise
> a path to dance beyond . . .
> a journey quest to selfhood . . .
> a love supremely unafraid . . .
> black bright, and binding
> ear to sight unseen.

The first stanza of this strong poem is jubilant with flowing lines and images of Africa, precious, but hidden. The use of Nommo becomes its own meaning: the word, the power of the word, communication. He mixes his metaphors and if one is familiar with the music of John Coltrane, one will understand his reversal of images and double use of allusion: "a love supremely unafraid." And again his mixing of metaphor: "black bright, and binding ear to sight unseen." Whereas Coltrane becomes an image of links and heritage, and not a weird extension of a Western musician.

Toward the end of the sixties, we were introduced to poets such as Nikki Giovanni, S. E. Anderson, Jayne Cortez, June Meyer, Audre Lorde, Sterling Plumpp, Mae Jackson, Julia Fields, Marvin X, Alicia L. Johnson, Jon Eckels, Charles K. Moreland, Jr., Rockie D. Taylor, Xavier Nicholas, Askia Muhammed Touré, Doc Long, Ted Joans, and Larry Neal, with the stronger voices of Etheridge Knight, Sonia Sanchez, Carolyn Rodgers, Norman Jordan, Keorapetse Kgositsile, and Johari Amini (Jewel C. Latimore) that continued to deafen us.

Sonia Sanches has moments of personal loneliness that are not akin to some philosophical abstraction, but come because of the absence of someone, her man, which is real. She is also intense and able to do many things at the same time, as in *Short Poem*, from her first published book, *Homecoming:*

> My old man
> tells me i'm
> so full of sweet
> pussy he can
> smell me coming.
> maybe
>   i
>   shd
>   bottle
>   it   and
>   sell it
>   when he goes.

It screams the fertile sense of being a woman desired; irony suggests an attitude toward a sex life that's natural (it can't be sold): revealing-self blues—obscenity that's funny and easy to relate to if you are black.

On the other hand, there is the formality and traditional verse form of Etheridge Knight. Gwendolyn Brooks said of Brother Knight: "[his] poetry is a major announcement. And there is blackness, inclusive, possessed and given: freed and terrible and beautiful."

Blackness:

> Hard Rock was "known not to take no shit
> From nobody," and he had the scars to prove it:
> Split purple lips, lumped ears, welts above
> His yellow eyes, and one long scar that cut
> Across his temple and plowed through a thick
> Canopy of kinky hair.

Freed:

> He sees through stone
> he has the secret
> eyes this old black one
> who under prison skies
> sits pressed by the sun
> against the western wall
> his pipe between purple gums.

Terrible and Beautiful:

> Now you take ol Rufus. He beat drums,
> was free and funky under the arms,
> fucked white girls, jumped off a bridge
> (and thought nothing of the sacrilege),
> he copped out—and he was over twenty-one.

We get a great deal in the poetry of Etheridge Knight; it's folkish as an African folk tale. It is simple/deep, as though the man has actually lived his words. He uses traditional lines, and we can see that obvious care is taken to bring forth the most meaning. He has the ability to say much in a few words. Each poem becomes a complete story that is not over- or understated.

Because of space limitations, I can't deal with other poets of merit. But I would like to mention that poets such as Lucille Clifton, Barbara D. Mahone, Zack Gilbert, Arthur Pfister, Jr., Ahmed Legraham Alhamisi, Stanley Crouch, Jay Wright, Kirk Hall, Edward S. Spriggs, Ron Wellburn, Lance Jeffers, Carol Freeman, D. L. Graham, and Bob Hamilton will be, along with the others mentioned earlier, poets to watch in the seventies. The seventies will be the decade of nation building for black people. The poets, with their special brand of insight and courage, will be in the forefront. Also, we'll see a deeper appreciation of Africa and that which is African. African literature as well as African-American literature will be placed in the positive context both deserve; bringing forth African poets like Léopold Senghor, David Diop, John Pepper Clark, Christopher Okigbo, Wole Soyinka, Léon Damas, and Aimé Césaire—all of whom are already established poets in their respective homelands, but relatively unknown in the United States.

Finally, the Black Aesthetic cannot be defined in any definite way. To accurately and fully define a Black Aesthetic would automatically limit it. What we've tried to do is relate specific points of reference. After all, that which is called the white (Western) aesthetic is continuously reconsidered every time a new writer, painter, or what they call a musician comes on the scene. We now know that there are nuances and ideas that are purely African. In the same vein, we can see things and ideas that are purely black, or African-American. We've talked about the music and we've seen it in the poetry, but that which we consider uniquely black can also be viewed in the way we prepare and eat food, the way we dance, our mode of dress, our loose walk, and in the way we talk and relate to each other.

What most of the young writers are doing is taking the lead in defining that which is of value to them, and doing this gives legitimacy to the community from which it stems. Therefore, these writers undertake a rather pragmatic and realistic look at the real world. Most of them grew up on Malcolm X and Frantz Fanon, and they non-romantically understand that we are an African people, but are also aware of the precariousness of the great African-past cult. As Fanon states, "I admit that all the proofs of a wonderful Songhai civilization will not change the fact that today the Songhais are underfed and illiterate, thrown between sky and water with empty heads and empty eyes." And what the younger writers of the sixties (most under thirty-five) are saying is that in order for the heads and eyes to be filled, we have to develop that which is necessary to fill them. Nation-building is the call; understanding how others have survived in this country, we as writers must contribute to the positive direction that is needed. Creativity and individuality are the two nouns most often used to describe an artist of any kind. Black poets ascribe to both, but understand that both must not interfere with *us,* black people, as a whole. Black poets of the sixties have moved to create images that reflect a positive movement for black people and people of the world. The poets understand their own growth and education from a new perspective. They comprehend that if all you are exposed to is Charlie Chan, you'll have Charlie Chan mentality. John Legett, in *The New York Times Book Review,* talking about the WASP vision, said: "I practice the Wasp novel. I can hardly do otherwise. I write of a Wasp world for the good and simple reason that I know it best." Just as there are the French writer, the Jewish writer, the Russian writer, the African writer, we have the black, or African-American, writer. Black poets have discovered their uniqueness, their beauty, their tales, their history, and have diligently moved to enlighten their people and the world's people in an art form that's called poetry, but to them is another extension of black music.

PATHS TO THE FUTURE
William Keorapetse Kgositsile

There are new voices very different from the ones that were around before. Different not only in the sense that they are new but essentially because of their attitude and intended purpose; precise as tools in the hands of skillful artisans. Lebert Bethune ". . . tired of strange ghosts/Whose cool bones/ Lived on the green furnace of my blood" makes "a juju of my own" as one of the means of ". . . baking my destiny to a lullaby. . . ." He continues his song:

> So she warned me—my grandmother,
> And now and now
> When I kindle again her small eyes with their
> quick lights
>
> Darting ancient love into my infancy
> And when I break through to her ancient voice
> That voice like the pliant red clay she baked
> She sings the only lullaby she sang me
>
> 'Me no care for Bakra whip
> Me no care fe fum-fum
> Come Juju come

> So I am fashioning this thing
> My own Juju
> Out of her life and our desire
> Out of an old black love
> I am baking my destiny to a lullaby—

Lebert Bethune in *Juju of My Own,* a slim volume of robust poetry. Like most of his peers he has been through American institutions of higher learning and come back disillusioned. It is no secret today that any honest Blackman in any western institution learns, sooner or later, that there is a calculated denial of his history, of his experience, by his oppressor. He is taught to aspire to Western ideals. Finally he is taught to understand and interpret his historical experience, his present existence and his possibilities through white eyes.

But any Time is with us. And if we take control to shape our attitudes and reshape our memories, that time is always NOW —Our Time for the best possible uses of our lives. "Show the chains. Let them see the chains as object and subject, and let them see the chains fall away," says LeRoi Jones. So there are these voices which attempt to move us in a very specific direction, criticizing us here, encouraging us there, clarifying for us elsewhere. You might say that they are voices from the future and they attempt to prepare us because they know that the future will not change to make room for the undesirable. The weak will be strengthened if there is any life left in them. And memories, of past or future or any time, are made of very specific selections from your sensibility. Memories move us, the best possible uses of our lives move us. And if we are ahead of the times the responsibility is ours to make the present Our Time lest we be destroyed. Gloria House celebrates the new day, our time:

> Look for mind seering into the future with
>   the intensity of their satellites in orbit
> And you will find it in our heads

And for power, latent and imminent like the panther's
In our bodies.

"We were not made eternally to weep!"

Steady, slow, knowing, like Ma Rainey with her man
The forces of time move on to Our Time
And in these days—
    uncovered, the great deceits of the man's monstrous
                                                    mind

    uprooted, his stone monuments to himself
    destroyed, the armies of the psychotic, decadent
    dead, a race of devils.

Yes, this decade—the Sixties—has produced a different caliber
of Black poets in America. The majority of them have been influenced by Negritude and protest poets and writers like Césaire,
Senghor, David Diop, Langston Hughes, Claude McKay,
W. E. B. DuBois, and others. These young poets felt the inade-
quacy of a purely "cultural" or artistic self-determination because the arguments for it and its artifacts generally boil down to
an academic masturbation or deviation, a kind of mannerism—
fornicating with the white eye and then emerging on some stage
with Western arguments for the validity and glory of a Black
virginity. (Césaire, though among the Negritude poets, is above
this because he is right there, "seering into the future" with
the best of the younger poets.) In practical terms, for instance,
the younger poets realize that the most beautiful poem Senghor
can write about the validity of the existence of a glorious Black
culture, without attempting to make the social institutions in
Senegal actually African, actually liberated from France, does
not even improve the diet of a single undernourished black
child anywhere in the world where black people are colonized
by Caucasians; most probably not even in "independent" Senegal.

This does not mean that Negritude and/or protest poetry is
not valid or functional. It is. But it is inadequate in terms of its

best possible social relevance or uses because it is limited to vision. It justifies Black Art and Black Experience to a white audience. Here again, Aimé Césaire is clean because, to him, Negritude was an introductory element, a prelude, to the re-emergence of the Blackman on the stage of history. The young Afro-American poets whose consciousness was awakened and facilitated by Negritude and protest poetry, among other influences, feel an urgency to make their art as potent a weapon as any in the assertion, not birth, of their humanism. In a poem titled, *The People Burning*, LeRoi Jones realizes:

> ". . . . . It is choice, now, like a philosophical problem. It is choice, now, and the weight is specific and personal. It is not an emotional decision. There facts, and who was it said, that this is a scientific century."

Jones is not addressing white America or some ideal universal intellect or conscience. He is talking to his people about his condition, finally theirs, because he is his people.

Most of these young writers of this decade, after verifying the facts with all the historical evidence necessary, emerge strongly convinced of the inhumanity of the Western world. They come out of Western institutions of higher learning strongly convinced that the university in the west is an extension of racism and the so-called Cold War which they detest. Quite often, the war is hot past any possible argument for or against it. Emmett Till. James Powell. Lumumba. Malcolm. Little babies charred while worshipping a Western God, for the perverted amusement of the deranged maniacs. And the Black poet's sensibility explodes. The weight becomes specific and personal. But the poet does not have explosives for the physical destruction of the West in general, and America in particular. Not yet. Thus the immediate resort for the Black poet is applied poetry. He uses his sensibility as ammunition. Brotherly love. Virtue. Construction which, by definition, embraces and transcends the necessary destruction. Restoration of human and humane values for the salvation of man. NOW.

> Now, I see it like this:
> You see da tree ou der?
> It's a good shade tree in ne summertime
> An you know, don nobody like to see dey
>   shade tree cud down

Thus Gloria House, in her "Alabama Farmer's Dialectic." The Alabama farmer, like any other colonized person, knows that the struggle for liberation is not easy because the oppressor does not want him to be liberated—"don nobody like to see dey shade tree cud down." It is recognition and acknowledgement. It leads to resolution. It is *dialectic.* After the farmer has looked around and observed some truths, "we been dat tree for dem folk/for a lotta summers," for instance, he makes the necessary resolution:

> Well, I cain be no shade tree *all* my life!
> Dat tree got to come down one a dese days
> Ain't dat right?

For Gloria, the making of a poetry is not escapist exploration or fantasy that could be shattered to smitherings the moment she ventures into the real world of the beauty of concrete human possibilities or the slime of decadent brutes. She never leaves actuality. Her language reflects this. The words she chooses to mold and project the images and symbols to celebrate the nature of her revelations/acts are very contemporary; that is, they come directly from the world around her. Her sensibility is informed by the pulse of actual, not imagined or imaginary, people from Alabama and all points white of her vision. She was down in Alabama giving that pulse form, direction. She lived and worked with communities in Alabama. She has been in Southern jails for attempting to help the people to "cud dat tree down." She was working with SNCC (Student Nonviolent Co-ordinating Committee) down South when SNCC graduated from the civil rights schools. And late in 1966, she came to New York to tell a conference of civil rights lawyers why it was time for SNCC to be unconditionally an Afro-American revolutionary Movement.

Gloria has lived elsewhere with her eyes open, sensitive to her condition as a Black woman under white domination, as witness, "DIRECTION/(Political advice for young Brothers)":

> It's like where you live, man
> And who lives there with you
> For example:
> You from Harlem?
> Yeah? Well, coulda been Johannesburg or Birmingham,
>   Alabama, you know. It's all the same. I'm from Fillmore.
> That makes us brothers, man
> Like we grew up in the same family. You dig?

Like every attuned-to-the-twentieth-century, self-respecting Black man and woman, Gloria believes in Unity and Pan-Africanism. And she realizes that "young Brothers"—young in terms of awareness of the world we live in—have problems of identity, especially if they grew up in Western "democratic" societies:

> I mean, like if you get shaky
> About stuff like who you are and
> Where you're going
> Ask somebody who lives near you
> Cause that's where it's at! man
> They'll set you straight!
> You can't just go and ask anybody, man
> Cause, dig, they just don't know
> They ain't been where you go
> EVERYDAY

Very intimate and direct. This is education because in any culture education serves to prepare people to be clear about their roles, to tap their potential so that their lives can be meaningful; so that they can better consolidate their resources and be productive in, and useful to, their communities.

The colonial situation is changing the world over. The relations between colonizer and colonized are changing, in America and elsewhere. Gloria observes and informs us that:

> They already dance to our drums,
> Elemental rhythm of life
> Attuned to the movement of the earth.

The language in this poem, like the period it celebrates, is dramatic and pulsates with a divine arrogance. It is not, however, a declaration of war. The war is on—has been on. This is a song celebrating CHANGE, the images bathed in the blood that flows when slaves turn men, burning plantations, be they in Newark or Kinsangani:

> There is a new Chief in the land
> And all the people will imitate the customs of His tribe
> And dancing to His heartbeat in His own compound,
> One Night, at The Time, they will see His face
> And they will be astounded that it is black.
>
> But there are signs of the revolution
>
> The young turks of the nation are Ours.

Gloria's clarity of vision also enables her to see our internal contradictions. As a result, she can be boldly critical of our mistakes and/or hang-ups as in "Woman":

> Has the length of one man alone
> So blurred your view?
> Can you leave the sons and daughters of Our Time
> Motherless?—no poems, no brown daughter, no acts of violence?
> For love squandered on one man?

You see, you have to clearly understand that because we do not have a long, active, collective memory of popular revolutionary movements; because we have endured abuse and all sorts of other perversions so long; because we were dehumanized and depersonalized to a point where we didn't really believe that we could rise as powerful men to threaten and damage the power of the oppressor, we developed a tendency to put all our hopes in individual courageous men who better reflected the desires and aspirations we were too afraid to own up to. To name a few from contemporary history, for instance: Malcolm, Muhammad Ali, Patrice Lumumba, Kwame Nkrumah, Rap Brown. The danger in this sort of tendency is that, should the given hero die, or should he be killed or run out of the country, we are left without direction, without even the necessary self-confidence; which would mean that we had shifted all our necessary responsibility from our shoulders to those of a given personality. This is criminal. This makes us traitors to our cause, virtually—Gloria comments:

> This is not Malcolm's sister
> Who sits sobbing for the love of one man
> While the nation groans for birth!

Yes, you see, Gloria House is striving for TRUTH, a *measure*, to facilitate her explorations, forever digging past pretenses and whatever superficial images of ourselves, our world and our possibilities. As Barbara Simmons might say, "This ain't art/ it's real movin." There are other forces in Gloria's company. Here is A. B. Spellman, for instance, looking into himself and other similar victims. He readily acknowledges the ugliness he sees:

```
. . . how stay clear in this      place
do not eat soap      relevance pays      there squats
mundanity      kick it in the nuts      its crotch swallow
your foot      now where are you      footless
his of the hideous      you goofed in the tactic      a.b.
you're still too quiet      break something larger
```

But there is more to us than those hideous tendencies we detest . . . if we are honest. A.B., moved by one of our spiritual heroes, John Coltrane, sings him "an impartial review":

> may he have new life like the fall
> fallen tree, wet moist rotten enough
> to see shoots stalks branches & green
> leaves (& may the roots) grow into his side

Jones says poetry is music made less abstract. And I agree. Because poems don't "mean" if they are honest like the honest explorations of music throbbing with life. Does a Charlie Parker riff mean anything? Poems are acts in motion. And acts, processes which involve action and reaction, lead inevitably to other acts. Confrontation forever moving towards resolving whatever other contradiction. And I learned that recently, after sufficient soul-searching, A. B. Spellman left New York to be involved in more direct, concrete and relevant acts in black communities in the South. Listen a little more often to Coltrane.

And then there is Edward Spriggs whose poetry is adequately representative of the *sentiments* of the younger Afro-American poets. Edward S. Spriggs is New York editor of Black Dialogue, "a meeting place for voices of the Black community—wherever that community may exist." Spriggs states unequivocally: "My forefathers brought upon this continent physical strength, intelligence, creativity, beauty, humanism, an unparalleled faith, and more. Only the physical strength and that faith has been allowed to function in this consciousless place . . . our intelligence, our creativity, our beauty and our humanism must be forced now, by us, upon the universe—upon ourselves even."

Spriggs argues that anything representative of America as she exists now is a threat to keep the Blackman in perpetual bondage, psychological and physical. Even the symbols of American liberty must be destroyed because white America's concept of liberty and justice is a perversion that must be irrevocably shoved out of our existence. "The statue of liberty must go. That bitch must vacate our minds." Spriggs has no explanations to make to the white world. His dialogue is strictly with black people. If he incites, excites, instructs or entertains, he does so to and for black people. His ability to look at the mirror of life boldly and shamelessly, his sensibility's functioning as an inevitable receptacle of his people's collective soul, makes him one of our spokesmen.

He is, hopefully, not preoccupied with merely analyzing and articulating our misery. Wright, Baldwin, Killens and many others—their shortcomings aside—have done that fairly competently already. He looks at America and sees in her ghettos all of the material conveniences of the Western world. He observes, for instance, in a short photographic poem on Harlem, the Jew-owned bars, barbecue joints and many other enterprises where black people live in squalor. Finally, he reveals that the only thing owned by black people in Harlem is death. This is the American experience which molded his sensibility. He lives in a period during which millions of people are murdered at random for the preservation of American dollarism. Sharpeville, Vietnam, Santo Domingo, Harlem, Watts, Detroit, Newark and many more places. Responsibility to see his people move from all things "South" imposes itself upon him with an unrelenting passion. He apparently has a Black conscience. Chauvinism? It depends on what the reader of Spriggs relates to. After all, even the oppressor taught him that cleanliness begins at home. He is far from being sentimental. He expresses the collective soul of the "ghetto" and tries to give direction because he is inherently part and parcel of the moving black mass. He does not appeal to the conscience of white America because white America has no conscience. Instead he appeals to his people to:

> Pray not for the Poet
> saints
> Pray instead
> Saints, for his critics.

The critics, of course, are the white murderers who want to control everything, including the Black poet's creativity. But Spriggs' creativity cannot be checked by adolescent fascists disguised as literary critics because he is the bearer of TRUTH. Spriggs asserts:

> A poet must & would
> give truth substance & form
> Truth needs a second career
> SO CRACK THE OTHER SIDE
> Black Poet
> that it be felt
> that it be looked at
> & into . . .

Evidently poets like Spriggs know the TRUTH is essentially the poet's business. Spriggs also believes that after the poet has stood Truth on her feet again, unveiled, unadulterated, a lot of cleaning up remains to be done. The Western white man has made the world a filthy place. Because of the damage done by the Western white man, the Blackman is even alienated from himself. So, in order that the job ahead be done efficiently,

> Black poets must make sons quick:
> using magic substances . . .
> Black poets must make soul anew . . .
> must crack the pods & let the semen fly . . .
> must carve epitaphs on their volume & numbers

Spriggs seems to have undergone a psychological and creative rebirth. He got rid of the Western *bourgeois* aesthetic. He is, then, a modern day "witchdoctor" whose art and expression are a way of life. Pulsating with love of life and love. Since he cannot relate to it, he rejects the white frame of reference he was programmed into from the very first day he went to kindergarten. He seems to have established a new frame of reference—ghetto-oriented, because the Black community in a white-dominated society is what he directly relates to.

Spriggs' language is free, is full of the free "ghetto" cadence and colorful beauty, is Afro-American, is delicately sensitive even in the midst of his unrelenting fury, is mystic, is magical, is moving—not in search of, but in the assertion and restoration of Truth, is present like the condition that molded his mind:

TRUTH IS PRESENT-HAPPENING LANGUAGE-PULSE:
is heart
    is myth
is vatic
    is Poetry.

Poetry, like any other "art" form, is meaningless, that is, has no use—beauty and good, inseparable—unless it be a specific act actual as dance or childbirth, carved bleeding from history, our experience. Tears scorched to deep tracks on the mine laborer's back recording the national epitaph. Walls and what shapes people your memory. Clarity is not a thought process but a way of life.

There are many, many more young men and women with a sense of mission across these United States. You might run into some of them in small magazines like Negro Digest, Soulbook, Black Dialogue, The Journal of Black Poetry, Freedomways, Liberator, Presence Africaine, Transition, the back issues of Black Orpheus and The New African. Yet others you might run into only at poetry readings in Harlem or Newark or some other black community across this country.

These are transitional men and women moving to the "elemental rhythms of Our Time." Transitional, because they are trying in our time, through their rhythms, to deniggerfy us, to bathe our pulse in revolutionary passions; attempting, as LeRoi Jones would sing, to "look into Black skulls and teach white people their death." But before one can be most effectively instrumental in freeing a people, he must first himself be free, so that he strives to assert and live up to what he has and its possibilities, not what he in frustration desires to have. One looks forward to a period when the majority of these young poets abandon mannerism and get directly involved in very concrete community action; when *"the state of black desire"* becomes an everyday act to satisfy that desire and split the skies with human and humanistic possibilities. They will be free then like their rhythms. And so will be the rest of us; the rhythms coming directly from the way we live. Then we will join Nina Simone and sing:

> And now we are one
> Let my soul rest in peace
> At last it is done
>
> My soul has been renewed . . .

IV   Drama

THE NEGRO AND THE AMERICAN THEATRE
(1927)
Alain Locke

In the appraisal of the possible contribution of the Negro to
the American theatre, there are those who find the greatest
promise in the rising drama of Negro life. Others see possibilities
of a deeper, though subtler influence upon what is after all
more vital, the technical aspects of the arts of the theatre.
Until very recently the Negro influence upon American drama
has been negligible, whereas even under the handicaps of
second-hand exploitation and restriction to the popular amusement stage, the Negro actor has already considerably influenced
our stage and its arts. One would do well to imagine what
might happen if the art of the Negro actor should really become
artistically lifted and liberated. Transpose the possible resources
of Negro song and dance and pantomime to the serious stage,
envisage an American drama under the galvanizing stimulus of
a rich transfusion of essential folk-arts and you may anticipate
what I mean.

A race of actors can revolutionize the drama quite as definitely and perhaps more vitally than a coterie of dramatists.

(*The late Alain Locke's essay is here reprinted by permission of the author's estate from* Theatre: Essays on the Arts of The Theatre, *edited by
Edith J. R. Isaacs, Boston: Little, Brown, 1927*).

The roots of drama are after all action and emotion, and our modern drama, for all its frantic experimentation, is an essentially anemic drama, a something of gestures and symbols and ideas and not overflowing with the vital stuff of which drama was originally made and to which it must return for its rejuvenation cycle after cycle.

Primarily the Negro brings to the drama the gift of a temperament, not the gift of a tradition. Time out of mind he has been rated as a "natural born actor" without any appreciation of what that statement, if true, really means. Often it was intended as a disparaging estimate of the Negro's limitations, a recognition of his restriction to the interpretative as distinguished from the creative aspect of drama, a confinement, in terms of a second order of talent, to the status of the mimic and the clown. But a comprehending mind knows that the very life of drama is an instinct and emotion, that drama begins and ends in mimicry, and that its creative force is in the last analysis the interpretative passion. Welcome then as is the emergence of the Negro playwright and the drama of Negro life, the promise of the most vital contribution of our race to the theatre lies, in my opinion, in the deep but still unemancipated resources of the Negro actor, and the folk arts of which he is as yet only a blind and hampered exponent. Dramatic spontaneity, the free use of body and the voice as direct instruments of feeling, a control of body plastique that opens up the narrow diaphragm of fashionable acting and the conventional mannerisms of the stage—these are indisputably strong points of Negro acting. Many a Negro vaudevillian has greater store of them than finished masters of the polite theatre. . . .

Unfortunately it is the richest vein of Negro dramatic talent which is under the heaviest artistic impediment and pressure. The art of the Negro actor has had to struggle up out of the shambles of minstrelsy and make slow headway against very fixed limitations of popular taste. Farce, buffoonery, and pathos have until recently almost completely overlaid the folk comedy and folk tragedy of a dramatically endowed and circumstanced people. These gifts must be liberated. . . . In the sensational successes of *Emperor Jones* and *All God's Chillun Got Wings* there have been two components—the fine craftsmanship and clairvoyant genius of O'Neill and the acting gifts of Charles Gilpin and Paul Robeson. From the revelation of the emotional power of the Negro actor by Opal Cooper and Inez Clough in the Ridgely Torrence plays in 1916 to the more recent half-successful attempts of Raymond O'Neill's Ethiopian Art Theatre and the National Ethiopian Art Theatre of New York, with Evelyn Preer, Rose McClendon, Sidney Kirkpatrick, Charles Olden, Frances Corbie, Julius Bledsoe, and, more lately, in the production of Paul Green's *In Abraham's Bosom,* an advanced section of the American public has become acquainted with the possibilities of the Negro in serious dramatic interpretation.

But the real mine of the Negro dramatic art and talent is in the subsoil of the vaudeville stage, gleaming through its slag and dross in the unmistakably great dramatic gifts of a Bert Williams, a Florence Mills, or a Bill Robinson. Give Bojangles Robinson or George Stamper, pantomime dancers of genius, a Bakst or an expressionist setting; give Josephine Baker, Eddie Rector, Abbie Mitchell, or Ethel Waters a dignified medium, and they would be more than a sensation, they would be artistic revelations. Pantomime, that most essential and elemental of the dramatic arts, is a natural *forte* of the Negro actor, and the use of the body and voice and facile control of posture and rhythm are almost as noteworthy in the average as in the exceptional artist. When it comes to pure registration of the emotions, I question whether any body of actors, unless it be the Russians, can so completely be fear or joy or nonchalance or grief.

With his uncanny instinct for the theatre, Max Reinhardt saw these possibilities instantly under the tawdry trappings of such musical comedies as *Eliza, Shuffle Along,* and *Runnin' Wild,* which were in vogue the season of his first visit to

New York. "It is intriguing, very intriguing," he told me then, "these Negro shows that I have seen. But remember, not as achievements, not as things in themselves artistic, but in their possibilities, their tremendous artistic possibilities. They are most modern, most American, most expressionistic. They are highly original in spite of obvious triteness, and artistic in spite of superficial crudeness. To me they reveal new possibilities of technique in drama, of the art-drama! . . . ."

I didn't enthuse. What Negro who stands for culture, with the hectic stress of a social problem weighing on the minds of an overserious minority, could enthuse! *Eliza, Shuffle Along, Runnin' Wild*—when I had come to discuss the possibilities of serious Negro drama, of the art-drama! I didn't outwardly protest, but raised a brow already too elevated perhaps, and shrugged the shoulder that carries the proverbial racial chip.

Herr Reinhardt read the gesture swiftly. "Ah, yes—I see. You view these plays for what they are, and you are right; I view them for what they will become, and I am more than right. I see their future. Why? Well, the drama must turn at every period of fresh creative development to an aspect which has been previously subordinated or neglected, and in this day of ours, we come back to the most primitive and the most basic aspect of drama for a new starting point, a fresh development and revival of the art—and that aspect is pantomime, the use of the body to portray story and emotion. And your people have that art—it is their special genius. At present it is prostituted to farce, to trite comedy—but the technique is there, and I have never seen more wonderful possibilities. Yes, I should like to do something with it."

With the New Russian Theatre experimenting with the "dynamic ballet" and Meyerhold's improvising or creative actor, with Max Reinhardt's own recently founded International Pantomime Society, with the entire new theatre agog over "mass drama," there is at least some serious significance to the statement that the Negro theatre has great artistic potentialities. What is of utmost importance to drama now is to control the primitive language of the art, and to retrieve some of the basic control which the sophisticated and conventionalized theatre has lost. It is more important to know how to cry, sob and laugh, stare and startle than to learn how to smile, grimace archly, and wink. And more important to know how to move vigorously and with rhythmic sweep than to pirouette and posture. . . .

Commenting on the work of the players of the Ethiopian Art Theatre, discerning critics noticed "the freshness and vigor of their emotional responses, their spontaneity and intensity of mood, their freedom from intellectual and artistic obsessions. . . ."

Without invoking analogies, we can see in this technical and emotional endowment great resources for the theatre. In terms of the prevalent trend for the serious development of race drama, we may expect these resources to be concentrated and claimed as the working capital of the Negro theatre. They are. But just as definitely, too, are they the general property and assets of the American theatre at large, if once the barriers are broken through. These barriers are slowly breaking down both on the legitimate stage and in the popular drama, but the great handicap, as Carl Van Vechten so keenly points out in his "Prescription for the Negro Theatre," is blind imitation and stagnant conventionalism. Negro dramatic art must not only be liberated from the handicaps of external disparagement but from its self-imposed limitations. It must more and more have the courage to be original, to break with established dramatic convention of all sorts. It must have the courage to develop its own idiom, to pour itself into new molds; in short, to be experimental.

This development may have to await the expected growth of the serious, worthwhile drama of Negro life, which for all the dramatic intensities of Negro experience has lagged lamentably until recently. There are many reasons for this; foremost, of course, the fact that drama, unless it develops in its own native soil, is the child of social prosperity and of cultural maturity. Negro life has only recently come to the verge of cultural self-expression, and has barely reached such a ripening point. . . . .

Propaganda, pro-Negro and anti-Negro, has scotched the dramatic potentialities of the subject. Especially with the few Negro playwrights has the propaganda motive worked havoc. In addition to the handicap of being out of actual touch with theatre, they have had the dramatic motive deflected at its source. Race drama has appeared to them a matter of race vindication, and pathetically they have pushed forward their moralistic allegories or melodramatic protests as dramatic correctives and antidotes for race prejudice.

A few illuminating plays, beginning with Edward Sheldon's *The Nigger* and culminating in *All God's Chillun Got Wings* and *In Abraham's Bosom* have already thrown into relief the higher possibilities of the Negro problem play. Similarly, beginning with Ridgely Torrence's *Three Plays for a Negro Theatre* and culminating in *The Emperor Jones* and *The No 'Count Boy*, a realistic study of Negro folk-life and character has been begun, and with it the inauguration of the artistic Negro folk play. The outlook for a vital and characteristic expression of Negro life in drama thus becomes more promising. . . .

The creative impulse is for the moment caught in this dilemma of choice between the drama of discussion and social analysis and the drama of expression and artistic interpretation. But despite the present lure of the problem play, it ought to be apparent that the real future of Negro drama lies with the development of the folk play. Negro drama must grow in its own soil and cultivate its own intrinsic elements; only in this way can it become truly organic, and cease being a rootless derivative. For the Negro it is futile to expect fine problem drama as an initial stage before the natural development in due course of the capacity for self-criticism. The Negro dramatist's advantage of psychological intimacy is for the present more than offset by the disadvantage of the temptation to counter partisan and propagandist attitudes. The white dramatist can achieve objectivity with relatively greater ease, though as yet he seldom does, and has temporarily an advantage in the handling of this material as drama of social situation. Proper development of these social problem themes will require the objectivity of great art. Even when the crassest conventions are waived at present, character stereotypes and deceptive formulae still linger; only genius of the first order can hope to penetrate to the material of high tragedy—and, for that matter, high comedy also—that undoubtedly are there. For with the difference that modern society decrees its own fatalisms, the situations of race hold tragedies and ironies as deep and keen as those of the ancient classics. Eventually the Negro dramatist must achieve mastery of a detached, artistic point of view, and reveal the inner stresses and dilemmas of these situations as from the psychological point of view he alone can.

The folk play, on the other hand, whether of the realistic or the imaginative type, has no such conditioned values. It is the drama of free self-expression and imaginative release, and has no objective but to express beautifully and colorfully race folk life. . . .

In all of these plays as yet, there still comes the impression that the drama of Negro life has not become as racy, as gaily unconscious, as saturated with folk ways and the folk spirit as it could be, as it eventually will be. Decidedly it needs more of that poetic strain whose counterpart makes the Irish folk drama so captivating and irresistible, more of the joy of life even when life flows tragically, and, even should one phase of it remain realistic peasant drama, more of the emotional depth of pity and terror. This clarification will surely come as the Negro drama shifts more and more to the purely aesthetic attitudes. With life becoming less a problem and more a vital process for the younger Negro, we shall leave more to the dramatist not born to it the dramatization of the race problem and concern ourselves more vitally with expression and its interpretation. . . .

The finest function, then, of race drama would be to supply an imaginative channel of escape and spiritual release, and by some process of emotional re-enforcement to cover life with the illusion of happiness and spiritual freedom. Because of the lack of any tradition or art to which to attach itself, this reaction has never functioned in the life of the American Negro except at the level of the explosive and abortive release. With the fine African tradition of primitive ritual broken and with the inhibitions of Puritanism snuffing out even the spirit of a strong dramatic and mimetic heritage, there has been little prospect for the development of strong native dramatic traits. But the traces linger to flare up spectacularly when the touch of a serious dramatic motive once again touches them. One can scarcely think of a complete development of Negro dramatic art without some significant artistic re-expression of African life, and the tradition associated with it. . . .

It may seem a far cry from the conditions and moods of modern New York and Chicago and the Negro's rapid and feverish assimilation of all things American. But art establishes its contacts in strange ways. The emotional elements of Negro art are choked by the conventions of the contemporary stage; they call for freer, more plastic material. They have no mysterious affinity with African themes or scenes, but they have for any life that is more primitive and poetic in substance. So, if, as seems already apparent, the sophisticated race sense of the Negro should lead back over the trail of the group tradition to an interest in things African, the natural affinities of the material and the art will complete the circuit and they will most electrically combine. Especially with its inherent color and emotionalism, its freedom from body-hampering dress, its odd and tragic and mysterious overtones, African life and themes, apart from any sentimental attachment, offer a wonderfully new field and province for dramatic treatment. . . .

But when our serious drama shall become as naïve and spontaneous as our drama of fun and laughter, and that in turn genuinely representative of the folk spirit which it is now forced to travesty, a point of classic development will have been reached. It is fascinating to speculate upon what riotously new and startling things may come from this. Dramatic maturings are notably sudden. Usually from the popular sub-soil something shoots up to a rapid artistic flowering. Of course, this does not have to occur with the American Negro. But a peasant folk art pouring out from under a generation-long repression is the likeliest soil known for a dramatic renascence.

THE BLACK ARTS MOVEMENT
Larry Neal

1.

The Black Arts Movement is radically opposed to any concept of the artist that alienates him from his community. Black Art is the aesthetic and spiritual sister of the Black Power concept. As such, it envisions an art that speaks directly to the needs and aspirations of Black America. In order to perform this task, the Black Arts Movement proposes a radical reordering of the western cultural aesthetic. It proposes a separate symbolism, mythology, critique, and iconology. The Black Arts and the Black Power concept both relate broadly to the Afro-American's desire for self-determination and nationhood. Both concepts are nationalistic. One is concerned with the relationship between art and politics; the other with the art of politics.

Recently, these two movements have begun to merge: the political values inherent in the Black Power concept are now finding concrete expression in the aesthetics of Afro-American dramatists, poets, choreographers, musicians, and novelists. A main tenet of Black Power is the necessity for Black people to define the world in their own terms. The Black artist has made the same point in the context of aesthetics. The two movements postulate that there are in fact and in spirit two Americas—one black, one white. The Black artist takes this to mean that his primary duty is to speak to the spiritual and cultural needs of Black people. Therefore, the main thrust of this new breed of contemporary writers is to confront the contradictions arising out of the Black man's experience in the racist West. Currently, these writers are re-evaluating western aesthetics, the traditional role of the writer, and the social function of art. Implicit in this re-evaluation is the need to develop a "black aesthetic." It is the opinion of many Black writers, I among them, that the Western aesthetic has run its course: it is impossible to construct anything meaningful within its decaying structure. We advocate a cultural revolution in art and ideas. The cultural values inherent in western history must either be radicalized or destroyed, and we will probably find that even radicalization is impossible. In fact, what is needed is a whole new system of ideas. Poet Don L. Lee expresses it:

> . . . We must destroy Faulkner, dick, jane, and other perpetuators of evil. It's time for DuBois, Nat Turner, and Kwame Nkrumah. As Frantz Fanon points out: destroy the culture and you destroy the people. This must not happen. Black artists are culture stabilizers; bringing back old values, and introducing new ones. Black Art will talk to the people and with the will of the people stop impending "protective custody."

The Black Arts Movement eschews "protest" literature. It speaks directly to Black people. Implicit in the concept of "protest" literature, as Brother Knight has made clear, is an appeal to white morality:

> Now any Black man who masters the technique of his particular art form, who adheres to the white aesthetic, and who directs his work toward a white audience is, in one sense, protesting. And implicit in the act of protest is the belief that a change will be forthcoming once the masters are aware of the protestor's

"grievance" (the very word connotes begging, supplications to the gods). Only when that belief has faded and protestings end, will Black art begin.

Brother Knight also has some interesting statements about the development of a "Black aesthetic":

Unless the Black artist establishes a "Black aesthetic" he will have no future at all. To accept the white aesthetic is to accept and validate a society that will not allow him to live. The Black artist must create new forms and new values, sing new songs (or purify old ones); and along with other Black authorities, he must create a new history, new symbols, myths and legends (and purify old ones by fire). And the Black artist, in creating his own aesthetic, must be accountable for it only to the Black people. Further, he must hasten his own dissolution as an individual (in the Western sense)—painful though the process may be, having been breast-fed the poison of "individual experience."

When we speak of a "Black aesthetic" several things are meant. First, we assume that there is already in existence the basis for such an aesthetic. Essentially, it consists of an African-American cultural tradition. But this aesthetic is finally, by implication, broader than that tradition. It encompasses most of the useable elements of Third World culture. The motive behind the Black aesthetic is the destruction of the white thing, the destruction of white ideas, and white ways of looking at the world. The new aesthetic is mostly predicated on an Ethics which asks the question: whose vision of the world is finally more meaningful, ours or the white oppressors'? What is truth? Or more precisely, whose truth shall we express, that of the oppressed or of the oppressors? These are basic questions. Black intellectuals of previous decades failed to ask them. Further, national and international affairs demand that we appraise the world in terms of our own interests. It is clear that the question of human survival is at the core of contemporary experience. The Black artist must address himself to this reality in the strongest terms possible. In a context of world up-heaval, ethics and aesthetics must interact positively and be consistent with the demands for a more spiritual world. Consequently, the Black Arts Movement is an ethical movement. Ethical, that is, from the viewpoint of the oppressed. And much of the oppression confronting the Third World and Black America is directly traceable to the Euro-American cultural sensibility. This sensibility, anti-human in nature, has, until recently, dominated the psyches of most Black artists and intellectuals; it must be destroyed before the Black creative artist can have a meaningful role in the transformation of society.

It is this natural reaction to an alien sensibility that informs the cultural attitudes of the Black Arts and the Black Power movement. It is a profound ethical sense that makes a Black artist question a society in which art is one thing and the actions of men another. The Black Arts Movement believes that your ethics and your aesthetics are one. That the contradictions between ethics and aesthetics in western society is symptomatic of a dying culture.

The term "Black Arts" is of ancient origin, but it was first used in a positive sense by LeRoi Jones:

> We are unfair
> And unfair
> We are black magicians
> Black arts we make
> in black labs of the heart
>
> The fair are fair
> and deathly white
>
> The day will not save them
> And we own the night

There is also a section of the poem "Black Dada Nihilismus" that carries the same motif. But a fuller amplification of the nature of the new aesthetics appears in the poem "Black Art":

> Poems are bullshit unless they are
> teeth or trees or lemons piled
> on a step. Or black ladies dying
> of men leaving nickel hearts
> beating them down. Fuck poems
> and they are useful, would they shoot
> come at you, love what you are,
> breathe like wrestlers, or shudder
> strangely after peeing. We want live
> words of the hip world, live flesh &
> coursing blood. Hearts and Brains
> Souls splintering fire. We want poems
> like fists beating niggers out of Jocks
> or dagger poems in the slimy bellies
> of the owner-jews . . .

Poetry is a concrete function, an action. No more abstractions. Poems are physical entities: fists, daggers, airplane poems, and poems that shoot guns. Poems are transformed from physical objects into personal forces:

> . . . Put it on him poem. Strip him naked
> to the world. Another bad poem cracking
> steel knuckles in a jewlady's mouth
> Poem scream poison gas on breasts in green berets . . .

Then the poem affirms the integral relationship between Black Art and Black people:

> . . . Let Black people understand
> that they are the lovers and the sons
> of lovers and warriors and sons
> of warriors Are poems & poets &
> all the loveliness here in the world

It ends with the following lines, a central assertion in both the Black Arts Movement and the philosophy of Black Power:

We want a black poem. And a
Black World.
Let the world be a Black Poem
And let All Black People Speak This Poem
Silently
Or LOUD

The poem comes to stand for the collective conscious and unconscious of Black America—the real impulse in back of the Black Power movement, which is the will toward self-determination and nationhood, a radical reordering of the nature and function of both art and the artist.

2.

In the spring of 1964, LeRoi Jones, Charles Patterson, William Patterson, Clarence Reed, Johnny Moore, and a number of other Black artists opened the Black Arts Repertoire Theatre School. They produced a number of plays including Jones' *Experimental Death Unit ⚹ One, Black Mass, Jello,* and *Dutchman.* They also initiated a series of poetry readings and concerts. These activities represented the most advanced tendencies in the movement and were of excellent artistic quality. The Black Arts School came under immediate attack by the New York power structure. The Establishment, fearing Black creativity, did exactly what it was expected to do—it attacked the theatre and all of its values. In the meantime, the school was granted funds by OEO though HARYOU-ACT. Lacking a cultural program itself, HARYOU turned to the only organization which addressed itself to the needs of the community. In keeping with its "revolutionary" cultural ideas, the Black Arts Theatre took its programs into the streets of Harlem. For three months, the theatre presented plays, concerts, and poetry readings to the people of the community. Plays that shattered the illusions of the American body politic, and awakened Black people to the meaning of their lives.

Then the hawks from the OEO moved in and chopped off the funds. Again, this should have been expected. The Black Arts Theatre stood in radical opposition to the feeble attitudes about culture of the "War On Poverty" bureaucrats. And later, because of internal problems, the theatre was forced to close. But the Black Arts group proved that the community could be served by a valid and dynamic art. It also proved that there was a definite need for a cultural revolution in the Black community.

With the closing of the Black Arts Theatre, the implications of what Brother Jones and his colleagues were trying to do took on even more significance. Black Art groups sprang up on the West Coast and the idea spread to Detroit, Philadelphia, Jersey City, New Orleans, and Washington, D.C. Black Arts movements began on the campuses of San Francisco State College, Fisk University, Lincoln University, Hunter College in the Bronx, Columbia University, and Oberlin College. In Watts, after the rebellion, Maulana Karenga welded the Blacks Arts Movement into a cohesive cultural ideology which owed much to the work of LeRoi Jones. Karenga sees culture as the most important element in the struggle for self-determination:

Culture is the basis of all ideas, images and actions. To move is to move culturally, i.e. by a set of values given to you by your culture.
Without a culture Negroes are only a set of reactions to white people.
The seven criteria for culture are:
1. Mythology
2. History
3. Social Organization
4. Political Organization
5. Economic Organization
6. Creative Motif
7. Ethos

In drama, LeRoi Jones represents the most advanced aspects of the movement. He is its prime mover and chief designer.

In a poetic essay entitled "The Revolutionary Theatre," he outlines the iconology of the movement:

> The Revolutionary Theatre should force change: it should be change. (All their faces turned into the lights and you work on them black nigger magic, and cleanse them at having seen the ugliness. And if the beautiful see themselves, they will love themselves.) We are preaching virtue again, but by that to mean NOW, toward what seems the most constructive use of the word.

The theatre that Jones proposes is inextricably linked to the Afro-American political dynamic. And such a link is perfectly consistent with Black America's contemporary demands. For theatre is potentially the most social of all of the arts. It is an integral part of the socializing process. It exists in direct relationship to the audience it claims to serve. The decadence and inanity of the contemporary American theatre is an accurate reflection of the state of American society. Albee's *Who's Afraid of Virginia Woolf?* is very American: sick white lives in a homosexual hell hole. The theatre of white America is escapist, refusing to confront concrete reality. Into this cultural emptiness come the musicals, an up-tempo version of the same stale lives. And the use of Negroes in such plays as *Hello Dolly* and *Hallelujah Baby* does not alert their nature; it compounds the problem. These plays are simply hipper versions of the minstrel show. They present Negroes acting out the hang-ups of middle-class white America. Consequently, the American theatre is a palliative prescribed to bourgeois patients who refuse to see the world as it is. Or, more crucially, as the world sees them. It is no accident, therefore, that the most "important" plays come from Europe—Brecht, Weiss, and Ghelderode. And even these have begun to run dry.

The Black Arts theatre, the theatre of LeRoi Jones, is a radical alternative to the sterility of the American theatre. It is primarily a theatre of the Spirit, confronting the Black man in his interaction with his brothers and with the white thing.

Our theatre will show victims so that their brothers in the audience will be better able to understand that they are the brothers of victims, and that they themselves are blood brothers. And what we show must cause the blood to rush, so that pre-revolutionary temperaments will be bathed in this blood, and it will cause their deepest souls to move, and they will find themselves tensed and clenched, even ready to die, at what the soul has been taught. We will scream and cry, murder, run through the streets in agony, if it means some soul will be moved, moved to actual life understanding of what the world is, and what it ought to be. We are preaching virtue and feeling, and a natural sense of the self in the world. All men live in the world, and the world ought to be a place for them to live.

The victims in the world of Jones' early plays are Clay, murdered by the white bitch-goddess in *Dutchman,* and Walker Vessels, the revolutionary in *The Slave.* Both of these plays present Black men in transition. Clay, the middle-class Negro trying to get himself a little action from Lula, digs himself and his own truth only to get murdered after telling her like it really is:

Just let me bleed you, you loud whore, and one poem vanished. A whole people neurotics, struggling to keep from being sane. And the only thing that would cure the neurosis would be your murder. Simple as that. I mean if I murdered you, then other white people would understand me. You understand? No. I guess not. If Bessie Smith had killed some white people she wouldn't needed that music. She could have talked very straight and plain about the world. Just straight two and two are four. Money. Power. Luxury. Like that. All of them. Crazy niggers turning their back on sanity. When all it needs is that simple act. Just murder. Would make us all sane.

But Lula understands, and she kills Clay first. In a perverse way it is Clay's nascent knowledge of himself that threatens the existence of Lula's idea of the world. Symbolically, and in fact, the relationship between Clay (Black America) and

Lula (white America) is rooted in the historical castration of black manhood. And in the twisted psyche of white America, the Black man is both an object of love and hate. Analogous attitudes exist in most Black Americans, but for decidedly different reasons. Clay is doomed when he allows himself to participate in Lula's "fantasy" in the first place. It is the fantasy to which Frantz Fanon alludes in *The Wretched of the Earth* and *Black Skins, White Mask*: the native's belief that he can acquire the oppressor's power by acquiring his symbols, one of which is the white woman. When Clay finally digs himself it is too late.

Walker Vessels, in *The Slave*, is Clay reincarnated as the revolutionary confronting problems inherited from his contact with white culture. He returns to the home of his ex-wife, a white woman, and her husband, a literary critic. The play is essentially about Walker's attempt to destroy his white past. For it is the past, with all of its painful memories, that is really the enemy of the revolutionary. It is impossible to move until history is either recreated or comprehended. Unlike Todd, in Ralph Ellison's *Invisible Man*, Walker cannot fall outside history. Instead, Walker demands a confrontation with history, a final shattering of bullshit illusions. His only salvation lies in confronting the physical and psychological forces that have made him and his people powerless. Therefore, he comes to understand that the world must be restructured along spiritual imperatives. But in the interim it is basically a question of *who* has power:

EASLEY. You're so wrong about everything. So terribly, sickeningly wrong. What can you change? What do you hope to change? Do you think Negroes are better people than whites . . . that they can govern a society *better* than whites? That they'll be more judicious or more tolerant? Do you think they'll make fewer mistakes? I mean really, if the Western white man has proved one thing . . . it's the futility of modern society. So the have-not peoples become the haves. Even so, will that change the

essential functions of the world? Will there be more love or
beauty in the world . . . more knowledge . . . because of it?

WALKER. Probably. Probably there will be more . . . if more people
have a chance to understand what it is. But that's not even
the point. It comes down to baser human endeavor than any
social-political thinking. What does it matter if there's more love
or beauty? Who the fuck cares? Is that what the Western ofay
thought while he was ruling . . . that his rule somehow brought
more love and beauty into the world? Oh, he might have thought
that concomitantly, while sipping a gin rickey and scratching
his ass . . . but that was not ever the point. Not even on the
Crusades. The point is that you had your chance, darling, now
these other folks have theirs. *Quietly.* Now they have theirs.

EASLEY. God, what an ugly idea.

This confrontation between the black radical and the white
liberal is symbolic of larger confrontations occurring between
the Third World and Western society. It is a confrontation
between the colonizer and the colonized, the slavemaster and
the slave. Implicit in Easley's remarks is the belief that the
white man is culturally and politically superior to the Black
Man. Even though Western society has been traditionally violent in its relation with the Third World, it sanctimoniously
deplores violence or self assertion on the part of the enslaved.
And the Western mind, with clever rationalizations, equates
the violence of the oppressed with the violence of the oppressor.
So that when the native preaches self-determination, the Western
white man cleverly misconstrues it to mean hate of *all* white
men. When the Black political radical warns his people not
to trust white politicians of the left and the right, but instead
to organize separately on the basis of power, the white man
cries: "racism in reverse." Or he will say, as many of them do
today: "We deplore both white and black racism." As if the
two could be equated.

There is a minor element in *The Slave* which assumes great

importance in a later play entitled *Jello*. Here I refer to the emblem of Walker's army: a red-mouthed grinning field slave. The revolutionary army has taken one of the most hated symbols of the Afro-American past and radically altered its meaning.* This is the supreme act of freedom, available only to those who have liberated themselves psychically. Jones amplifies this inversion of emblem and symbol in *Jello* by making Rochester (Ratfester) of the old Jack Benny (Penny) program into a revolutionary nationalist. Ratfester, ordinarily the supreme embodiment of the Uncle Tom Clown, surprises Jack Penny by turning on the other side of the nature of the Black man. He skillfully, and with an evasive black humor, robs Penny of all of his money. But Ratfester's actions are "moral." That is to say, Ratfester is getting his back pay; payment of a long over-due debt to the Black man. Ratfester's sensibilities are different from Walker's. He is *blues people* smiling and shuffling while trying to figure out how to destroy the white thing. And like the blues man, he is the master of the understatement. Or in the Afro-American folk tradition, he is the signifying Monkey, Shine, and Stagolee all rolled into one. There are no sterotypes any more. History has killed Uncle Tom. Because even Uncle Tom has a breaking point beyond which he will not be pushed. Cut deeply enough into the most docile Negro, and you will find a conscious murderer. Behind the lyrics of the blues and the shuffling porter loom visions of white throats being cut and cities burning.

Jones' particular power as a playwright does not rest solely on his revolutionary vision, but is instead derived from his

* In Jones' study of Afro-American music, *Blues People*, we find the following observation: ". . . Even the adjective *funky*, which once meant to many Negroes merely a stink (usually associated with sex), was used to qualify the music as meaningful (the word became fashionable and is now almost useless). The social implication, then, was that even the old stereotype of a distinctive Negro smell that white America subscribed to could be turned against white America. For this smell now, real or not, was made a valuable characteristic of 'Negro-ness.' And 'Negro-ness,' by the fifties, for many Negroes (and whites) was the only strength left to American culture."

deep lyricism and spiritual outlook. In many ways, he is fundamentally more a poet than a playwright. And it is his lyricism
that gives body to his plays. Two important plays in this regard
are *Black Mass* and *Slave Ship*. *Black Mass* is based on the
Muslim myth of Yacub. According to this myth, Yacub, a Black
scientist, developed the means of grafting different colors of
the Original Black Nation until a White Devil was created.
In *Black Mass*, Yacub's experiments produce a raving White
Beast who is condemned to the coldest regions of the North.
The other magicians implore Yacub to cease his experiments.
But he insists on claiming the primacy of scientific knowledge
over spiritual knowledge. The sensibility of the White Devil
is alien, informed by lust and sensuality. The Beast is the
consummate embodiment of evil, the beginning of the historical
subjugation of the spiritual world.

Black Mass takes place in some pre-historical time. In fact,
the concept of time, we learn, is the creation of an alien
sensibility, that of the Beast. This is a deeply weighted play,
a colloquy on the nature of man, and the relationship between
legitimate spiritual knowledge and scientific knowledge. It is
LeRoi Jones' most important play mainly because it is informed
by a mythology that is wholly the creation of the Afro-American
sensibility.

Further, Yacub's creation is not merely a scientific exercise.
More fundamentally, it is the aesthetic impulse gone astray.
The Beast is created merely for the sake of creation. Some
artists assert a similar claim about the nature of art. They
argue that art need not have a function. It is against this
decadent attitude toward art—ramified throughout most of Western society—that the play militates. Yacub's real crime, therefore,
is the introduction of a meaningless evil into a harmonious
universe. The evil of the Beast is pervasive, corrupting everything and everyone it touches. What was beautiful is twisted
into an ugly screaming thing. The play ends with destruction
of the holy place of the Black Magicians. Now the Beast and
his descendants roam the earth. An off-stage voice chants a

call for the Jihad to begin. It is then that myth merges into legitimate history, and we, the audience, come to understand that all history is merely someone's version of mythology.

Slave Ship presents a more immediate confrontation with history. In a series of expressionistic tableaux it depicts the horrors and the madness of the Middle Passage. It then moves through the period of slavery, early attempts at revolt, tendencies toward Uncle Tom-like reconciliation and betrayal, and the final act of liberation. There is no definite plot (LeRoi calls it a pageant), just a continuous rush of sound, groans, screams, and souls wailing for freedom and relief from suffering. This work has special affinities with the New Music of Sun Ra, John Coltrane, Albert Ayler, and Ornette Coleman. Events are blurred, rising and falling in a stream of sound. Almost cinematically, the images flicker and fade against a heavy back-drop of rhythm. The language is spare, stripped to the essential. It is a play which almost totally eliminates the need for a text. It functions on the basis of movements and energy—the dramatic equivalent of the New Music.

Slave Ship's energy is, at base, ritualistic. As a matter of fact, to see the play any other way is to miss the point. All the New York reviewers, with the possible exception of John Lahr, were completely cut off from this central aspect of the play when it was performed at the Brooklyn Academy under the brilliant direction of Gilbert Moses. One of the prime motivations behind the work is to suck the audience into a unique and very precise universe. The episodes of this "pageant" do not appear as strict interpretations of history. Rather, what we are digging is ritualized history. That is, history that allows emotional and religious participation on the part of the audience. And, like all good ritual, its purpose is to make the audience stronger, more sensitive to the historical realities that have shaped our lives and the lives of our ancestors. The play acts to extend memory. For black people to forget the realities posed by *Slave Ship* is to fall prey to an existential paralysis.

History, like the blues, demands that we witness the painful
events of our prior lives; and that we either confront these
painful events or be destroyed by them.

3.

LeRoi Jones is the best known and the most advanced
playwright of the movement, but he is not alone. There are
other excellent playwrights who express the general mood of
the Black Arts ideology. Among them are Ron Milner, Ed Bullins, Ben Caldwell, Jimmy Stewart, Joe White, Charles Patterson,
Charles Fuller, Aisha Hughes, Carol Freeman, and Jimmy Garrett.

Ron Milner's *Who's Got His Own* is of particular importance.
It strips bare the clashing attitudes of a contemporary Afro-
American family. Milner's concern is with legitimate manhood
and morality. The family in *Who's Got His Own* is in search
of its conscience, or more precisely its own definition of life.
On the day of his father's death, Tim and his family are forced
to examine the inner fabric of their lives: the lies, self-deceits,
and sense of powerlessness in a white world. The basic conflict,
however, is internal. It is rooted in the historical search for
black manhood. Tim's mother is representative of a generation
of Christian Black women who have implicitly understood the
brooding violence lurking in their men. And with this understanding, they have interposed themselves between their men
and the object of that violence—the white man. Thus unable
to direct his violence against the oppressor, the Black man
becomes more frustrated and the sense of powerlessness deep-
ens. Lacking the strength to be a man in the white world, he
turns against his family. So the oppressed, as Fanon explains,
constantly dreams violence against his oppressor, while killing
his brother on fast weekends.

Tim's sister represents the Negro woman's attempt to acquire
what Eldridge Cleaver calls "ultrafemininity." That is, the attributes of her white upper-class counterpart. Involved here is

a rejection of the body-oriented life of the working class Black man, symbolized by the mother's traditional religion. The sister has an affair with a white upper-class liberal, ending in abortion. There are hints of lesbianism, i.e., a further rejection of the body. The sister's life is a pivotal factor in the play. Much of the stripping away of falsehood initiated by Tim is directed at her life, which they have carefully kept hidden from the mother.

Tim is the product of the new Afro-American sensibility, informed by the psychological revolution now operative within Black America. He is a combination ghetto soul brother and militant intellectual, very hip and slightly flawed himself. He would change the world, but without comprehending the particular history that produced his "tyrannical" father. And he cannot be the man his father was—not until he truly understands his father. He must understand why his father allowed himself to be insulted daily by the "honky" types on the job; why he took a demeaning job in the "shit-house"; and why he spent on his family the violence that he should have directed against the white man. In short, Tim must confront the history of his family. And that is exactly what happens. Each character tells his story, exposing his falsehood to the other until a balance is reached.

Who's Got His Own is not the work of an alienated mind. Milner's main thrust is directed toward unifying the family around basic moral principles, toward bridging the "generation gap." Other Black playwrights, Jimmy Garrett for example, see the gap as unbridgeable.

Garrett's *We Own the Night* (see this issue of TDR, pp. 62–69) takes place during an armed insurrection. As the play opens we see the central characters defending a section of the city against attacks by white police. Johnny, the protagonist, is wounded. Some of his Brothers intermittently fire at attacking forces, while others look for medical help. A doctor arrives, forced at gun point. The wounded boy's mother also comes. She is a female Uncle Tom who berates the Brothers and their cause. She tries to get Johnny to leave. She is hysterical. The whole idea of Black people fighting white people is totally outside of her orientation. Johnny begins a vicious attack on his mother, accusing her of emasculating his father—a recurring theme in the sociology of the Black community. In Afro-American literature of previous decades the strong Black mother was the object of awe and respect. But in the new literature her status is ambivalent and laced with tension. Historically, Afro-American women have had to be the economic mainstays of the family. The oppressor allowed them to have jobs while at the same time limiting the economic mobility of the Black man. Very often, therefore, the woman's aspirations and values are closely tied to those of the white power structure and not to those of her man. Since he cannot provide for his family the way white men do, she despises his weakness, tearing into him at every opportunity until, very often, there is nothing left but a shell.

The only way out of this dilemma is through revolution. It either must be an actual blood revolution, or one that psychically redirects the energy of the oppressed. Milner is fundamentally concerned with the latter and Garrett with the former. Communication between Johnny and his mother breaks down. The revolutionary imperative demands that men step outside the legal framework. It is a question of erecting *another* morality. The old constructs do not hold up, because adhering to them means consigning oneself to the oppressive reality. Johnny's mother is involved in the old constructs. Manliness is equated with white morality. And even though she claims to love her family (her men), the overall design of her ideas are against black manhood. In Garrett's play the mother's morality manifests itself in a deep-seated hatred of Black men; while in Milner's work the mother understands, but holds her men back.

The mothers that Garrett and Milner see represent the Old Spirituality—the Faith of the Fathers of which DuBois spoke. Johnny and Tim represent the New Spirituality. They appear to be a type produced by the upheavals of the colonial world

of which Black America is a part. Johnny's assertion that he is
a criminal is remarkably similar to the rebel's comments in
Aimé Césaire's play, *Les Armes Miraculeuses* (*The Miraculous
Weapons*). In that play the rebel, speaking to his mother,
proclaims: "My name—an offense; my Christian name—humilia-
tion; my status—a rebel; my age—the stone age." To which the
mother replies: "My race—the human race. My religion—brotherhood." The Old Spirituality is generalized. It seeks to recognize
Universal Humanity. The New Spirituality is specific. It begins
by seeing the world from the concise point-of-view of the
colonialized. Where the Old Spirituality would live with oppression while ascribing to the oppressors an innate goodness,
the New Spirituality demands a radical shift in point-of-view.
The colonialized native, the oppressed must, of necessity, subscribe to a *separate* morality. One that will liberate him and
his people.

The assault against the Old Spirituality can sometimes be
humorous. In Ben Caldwell's play, *The Militant Preacher*, a
burglar is seen slipping into the home of a wealthy minister.
The preacher comes in and the burglar ducks behind a large
chair. The preacher, acting out the role of the supplicant minister
begins to moan, praying to De Lawd for understanding.

In the context of today's politics, the minister is an Uncle Tom,
mouthing platitudes against self-defense. The preacher drones
in a self-pitying monologue about the folly of protecting oneself
against brutal policemen. Then the burglar begins to speak.
The preacher is startled, taking the burglar's voice for the voice
of God. The burglar begins to play on the preacher's old time
religion. He *becomes* the voice of God insulting and goading
the preacher on until the preacher's attitudes about protective
violence change. The next day the preacher emerges militant,
gun in hand, sounding like Reverend Cleage in Detroit. He now
preaches a new gospel—the gospel of the gun, an eye for an
eye. The gospel is preached in the rhythmic cadences of the
old Black church. But the content is radical. Just as Jones
inverted the symbols in *Jello*, Caldwell twists the rhythms

of the Uncle Tom preacher into the language of the new militancy.

These plays are directed at problems within Black America. They begin with the premise that there is a well defined Afro-American audience. An audience that must see itself and the world in terms of its own interests. These plays, along with many others, constitute the basis for a viable movement in the theatre—a movement which takes as its task a profound re-evaluation of the Black man's presence in America. The Black Arts Movement represents the flowering of a cultural nationalism that has been suppressed since the 1920's. I mean the "Harlem Renaissance"—which was essentially a failure. It did not address itself to the mythology and the life-styles of the Black community. It failed to take roots, to link itself concretely to the struggles of that community, to become its voice and spirit. Implicit in the Black Arts Movement is the idea that Black people, however dispersed, constitute a *nation* within the belly of white America. This is not a new idea. Garvey said it and the Honorable Elijah Muhammad says it now. And it is on this idea that the concept of Black Power is predicated.

Afro-American life and history is full of creative possibilities, and the movement is just beginning to perceive them. Just beginning to understand that the most meaningful statements about the nature of Western society must come from the Third World of which Black America is a part. The thematic material is broad, ranging from folk heroes like Shine and Stagolee to historical figures like Marcus Garvey and Malcolm X. And then there is the struggle for Black survival, the coming confrontation between white America and Black America. If art is the harbinger of future possibilities, what does the future of Black America portend?

I WORK HERE TO PLEASE YOU
Loften Mitchell

During my school days I worked at terrible jobs that I would not give to a Mississippi Dixiecrat. I assisted my father in being janitor of a building, moving black folks' garbage, and then I became the assistant janitor in a white building, where I moved white folks' garbage. I ran an elevator in a building where I took white folks up and down, and all the time I felt as though I were going down, down. I delivered lunches to Wall Street offices where white fellow students sat with their feet thrown across desks, and I set pins in a bowling alley where white men flung black balls down the lanes at me and occasionally a measly tip. I mopped floors and cleaned toilets and hopped bells and bussed tables and finally I graduated and became a waiter.

I liked waiting tables, because it gave me a chance to dish out smart remarks to customers as well as food. But the thing I liked most about waiting tables was the opportunity it gave me to listen to older black waiters and their words of wisdom. Sometimes, even today, their words ring in my brain and I find myself smiling.

On one occasion, I worked in a swank hotel where the waiting staff was integrated. You see, in those days white people actually worked for a living. Well, in this hotel there was a wise waiter named Dan who carried the weight of sixty years of being black in white America. He was the most efficient waiter I have ever known. One morning, Dan got ready for his set-up. He put his forks and knives on his tray, then his napkins and his juices, and then he went for his rolls. When he did that, a white waiter calmly went to Dan's tray and began to remove things from it and place them on his own tray. I stood there, watching him steal from Dan's tray, in naïve amazement. Dan sauntered back just as the white waiter was removing his forks and knives. The white waiter turned to Dan and said innocently: "Oh! I didn't know this was *your* tray!"

Dan's tones were acidic. He said: "Oh, that's all right, white boy. I work here to please you."

"I work here to please you." I laughed at this remark for years. After all, it was what we in Harlem called a "good backcap." Those were the days, of course, when we got our kicks by telling off white folks, then going uptown and telling our brothers what we had told the whites. Sometimes I think we were more interested in *beating* the system that we were in changing it. In fact, sometimes I think we were so interested in beating the system that we beat up white folks and black folks rather than change the system.

"I work here to please you." Accurate, indeed, were the words of that old black waiter, for the "you" is the system built on power and profits, and we are all slaves to it, even those who rebel against it. For, in the last analysis, as Dr. W. E. B. DuBois has said, in *Black Reconstruction,* ministers, teachers, and confirmed pacifists will resort to war—in spite of all their utterances. I have no right to add to Dr. DuBois' statement, but I am going to do just that: In the last analysis, nearly all American revolutionists, black and white, can be *bought.* For this is a land where the dollar is God, and many a one hundred pennies is hustled in His name.

"I work here to please you." And though these words came

from the lips of a black waiter, they might well have been
uttered by every American who reached these shores. An im-
poverished Europe sought a new route to India, seeking endless
wealth. This Europe found a new land to the west, and it
claimed this land and called the red people "Indians," although
they knew full well they had not found a new route to India.
Indeed, it is said that Christopher Columbus heard of this new
land to the west from his contact with Africans. But Western
world history is made up of myths and lies. We have first the
vicious deed, and then we have to make it respectable. This
underlines the actions of a horse thief named Cornelius Vander-
bilt, who built Grand Central Station, then had his descendants
try to clean up his name. This is explained today when one
looks at that crook named John D. Rockefeller, whose children,
grandchildren, and great-grandchildren have tried to "clean up
his name."

Right there we see why Nelson Rockefeller will never become
President of the United States and why his governorship of
New York State is a mealy-mouthed act of placating the upstate
power structure that makes the greatest city in the world into
a pit of slime.

"I work here to please you." This statement has underlined
too much of the Black Aesthetic. At the end of the nineteen
sixties we find black men walking around in dashikis made by
white companies. We find them walking around with hair
nature made for close cropping in order to ward off the sun's
unrelenting rays, now long, defiantly long, defensively long. We
find black folks "doing their thing," which—to quote my
wife, Marjorie—is "no thing" or "nothing." And, to further quote
Marjorie, "the white folks are paying for it through foundations
and anti-poverty funds, which means that that 'thing' is a white-
influenced thing." In other words, subconsciously, black folks
exist to please white folks.

Marjorie is a charming, intelligent woman, but when she uttered these words, I could not help thinking that that has been
the historic role of black people in this country. Their primary

function is to make profits for white people—from slavery time
to the present, from the cotton fields to the industrial swamps
to liquor to heroin. Doing your thing is welcome, indeed, as
long as it fills the coffers of white folks.

This was apparent when America was founded. The so-called
Founding Fathers ignored landless whites when they founded
this nation, and they considered black people as "three-fifths"
human. Those moneygrubbers who founded this nation were
unwilling to cut the King of England in on a share of the
profits. And they went to war, yelling about "Give me liberty
or give me death." And therein lies one of the ironies of history.
Five thousand black men and women fought in that war and
helped to turn the tide of the American Revolution.

Why???

Were they really naïve? Were the red people naïve when
they welcomed the white people and taught them to grow
corn? Why, indeed? And speculation can only enter here. The
black man, like the red man, was community-minded, believing
that all belong to the land and the land to all. If you knocked
on the door and offered a friendly hand, you were invited
into the house and you could partake of all that was there.
The suspicion cannot be avoided, therefore, that the white
stranger who knocked on the door did so with malice afore-
thought, seeking to obsequiously make his way inside the door
and to "take control." This was, in short, a hungry, desperate,
deceiving rat who was to chase the art-minded Jew from land
to land, enslave the black man, kill the red man, milk the Asian,
and make the Irish, the Italian, and the Polish into flunkies in
his power structure.

The first black men to reach the American shores must have
harbored dreams that are yet unfulfilled. The ancient works
of Latin American artists suggest that Africans reached America
long before Christopher Columbus. It is a matter of record,
however, that one of Columbus' ships was captained by a
black man, that there was a black man with Ponce de León
when he "discovered" Florida and one with Balboa when he

"discovered" the Pacific Ocean. Contrary to the lies of history, black people were in the New World long before the first slaves arrived at Jamestown in 1619.

New York City when it was a Dutch colony known as New Amsterdam had black people. Peter Stuyvesant said, "all is well, thanks to the employment of Negroes," and when he left for Holland, he wrote, "Let the company's Negroes keep good watch on my Bowery!"

In short, slavery in America was "integrated." Black people and white people were indentured servants, and slavery was a matter of labor, not color. In fact, there are records that document that well-to-do black people owned slaves. The British conquest of New Amsterdam in 1664 led to the introduction of chattel slavery. A badge was placed on color, and the Negro's visibility marked him as the man who was going to be betrayed in the search for the American Dream.

But this dream burned bright in the hearts of black breasts. How else can one explain Phillis Wheatley's lines of verse to General George Washington? How else can one explain Phoebe Fraunces saving the life of Washington when an Irish traitor tried to poison him? How else can one explain Phoebe's father, Sam Fraunces, giving up a lucrative restaurant business and joining the staff of President Washington? How else can we explain that five thousand black men and women fought in the American Revolution while chattel slavery existed in the South?

We see, then, that black Americans had bought the American Dream. We see the meaning of the words: "I work here to please you."

And, indeed, we did. The theater illustrates this in sharp, significant terms. In the eighteenth century, the American theater attempted to deal with black people in *The Fall of British Tyranny*. In that play, black slaves were offered their freedom if they joined in the British cause during the American Revolution. Many did, including some of George Washington's slaves, and the British later freed them and settled them in Nova Scotia, where their descendants live now. But the tone set there was not to last. Murdock's *The Triumph of Love* introduced a shuffling, cackling "darky," and the rape of the black image—and, indeed, of the Black Aesthetic—had begun!

Bold attempts were made thereafter to laugh at the Negro's features, his habits, his very being. He was a creature to be scorned, humiliated, assailed from pulpits and public lecterns. He was, therefore, placed on the defensive—a position he occupies to this day. And his songs about freedom are sad songs, for he himself does not know the true meaning of freedom; nor will he, unless, in the words of Dr. DuBois, there comes to America "a vast social change."

This defensive action by black people led to interesting cultural activities. One of the very first occurred in 1821, when black tragedian James Hewlett spearheaded the founding of the African Grove Theatre in New York City. This theater was located at Bleecker and Grove streets, and here the classics were performed for black people. The theater was a source of inspiration for that great black actor Ira Aldridge. But the police harassed the company, often arresting actors in the middle of a performance. The actors returned when they were released from jail, and they performed again. White hoodlums created disturbances in the theater, and the management was compelled to post a sign asking whites to sit in the rear of the theater because "white people do not know how to conduct themselves at entertainment designed for ladies and gentlemen of colour."

White hoodlums eventually wrecked the African Grove Theatre and, with its destruction, Ira Aldridge realized that America offered little to the black creative artist. He sailed for Europe, where he was acclaimed by royalty. It is significant to note that, two years after he left these shores, the shuffling, cackling black stereotype was acclaimed on the New York stage, projected by a white man in "blackface."

Long, bleak moments followed—in terms of the black man's creative activity. He had been creating for a long time. Sometime during the eighteenth century, black slaves on southern plantations had created the minstrel pattern. This form—the forerunner of the American musical comedy pattern—was designed by slaves to satirize slavemasters. Minstrelsy was a unique, fast-moving, devastating art form until whites saw it, copied it, then used that form to caricature the black man. The black man's protest form was therefore used to destroy his image. And when black men joined the theater at the end of the Civil War, they had to do so as minstrels, blacken their faces, and, in the words of James Weldon Johnson, they became "a caricature of a caricature."

They, in short, worked here to please you.

There were exceptions. William Wells Brown, an ex-slave, wrote *The Escape, or A Leap to Freedom*. William Lloyd Garrison wrote in *The Liberator* in 1853 of the playwright's power and eloquence. Minstrelsy, however, was the order of the day. James Bland, composer of *Carry Me Back to Old Virginny* and *In the Evening by the Moonlight*, was a Long Island Negro, a minstrel man. And many were the minstrel companies headed by black men. It was not until the latter part of the nineteenth century that a group of black men set out to deliberately destroy the minstrel tradition. Among these were: Bert Williams, George Walker, Jesse Shipp, Alex Rogers, Bob Cole, J. Rosamond Johnson, Will Marion Cook, and Paul Laurence Dunbar. But—and this is easy to say in the nineteen sixties—theirs was a defensive action, geared toward capturing white audiences without alienating them. They had no love scenes in their plays, because they felt that white audiences would not accept black people mating romantically. They were pleasing the you of you.

There seems to be a popular illusion that the black playwright is a recent phenomenon. Actually, he has been a part of the theater as long as its has existed. Bob Cole, along with J. Rosamond Johnson, composer of *Lift Every Voice and Sing*, created the operas *The Red Moon* and *The Shoofly Regiment*. In April 1898, Mr. Cole offered a vehicle known as *A Trip to Coontown*, at the Third Avenue Theatre. Will Marion

Cook, the composer, and Paul Laurence Dunbar must be considered among black theater writers. Their *Clorindy—the Origin of the Cakewalk* was particularly well received. During this era, Jesse Shipp and Alex Rogers were creating works for Bert Williams and George Walker. The Williams and Walker Company "crashed" Broadway with an original musical, *In Dahomey,* which went on to London, where it was presented at a command performance at Buckingham Palace in 1903. The company's next musical, *In Abyssinia,* with a book by Jesse Shipp and Alex Rogers, opened in New York City with a soaring musical number by Will Marion Cook known as "Song of Reverence to the Setting Sun." One New York critic blatantly described this work as a "little too high-brow for a darky show."

Williams and Walker followed this work with *Bandanna Land,* during which George Walker became ill and gave up the theater. Bert Williams went alone into *Mr. Lode of Kole,* then later, at the invitation of Abraham Erlanger, joined the cast of the *Follies.*

To my knowledge, Bert Williams was the only black artist who worked in the Broadway theater between the years 1910 and 1917. Black people were excluded from Broadway as performers and patrons. Nor was this an accident. It was a product of the sabotaging of the Reconstruction Era, of the same type of backlash faced by black people in the United States today. The United States Supreme Court was then an oracle for the rights of white people and rampant racism, highlighted by its *Plessy* v. *Ferguson* decision, in which it upheld the separate-but-equal doctrine. The American power structure had placed a "badge" on color, and it became fashionable to attack black people. Lynch mobs rode the southern night, and Jim Crow laws appeared on the statute books of southern states. Race riots flared in cities, and the rape of the black American continued.

Big business assumed control of the American theater. A powerful group known as the Theatrical Trust Syndicate took control of all bookings, hirings, and firings. They punished prominent white stars who failed to cooperate with them, forcing the great Sarah Bernhardt and Mrs. Dwight Fiske to perform in second-rate theaters. This, then, was the tone of the nation of the robber barons.

The attack on black people in New York City was merciless. White hoodlums crashed into black homes, beating women and children. Black workers had to meet on street corners and walk home together to prevent attacks. This type of terror made many black people welcome the black development of the community known as Harlem.

From 1910 through 1917, black theatrical artists worked primarily in the Harlem area. In 1909, writer-actor-producer Eddie Hunter offered shows at the Crescent Theatre, on the site of the present-day Lenox Terrace apartments. Many of the shows produced at the Crescent were by Mr. Hunter, notably *Going to the Races* and *The Battle of Who Run.* There were also such ventures as Harry Lawrence Freeman's opera *An African Kraal.* And down the street, near Lenox Avenue, stood the Lincoln Theatre, where Henry Kramer and S. H. Dudley had their plays produced.

White America is paradoxical. Inconsistency—and, indeed, ambivalence—is its middle name when it comes to black people. It wants black people off to themselves in slave cabins, shacks, ghettos; wants to hear them sing the blues and spew out their hatred of white America, yet white America is *compelled* to follow black people into these areas, wanting to know what they are thinking, wanting to be loved and understood by black people. It is, indeed, the modern slave system, the old plantation system updated. It is a modern translation of the slavemaster who beat his slaves, then wanted them to love him. In fact, one can get Freudian here in terms of love-hate relationships . . .

At any rate, white people followed black people to Harlem to see shows and sit in black night clubs. In 1913, when J. Leubrie Hill's *Darktown Follies* opened at the Lafayette

Theatre, on Seventh Avenue and 132d Street, one critic wrote: "It looked like a Broadway opening." Florenz Ziegfeld bought the Finale of that show for use in his own *Follies*. Another Lafayette show, *Darkydom*, by Aubrey Lyles and Flournoy Miller, saw many of its sketches sold to Broadway.

Now, a note must be added here in terms of the Black Aesthetic. At the outset, these Harlem ventures were black indeed—created by black people for the enjoyment of black people. In short, jokes could be heard and music played and sung in terms of the black idiom. But the invasion by whites into the Harlem area brought rank commercialism to the fore. Many black artists changed their repertories to conform to *what whites expected of them*. Here we see the pleasing of whites, expressed too often by the most militant of blacks in these terms: "You've got to deal with whites because they have the money." And this philosophy undercut and vitiated the movement of a people in the direction of creating a truly black theatrical form.

But the excitement and vitality of black life was too apparent for a dramatist to ignore. And so Eugene O'Neill wrote his *The Emperor Jones*, which I consider a bad play with a magnificent acting role for a Negro. It was performed by Charles Gilpin at the Provincetown Playhouse in 1920. This was the same Mr. Gilpin who had appeared in *Abraham Lincoln* in 1917 and marked the Negro performer's return to the downtown area. The latter work, along with Ridgely Torrence's *Three Plays for a Negro Theatre* in 1917 indicated that white dramatists saw the dramatic possibilities of Negro life.

In 1921, *Shuffle Along*, by Aubrey Lyles and Flournoy Miller, with music and lyrics by Noble Sissle and Eubie Blake, opened in New York and became a smash hit. It launched the period that came to be known at the Black Renaissance, in which black-authored books, sculpture, and music held sway. Several editions of *Shuffle Along* followed, as well as *Blackbirds*. In 1923, Eddie Hunter's *How Come?* was seen on Broadway with that great jazz musician Sidney Bechet.

Many fine black playwrights appeared during this period. Willis Richardson, author of *The Chipwoman's Fortune;* Garland Anderson, author of *Appearances;* Wallace Thurman, coauthor of *Harlem;* and Eulalie Spence and Randolph Edmonds had their work performed. These were serious writers at a time when the musical theater was in vogue. Their work was followed into the nineteen thirties and forties by such plays as Langston Hughes's *Mulatto* and Hall Johnson's *Run, Little Children,* both seen on Broadway; and in Harlem there were works by J. Augustus Smith, Rudolph Fisher, George Norford, Abram Hill, William Ashley, and Ferdinand Voteur. Some of these plays were directed by Dick Campbell at the Rose McClendon Players Workshop. The American Negro Theatre later produced the plays of Abram Hill, Theodore Browne, and Owen Dodson, and it is said that veteran actor John Proctor practically wrote *Anna Lucasta* for the American Negro Theatre.

In the nineteen fifties there were numerous plays: William Branch's *A Medal for Willie* and *In Splendid Error;* Alice Childress' *Just a Little Simple, Gold Through the Trees,* and *Trouble in Mind;* Theodore Ward's *John Brown;* Louis Peterson's *Take a Giant Step;* Sidney Easton's *Miss Trudie Fair;* Sallie Howard's *The Jackal;* as well as plays by Virgil Richardson, Gertrude Jeanette, Oliver Pitcher, Harold Holifield, Julian Mayfield, Ossie Davis, and this writer.

Broadway saw Charles Sebree's *Mrs. Patterson.* Langston Hughes's hilarious *Simply Heavenly* was first seen off Broadway; then it moved to Broadway. In 1959 came Lorraine Hansberry's first play, *A Raisin in the Sun,* a smash hit that won the New York Drama Critics' Circle Award and set into motion a series of critiques that reverberate until the present. What Miss Hansberry wrote was an honest, moving, human drama, and she well deserved the acclaim accorded her. What she did not deserve was the many misinterpretations of her work. For example, some critics said openly that this play about a ghettoized black family was a "Negro *Cherry Orchard*" or a "Negro *Awake and Sing.*" Louis Peterson faced the same indignity when some critic wrote that his *Take a Giant Step* was a "Negro *Ah, Wilderness.*" Such categorizing is unique to the Black Aesthetic and the black experience. One can search volumes of criticism and never see such statements as Chekhov's *The Sea Gull* being a "Russian *Wild Duck*" or Maxwell Anderson's *Winterset* being an "American *Hamlet.*" There is, indeed, an attempt, conscious or unconscious or subconscious, to reduce the Black Aesthetic to an imitative level, to deny it its originality!

The success of Miss Hansberry's work brought waves of scripts allegedly dealing with the black experience, written, of course, by whites. Ironically, it was six years before Miss Hansberry had another play done on Broadway. This was *The Sign in Sidney Brustein's Window,* and she died of cancer during its run.

Miss Hansberry's work was monumental in terms of commitment, of "standing up and being counted." She was positive and unflinching, deadly serious, and, in the words of her colleague Alice Childress, "She did not wear the garments of this world loosely." Another colleague, Julian Mayfield, described her as ". . . a ball of fire, visiting places as though she had only one time to do so." It is almost simplistic to say—and, indeed, deserves an apology—that she created for a broad audience the reality of the black experience in the drama. I say this with apology, for, having known her, I know she would say, "So did many others before me."

Between and after *A Raisin in the Sun* and *The Sign in Sidney Brustein's Window,* there were other Negro-authored works that reached professional stages. Ossie Davis' *Purlie Victorious* romped onto the Broadway stage. *Ballad for Bimshire,* which I wrote with Irving Burgie (Lord Burgess), opened in the downtown area. There were also William Hairston's *A Walk in Darkness,* Langston Hughes's *Tambourines to Glory,* Adrienne Kennedy's *The Funny House of a Negro,* the James V. Hatch-C. Bernard Jackson musical *Fly, Blackbird,* and *Ballad of the Winter Soldier,* which I wrote with John Oliver Killens. The civil rights movement was in high gear by then, and

people were interested in what black people had to say—
or at least in what they *thought* black people had to say
if it conformed to what they *wanted* them to say.

By this time, however, white America was doing some trembling. Someone managed to get the message that the plays
black writers had been writing for many years had at their
very hearts the reality of the saying, "We don't want to get
integrated into a burning building." That did it! That spelled
rejection of white values and white people. And the last thing
the American white man can stand is *rejection*—especially by
his slave. What else, indeed, would make him think he is
a man unless he had a poor slave? The martini he has late
afternoon wears off by morning, but the slave—the slave should
be there.

He wasn't there, and the young crop of black writers let him
know why the slave wasn't there. LeRoi Jones ripped at his
values in *Dutchman* and held his precious white woman up
to be a sex-teaser, slanderer, and a false-faced murderer. Then
Jones turned around, in *The Toilet,* and told him his society
was a foul toilet, and in *The Slave* he told him he had a
slave system. James Baldwin stuck daggers farther into him
with *Blues for Mr. Charlie* and *The Amen Corner,* and he
began to wonder what was going on with these young black
writers that he had promoted. While he was wondering, Douglas
Turner Ward brought *Happy Ending* and *Day of Absence* to
the stage. Then there followed the works of Ron Milner, Ed
Bullins, Marvin X, Ben Caldwell, Paul Harrison, William Welling-
ton Mackey, Clifford Mason, Ted Shine, Larry Neal, Sarah
Fabio, Lonne Elder, and others. And I suspect that the American white man began to wonder: *"Who* is working here to
please *me?"*

The question, of course, arises as to whether or not the
black man has ever *really* worked here to please the white
man. The question remains as to whether or not tactics were
not involved in a country that *talks* democracy and practices
totalitarianism on every level. The question this projects is the

following: Has the black man given up on the subtlety he practiced during the minstrel period, the musical-comedy period, and the well-made-play period? Has he said: You folks don't understand art, so let's get out here and fight it out?

It is a tantalizing thought. I do not pretend that I have an answer to that, but my suspicion is that subtlety and innuendo will not be the tools of black theater writers for a long time to come. I have a hunch that in this era, when we see more and more encroachments on civil liberties, and attacks on the press and on political groups, we shall realize the warnings raised not only by the present crop of black writers but those of years gone by. In his marvelous play about Frederick Douglass and John Brown, *In Splendid Error,* playwright William Branch has Douglass speaking to one of his characters, Loguen:

"Then, tell me, Loguen, how long this night? How long this dark, dark night when no man walks in freedom, without fear in this cradle of democracy, no man who's black? How will it happen, what will we have to do? Nat Turner tried it with guns and he failed. Dred Scott went to the high courts, and they hurled him back into slavery. Old John said it must be by blood, and tonight he lies wounded in a Virginia prison. When will it end, Loguen—how long this night?"

Loguen answers slowly: "Douglass, this I believe as surely as God gives me breath to speak it: No man lives in safety so long as his brother is in fear. Once arouse consciousness of that and there will be those living and those dead, there will be guns and blood and the high courts, too. . . . But it will come. I may not be here to see it, Douglass, but it will come."

And Douglass says: "How often do I wonder?"

How often do I wonder when the Black Aesthetic is no longer dependent upon defensive action, no longer dependent upon working here to please "you." How often, indeed, do I wonder, for the freedom of that Black Aesthetic might send our art forms soaring into undreamed-of realms beyond the petty commercialism that makes a mockery of art. Indeed, I wonder:

How long this night?

BLACK THEATER—GO HOME!
Ronald Milner

If a new black theater is to be born, sustain itself and justify its own being, it must go home. Go home psychically, mentally, esthetically, and, I think, physically.

Now what does all that mean? First off, what do I, myself, mean by a new *black* theater? I mean the ritualized reflection and projection of a unique and particular way of being, born of the unique and particular conditioning of black people leasing time on this planet controlled by white-men; and having something to do with the breaking of that "leasing-syndrome." A theater emerging from artists who realize that, for black people of this world, and, specifically, this country, every quote "universal" human malady, dilemma, desire, or wonder, is, by the heat of the pressure of white-racism, compounded and enlarged, agitated and aggravated, accented and distilled to make that omni-suffusing, grinding sense of being we once called the blues but might now just term: *blackness*. From this peculiar and particular extra-dimension of being, of experiences, of conditioning, will come the kind of theater I'm looking for.

Out of the fact that something as "universal" as the inner-drive and desire for success takes on a different shade, another prick-point, when it is beneath a black skin; there are some strange bi-level goals, some other, further obstacle considerations involved. Out of the fact that even Love vibrates to these ultra-earthy subterranean accents. Love for family, for woman, for friend, for self, are all touched somehow, somewhere, by this infra-shadow. And it is from this deep shadow that will come this new theater I am seeing; come in many brilliant new forms of enlightenment, illumination.

It will be a theater having to do with love of one's self, and one's personal, national, and international family; with wariness and hatred of one's personal, national, and international enemies; with, ideally, points as to how to break their grip and splatter their power.

Now, let me stay right in here a minute. I want to make sure I get across at least some hint of all the levels I see here; try a couple more parables, examples, similies, or whatever. All-right? So, let's take the French Film, *Black Orpheus.* A sweet, bright, touching thing. (Just good to see a woman like that in full color). But to make it Afro-American Orpheus there would have to be some extending and deepening of dimensions. Understand me? A writer in the new black theater might want to make the Hell, the Death, the girl's going into the White-World, rejecting not only Orpheus but all other cats and things black. That would be the Hell. And Orpheus going to get her back with just courage and con and a song would really be something, wouldn't it? And how could he not look back at the past, at the promises of the Devil? Yeh, deep stuff. Tragic. And neither Shaw, O'Neill, nor any of those other great ones, could write it. Not within this level of blackness I'm talking about. I can almost feel some of you thinking: Racism, pure racism. Well, I don't know, now. All the universal implications, messages, of the tale are still there. What this imaginary writer has done is to put Hell up on Earth where it belongs; and say that it has something to do with rejecting And if there is racism in it, it only makes it more validly of your own people and images for other people and images.

this time and of this world: Your fire driving others' fires out of your brain.

Now that little adaptation points at just one level of what I'm visualizing. But there will be so many other levels coming simultaneously. Levels of love and joy and strength and courage. Like, how did bighearted, big-bellied George Jones, this elevator-operator, Pullman-porter, foundry-flunky, keep that deep clean laughter going?—Raise all those kids and keep that strong groovy woman swept all those years on it? How did he do it? How come everybody in the barbershop, poolroom, workhouse, and everywhere is glad to see him coming? Turning to him to warm their psychic and spiritual hands? How? Why? Who? What? Can't you see him, in a blue-light, sitting up on the side of the bed, plotting next week's bill-dodging and bill-paying, with all of them asleep, except maybe her lying there touching his back now and then, telling him to get some rest? But in the morning, with still no answers in sight, he's got the right glowing laugh of confidence to send those kids on out ready to run through those prejudice teachers and all that other crap—to look for something he never saw. Now how does he do that? He knows what's happening.

He's been through a thousand hunky overseers on a thousand poisonous jobs. He's had to dodge and stall the buzzards so long he can smell 'em a month away. Now—how? He's some huge, terrific soul stretching his low-ceilinged cage all out of shape—defeating it even while it kills him. A peculiar and particularly tragic-hero; made both tragic and heroic by his way with a particularly peculiar poisonous situation. Getting George Jones, and that deep resilient lady of his and their indigo moments, on stage, is being in another level of the new black theater. So many levels. All levels.

Because there is no personal style, or hang-up, or revelation, that can't be worked out within and through the stances and situations of black people; through the questions and answers in the Right-Now relevance frequency we must tune ourselves and our audiences into in order to nurture race, self, and art.

A writer coming this way won't lack in his work any of those universals everyone screams about—not if he has any in him; (if you look for 'em you'll find 'em even in the comic strips) but he will become involved in the projection of a certain uniqueness that is his hard-earned birthright.

Now, any of you who know about writing, or about speech-making, probably realized that that was the return of the bridge back there: that stanza ending in that riff of—race, self, art. That brings me back to where I started. Where I said that if this theater is to be it must—psychically, mentally, aesthetically, and I feel, even physically—go home. I'm sure you know now what I mean by going home psychically and mentally. But, just in case, let me try to run a short, quick summary. By *psychically,* I mean coming away from your dues-paying to all those "outside influences" and going into the real, black, YOU, by way of those places, people, and experiences which began and had the most to do with the shaping of what is now yourself—mean, making works, theater, out of that and, in doing it, extending and validating that particular psychic. By mentally, I mean understanding that you and the experiences of you are in time and history collective repetitions, have been repeated and multiplied many times; so, as artists, you are to try to find the terms, and the pictures, which will most simply clarify those experiences and that knowledge for the *you's* who do not, or could not, understand what is, or was, happening to you, and to future you's who will need to be warned and directed in terms from inside that level we call: *blackness*—for it is within that level that most of the added, making or breaking, weight comes.

Going home aesthetically will follow naturally after those first two steps—since your aesthetics come out of your mental and psychic environment. So I won't go into the demand for new dynamics, for a new intensity of language and form, that the material and the desired atmosphere will make on you; ex-

cept to say that the further you go home, the more startlingly
new and black the techniques become: Musicians are pointing
that out to us.

Now, going home physically with the new theater means
just that. Probably I should have started here. For this new
theater must be housed in, sustained and judged by, and be
a useable projection of, and to, a black community! The community itself will be the theater, and the black artist's house
of drama like a weirdly fixed and pointed looking-glass, a
light-prism casting warnings, directions, fruitful memories and
marvelous imaginings on the walls of the doomed, or soon
to be recreated, buildings. Right there in the community are
your materials, your situations and conflicts—relevant and powerful.

When you stand on those streets feeling the human whimper-
ing going on under the beast's muzzle, when the myriad poisons
are part of your natural everyday elements, the needs will
either come bursting out of your pens onto your stages, or
they'll drive you sick with your own faggot cowardice.

The need to displace and replace pale and dark villains
and heroes, ideas and concepts, images and symbols; the need
for defined and dramatized, hugely-drawn, clearly shown, walking and talking details as to how to organize community,
county, nation, world for a shattering attack against the most
voracious power-machine the world has ever known. Details!
Not stunning poetic generalities. Details! Details should be
moving around those stages in all kinds of explicit images;
huffing and puffing and working themselves out of the killing situations—or showing why they cannot! Pictures of who
and what was the past; how it was called and who answered,
and why it all went down. Who were those heroes the kids
have got to know of and believe in before they can believe
that you, or any other black man, has anything to tell them?
What were the betrayals? How does Judas look when he's
black? Detailed pictures of who and what is doing the killing
now. And how it—awesome as it might seem—can be maneu-

vered into deathtraps. All the while you're singing about that woman, that buddy, those personal art-promises you made to yourself. All and any of it placed right in the context in which you found it, and from which you can only free it through direct confrontation—that is, America's ball-cutting racist vise.

You've grabbed every piece of beauty, thought, insight and style you've ever achieved in your life while dodging that crap. And to put it out of your work before it is out of your life is making a lie of your art—which is nothing but your life (thoughts, feelings, seeings, imaginings, doings) sent out to others with an imposed re-order. You will never have a theater, an art, a life really representative of the soul-beats and desire-lines of you and your kind until you and your kind have come together and pooled desires, plans, resources and capabilities to throw off the jailers.

The people, the communities, are trapped in both unconscious suicide and subtle, dedicated genocide. You have a tool that might be able to help. What're you going to do? Go out on a bridge halfway between realities and blow to yourself? Or serenade the downtown people and catch the pennies they throw at your feet? I hope not.

Speaking of pennies—and we have to—there is also a definite practical, economical, reason for the new theater going physically to the black communities. That is that Broadway doesn't want your blackness, wasn't designed or intended for it; definitely doesn't want any strange new forms inspired by that very blackness. She is a contented fat white cow. If you can slip in and milk her for a minute—well, then, more blackpower to you brother. But, I'm telling you—it's a weird price she's asking: She wants you to be a singing hyena, dancing on the graves of yourself and everyone you know. (Serious things, dramas, are things that come from some other country, some other century, and even then are best set in a mad-house. And (quote) black-comedy has nothing to do with Afro-Americans!) Broadway cannot support you, brothers and sisters; it would be against *their* interests.

If you're thinking that Off-Broadway is a haven, think again. It is, finally, as a perfect example of what America would have its artists involved in: a zoo, with a carnival, where the animals and the freaks play delightfully, curiously, shockingly, with lights, colors, words, forms, gestures, always with some ingrown aspect of themselves, never with anything in the outerworld should any relevance be uttered or implied it is usually done so with the utmost obscurity. Now and again, I have to admit, something disturbs that tranquil scene down there, something real and relevant—related to other peoples lives—seeps in; then everyone does a double-take and goes back wondering if maybe something could really be starting down there after all. But it's usually just something or someone healthy getting ready to break-out of there; nothing to be alarmed about; won't happen often. To round off my thinking on Off-Broadway, I tell you that art for art's sake is: incest! And the offsprings of that are usually strange and feeble.

We, black people, desperately need a healthy natural artform: art coming from an intercourse with life! Our lives! As we have, and must, live them. In order for our art, theater, to provide this for us, it must become an organic, functioning part of our communities. As black artists we must go home in every way; go wherever it is we most feel indigenous and organic and, therefore, a natural observer and commentor. It is there that our talents must pay dues and spend dividends. The communities, the people, can sustain, assist, and inspire us to essential and brilliant levels in our new black theater, our new visions. But only if we assist and inspire them to the same levels in the new black theater of their living, to new visions of their lives.

Ronald Milner, author of the article, "Black Theater—Go Home!", is author-in-residence at Lincoln University (Pennsylvania). His full-length play, *Who's Got His Own*, was produced at the New Lafayette Theatre in Harlem last fall. The play had been performed earlier at the American Place Theatre in New York.

ON BLACK THEATER
Clayton Riley

I. *Random Nigger Notes (Category D for Deception)*

Insignificant crimes are carried out in the realm, in America—are the denial of truth and reality for purposes no sane people would fail to recognize. Cultural lawbreakers, liars, and thieves must be called by their rightful names whether or not dressed in Balenciaga originals, fakes by Cardin and others, drifting as merchants and purchasers of death in Broadway graveyards, cemeteries called the LinCON SSSSSentah. (Make them memory, these freak palaces; let them burn.)

Wish them a shambles, smoldering wrecks, even for the Black prides of the missionary ethic; hope such places pass away quickly.

In such arenas, final resting place for those foolish enough to practice or take seriously the distortion called Christianity, Blacks, too, have longed to be welcome. Which is simply to reconstruct ambition by Blacks in all other places, where definition and acceptance demand whites sit patiently as juries —their confusions hanging out, glazed eyes wishing to be anywhere else.

These niggers, pretending to understand Shakespeare and

Kentucky Williams, or whatever his name really is. History as
a blind guide, spooks wandering in the general direction of
someone else's muse, seeking, out of experiences designed precisely to murder them, some measured states of grace. Yeah.
Refined colored people imagining the limitless value of playing
King Lear in their old age, Hamlet in their nearly endless
BOYhood. Or constructing for themselves an image reflecting
the cracked mirror of an oppressor, aping his contempt for
those who look exactly like these mimics, these copycoons.

As with the eightieth annual production of *The Glass Menag-
erie* at the Harlem Y—or Blood versions of *Fiddler on the Roof.*
Insignificant crimes, you say? Second-rate shoplifting—no need
to press charges. Let them be; assure their lives. And look
elsewhere for grand larceny, first-degree murder.

Somewhere around '63, bands of crazed field hands slip into
silver cities, sleepy golden villages, stoned on a new communion
wine, covered by the night and their own sense of darkness.
Thieves. Outlaws. The only heroes a thoroughly corrupt society
(America owns the patent) can logically produce. Bandits.
Ready to define the culture for the honest listener. As Bird
attempted, as Lady Day failed at trying; as with Coltrane,
Max Roach, others who bore genius into the wreckage of the
life offered them (Miles, in a strange way, breaking the pattern.)

Calling themselves playwrights, BLACK actors, throwing some
new shit in the fan. From this point in time we can measure,
beyond any terminology fashioned by anyone else but ourselves,
past any previous measures for success or failure, a fresh design
for artistic living.

Trail-blazing given a new meaning, frontier land-grabbing
offered a new shape. And were there no losers, nobody running
a game on the territorial inhabitants? Oh, yes. Some of them,
too. Without talent or honor. Black Frankensteins, as well. Rub-
bing everybody the wrong way, and teaching nothing. Far more
important, however, is the fact, the reality of emerging forces
and artistic personalities who have shaped what is today a black

theater whose strength resides primarily in the fact that it need not be compared to any other. What is more, it needs no borrowed standard of excellence or worth to be sustained. Its quarrels and loves are distinguished by a vitality that the general run of American theater does not possess and, in all likelihood, has not witnessed in the past.

Black theater, as opposed to the theater of Negro participation, has the distinct advantage of being responsible for its own mistakes and triumphs, has a unique degree of perceptive possibility and potential based on the fact of being peopled by a membership grown to adulthood with a clarity about America—Black and white—developed on the one hand by an exclusion resulting in a forced awareness, and by a self-awareness proceeding from a pride in knowing intimately of survival and endurance.

It is often an unsubtle, relentlessly candid theater, brutalized and brutalizing in the candor displayed, unsettling in the way it exposes truths long submerged and disquieting information we have deliberately closeted away. When functioning at maximum, black theater self-regulates with the rhythm of the lives responsible for its being, charges and recharges with a beat even those of us who can't really dance (but fake up a storm) dig for the recollections inspired, the yesterdays rediscovered and explained.

Black theater, if it served no other purpose, would prove invaluable for the steps it already has taken to legitimize for the illegitimate all phases and facets of their lives; in the most definitively humanist terms, it has stated with an arresting immediacy the essential worth of lives called valueless by those who have no right whatsoever to establish standards for anything but the technology of destruction. Black theater has, as perhaps nothing else but Black music has, worked to show Black people what they look like, and how much it is possible to love themselves for being what they are, for looking as they do. Black literature, whatever victories it has sought and/or won, has not really managed to accomplish this. Film, as yet, has not had the time to do so. These forms, in addition, have not developed their own language and rhythm, as has the Black theater. (Not in terms serviceable to the nation's Blood, certainly.)

The "legitimacy" I speak of can be seen in Black poetry, too, particularly in the spoken form, which is, by definition, a specialized rendering of a new (for this country) channel of theatrical expression.

That "legitimacy" implies, as well, an essential and previously unexplored region of blackness—determinedly pursuing what "self" can mean when we want to know. We are the descendants of people whose survival of this masked and often well-disguised asylum, this camouflaged dungeon, makes them, by standards we ourselves must propose and maintain, the most complete and enviable examples of contemporary heroism. In recognizing and, indeed, glorifying our existence, we do honor to those who produced us.

II. Artists and Outlaws

When LeRoi Jones presented to the world a one-act play called *Dutchman,* he struck a discordant note on an abandoned gong, a note residing within the chambers holding all our music, all our melodic frames of reference. The play introduced a vision of what had always been (within) and what would now stretch and exercise itself beyond all former artistic limitations. For the middle sixties, *Dutchman's* language was a shocking display—the most bluntly communicative and blackest outpouring of a vibrant heart. It was a language steeped in the purest traditionalism of America's original bandit population— nigger words, a crackling brush fire of secret native intelligence and total description. It stabbed America in every private place and part, quickly, with the urgent force of total commitment to such truths as the nation surely knew but hoped never to make public.

Clay, a middle-class suburban Negro youth, suffers an en-

counter with a white female representative of the country's
continually denied but genuinely truthful level of sanity, and
plays games with her on a subway train. Word games. A proces-
sion of documented examples of his precisely formulated training as well-spoken, well-mannered issue of a colonized tribal
group. From his dress to his speech, Clay is all America could
want to claim as a product of its emasculating social machinery.
He is, perhaps more than all those unemployed gas-station at-
tendants who double as the ruling class's assassin corps in
Mississippi, the being who makes the system work. He wants
no trouble, will sacrifice self-respect in small but lifelong doses
toward that end, and in his carefully developed and thoroughly
contrived sense of himself as charming and debonair, we bear
witness to the nation's force of arms in shaping life among its
house-servant class.

Jones wrote, in the introductory portion, of Clay's appearance
—a character who possessed both the ability to be painfully
recognizable to blacks who observed him, and one who was
completely believable and welcome to the consciousness of all
whites who watched his life unfold in perfectly understandable,
pleasing blandness before them.

Here was a colored fellow who didn't (quite obviously) carry
a knife—not surely in the classically flat pockets of an Ivy
League suit. Certainly, then, he could be beaten in a "fair"
fight, if it came to that, if things got out of hand, as they seem
always to do with even the best of "these people."

Moreover, he was reading a book—always an excellent sign;
can't be plotting much, with his nose in some approved reading
material. Wears glasses, too; a sign, perhaps, that he's not too
fit physically, not outstanding in the sheets, hopefully.

And he bears the girl's eventual insults quite well. Good, good.

LULA. What've you got that jacket and tie on in all this heat
for? And why're you wearing a jacket and tie like that? Did
your people ever burn witches or start revolutions over the price
of tea? Boy, those narrow-shoulder clothes come from a tra-

dition you ought to feel oppressed by. A three-button suit. What right do you have to be wearing a three-button suit and striped tie? Your grandfather was a slave; he didn't go to to Harvard.

. . . come on, Clay. . . . let's do the thing. . . . Clay! Clay! You middle-class black bastard. Forget you social-working mother for a few seconds and let's knock stomachs. Clay, you liver-lipped white man. You would-be Christian. You ain't no nigger, you're just a dirty white man. . . .

. . . That's all you know . . . shaking that wildroot cream-oil on you knotty head . . . so full of white man's words.

Yet the Clay we assign to the worst dreams we have, gets it all together. Brings things down front. Works his show.

CLAY. . . . you just shut the hell up . . . just shut up. You don't know anything. So just keep you stupid mouth closed.

Shit, you don't have any sense, Lula, nor feelings either. I could murder you now. Such a tiny ugly throat. I could squeeze it flat, and watch you turn blue, on a humble. For dull kicks. And all these weak-faced ofays squatting around here, staring over their papers at me. Murder them too. Even if they expected it. That man there. . . . I could rip that *Times* right out of his hand, as skinny and middle-classed as I am, I could rip that paper out of his hand and just as easily rip out his throat. It takes no great effort. For what? To kill you soft idiots? You don't understand anything but luxury.

. . . let me be who I feel like being. Uncle Tom. Thomas. Whoever. It's none of your business. You don't know anything except what's there for you to see. An act. Lies. Device. Not the pure heart, the pumping black heart. You don't ever know that. And I sit here, in this buttoned-up suit, to keep myself from cutting all you throats.

You great liberated whore! You fuck some black man and right away you're an expert on black people. What a lotta shit that is. The only thing you know is that you come if he bangs you hard enough. And that's all!

Spiels for days, and for the cotton-chopping spirit in every one of us. (Even Uncle Roy of the EN-DOUBLE HEY! has indicated, in recent times, his ability to "get an attitude.")

In the play's final stanza, Lula stabs Clay to death, and fixes her make-up in anticipation of another victim, who shortly appears and sits down near her.

Clay's death, on the heels of his explosive "great gettin' up" insured the play's success insofar as white audiences were concerned (dying is an act consistently present in Jones's work), who overlooked—as was correct and necessary for them to do—the rambling code messages throughout the piece, messages only Blood could really understand. (Jones's intention, one must assume.)

Listen:

Old bald-headed ofays popping their fingers . . . and don't know yet what they're doing. They say, "I love Bessie Smith." And don't even understand that Bessie Smith is saying, "Kiss my ass, kiss my black unruly ass." Before love, suffering, desire, anything you can explain, she's saying, and very plainly, "Kiss my black ass." And if you don't know that, it's you that doing the kissing.

All the hip white boys scream for Bird. . . . they sit there talking about the tortured genius of Charlie Parker. Bird would've played not a note of music if he just walked up to East Sixty-seventh Street and killed the first ten white people he saw.

. . . if Bessie Smith had killed some white people she wouldn't have need that music. She could have talked very straight and plain about the world.

Now who understands all this, whom is this intended for?

My people's madness. Hah! That's a laugh. My people. They don't need me to claim them. They got legs and arms of their own. Personal insanities. Mirrors. They don't need all those words. They don't need any defense. . . . tell this to your father, who's probably the kind of man who needs to know at once. So he can plan ahead. Tell him not to preach so much rationalism and cold logic to these niggers. Let them alone. Let them sing curses at you in code and see your filth as simple lack—lack of style. Don't make the mistake, through some irresponsible surge of Christian charity, of talking too much about the advantages of Western rationalism, or the great intellectual legacy of the white man, or maybe they'll begin to listen. And then, maybe one day, you'll find they actually do understand exactly what you are talking about, all these fantasy people. All these blues people. And on that day, as sure as shit, when you really believe you can "accept them into your fold, as half-white trusties late of the subject peoples . . . with no more blues except the very old ones, and not a watermelon in sight, the great missionary heart will have triumphed, and all of those ex-coons will be stand-up Western men, with eyes for clean hard useful lives, sober pious and sane, and they'll murder you. They'll murder you, and have very rational explanations. Very much like your own. They'll cut you throats and drag you out to the edge of your cities so the flesh can fall away from your bones, in sanitary isolation.

Jones brought to the theater a remarkable, stunning poetry, Black sensibilities defined beyond the traditionally acceptable American caldron. Prior to *Dutchman,* even the most iconoclastic white playwrights did not dare to utilize language as Jones did —could not dare, in fact—and no one had every presented a more concise and devastating view of what America is as opposed to what it pretends to be. The play was written to run approximately thirty-five minutes. In that time, in the characters of Clay and Lula, there is an offering of precision-tooled master craftmanship revealing all we could want to know of one facet of Black life in an encounter with a portion of the national state of mind.

So powerful is the work that no production of it seems able to completely capture and relate all the symbols within, not any production of it that I've seen or played in, that is. A difficult work, because it demands so much, because it speaks in shifting terminologies—codes, to be sure—some of which are more clarified by reading than by presentation. The complexities implicit for the actor preparing to work as Clay begin with the difficulty of playing (as nearly all actors dislike doing) an essentially unglamorous, certainly near-Tom, role for a good deal of the short one-acter. The monologue—the explosion near the end is relatively easy to play—plays itself to some extent, but the beginning, that sheepish, head-in-a-book beginning, is a *number*. One measure of Jones's genius is this duality, intricately structured and realized in the writing of an extremely brief piece. In Lula, one confronts even more complexity. Jones's text gives a perceptive actress the opportunity to render seemingly idle chatter into a primer on the nation's peculiar forms of "sanity."

In another of his works, *The Toilet*, Jones pulled off the incredible feat of bringing the world into the lavatory of a public school (or, perhaps, vice-versa) and making the words and activities there blaze with universal truths. Here, with outrageously blunt, razor-sharp delineation, a group of Black youths (and one non-black one) peel away the lies that protect America from what has been done to them; the resulting exposure brings into focus the frailties and the strengths proceeding from lives shaped by an oppressive regime. Once again, in this play, Jones displayed his brilliant facility with the language and rhythm implicit in the life-style he explored. No one, with the possible exception of Ed Bullins, deals with the sound of black life with more-formidable powers of persuasion. Even as Jones's design and purpose regarding his work have changed—or been redirected by him—the weight of his words and the soundness of his dramatic structure have traveled well with him to new stations. In his recent *Great Goodness of Life*, he has examined the crippling effects of the black civil-service mentality with a scalpel that somehow manages to penetrate with a retained measure of love for the legions of black men (of whom my father is one) who found in the Post Office some way to save both their lives and their beliefs, at a cost too dear for calculation. Court Royal, the protagonist, settles for all time any ques-

tions about the damage done and the price paid, when he
responds to an inquiry investigating whether or not he has
been harboring a criminal: "Of course I'm not guilty. I work in
the Post Office. . . . you must have the wrong man, I work in
the Post Office. . . . I've done nothing wrong, *I work in the
Post Office.* . . ."

The criminal is, finally, Court Royal's son—who is, in turn,
all the sons of all those men who went off on all those terrible
mornings, mumbling to themselves—"Badge, keys, do I have
everything?"—and left so many of us wonder if the Post Office
was indeed the only safe haven in the world.

Great Goodness was, as is most of Jones's work, a magnificent
example of an artist's ability to communicate in a manner
meant to force one to confront personal levels of awareness.
His work is relentlessly Black because it is concerned with a
response by Blacks, demands *their* attention, *their* recognition.
White audiences abandoned Jones when they discovered that
his primary concerns were not with them. Blacks moved toward
his art for precisely the same reason; what whites were not
into—so far as Jones was concerned—could turn Blood on for
having had their lives serve both as a source of inspiration and
congregation of review. In turning the theater onto new streets—
Black streets—Jones legitimized for many others the notion that
a play could be validated by the reaction of Black people
to it. He revamped a process in which the Black dramatist
needed a white decision on his work *before* anything Blacks
said about it had any relevance whatever.

The Black Arts Theater, which Jones was instrumental in
starting in Harlem, was of pivotal importance to the current
movement in Black drama. Although internal dissension ultimately brought the project to an end (with considerable assistance from outside sources in the local and federal governments),
the reality of a viable Black creative arena was furthered
by the fact of its existence. What Jones had begun with his
own work—in terms of an artistic and cultural forum distinctly
oriented to community interests—developed into a notably larger

and more ambitious experience for Black writers, particularly playwrights. For Jones's success, even that part of it growing out of the masochistic homage paid him (and subsequently withdrawn) by white liberal dilettantes, did much to create an atmosphere and a confidence conducive to the emergence of other artists. The difficulties he experienced during a period when his talents delighted downtown New York audiences, seemed to have an effect of producing a body of work by new Black writers who came to regard the stage as a proper, if not always easily handled, proscenium from which all ranges and levels of defiance could be mounted.

Such as Ed Bullins. And Ron Milner. Giants of a particular movement. Recognizing life in Black America as an experience without genuinely valuable creative documentation brings the work of Bullins and Milner toward us with an attending and awesome significance. Both writers have dealt with basic Black folks, the people in the phrase ALL POWER TO, those souls whose existence in this country touches all, I say all, bases in the ball game, who know of life from a continuing physical confrontation with it—no quarter ever given, no point missed in the range of things: pain, joy, anguish, terror, love—all these; the survivors, a collective will to continue in spite of, by all means, with any tools, having defined morality, sophistication, courage, as attributes as well determined (if not better) by the curriculum fashioned in the street as by any other.

Ed Bullins, with a one-act drama called *Clara's Old Man,* made terror and menace over into beauty: a South Philly kitchen as a purgatorial chamber, splendid and profane cathedral—worshippers without prayer, concocting evil ceremonies, riding off on the wine of their own communion. Here was Bullins as a new force. In that kitchen a tableau, a wandering ritual, as Clara, a young and attractive sister, brings home for a visit an innocent, Jack, who just doesn't know, even when faced with jeopardy, even when looking at Big Girl, Clara's "old man," just cannot see until the hard ones from the block, the neighborhood death merchants—teen street-hustlers—till they come and bring the revelation and the end. *Clara's Old Man* as a mystery with no detective, as a suspenseful episode filled with vibrating danger signs, remains a work of constant and consummate elegance. Style. A gloomy luster is attached to it throughout, the sort of fascination provoked by criminal personalities in mohair, in alligators, in real and thorough darkness. Bullins revealed here—and has continued to reveal—a nearly unparalleled ability to take lives he knows as he finds them, to stick with them and not shrink from whatever horror they may contain, thus creating in the "worst" folks a belief in themselves as legitimate human beings whose only credential for being worthy of acknowledgement and respect is that they live. They live, and more completely than most, with greater risks and less hope. Their lives are maintained precariously, yet are sturdy and vital; the fullest measure of the beauty and profound nature of what they are resides, we know, in the realization that all Christian virtue and righteousness would cease to be, were it not for the pimp and the whore, the thief and the junkie—all the criminal saints whose blasphemous acts allow others to see themselves as practicers of goodness, citizens of good will and charity, all because their crimes are carried out in secret and bear no public scrutiny.

Bullins, with *Goin' a Buffalo* and *In the Wine Time*, took us part way to the life, brought the rest to us. Both these plays took a long, unhurried look at the world of blacks forgotten, or deliberately ignored, or both—back-yard South Philly once again, (*Wine Time*) and hustlers in Los Angeles (*Buffalo*). The look was hard, straight. There was retained from his earlier piece a unique ability to design a dramatic situation that didn't need to depend simply on dialogue for the tense, sometimes quiet, always boiling, human encounters in his work. Again, all about Black. With no apologies. With a front calculated to get him into trouble with white people who look for reflections in his work and don't see the ones they remember from lily ponds in the country and the long ago.

Bullins was profoundly influenced and greatly encouraged

by the work of LeRoi Jones, and has, as is natural, moved even further into drama than his predecessor. He (Bullins) is as prolific a playwright as lives among us today, who writes long as well as short, with equal facility. The only poor example of his work I can recall is *The Gentleman Caller*, which was a lazy effort he filled with masked and painted ritual figures struggling amid the nation's mad living room, a play unlike his previously *acknowledged* ones in its obviously derivative quality, a kind of forced symbolism popular among self-styled avant-gardists.

The power of Bullins' work lies—*Goin' a Buffalo* is, I feel, the best example—in his bringing, indeed elevating, apparently ruined lives (in this instance, a nomadic band of lifers and their pimps), toward a profanely beautiful state of grace without romanticizing them. His use of language is expansive and brutal; he spares an audience (or himself) nothing in this respect. And by exploring the lives of his "fallen" heroines and heroes so thoroughly, he carves through every cliché and presumption about those who lead lives that many of us know only through our dreams and speculations.

Completing the triumvirate of playwrights having the greatest impact to date on the black theater, is Ron Milner. While the body of his presented work is small, his gifts and his perceptions are exceptionally large—vast, let us say. In speaking of him, we may refer only to *Who's Got His Own,* a big, sprawling family drama, and *The Warning: A Theme for Linda,* a shorter, sprawling family drama. Milner's forte and primary concern is the black family, more particularly the black family with recognizable southern roots—blues, the Baptist rhythm in living, the societal and imposed dislocations—existing, often badly, in a large city. Detroit, although specific mention of that Midwest city is seldom pushed, seems to be the place for Milner. He deals relentless hands of woe in these works, first with the Bronson family—mother, son, daughter—in the aftermath of the death of a husband and father who, in life, had been that incredibly complex, frustrated black personality James Baldwin

has detailed when he speaks of men putting their lives in a
fire every day of their lives. So it was, unquestionably, with
Tim Bronson. Milner made the man live, even though in his
casket (and, in some productions, the casket is on stage) when
the play begins. Rarely has a dead man spoken so eloquently
of his life, or had its intricate design articulated for him within
the context of a play. Through his son and daughter, whose
hatred and fear of their father has nearly squeezed their own
lives dry, we see the raging giant roaring around his home,
violently assaulting his children and woman in both word and
deed, and going off to work in the factory where he cleans
toilets for a living. His son, as a young boy, had seen the
father who struck such notes of terror in his own house, mocked
as a lackey by the whites on his job. "When," they asked of
Bronson, Sr., "when are you going to bring your boy around
and teach him your trade?"

A son cannot feel much more hate for a father than would
be induced by such a moment, could not endure much more
shame. Milner brought us all home who had, for this or other
imprecise reasons, discovered our own fathers at some unbearable juncture, some destroyed or destroying instant. And Milner
went further, opened the family's closets and its wounds, a
daughter whose disastrous affair with a white college student
had resulted in a near-fatal abortion and a subsequent relationship with an unusually affectionate woman, and a mother who
could only counsel her children against blaming their father for
too much, for seeing in the past all the possibility for claiming
vengeance on the future. "You can't," says the mother, "lay in
ambush for yesterday. . . . it's gone, ain't never coming back."

In a somewhat different way, *The Warning* found fruit on
the same plain, with a family essentially composed of women—
grandmother, mother, and daughter. This was another instance
of a work abounding with riches in the dialogue and the developing characters. The work came dangerously close to being
anti-male (more to the point, anti-Black man), which, I now
think, is often the result of careless playing by the actors, and

a failure to explore the very subtle texture of Milner's writing. A mixture of symbolic and naturalistic references revealed in Milner's work an especially well-developed dual sense of drama and black music—musical *BLACKNESS* as a sturdy vehicle for conveying a vision of our lives.

Vision. This, perhaps more than any other single quality, sets Jones, Bullins, and Milner apart from others in the Black theater movement. What they see is not simply a photographic view of the terrain, is not only an artistic duplication of the facts contained in the *LIFE;* the witness they bear leads them to elaborate on the quality of blackness in this country in a way that avoids the clinical approaches traditionally associated with such efforts. Moreover, they all serve a new artistic purpose, new for the reason that each has either begun at or moved to the point of designing art best judged by black audiences, while not necessarily excluding white ones. Jones has managed to speak to the black middle class (a misnomer if ever there was one, for being applied to a group of people who constitute no *class*, but simply a cracked reflection of the worst attributes of white America) in a way no writer has ever managed to do. He has managed this, particularly in *Dutchman* and *Great Goodness of Life,* by exposing the reality of the falsehoods implicit in an existence structured to accommodate evil and glorify inaction.

Bullins, by contrast, concentrates his sphere of concern upon the so-called criminal element in Black America, the outlaws whose life-style and maintenance of confrontations with the terms of their existence make them the only true frontier personalities and thoroughly honest people in the nation. (Genet succeeds in like fashion to convince white people that more than a little of their language, style, and social dispositions emanate from the outlaw sensibility: thieves offer romantic notions about courage, as do killers; homosexuals define the limits of tragedy and a hopeless form of bravery.)

Bullins also has been able to deal with ordinary Black people, street people, with an interest proceeding from genuine regard, as opposed to the flabby emotions connoted by sociological jargon—compassion, understanding, etc.

Through Milner, the Movement in Black Art has come to recognize and turn toward, instead of away from, the central ingredients that shaped so many Black personalities. The family as a Black crucible where so much was formed—and perhaps deformed as well—becomes a phenomenon from which new strengths can be derived. Milner is responsible for many of the heads sent drooping by the Moynihan Report rising up to look with clearer eyes at where they, not the social "scientists," have come from.

What others? Who else?

A number of playwrights have had productions of their work offered in the growing community of Black theater artists across the country. In New York, Ben Caldwell's short one-acter *The First Militant Minister*, which appeared as part of the off-Broadway production called *A Black Quartet*, was a notable work, well crafted and hilariously funny within the context of a specific message. In it, a burglar is surprised into playing the voice of God when a minister returns home during a heist. As a satirical departure, it was a brief, grand tour de force.

III. Where Else Are We Comin' From?

Black is, of course, more than theater. Or should be. One real situation developing—recently developed—is a belief on the part of many new participants in the struggle that plays can rise above the fact of being essentially limited things, incomplete things, designed to be encountered, and enjoyed, and learned from, and elevating, but more than anything else, constructed to take a less than primary place on the priority scale. Theater will play a role, if it is Black enough, in shaping the consciousness of black people, but at a level existing *this* side of activist considerations: nobody's gonna see a play and go into the streets to destroy the Guggenheim Museum (and it *needs* to fall), because theater cannot deal with reality that specifically. Black theater as a clarion (. . . "an' I'll hear the trumpet sound in the mornin' . . .") is no more than a continuing instigation, a provocation, an agitator—the playground signifier (you remember him) standing on the sidelines talking shit and getting people fucked up. Can you dig it? Recognizing theater for what it really is, an artifact, structured to take people away from basics, from fundamentals, into a special kind of chapel atmosphere for rituals and other procedures. Which is cool. As long as we remember where we're coming from. What we can do with that particular aspect of our lives. Great Black theater, like any other kind, can, and quite probably will, leave in its wake the same rotting tenements, the same killers of our dream, all the pain and loss we endure now. *Awareness* —pointing a finger at the scene for what it really is—ain't hardly enough.

Black theater is a theater of warfare. What if the battle is won? What do we do with an art form we have come to revere beyond the framework in which it remains usable? We must assign to theater a realistic place in a sector of our lives, recognizing what it can and cannot accomplish. (Seventh, maybe, on a scale of ten for living programs.) The vitality growing among black playwrights, actors (or Liberators, as they are called in Barbara Ann Teer's National Black Theater), directors, technicians, should not permit anyone the luxury of drifting away from the harsh and unrelenting immediacy present in the lives around us, lives on the sidewalk instead of in the third row.

One need only to read of the recent past in Negro theater—read the patronizing nonsense of Doris E. Abramson in her book *Negro Playwrights in the American Theater 1925–1959*, a book absurdly defective in its assumptions, and steeped in a plantation-oriented, thinly veiled contempt for plays and playwrights who could not live up to the standards she regards as the only important ones—those previously established by white artists. Thus, Doris Abramson can declare, as Scarlett O'Hara in *Gone With the Wind*, might have: "Louis Peterson's *Take a Giant*

Step . . . is a Negro *Ah, Wilderness!,* and Lorraine Hansberry's *A Raisin in the Sun,* a Negro *Awake and Sing!*" This, because Doris Abramson *has* no standard—no *life*—that is not controlled by norms established in the most racist terms, the most relentlessly *white* terms. As the book indicates, she deals in the past, when everything *colored* was an imitation dependent on the good graces of enlightened whites for an existence—let alone a life. She deals there, and still lives there.

We learn, then, from this. Black theater can both recognize itself in rational and realistic terms, and avoid the mistake of allowing those whose sensibilities and concerns have been shaped in other places, by other considerations, to formulate a system of critical judgment regarding Black works.

To the extent that a Doris Abramson will never be able to say that an Ed Bullins play is a Neal Simon comedy (although Ed should have Simon's money), or a Ron Milner observation of the family is consistent with those by Arthur Miller—to that extent will a Black theater exist, exist with sensible review and analysis. Exist and give us valuable new insights on both where we were and where we will be.

I wrote earlier of the Black theater's advantage of having the responsibilities for both mistakes and triumphs assigned solely to those participating in it. That advantage must be cultivated and maintained with self-generating standards, unflinching critical evaluations, and, finally, the ability to recognize the time and the possibility of stages—as we now use them—vanishing, passing away, into an oblivion brought on by more-genuine revolutions than theater can contain.

Teach—while you can. Do—when you must.

V Fiction

INTRODUCTION: BLUEPRINT FOR NEGRO WRITING
Richard Wright

1) The Role of Negro Writing: Two Definitions

Generally speaking, Negro writing in the past has been confined to humble novels, poems, and plays, prim and decorous ambassadors who went a-begging to white America. They entered the Court of American Public Opinion dressed in the knee-pants of servility, curtsying to show that the Negro was not inferior, that he was human, and that he had a life comparable to that of other people. For the most part these artistic ambassadors were received as though they were French poodles who do clever tricks.

White America never offered these Negro writers any serious criticism. The mere fact that a Negro could write was astonishing. Nor was there any deep concern on the part of white America with the role Negro writing should play in American culture; and the role it did play grew out of accident rather than intent or design. Either it crept in through the kitchen in the form of jokes; or it was the fruits of that foul soil which was the result of a liaison between inferiority-complexed Negro "geniuses" and burnt-out white Bohemians with money.

On the other hand, these often technically brilliant performances by Negro writers were looked upon by the majority of literate Negroes as something to be proud of. At best, Negro writing has been something external to the lives of educated Negroes themselves. That the productions of their writers should have been something of a guide in their daily living is a matter which seems never to have been raised seriously.

Under these conditions Negro writing assumed two general aspects: 1) It became a sort of conspicuous ornamentation, the hallmark of "achievement." 2) It became the voice of the educated Negro pleading with white America for justice.

Rarely was the best of this writing addressed to the Negro himself, his needs, his sufferings, his aspirations. Through misdirection, Negro writers have been far better to others than they have been to themselves. And the mere recognition of this places the whole question of Negro writing in a new light and raises a doubt as to the validity of its present direction.

2) *The Minority Outlook*

Somewhere in his writings Lenin makes the observation that oppressed minorities often reflect the techniques of the bourgeoisie more brilliantly than some sections of the bourgeoisie themselves. The psychological importance of this becomes meaningful when it is recalled that oppressed minorities, and especially the petty bourgeois sections of oppressed minorities, strive to assimilate the virtues of the bourgeoisie in the assumption that by doing so they can lift themselves into a higher social sphere. But not only among the oppressed petty bourgeoisie does this occur. The workers of a minority people, chafing under exploitation, forge organizational forms of struggle to better their lot. Lacking the handicaps of false ambition and property, they have access to a wide social vision and a deep social consciousness. They display a greater freedom and initiative in pushing their claims upon civilization than even do the petty bourgeoisie. Their organizations show greater strength, adaptability, and efficiency than any other group or class in society.

That Negro workers, propelled by the harsh conditions of their lives, have demonstrated this consciousness and mobility for economic and political action there can be no doubt. But has this consciousness been reflected in the work of Negro writers to the same degree as it has in the Negro workers' struggle to free Herndon and the Scottsboro Boys, in the drive toward unionism, in the fight against lynching? Have they as creative writers taken advantage of their unique minority position?

The answer decidedly is *no*. Negro writers have lagged sadly, and as time passes the gap widens between them and their people.

How can this hiatus be bridged? How can the enervating effects of this longstanding split be eliminated?

In presenting questions of this sort an attitude of self-consciousness and self-criticism is far more likely to be a fruitful point of departure than a mere recounting of past achievements. An emphasis upon tendency and experiment, a view of society as something becoming rather than as something fixed and admired is the one which points the way for Negro writers to stand shoulder to shoulder with Negro workers in mood and outlook.

3) *A Whole Culture*

There is, however, a culture of the Negro which is his and has been addressed to him; a culture which has, for good or ill, helped to clarify his consciousness and create emotional attitudes which are conducive to action. This culture has stemmed mainly from two sources: 1) the Negro church; and 2) the folklore of the Negro people.

It was through the portals of the church that the American Negro first entered the shrine of western culture. Living under slave conditions of life, bereft of his African heritage, the Negroes' struggle for religion on the plantations between 1820–60 assumed the form of a struggle for human rights. It re-

mained a relatively revolutionary struggle until religion began
to serve as an antidote for suffering and denial. But even today
there are millions of American Negroes whose only sense of a
whole universe, whose only relation to society and man, and
whose only guide to personal dignity comes through the archaic
morphology of Christian salvation.

It was, however, in a folklore moulded out of rigorous and in-
human conditions of life that the Negro achieved his most
indigenous and complete expression. Blues, spirituals, and folk
tales recounted from mouth to mouth; the whispered words of
a black mother to her black daughter on the ways of men, to
confidential wisdom of a black father to his black son; the swap-
ping of sex experiences on street corners from boy to boy in the
deepest vernacular; work songs sung under blazing suns—all these
formed the channels through which the racial wisdom flowed.

One would have thought that Negro writers in the last century
of striving at expression would have continued and deepened
this folk tradition, would have tried to create a more intimate and yet a more profoundly social system of artistic communication between them and their people. But the illusion
that they could escape through individual achievement the
harsh lot of their race swung Negro writers away from any
such path. Two separate cultures sprang up: one for the
Negro masses, unwritten and unrecognized; and the other for
the sons and daughters of a rising Negro bourgeoisie, parasitic
and mannered.

Today the question is: Shall Negro writing be for the Negro
masses, moulding the lives and consciousness of those masses
toward new goals, or shall it continue begging the question of
the Negroes' humanity?

4) The Problem of Nationalism in Negro Writing

In stressing the difference between the role Negro writing
failed to play in the lives of the Negro people, and the role
it should play in the future if it is to serve its historic function;

in pointing out the fact that Negro writing has been addressed in the main to a small white audience rather than to a Negro one, it should be stated that no attempt is being made here to propagate a specious and blatant nationalism. Yet the nationalist character of the Negro people is unmistakable. Psychologically this nationalism is reflected in the whole of Negro culture, and especially in folklore.

In the absence of fixed and nourishing forms of culture, the Negro has a folklore which embodies the memories and hopes of his struggle for freedom. Not yet caught in paint or stone, and as yet but feebly depicted in the poem and novel, the Negroes' most powerful images of hope and despair still remain in the fluid state of daily speech. How many John Henrys have lived and died on the lips of these black people? How many mythical heroes in embryo have been allowed to perish for lack of husbanding by alert intelligence?

Negro folklore contains, in a measure that puts to shame more deliberate forms of Negro expression, the collective sense of Negro life in America. Let those who shy at the nationalist implications of Negro life look at this body of folklore, living and powerful, which rose out of a unified sense of a common life and a common fate. Here are those vital beginnings of a recognition of value in life as it is *lived*, a recognition that marks the emergence of a new culture in the shell of the old. And at the moment this process starts, at the moment when a people begin to realize a *meaning* in their suffering, the civilization that engenders that suffering is doomed.

The nationalist aspects of Negro life are as sharply manifest in the social institutions of Negro people as in folklore. There is a Negro church, a Negro press, a Negro social world, a Negro sporting world, a Negro business world, a Negro school system, Negro professions; in short, a Negro way of life in America. The Negro people did not ask for this, and deep down, though they express themselves through their institutions and adhere to this special way of life, they do not want it now. This special existence was forced upon them from without by lynch rope, bayonet and mob rule. They accepted these negative conditions with the inevitability of a tree which must live or perish in whatever soil it finds itself.

The few crumbs of American civilization which the Negro has got from the tables of capitalism have been through these segregated channels. Many Negro institutions are cowardly and incompetent; but they are all that the Negro has. And, in the main, any move, whether for progress or reaction, must come through these institutions for the simple reason that all other channels are closed. Negro writers who seek to mould or influence the consciousness of the Negro people must address their messages to them through the ideologies and attitudes fostered in this warping way of life.

5) *The Basis and Meaning of Nationalism in Negro Writing*

The social institutions of the Negro are imprisoned in the Jim Crow political system of the South, and this Jim Crow political system is in turn built upon a plantation-feudal economy. Hence, it can be seen that the emotional expression of group-feeling which puzzles so many whites and leads them to deplore what they call "black chauvinism" is not a morbidly inherent trait of the Negro, but rather the reflex expression of a life whose roots are imbedded deeply in Southern soil.

Negro writers must accept the nationalist implications of their lives, not in order to encourage them, but in order to change and transcend them. They must accept the concept of nationalism because, in order to transcend it, they must *possess* and *understand* it. And a nationalist spirit in Negro writing means a nationalism carrying the highest possible pitch of social consciousness. It means a nationalism that knows its origins, its limitations; that is aware of the dangers of its position; that knows its ultimate aims are unrealizable within the framework of capitalist America; a nationalism whose reason for being lies in the simple fact of self-possession and in the consciousness of the interdependence of people in modern society.

For purposes of creative expression it means that the Negro writer must realize within the area of his own personal experience those impulses which, when prefigured in terms of broad social movements, constitute the stuff of nationalism.

For Negro writers even more so than for Negro politicians, nationalism is a bewildering and vexing question, the full ramifications of which cannot be dealt with here. But among Negro workers and the Negro middle class the spirit of nationalism is rife in a hundred devious forms; and a simple literary realism which seeks to depict the lives of these people devoid of wider social connotations, devoid of the revolutionary significance of these nationalist tendencies, must of necessity do a rank injustice to the Negro people and alienate their possible allies in the struggle for freedom.

6) *Social Consciousness and Responsibility*

The Negro writer who seeks to function within his race as a purposeful agent has a serious responsibility. In order to do justice to his subject matter, in order to depict Negro life in all of its manifold and intricate relationships, a deep, informed, and complex consciousness is necessary; a consciousness which draws for its strength upon the fluid lore of a great people, and moulds this lore with the concepts that move and direct the forces of history today.

With the gradual decline of the moral authority of the Negro church, and with the increasing irresolution which is paralyzing Negro middle class leadership, a new role is devolving upon the Negro writer. He is being called upon to do no less than create values by which his race is to struggle, live and die.

By his ability to fuse and make articulate the experiences of men, because his writing possesses the potential cunning to steal into the inmost recesses of the human heart, because he can create the myths and symbols that inspire a faith in life, he may expect either to be consigned to oblivion, or to be recognized for the valued agent he is.

This raises the question of the personality of the writer. It means that in the lives of Negro writers must be found those materials and experiences which will create a meaningful picture of the world today. Many young writers have grown to believe that a Marxist analysis of society presents such a picture. It creates a picture which, when placed before the eyes of the writer, should unify his personality, organize his emotions, buttress him with a tense and obdurate will to change the world.

And, in turn, this changed world will dialectically change the writer. Hence, it is through a Marxist conception of reality and society that the maximum degree of freedom in thought and feeling can be gained for the Negro writer. Further, this dramatic Marxist vision, when consciously grasped, endows the writer with a sense of dignity which no other vision can give. Ultimately, it restores to the writer his lost heritage, that is, his role as a creator of the world in which he lives, and as a creator of himself.

Yet, for the Negro writer, Marxism is but the starting point. No theory of life can take the place of life. After Marxism has laid bare the skeleton of society, there remains the task of the writer to plant flesh upon those bones out of his will to live. He may, with disgust and revulsion, say *no* and depict the horrors of capitalism encroaching upon the human being. Or he may, with hope and passion, say *yes* and depict the faint stirrings of a new and emerging life. But in whatever social voice he chooses to speak, whether positive or negative, there should always be heard or *over*-heard his faith, his necessity, his judgement.

His vision need not be simple or rendered in primer-like terms; for the life of the Negro people is not simple. The presentation of their lives should be simple, yes; but all the complexity, the strangeness, the magic wonder of life that plays like a bright sheen over the most sordid existence, should be there. To borrow a phrase from the Russians, it should have a *complex simplicity*. Eliot, Stein, Joyce, Proust, Hemingway, and

Anderson; Gorky, Barbusse, Nexo, and Jack London no less than the folklore of the Negro himself should form the heritage of the Negro writer. Every iota of gain in human thought and sensibility should be ready grist for his mill, no matter how far-fetched they may seem in their immediate implications.

7) *The Problem of Perspective*

What vision must Negro writers have before their eyes in order to feel the impelling necessity for an about face? What angle of vision can show them all the forces of modern society in process, all the lines of economic development converging toward a distant point of hope? Must they believe in some "ism"?

They may feel that only dupes believe in "isms"; they feel with some measure of justification that another commitment means only another disillusionment. But anyone destitute of a theory about the meaning, structure and direction of modern society is a lost victim in a world he cannot understand or control.

But even if Negro writers found themselves through some "ism," how would that influence their writing? Are they being called upon to "preach"? To be "salesmen"? To "prostitute" their writing? Must they "sully" themselves? Must they write "propaganda"?

No; it is a question of awareness, of consciousness; it is, above all, a question of perspective.

Perspective is that part of a poem, novel, or play which a writer never puts directly upon paper. It is that fixed point in intellectual space where a writer stands to view the struggles, hopes, and sufferings of his people. There are times when he may stand too close and the result is a blurred vision. Or he may stand too far away and the result is a neglect of important things.

Of all the problems faced by writers who as a whole have never allied themselves with world movements, perspective is the most difficult of achievement. At its best, perspective is a pre-conscious assumption, something which a writer takes for granted, something which he wins through his living.

A Spanish writer recently spoke of living in the heights of one's time. Surely, perspective means just *that*.

It means that a Negro writer must learn to view the life of a Negro living in New York's Harlem or Chicago's South Side with the consciousness that one-sixth of the earth surface belongs to the working class. It means that a Negro writer must create in his readers' minds a relationship between a Negro woman hoeing cotton in the South and the men who loll in swivel chairs in Wall Street and take the fruits of her toil.

Perspective for Negro writers will come when they have looked and brooded so hard and long upon the harsh lot of their race and compared it with the hopes and struggles of minority peoples everywhere that the cold facts have begun to tell them something.

8) *The Problem of Theme*

This does not mean that a Negro writer's sole concern must be with rendering the social scene; but if his conception of the life of his people is broad and deep enough, if the sense of the *whole* life he is seeking is vivid and strong in him, then his writing will embrace all those social, political, and economic forms under which the life of his people is manifest.

In speaking of theme one must necessarily be general and abstract; the temperament of each writer moulds and colors the world he sees. Negro life may be approached from a thousand angles, with no limit to technical and stylistic freedom.

Negro writers spring from a family, a clan, a class, and a nation; and the social units in which they are bound have a story, a record. Sense of theme will emerge in Negro writing when Negro writers try to fix this story about some pole of meaning, remembering as they do so that in the creative process meaning proceeds *equally* as much from the contemplation of the subject matter as from the hopes and apprehensions that rage in the heart of the writer.

Reduced to its simplest and most general terms, theme for Negro writers will rise from understanding the meaning of their being transplanted from a "savage" to a "civilized" culture in all of its social, political, economic, and emotional implications. It means that Negro writers must have in their consciousness the foreshortened picture of the *whole*, nourishing culture from which they were torn in Africa, and of the long, complex (and for the most part, unconscious) struggle to regain in some form and under alien conditions of life a *whole* culture again.

It is not only this picture they must have, but also a knowledge of the social and emotional milieu that gives it tone and solidity of detail. Theme for Negro writers will emerge when they have begun to feel the meaning of the history of their race as though they in one life time had lived it themselves throughout all the long centuries.

9) *Autonomy of Craft*

For the Negro writer to depict this new reality requires a greater discipline and consciousness than was necessary for the so-called Harlem school of expression. Not only is the subject matter dealt with far more meaningful and complex, but the new role of the writer is qualitatively different. The Negro writers' new position demands a sharper definition of the status of his craft, and a sharper emphasis upon its functional autonomy.

Negro writers should seek through the medium of their craft to play as meaningful a role in the affairs of men as do other professionals. But if their writing is demanded to perform the social office of other professions, then the autonomy of craft is lost and writing detrimentally fused with other interests. The limitations of the craft constitute some of its greatest virtues. If the sensory vehicle of imaginative writing is required to carry too great a load of didactic material, the artistic sense is submerged.

The relationship between reality and the artistic image is not always direct and simple. The imaginative conception of a historical period will not be a carbon copy of reality. Image and emotion possess a logic of their own. A vulgarized simplicity constitutes the greatest danger in tracing the reciprocal interplay between the writer and his environment.

Writing has its professional autonomy; it should complement other professions, but it should not supplant them or be swamped by them.

10) *The Necessity for Collective Work*

It goes without saying that these things cannot be gained by Negro writers if their present mode of isolated writing and living continues. This isolation exists *among* Negro writers as well as *between* Negro and white writers. The Negro writers' lack of thorough integration with the American scene, their lack of a clear realization among themselves of their possible role, have bred generation after generation of embittered and defeated literati.

Barred for decades from the theater and publishing houses, Negro writers have been *made* to feel a sense of difference. So deep has this white-hot iron of exclusion been burnt into their hearts that thousands have all but lost the desire to become identified with American civilization. The Negro writers' acceptance of this enforced isolation and their attempt to justify it is but a defense-reflex of the whole special way of life which has been rammed down their throats.

This problem, by its very nature, is one which must be approached contemporaneously from *two* points of view. The ideological unity of Negro writers and the alliance of that unity with all the progressive ideas of our day is the primary prerequisite for collective work. On the shoulders of white writers and Negro writers alike rest the responsibility of ending this mistrust and isolation.

By placing cultural health above narrow sectional prejudices, liberal writers of all races can help to break the stony soil of aggrandizement out of which the stunted plants of Negro nationalism grow. And, simultaneously, Negro writers can help to weed out these choking growths of reactionary nationalism and replace them with hardier and sturdier types.

These tasks are imperative in light of the fact that we live in a time when the majority of the most basic assumptions of life can no longer be taken for granted. Tradition is no longer a guide. The world has grown huge and cold. Surely this is the moment to ask questions, to theorize, to speculate, to wonder out of what materials can a human world be built.

Each step along this unknown path should be taken with thought, care, self-consciousness, and deliberation. When Negro writers think they have arrived at something which smacks of truth, humanity, they should want to test it with others, feel it with a degree of passion and strength that will enable them to communicate it to millions who are groping like themselves.

Writers faced with such tasks can have no possible time for malice or jealousy. The conditions for the growth of each writer depend too much upon the good work of other writers. Every first rate novel, poem, or play lifts the level of consciousness higher.

THE NEW BLACK LITERATURE:
PROTEST OR AFFIRMATION
Hoyt W. Fuller

There is a revolution in black literature in America. It is nationalist in direction, and it is pro-black. That means, in effect, that it is deliberately moving outside the sphere of traditional Western forms, limitations, and presumptions. It is seeking new forms, new limits, new shapes, and much of it now admittedly is crude, reflecting the uncertainty, the searching quality of its movement. But, though troubled and seeking, it is very, very vital.

The creators of the new black literature are deeply concerned with image and myth. They are about the business of destroying those images and myths that have crippled and degraded black people, and the institution of new images and myths that will liberate them. In the article "The Black Writer and His Role" (*Negro Digest*, January 1969), critic Carolyn Fowler Gerald explains that image is important to black Americans because ". . . image is central to a man's self-definition." Says Mrs. Gerald: "Because all images, and especially created images, represent a certain way of focusing on the world outside . . . they represent a certain point of view. Now, if we hold a certain point of view, we have automatically emphasized some aspects of reality, blocked out others, and glossed over the rest, and the image which we project or which we perceive is not objective reality but our own—or someone else's—reshaping of reality. If it is someone else's reshaping of reality which we perceive, then we are within that other person's sphere of influence and can be led to believe whatever he wishes us to believe: that a rose bush is pleasant because it has a fragrant smell, or that it is unpleasant because it has thorns. If these two images of the rose bush are combined into a metaphor, we have created images which lead us to make an association between the reality of the rose bush and another level of reality, and we can be influenced, for instance, on a moral level: 'Pleasant-smelling roses have unpleasant thorns; therefore, beware the sweet fragrance of pleasure for underneath it lie hidden the thorns of destruction.' In this way, the association made in the mind of the hearer or reader is controlled. By guiding, by controlling our associations, the image-maker can, and usually does, shape our view of reality, because the images the words conjure up when they are put together artistically provoke an immediate emotional response in us, and dim out of our consciousness all the untold other points of view at our disposal."

Black Americans grow up in a world where white people have projected white images everywhere, leaving black people with what Mrs. Gerald calls "a zero image" of themselves. "The black child growing into adulthood through a series of weekend movies, seeing white protagonists constantly before him projecting the whole gamut of human experience, is, in extreme cases, persuaded that he too must be white, or (what is more likely) he experiences manhood by proxy and in someone else's image. He sees, in other words, a zero image of himself. If there are black people on the screen, they are subservient to, uncomfortably different from, or busy emulating the larger, all-inclusive white culture. In that case, our young person sees a negative image of himself . . ."

Mrs. Gerald points out that Western culture's projection of white images upon the universe, conditioning those within its sphere to ". . . accept white as the symbol of goodness and purity; black as the symbol of evil and impurity," has been very deliberate in design. "The white man has developed a myth of superiority based on images which compare him symbolically with the black man," she says. "The very fact of this interconnection is at once a holdover from previous bondage and the most effective means of perpetuating that bondage. We realize now that we are involved in a black-white war over the control of image. For to manipulate an image is to control a peoplehood. Zero image has for a long time meant the repression of our peoplehood."

In the recently published anthology *Black Fire,* James T. Stewart, another of the new black critics, talks about the importance of image—or models—in the creative process. "The dilemma of the 'Negro' artist is that he makes assumptions based on the wrong models," Mr. Stewart says. "He makes assumptions based on white models. These assumptions are not only wrong, they are even antithetical to his existence. The black artist must construct models which correspond to his own reality. The models must be non-white. Our models must be consistent with a black style, our natural aesthetic styles, and our moral and spiritual styles. In doing so, we will be merely following the natural demands of our culture. These demands . . . are found in our music and and in our spiritual and moral philosophy. Particularly in music, which happens to be the purest expression of the black man in America. . . ."

Larry Neal, co-editor of *Black Fire* and one of the strongest of the new poet-critics, feels that the new black literature aims at nullifying the influence of the white image by destroying the "double consciousness" of black people—the dilemma of being both black and American. In his classic book *The Souls of Black Folk,* the great W. E. B. DuBois described this dilemma as ". . . two souls, two thoughts, two unreconciled strivings; two warring ideas in one dark body, whose dogged strength alone keeps it from being torn asunder." But Neal feels that the black revolutionaries of today are no longer concerned about that part of their identity which is "American," that is, of European derivation, because "It is almost axiomatic that most of what the West considers important endangers the more humane world we feel ours to be." The new black writers are concerned with "consolidating the African-American personality," and they look upon the West ". . . as a dying creature, totally bereft of spirituality. This being the case, the only hope is some kind of psychic withdrawal from its values and assumptions."

Mr. Neal emphasizes that the new black literature, which is "primarily directed at the consciences of black people," is not "essentially a literature of protest." It is, to be sure, a literature of affirmation.

The trouble with black literature in America is—and always has been—the white literary establishment. If that idea seems shocking at first, then consider it for a moment. Literature, after all, is not separate from life, although many white critics seem to want to separate black literature from the realities of black life. The literature of any people grows organically out of the experiences of that people, informed by imagination and wit—the gift, in short, of artistry. Black literature in America is, and always has been, handicapped by literary colonialism. The rules of literature and the criteria for literary achievement are established by white critics and scholars who share a general experience and perspective; these rules and criteria are then imposed on the works of black writers, who have qualitatively different experiences and who approach these experiences from an essentially different angle of vision. If, theoretically, the values underlying both white and black experiences are the same, then the area between the white and black interpretations of those values is vast, perhaps beyond bridging.

Consider: America is a racist society. That is, opportunities and rewards are apportioned, for the most part, according to race and color. The preferred and the privileged are white; the rejected and the degraded are non-white. The whites, who are in the majority and hold the power, proceed under the very natural assumption that the nation's vaunted principles, creeds, and institutions are both valid and operative. The non-whites understand that much of "the good life" for white Americans is bought at the price of their continued subjugation. In Chicago, for example, hundreds of thousands of ordinary white people have access to high-paying jobs because they do not have to compete for those jobs with the million black people who live in the city. Those million black people know they are being debased and cheated, and that knowledge shapes their attitude toward both the people who cheat and debase them and the society that condones it. The white boy who grows up as writer might fashion prose or poetry that strikes at the fabric of the social structure that insures injustice against his non-white fellow citizens, but he does not, at the same time, remove himself from his position in the society that brings him the benefits of that very injustice. His, then, is a moral stance, and though he may be serious enough to take certain real risks to his person or to his position in defense of it, he cannot reject the privileged status that is the gift of his whiteness. On the other hand, the black boy who grows up to be a writer is fighting for his life both literally and literarily, and while he certainly feels that morality is on his side in the struggle, his stance can never be merely moral. Choice in that matter is a luxury forever denied him. The white boy can approach the great question of racism with a certain detachment; his conscience is under siege, not his very being; he could, at some conceivable point, reverse his attitude toward the whole question of racism and injustice without serious consequence to his image of his own humanity. But the black boy who manages to divest himself of his outrage must, in the process, diminish his own humanity, to say nothing of his manhood; his detachment must be achieved at considerable cost to his sense of self.

Conscious and unconscious white racism is everywhere, infecting all the vital areas of national life. But the revolutionary black writer, like the new breed of militant activist, has decided that white racism will no longer exercise its insidious control over his work. If the tag of "racist" is one the white critic will hang on him in dismissing him, then he is more than willing to bear that. He is not going to separate literature from life.

When the novel *The Confessions of Nat Turner* was published, the black intellectual community exploded in a fury of outrage. A white author, William Styron, had taken a black man who is a hero to black people, filtered the man's life through a white sensibility, and produced a book that black people feel slanders and diminishes their hero. The white critical community lavished praise upon the book; and when black intellectuals expressed their anger, resorting finally to the device of publishing a counterbook, *Ten Black Writers Respond*, the white critical community dismissed the black reaction as so much "black racism" and "hysteria." One of the more highly regarded of the white critics, Philip Rahv, writing in *The New York Review of Books*, acclaimed the book a masterpiece and said, ". . . only a white Southern writer could have brought it off." Then, incredibly, this writer of Jewish extraction, forgetting his own people's history of repression and their long struggle for dignity and self-expression, wrote the following: "A Negro writer, because of a very complex anxiety . . . would have probably stacked the cards, producing in a mood of unnerving rage and indignation, a melodrama of saints and sinners." *Would have probably stacked the cards!* One wondered if Mr. Rahv would have looked back on the *Diary of Anne Frank*, or on all that library of volumes by Jews describing in fact and fiction the horrors of pogroms through which they have passed, and concluded that the Jewish writers *stacked the cards*. But it was a black critic, June Meyer, writing in *The Nation*, who got to the core of the problem. The white critical establishment preferred William Styron's version of Nat Turner and his revolt because white America has never been willing to listen to the authentic voice of black America. "The definitely *preferred* form of communication, black to white, is *through* a white intermediary—be he sociologist or William Styron," Miss Meyer wrote. The authentic black voice is not wanted: it is too harsh, too accusing, too haunting, too full of "unnerving rage and indignation."

Black literature, as written literatures go, is not very old. Prior to the Civil War, a few novels by black writers were published, and so were some poems, the best known of which were works of Phillis Wheatley, the celebrated house slave. There were some newspapers published by blacks, including one in New Orleans that was bilingual (French and English), and a number of journals. The writings of Frederick Douglass were rather well known, and his autobiography remains a work of distinction. There were some notable histories, slave narratives, and a few novels. However, it was not until the advent of Paul Laurence Dunbar and Charles W. Chesnutt, toward the end of the nineteenth century, that works that qualified as literature according to those whose prerogative it is to make such judgments, were published. Each man produced several novels, and Dunbar, of course, gained considerable eminence for his poetry, especially for that written in dialect. In the years between 1900 and the early twenties, a number of black novelists and poets were published, with even the great scholar W. E. B. DuBois trying his hand at "creative writing" (*The Quest of the Silver Fleece,* 1911). Robert A. Bone, the white professor whose book *The Negro Novel in America* has long been considered the definitive work on the subject, wrote, ". . . most Negro novelists will produce only one or two novels in any case," backing up that declaration with the observation, "Of 62 novelists writing between 1853 and 1952, 40, or two-thirds, have published only one novel. Eleven more have published only two novels; only 11 have published more than two." This information is offered in Mr. Bone's book with no qualifications, and it is rather typical of the critical approach to black writers and writing that has proven so damaging over the years. Now, apart from the fact that Mr. Bone offered no comparable statistics of the productivity of "most" white writers, which might have made his statistics on black productivity irrelevant in any case, the implications of his statements are rather insidious. The suggestion is that some defect in the nature or character or industry of black writers prevented them from producing more novels. But the truth is that Mr. Bone has simply compiled his statistics without reference to his own data on the socioeconomic conditions under which black people lived between 1853 and 1952. And those conditions explain everything.

To begin with, the hundred-year period covered by Mr. Bone's statistics included the Civil War, Reconstruction, the post-Reconstruction era during which the South virtually stripped black people of all their Constitutional rights, the rise of the Ku Klux Klan, the two great migrations of blacks from the rural South to the urban North, the two world wars, and the Depression. During much of this time, middle-class black communities of some size and importance existed in only a few centers, such as Atlanta, Georgia, and Washington, D.C., and the audience for books by black authors was small indeed. There were no black-owned trade-book publishing firms, and those books that black authors produced had to be acceptable to white publishers, few of whom were known for their sympathy for black people. When it is realized that even today, in this relatively enlightened era of broadly expressed liberal sentiments, many publishers are less than ecstatic over the prospect of publishing certain books by black writers, it is not difficult to understand how novels dealing with black life were not welcomed, say, in the early 1900s, when lynchings were a kind of grim pastime in the South and black people were confined systematically to clearly defined enclaves in northern cities. The novels of Dunbar and Chesnutt reflected very dramatically the pressures under which the authors were published. Dunbar, though born and brought up in Ohio, deliberately chose to write in dialect partly because dialect stories about black people were more readily accepted by both publishers and readers. Chesnutt, who was a well-educated man with skin so pale that he easily passed for white, often wrote of black people with the same kind of condescension

that was routine for white writers at the time. Neither Dunbar
nor Chesnutt created black characters who smoldered with the
repressed rage that black men have always felt, for there is
little likelihood that such novels would ever have been published
at that time.

Despite those concessions that black writers were forced
to make in order to see their works in print, they did not
attempt to totally exclude from their work the natural sentiments
of black people. The poems and novels of black writers reflected
the anguish and bitterness black people felt within a society
that would not leave them free to pursue their lives; the poems
and stories also expressed the hope, tenaciously held, that the
nation would live up to its laws, which promised equality of
opportunity and treatment to all its citizens; and black literature
faithfully recorded the experiences of black people who, no
matter how accomplished or distinguished, inevitably found
themselves at some point or time frustrated by a racial wall
that no power on earth could obliterate. This refusal of black
writers to withhold from their works the harsh reality of race
or their failure to soften its impact by glossing it over, did
not serve to endear black writing to the critics. In his highly
praised little book *Black on White: A Critical Survey of Writing
by American Negroes*, David Littlejohn used a great deal of
space describing the "pain" a white reader is likely to feel
upon reading black writing. "A white reader is saddened, then
burdened, then numbed by the deadly sameness, the bleak
wooden round of ugly emotions and ugly situations; the same
small frustrated dreams, the same issues and charges and
formulas and events repeated over and over, in book after
book," he writes. Mr. Littlejohn reluctantly admits that the
white reader—and critic—is likely to try to evade the pain of
black writing by a number of "escapes," and he lists the following as the most "sophisticated" of many: the escape of literary
judgment. "'It's poorly done,'" the critic will say of the poem
or the story or the novel. "Amen. End of problem. One tends
to fall back on this last evasion (if it is an evasion) quite

frequently in the case of the more militant Negro literature: It isn't literature. Propaganda with a plot (or in rhyme, or in acts). Unconvincing; lifeless, unearned; unfelt; uncrafted. Such criticisms are often only illicit self-defenses against pain," Mr. Littlejohn continues; "a reader slips on the rubber gloves of criticism to avoid the sting. But has he, the white reader, then, no right to make literary judgments—in wartime, as it were? Many of these critiques, interior or in print, are of the nature of moral evasions; but many of the wounds being evaded are illicit and unfair. Is the white reader simply to sit there, turning pages and squirming?"

Well, what the white critic has done, providing a convenient evasion for the white reader, is to characterize as "protest" all writing by black authors which deals honestly and passionately with the black experience. As "protest," this literature can be dismissed, placed in a special category somewhere on the far periphery of art. And in not confronting the literature as art, it is then somehow possible to take less seriously what it says and means. Black literature accuses, and its charges must be denied. Jean Paul Sartre, the French philosopher-novelist, has posed in general terms the question black literature asks white America: How can our century possess a conscience and yet live with the monstrous crimes it commits?

Countless black writers have foundered and failed in an effort to please the critics—and, of course, the publishers—by shielding their work from the abrasiveness that the critics describe as "protest." The critics for a long while advised black writers to choose "universal" subjects, to write about characters and situations with whom readers (meaning white readers) could identify, and because black writers have egos as large as any other writers', and because they want to eat, some of the best of them did the critics' bidding. Ann Petry, Zora Neale Hurston, William Attaway, and even Richard Wright wrote books in the forties and fifties that had no black characters, and Willard Motley and Frank Yerby built literary careers writing about whites. This was in the wake of World War II, when many blacks, having helped to win the struggle against fascistic tyranny in Europe, truly believed that a new era of brotherhood and unity had been ushered in at home. The philosophy abroad in the land taught that all men were really the same under the skin, and black people wanted to believe. Even James Baldwin, one of the best writers of this generation, bought the assimilationist philosophy and proceeded to launch a brilliant literary attack against the works of Richard Wright in particular and all "protest" literature in general. He lived to regret it. He soon discovered, as he found fame, that the same critics who had lavished praise on him for his assault on "protest" literature now lumped his own works under that label. Mr. Baldwin doesn't talk about protest any more.

It was in the early twenties, at the beginning of the so-called Harlem Renaissance, that black writers first made their declaration of independence from both the dictatorial literary establishment and the latent urge to whiteness. The credo was stated by a young Langston Hughes, the best-known writer of that movement. "To my mind, it is the duty of the younger Negro artist . . . to change through the force of his art that old whispering 'I want to be white,' hidden in the aspirations of his people, to 'Why should I want to be white? I am a Negro— and beautiful!' So I am ashamed for the black poet who says, 'I want to be a poet, not a Negro poet,' as though his own racial world were not as interesting as any other world. I am ashamed, too, for the colored artist who runs from the painting of Negro faces to the painting of sunsets after the manner of academicians because he fears the strange unwhiteness of his own features. An artist must be free to do what he does, certainly, but he must also never be afraid to do what he might choose. . . . We younger Negro artists who create now intend to express our individual dark-skinned selves without fear or shame. If white people are pleased, we are glad. If they are not, it doesn't matter either. We build our temples for tomorrow, strong as we know how, and we stand on top of the mountain, free within ourselves."

Langston Hughes kept to that creed all his life, although he watched writers younger than himself abandon or reject it; and it must have been gratifying to him in his final years when he saw a new crop of black artists emerging upon the scene who, though ignorant of the credo, began to speak out in words very similar to his own. The young writers of the black revolution, at last, are able to do what the militant young writers of Langston Hughes's generation merely dreamed of doing. The most important element of difference between 1920 and 1960 is geopolitical: The white world no longer holds unlimited hegemony over the hundreds of millions of black and brown and yellow peoples of the world. The voices and opinions of non-white people must be heard in the chambers of world councils of nations, and their wishes must be respected. As the leading nation of the West, the white world, the United States is, in effect, on exhibit, and it must pay, in terms of influence and investments, when its practices at home conflict too sharply with the principles with which it persuades the rest of the world of its worthiness to lead. And the political freedom of India, Pakistan, the rest of Asia, and most of Africa, has taught black writers in America that they now have prospects and possibilities. To begin with, they have an audience; books by black writers sell very well in the growing number of black-owned bookshops in cities across the nation, and a number of lively black journals publish the poems and stories they produce; black theater companies are organized in the ghettos to produce the plays; and writers' conferences are held periodically so that the writers can come together and exchange ideas and reinforce one another in the drive toward literary independence. Where the writers of another generation were persuaded to seek "universal" subjects and themes, the new black writers are deliberately delving into their own folk culture and traditions, exploring their own history, creating their own myths. The new poetry is a poetry of exhortation and celebration, and the new prose is a prose of affirmation. The new literature is characterized by a spirit of rejection—rejection of values that have proven useless or destructive or debasing—but there is no "protest," as protest, in it. And the new poetry is a celebration of blackness and the spirit of pan-Africanism, as in the works of Willie Kgositsile, the brilliant young South African writer:

I. The Elegance of Memory

Distances separate bodies not people. Ask
Those who have known sadness or joy
The bone of feeling is priced open
By a song, the elegance
Of color, a familiar smell, this
Flower or the approach of an evening . . .

All this is NOW

I used to wonder
Was her grave warm enough,
'Madikeledi, my grandmother,
As big-spirited as she was big-legged,
She would talk to me. She would . . .
How could I know her sadness then
Or who broke my father's back?
But now . . .

The elegance of memory,
Deeper than the grave
Where she went before I could
Know her sadness, is larger
Than the distance between
My country and I. Things more solid
Than the rocks with which those sinister
Thieves tried to break our back

I hear her now. And I wonder
Now does she know the strength of the fabric
She wove in my heart for us? . . . Her
Voice clearer now than then: 'Boykie,
Don't ever take any nonsense from them,
You hear!'

> There are memories between us
> Deeper than grief. There are
> Feelings between us much stronger
> Than the cold enemy machine that breaks
> The back. Sister, there are places between us
> Deeper than the ocean, no distances.
> Pry your heart open, Brother, mine too,
> Learn to love the clear voice
> The music in the memory pried
> Open to the bone of feeling, no distances

Like Langston Hughes, who was a true blues and jazz poet, some of the new poets are obsessed with the idea of unifying their poetry with basic black musical forms. ". . . If one is to judge poetry on the basis of meters and music, we must decide which music we're talking about," says California poet Stanley Crouch. "That is, the high floating sound from Bach, Brahms, Mozart, etc., is fine for Yeats, Pound, Williams, *et. al.*, but we Black People season our ears on different sound-rhythm arrangements. That is, if a song like [Charlie] Parker's 'Ornithology' is considered 'flat,' then poetry sprung from that sound is, also, 'flat,' flat as be-bop which, we all know by now I hope, was and is beautiful. . . ."

Mr. Crouch says that the above is why a new poet, Jayne Cortez, is so exciting. Here is a poem by Miss Cortez that he feels illustrates his thesis:

Lonely Woman

> A wasted flow of water hiding
> Sliding
> down the face
> of a lone-ly one
>
> This black woman's
> oblong tears
> render
> softly felt wetness

warm like sperm
to melt
the calling–calling
flesh

Is there any reason
for this not so
Dry–dry season

Cutting tongue of fear
please–
won't you hear
the stretch marks
of Loneliness
bent–in this
cold woman's tear
Night Raining
in
The Woman's Quarters
listening to
crickets
small–weak
dark like me
–sit–
Stripped–Nude
from the trembling cadence of fire
Lit–
in Ornette's horn

Crickets that cry
Come–weep–with–us
come–weep with us
come weep with us
Lonely wo-man
Lonely Woman
come weep with us

Says Mr. Crouch of Miss Cortez's poetry: "She's got bop, boogie, blues, and the new Black Music flowing through her lines— she achieves those sounds and rhythms and, thereby, comes

up with a prismatic, swinging sound as varied in color as
the everglades. She, as far as I can see, is our new blues
singer, our new Aretha. In verse. Stories piled high as sky-
scrapers, foot tappers, swinging cymbals. Bells. . . ."

And, in *Too Late Blues* (*ain't no ambulances for no nigguhs
tonite*), Mr. Crouch demonstrates his own poetic oneness with
the blues:

TOO LATE BLUES
(*ain't no ambulances for no nigguhs tonite*)

The jitterbug ditty bops thought
they was off in the boogie
but it was another
dance altogether
to the devil
so as Bo Dolla, Bo Pette & the others
grinded against their women
they fell perforated
under the flames of
BABY! BABY! BABY!

Horns as tall as cornstalks
had sprung from the head of the beast
his tail made a tunnel
through his striped pants
and flapped through the vent
of his frock coat
his fangs came forward
and he french-tongued
his dogs before coming
down in lead rain
on the rest of dark
town

Monkey Junior was ready
when it went down, but,
couldn't get nobody to go
with him
the sun shone across the

livid face of white america
was when the torture took off
came out of the blocks of gun barrels
runnin *fast*
didn't stop for nobody
swept all the nigguhs in Watts
out of Will Rogers Park
hummed their sirens
and came down too cold on the boulevard
100 & 3rd Street
blowing people away
and they, the wooly-headed
would-be lovers
would-be warriors
bit concrete
under the fast creepin
bullets
for goddam sure
out to kill every nigguh they could

and they carried a victim
dripping red up the steps
of the police station
asking only for an ambulance
but the beast manning the valiant Watts Station said
No Ambulances For No Nigguhs Tonite

No one went wild
they had been too busy getting high
they could not see the pink face
of the oppressor sitting on the bull's eye
of the black night
therefore, whatever guns
the dumb and high had, did
uh uh:
No good,
merely helped pave the way
for tombstones)

The Devil Ages were the days now that we were in
never too cool to kill a brother
but always
dropping the gun
when the beasts with the badges arrived
(and they shot little Fats all of nine times
after having made him get down on his knees
and raise his arms in prayer)

Fashion plate nationalists were too busy
making money selling clothes
to notice.
They died in their bright African colors,
swahili curses dripping from their mouths

Many revolutionaries
got theirs in the ass
another bourgeois bitch.
Preparing her for the revolution.

Many who slipped in college
and skated out with degrees
were huff puffing their way
up the Mt. Everest
of the middle class
when the tongue rope
red up the honkies' ass was cut
and they landed on sabres.
OW!
But it wasn't bebop.

And Monkey Junior found himself
almost alone
but the nigguh did
get on his job—
                    straight out Mau Mau
Nat Turner madness:
The red that passed for blood
in the devils' veins
laid out everywhere:

He caught them
in kitchens grinning at the massacre
over the radio—
the housewives, the daughters, the babies
ALL THEIR HEADS—YEA—
set up in their windows like pumpkins
Their bodies stuffed in their washing machines,
piled in their bathtubs.
And he masqueraded:
White men stabbed in
the belly by the shoe shine boy
he pretended to be
or spikes run through their mouths
nailing their heads to the floor
by elevator boys
with bloody gloves
running up the alley.
He dismembered babies
and shitted on their bodies—
Monkey Junior was a wild
madman, a black hurricane
carrying knives and dancing
through the white cities.
He, alone, and no others,
was the only one to survive.

And the sun
which had grasped its light
reflected from the eyes of Black Women
and its heat from the love of their
men, the sun went skinny
and fell wheezing into the sea
warming it to a pallid soup of dead fish & melted pearls.

The beasts did not adapt to darkness
starved
finding no one else to kill.
And Monkey Junior, on his knees,
the only man left,
prayed.

While the new black literature is, where it is most dynamic, informed by a spirit of nationalism, some of the best of the current novelists manage to bridge rather effectively the generation of Langston Hughes and that of the exciting young writers who, for the most part, have been published only in the new black journals and a few anthologies. Outstanding among this group are William Melvin Kelley, Kristin Hunter, and Ronald Fair. Mr. Kelley and Miss Hunter, while increasingly "nationalistic" in their personal outlook, have not yet moved to the point where their characters do not react directly to the overwhelming presence of whites. Mr. Kelley's latest novel, *Dem*, is a satirical look at middle-class white America, and Miss Hunter's latest novel for adults, *The Landlord*, deals with the adventures of a liberal white man who chooses to involve his life with the lives of some denizens of a black-occupied apartment house. However, Miss Hunter's newest book is a novel for juveniles, *The Soul Brothers and Sister Lou*, for which she won the 1968 award of the Council on Interracial Books for Children. This book is important in that it represents Miss Hunter's concrete break from being "just a writer, not a Negro writer." Like so many intellectuals of her age (middle thirties), Miss Hunter has "come back home." In a special article published in *Publishers' Weekly* in connection with her new book and the award, Miss Hunter discusses her personal "identity crisis." ". . . My generation was the last to make an all-out effort to be white," she says, "and as the last in line of this thrust, we traveled the farthest and suffered the most when we were eventually, inevitably, brought up short. We went to Ivy League schools; we spoke almost too-perfect English as well as French; we traveled in Europe; we socialized with whites; some of us even married them. Then came the inevitable day when we realized, individually and collectively, that it had all been to no avail." Miss Hunter wrote her book for young blacks because she feels that—unlike her generation—"the youngest black people have already gone through this crisis and come out whole." In his second novel, *Hog Butcher*, Ronald Fair's hero is a young black boy who is thrown into the mire of political sordidness in the Chicago ghetto, but who emerges both whole and strong. All these books have characters who fit the mold of the new image of black manhood that the militant black public is demanding.

Perhaps the best of the current non-nationalist black novelists is Ernest J. Gaines of San Francisco, author of two excellent novels (*Catherine Carmier* and *Of Love and Dust*) and a collection of short stories (*Bloodline*). The protagonists in Mr. Gaines's two novels are very different kinds of men, but they share a fiber and strength that, though always present in black men of their backgrounds, have rarely been portrayed in fiction. The one is college-bred, assured, reflective, returned to his native Louisiana to reassess his past in order to determine his future; the other is a hard-bitten rebel, but a man sure of his personal magnetism and of his manhood and determined to diminish neither. Mr. Gaines's themes are love, endurance, and the tragedy inherent in the human resistance to inevitable change. His style is lucid; his technique, quiet and sure.

Some of the more talented of the writers spawned by the black revolution are women. Outstanding among these are Nikki Giovanni, Alice Walker, Jean Wheeler Smith, Jane Stembridge, and Carolyn Rodgers. Several of them have novels in progress. Four (all but Miss Stembridge) have published short stories, and four (all but Mrs. Smith) have published volumes of poetry. Mrs. Smith, a veteran of the SNCC campaigns in Mississippi, has written movingly of the struggle for manhood among the young SNCC workers under siege in the South and of the women whose spirits are bent on the altar of that manhood. Miss Rodgers, a member of a writers' group concerned with the articulation of a black aesthetic (OBAC), concentrates on capturing in her stories and short plays the soulful essence of the black experience.

Writing of Richard Wright, young Cecil M. Brown, one of the new black novelist-critics, states that the famed novelist ". . . wrote about Chicago in the manner that he did because that was what white America was ready to accept (in terms of literary fashion and social imagery), or, more accurately, *needed* to accept. White America branded Wright the Official Negro Protester, the genuine article," Mr. Brown says; "to reject him was to reject official, genuine Negro protest, no matter what your own experience as a Negro might have been. . . ." But Mr. Brown is not opposed to protest, he is opposed to what he terms "negative protest." He rejects "the white man's concept of protest, which is that of a raging, ferocious, uncool, demoralized black boy banging on the immaculate door of White Society, begging, not so much for political justice as for his own identity, and in the process consuming himself, so that in the final analysis, his destiny is at the mercy of the White Man."

The new black writers have decided that their destiny is not at the mercy of the white man, that they live in a world with options. This does not mean that they have ceased to protest the indignities they still experience. "Every black person who realizes how sick American white society is, by the logic of this awareness, makes a protest, a positive protest," Mr. Brown says. "This is a delicate point which the oversimplification of Wright's social reality has obscured. Positive protest that creates as it eliminates: it deals with the opposition's ugliness by concentrating on its own beauty. LeRoi Jones' prose is positive protest because it is witty and beautiful to black people —which means simply that white people can't understand it. . . ."

And former *Ebony* magazine writer David Llorens says the following:

"The contemporary black writer understands that, as white people lose control over our lives, their last recourse, their final imposition, will perhaps be an attempt to insure that our deaths are in accordance with their will. A love poem to a man who is being choked is a poem that teaches him how to get the damned hands from around his neck, and, moreover, teaches him how to create an order in which he will never again be choked. Drawing from an experience that is far wider than that of the white American, and understandably beset with an ambivalence more painful than artists anywhere have known, the black writer is about his work."

There is a great deal of literary excitement in the black communities of America, and out of it will come a fresh and mature literature that can only expand the dimensions of art and consciousness in America. The plays of LeRoi Jones, the poems of Sonia Sanchez and Don L. Lee, the novels of Ishmael Reed and Sam Greenlee, and the prose of Julius Lester are strong and viable works that speak directly to the revolutionary black sensibility. And now, of course, the white critics, having failed to destroy the buds of this new literature, are beginning to find a slot in which to isolate it and thus avoid the "pain" it gives them. In an extraordinary series of essays published recently in the *New Republic,* critic Richard Gilman all but admitted that Eldridge Cleaver's book *Soul on Ice* had forced him to consider if, perhaps, black writing is not, after all, beyond his competence to judge. A few years earlier, as drama critic of *Newsweek* magazine, Mr. Gilman had told a group of black writers that they were incapable of creating mature drama. What he meant, of course, was that black drama did not speak to him with the cadence, substance, and style by which he measured the worth of plays. Now Mr. Gilman is willing to admit that, just possibly, this forceful and disturbing black literature requires a different yardstick. The revolutionary black writers will be the first to agree that the traditional Western criteria are not always relevant to their work, but they will also resist the efforts of the Richard Gilmans of this world ever again to establish criteria for them.

For the simple fact is this: The black writer can only further demean himself and reinforce the arrogance and presumption of the critics by seeking to bend his vision and his art to the shape the critics hold up as example. The critic's country is not the black writer's country, and the goals of the two separate and essentially antagonistic territories are far from identical.

Writing of the anthology *Soon, One Morning* in the September 1963 issue of *Midstream*, Cynthia Ozick, one of the few white critics with real insight into the American racial mire, stated the proposition with unusual eloquence: "It is a commonplace but curious law of the Outsider that the more he strives to fashion himself emotionally after the Insider, the more he proves himself Outside—and without benefiting his real condition," she said. "The Negro is not yet inside America—which is what the shouting is all about. [That is, in 1963, that was what the shouting was all about.] Until he is, his good manners will be bad manners, his decency will be an indecency, and his sense of the proprieties will be the most shocking impropriety it is possible for him to commit against himself and against the idea of a human being."

The best of the young black writers know this to be true. It is time that the critics—and the professors—also understood it.

THE BLACK WRITER AND HIS ROLE
Carolyn F. Gerald

*"What is new (in black literature) is the deliberate desecration
and smashing of idols, the turning inside-out of symbols . . .
Bitterness is being replaced by wrath; a sense of frustration
giving way before a sense of power"*

Image is a term which we are using more and more in the
black community because we are discovering that the image
we have of ourselves controls what we are capable of doing.
Image, in this sense, has the meaning of self-concept. We are
giving cause and effect the same name. But the word image
is properly speaking a concrete term meaning the projection or
representation of an object; the image is the mirror of some
aspect of reality.

At this point, we should draw a distinction between real
and created images. Both are projections of reality, but the
created image is projected by the imagination of man, and by
the recall and associative power of his five senses. For instance,
I can hold out a rose before you; the image of that rose is
mirrored in your eye; it is a real image. Or I can describe
a rose to you, and my words will create an image which
you can visualize mentally. Perhaps you will even imagine the
smell and the feel; the words I choose and the way I build
them into the image will determine this. Usually a whole complex
of associations builds up around an image, secondary images are
evoked, until well-defined patterns of associations based upon

sensory perceptions pervade in a very vague way the whole area of a man's experience.

Why is image so central to a man's self-definition? Because all images, and especially created images, represent a certain way of focusing on the world outside, and therefore they represent a certain point of view. Now, if we hold a certain point of view, we have automatically emphasized some aspects of reality, blocked out others, and glossed over the rest, and the image which we project or which we perceive is not objective reality but our own—or someone else's—reshaping of reality. If it is someone else's reshaping of reality which we perceive, then we are within that other person's sphere of influence and can be led to believe whatever he wishes us to believe: that a rosebush is pleasant because it has a fragrant smell, or that it is unpleasant because it has thorns. If these two images of the rosebush are combined into a metaphor, we have created images which lead us to make an association between the reality of the rosebush and another level of reality, and we can be influenced, for instance, on a moral level: "Pleasant-smelling roses have unpleasant thorns; therefore, beware the sweet fragrance of pleasure for underneath it lie hidden the thorns of destruction." In this way, the association made in the mind of the hearer or reader is controlled. By guiding, by controlling our associations, the image-maker can, and usually does, shape our view of reality, because the images the words conjure up when they are put together artistically provoke an immediate emotional response in us, and dim out of our consciousness all the untold other points of view at our disposal.

Image-making is part of all human experience. However, we are speaking here of the image created by the magic of words. We are considering image not so much as life but as literary art. Art reshapes the raw materials of nature and of human interaction and, in so doing, interprets reality in a non-analytical, non-intellectual way. Art thus makes a direct appeal to the senses and calls forth a spontaneous emotional identification with other men and with the universe. Therefore, the effects

of the literary image are most often intuitive, deep beyond
the threshold of reason and common sense. When we spoke of the
sweet fragrance of pleasure and the thorns of destruction, we
made an appeal not to reason but to the emotional attractiveness
of the images. In this way, we develop, quite aside from our
rational perception, an intuitive view of nature and of the
cosmos, and our own relation to it. The rose is an old, familiar
example of how our attitude toward the surrounding environment takes form and grows. The body of imagery surrounding
the rose is rooted historically deep in Western cultural patterns
of looking at the world. The rose symbolizes beauty on the
physical level, and purity and freshness on the moral level.
Because this imagery is traditional the associations are unquestioned, and because they are unquestioned, they take on
the quality of myth. In the case of the rose, the imagery
may seem harmless but we will see in a moment how such
myth-building images can be the very death of self-concept.

Notice too, in the case of the rose, that man has projected
himself into his imagery. The purity, beauty and freshness of
the rose are usually compared to an idealized womankind. This
is because the natural impetus of man is to impart to the whole
cosmos the qualities which he possesses. Man's imagery is thus
anthropomorphic; he sees himself or his behavior in every projection he makes. Thus, a flower *dances* in the breeze; the
thunder rushes *angrily* through the skies; the sun *smiles* down
on the *sleepy* noontime village; *Mother* earth *provides* for us.
It follows that man's self-concept must inevitably be tied to
his view of the universe, since he sees his own reflection in
it at every moment. And a reflection of ourselves cannot be
neutral; it cannot be objective; it is either positive or negative.
How we regard the phenomena of nature is an indication of
what we think of ourselves. The *howling* wind, for example,
is not the same image as the *whining* wind. If our literary
tradition stresses the howling wind, then we feel emotively that
a mysterious prowling creature stalks through our universe. If

the whining wind is stressed, we feel the presence of a weak but persistent creature following us constantly around.

We've said that man projects his image upon the universe. But man does not exist in isolation. It is far more accurate to say that man projects his cultural and racial images upon the universe and he derives a sense of personal worth from the reflection he sees gazing back at him. For he defines himself and the world in terms of others like him. He discovers his identity within a group.

And now we come to the heart of the matter, for we cannot judge ourselves unless we see a continuity of ourselves in other people and in things and concepts. We question our very right to exist without other existences like our own. This is why image is so important to African Americans. We are black people living in a white world. When we consider that the black man sees white cultural and racial images projected upon the whole extent of his universe, we cannot help but realize that a very great deal of the time the black man sees a zero image of himself. The black child growing into adulthood through a series of week-end movies, seeing white protagonists constantly before him projecting the whole gamut of human experience, is, in extreme cases, persuaded that he too must be white, or (what is more likely), he experiences manhood by proxy and in someone else's image. He sees, in other words, a zero image of himself. If there are black people on the screen, they are subservient to, uncomfortably different from, or busy emulating the larger, all-inclusive white culture. In that case, our young person sees a negative image of himself. Nor are the images which control personal worth always so direct or obvious. The very same image-myth process which we discovered through the example of the rose is present in the extensive body of color imagery in Western culture. Those associations with black and white have conditioned us to accept white as the symbol of goodness and purity; black as the symbol of evil and impurity.

This did not just happen. It is the result of white racial

projection of its own best image upon the universe. Concomitant
with that projection for several hundred years—ever since the
black man has come within the sphere of influence of the white—
the moral and aesthetic associations of black and white have
been mixed up with race. Thus, the negative reflection of
ourselves is, in the white man's system, the reverse side of his
positive projection of himself. The white man has developed a
myth of superiority based on images which compare him symbolically with the black man. The very fact of this interconnection is at once a holdover from previous bondage and
the most effective means of perpetuating that bondage. We
realize now that we are involved in a black-white war over the
control of image. For to manipulate an image is to control a
peoplehood. Zero image has for a long time meant the repression of our peoplehood.

Of course, the black American has not relied totally on the
image projected by white culture. He has developed a literature,
and that literature gives him a certain sense of self. We have,
however, in spite of ourselves, not been successful in destroying
zero image, for we have not been able to convince ourselves
that our image is projected on any but a small and segregated
strip of the universe. When a self-definition has proceeded
spontaneously, the literature will reflect not only a group consciousness, shared points of view, common ancestry, common
destiny and aspirations, but it reflects these in spiritual oneness with whatever natural and/or supernatural powers preside
over and guide that destiny. For the black writer, the only
possibility for spiritual oneness has been non-race or religious
literature. But non-race or religious literature takes on insidiously
the image projected by what is called the larger culture, and
so takes on a white image. Black writers have also attempted
to reflect spiritual oneness by writing within a totally black
framework. But white images are implanted at the core of
black life, the most obvious example being that of the Church,
where God is white. Moreover, the black community is not

self-sustaining, and a literature which would circumvent this essential feature of peoplehood cannot cope with the forces that shape us. For the most part though, black writers have avoided these two pitfalls, and our literature has been, as we have, slowly, painfully coming out of bondage and has been contributing to our growing sense of peoplehood. If black writers have historically concentrated on white-black animosity, it is because that animosity is an everyday fact of life and functional part of our universe.

The artist then, is the guardian of image; the writer is the myth-maker of his people. We still at times are not sure as to how much of our image is us; to what extent we are the sole authors of our myth, our peoplehood. There are those white people who would nullify any argument we advance on the basis that it is advanced in a white language. And it is true that languages project a specific cultural image. But I believe that we have arrived at a stage of self-awareness in our writing which sees this type of argument as irrelevant. Our very plain answer to this sophisticated argument is simply that we will not let white men define our peoplehood by telling us we're still using white tools to create it. Similarly, we must reject white attempts at portraying black reality. They are valid only in terms of the white man's projection of himself. They have no place in the definition of blackness, for they reveal the white writer's attempt to work through his own cultural guilt, fascination with blackness, or sense of spiritual emptiness. This includes all latterday Harriet Beecher Stowes. No one can hand us a peoplehood, complete with prefabricated images.

Even the word *black* is a translation from the Portuguese slave term *negro*, gone into the English language as Negro. But black is also the generalized term which we use to symbolize unity of origin, whether we are called Anglophone, Francophone, coloured, mulatto, West Indian or American Negro by the white image-makers. *Black* is the highly imagistic term we use to do away with all such divisionary euphemisms. It is the term we use to destroy the myth based on the complex of images which polarize black and white. These images must be mythically torn down, ritually destroyed. We cannot bury our heads before the existing body of myth, nor before our own Europeanization. Therefore, we cannot return nostalgically to a past heritage and pretend that historical continuity exists in anything but fragmentary form. We cannot block out the black-white struggle for control of image and create a utopianized world of all-black reflections. Our work at this stage is clearly to destroy the zero and the negative image-myths of ourselves by turning them inside out. To do this, we reverse the symbolism, and we use that reverse symbolism as the tool for projecting our own image upon the universe.

Zero image, and the need to work through it, is not a new concept. Many black writers have understood the importance of image, and Ralph Ellison in the early fifties stated the same intent metaphorically in the title and outer structure of his novel, *Invisible Man.* What is new, I believe, is the deliberate desecration and smashing of idols, the turning inside-out of symbols, to which black writers are now proceeding with a vengeance. Bitterness, which runs through the whole of black literature, is being replaced by wrath; a sense of frustration is giving way before a sense of power. It is the sense of power which proceeds from a mythic consciousness based on a people's positive view of themselves and their destiny.

Perhaps we can best conclude with an illustration of the processes we've been discussing. The following poem attempts to desecrate the mythical and beautiful figure of the muse, entrenched in white culture since the time of its earliest flowering, Greco-Roman antiquity.

> Dress the muse in black . . .
>   No!
>   Kill her!
>
> Make her jump
>   Burning bright white bitch
>   From the pitched peaks of our houses

Let her shriek
    Pale old faded biddy . . .
Hear her?
    Stomping her feet round
        On our rooftops all these years?

And we, inside. Yassuh meek
    Warming our hands by the fire (like sheep)

Phony 'fay!

Look at her!
    Running past
        Blond flames waving in the wind

Blow on her!

Grab a torch up in your hand and come outside
    And watch her burn
        And crackle
            And topple
                And lie

Fallen
    Off our rooftops
        Into the flame

Look up
    And gather round
        And shake your torch up at her!

Tease her like a yellow cat
    Crouching on the roof

Make her jump
    Make her howl
        Make her yowl
            Falling in the fire

Make it hot . . .
    Make it hate.
Clap and stomp round the fire
    And shout the spirit out of her.
        And draw your circle close
            For we'll kill us a devil tonight.

Come on away, now!
   Now!
      We'll find our own saint
         (or another name for her)
No need for hell's fire now

The fire's weak
   And burned out
      The universe is black again.

Carolyn F. Gerald, the perceptive critic and author of "The Black Writer and His Role," lives and works in Philadelphia, Pa.

THE BLACK WRITER
VIS-À-VIS HIS COUNTRY
John Oliver Killens

I believe it was George Bernard Shaw who once said that America was the first country in history to move from barbarism to decadence without going through civilization. I construe the statement of this estimable British gentleman of letters to mean that our country has been in such a hurry becoming the wealthiest and the most powerful nation in the world, it has hardly had the time or stomach for the niceties of culture and civilization. Indeed, it has been in such unseemly haste, it has not even taken the time to bring into reality some of the most magnificent literature ever written about the rights of men. I refer, of course, to the Bill of Rights, the Declaration of Independence, and the Constitution of the United States.

So a cultural revolution is desperately needed, here and now, to un-brainwash the entire American people, black and white. For the people of this land have been the victims of a mighty brainwash that has continued unabated for the last four hundred years. Perhaps Negro artists must assume an uneven load in this cultural revolution because, as black folk, they know America better than she knows herself. The laws of survival dictate that the slave must know the many turns and twists and quirks of his master. Moreover, the Negro remembers better

than anybody else the American dream, deferred and forgotten
by most Americans. He remembers, because he lives constantly
the dream's negation, yet lives for the day when the dream
will become a reality. He could never take for granted the
Declaration of Independence, the Bill of Rights, the Constitution
of these United States. He could never become blasé about the
dream. In a word, your humble servant, the black American, has
borne the brunt of the millions of little white lies America has
told the world about herself and about the Negro.

Since the so-called American Indian is practically extinct, it
is highly probable that the only indigenous American culture
is that of the American Negro. The Negro was invented in
America. Only in America. In the main, his has been a culture
of revolt, of protest and revolution; a culture that is expressed
very clearly in the Negro spirituals. More often than not, they
are still interpreted as songs of a happy, childlike people,
satisfied with their lot in this world and looking forward to the
Hereafter, where the streets would be paved with gold and
overflow with milk and honey. Why do Americans still hang
on in desperation to the image of the happy and contented
slave? "DIDN'T MY LORD DELIVER DANIEL? WHY NOT
EVERY MAN?" is not exactly a happy and contented lyric!

From all sides pressure is put upon the Negro artist to deny
his culture, his roots, his selfhood. How many black writers
have you heard engage in this abject self-denial: "I am not a
Negro writer. I am a writer who happens to be a Negro." But
the truth of the matter is that we black Americans are all
Negroes (African-Americans, if you prefer) who happen to
have become writers, painters, lawyers, subway motormen,
doctors, teachers, ditch-diggers, pickpockets, hustlers, or whatever. We see life from the vantage point of being Negro. A creative writer writes out of his particular frame of reference, which
is the sum total of his life's experience, and he had better
come to terms with it as hurriedly as possible.

Yet from Hollywood to Broadway to Madison Avenue, I hear
variations of the same refrain: "John, why do you insist upon

writing about Negroes? Why don't you write about people?" As often as I've heard that one, it never fails to jar me, laboring, as I always have, under the illusion that Negroes *are* people. Another goes like this: "The thing I liked about your story, John, it was universal. It could have been about anybody."

Well—I submit that a story that could have been about anybody is probably about precisely nobody at all. Negroes are the only people in this world who are set apart because of who they are, and at the same time told to forget who they are by the same people who set them apart in the first place.

Now, then, how could I, John Killens, write a valid story about a Chinese peasant in the hinterlands of China? No matter how *universal* my literary approach, I would never be able to get close to the Chinese peasant's specifics, the cultural and the idiomatic meanings of his life, the unique Chineseness of him, which are his and only his. Besides, I could never muster up that much racial arrogance.

I am convinced that when Western man speaks of universality, he is referring to an Anglo-Saxon universality, which includes a very meager sector of this young and aging universe. Every line of Sean O'Casey's works exudes a sense of Irishness. Dostoevski bared the Russian soul. No critic ever questioned their universality. But to write out of the frame of reference of an American Negro is *ipso facto* anti-universal.

Herbert Hill, newly blossoming literary expert on Negro affairs, in his introduction to *Soon, One Morning*, an anthology of "New Writing by American Negroes," acclaimed Ralph Ellison for all the wrong reasons, because Ellison's work, according to Hill, "transcends the traditional preoccupations of the Negro writer. . . . Today the Negro artist, as he enters into the mainstream of contemporary literature, feels a new strength and refuses to be limited to racial protest. . . . As the Negro writer moves beyond his anger, he develops a new concern for literary discipline and control . . ."

Well, Mr. Hill, the American mainstream contains some rather sickly fish; if Ellison did indeed enter the "mainstream," the

mainstream got more than it gave. It is a pretty puny achievement to join the mainstream, and a puny achievement is precisely what Ellison's novel was not.

The mainstream is jammed with writers like Updike and
Salinger, who write page after page of precious prose about
absolutely nothing. With the whole Western world as their
potential canvas, and swiftly going to pot and trying desperately
to take the rest of civilization with it, such writers flee in
panic because the New World is becoming too much for them.
They escape into minutiae of tight little islands of personal in-
significance and Oedipus complexes. The American mainstream
has come up with a crop of literary nitpickers, most of them
entirely without testicles. So now they want to castrate the
Negro writer, too. Is this the stream Herb Hill would lead
black writers into?

But the motley crew of little white fathers are saying nothing
new. They merely repeat the old refrains pontifically, as if
they're saying something startling and fresh. You say to yourself,
I've heard that song before, for underneath there is always
this veiled admonition to black writers: "You'll never win the
prizes or the critics' adulation unless you cool your anger and
lay that pistol down. Keep criticizing society and you'll continue
to incur the wrath of us white reviewers, who are not bad
fellows at all and would really like to bring you into the fold.
Oh yes, in spite of the fact that you are a Negro, you too
can join the club if you'll just play down your Negro-ness."

But a writer who writes to get into the mainstream and win
National Book Awards and plaudits from the critics is in
trouble with his muse. A creative writer is not a statesman.
He must tell as much of the truth as he knows the painful
truth to be, and let the flak fall where it may. Writing is a hazard-
ous pursuit. The flak might very well fall back on the writer
and put a large hole in his head. It has something to do
with the law of gravity. What goes up must come down. Artists
are forever at war with society, and if the artist is a black man
in the Free World he is doubly at war and the war's con-

sequences are especially dangerous for him. But he must fight in any event, for the consequences of his temporizing are fraught with even greater danger.

When Ernest Hemingway was interviewed by the *Paris Review* a few years before he died and asked what kind of advice he would give young writers, he answered that a writer needed two things—a sense of justice and a built-in, shockproof shit detector. Obviously a writer also needs artistic talent, but granting his talent, he desperately needs these two attributes Mr. Hemingway so graphically described.

As a writer, I must believe with all my mind and heart and soul in the ancient adage "You shall know the truth and the truth shall set you free." In a far deeper sense even than men of the cloth, writers must be searchers for the truth; men and women whose life's mission is to explore the truth of man's relationship to man. And I, for one, believe the basic truth of what my grandmother used to say. "Aah Lord, honey, the half ain't never been told." There is nothing in the world that I believe more than the wisdom of that statement. If I believed, as some Western men continually assert, that everything has already been said and it's just a question now of how differently you say it, that all is semantics from now on, I would put the cover on my typewriter and never uncover it again. As a writer, I must believe that most of what has already been said is a pack of lies, or, in some instances, mistakes, to be more charitable to makers of the myths. It is up to the writer to create a new vision for mankind. He must be forever asking questions. He must ask the unaskable. Was "Plato's Republic" a Republic? Was Jefferson democrat or slaveholder? This world can't possibly be man's best effort, or we're all doomed to destruction or the madhouse. Life must make more sense than it has up to this point.

Did Shakespeare's "Macbeth" utter an everlasting truth? Have all our yesteryears lighted fools the way to dusty death? "Out, out, brief candle!" Macbeth shouts. "Life's but a walking shadow; a poor player, that struts and frets his hour upon the stage, and then is heard no more: it is a tale told by an idiot, full of sound and fury, signifying nothing." Or did Langston Hughes come closer to *our* truth when he asked: "What happens to a dream too long deferred?"

I am a writer, first of all, and precisely because the world stinks and I want to change it. Yes, I mean it, and any writer worth his salt is up to the same subversive business. This is the way things always were, the eternal confrontation between the artist and society. Every time I sit down to the typewriter, with every line I put on paper, I am out to change the world, to capture reality, to melt it down and forge it into something entirely different. The portrait of the artist as a human being is one of profound frustration, because although he knows that "change" is one of the inevitable laws of the universe in the context of time and space, change in human nature is imperceptible. That is why the French have a saying: "The more things change the more they remain the same." But the earth *does* move. And things *do* change.

Since everybody "knows" the artist is the maladjusted one, I plead guilty to the charge. To be perfectly adjusted in a crazy, impractical, unreasonable society hellbent for its own annihilation seems tantamount to remaining blissful in a raging booby hatch. This is what drove Van Gogh to suicide. He was naïve enough to want to make sense in a crazy world. His sin was that he took life seriously and he loved mankind. *Ergo,* he was an idiot before his peers. He wanted to make sense out of a senseless society, and therefore he was a damn fool. But what is the verdict a century after he departed? Whom does the world remember, Van Gogh or his contemporaries?

But despite the current Negro Revolt, which is not yet a revolution, rumors to the contrary, the American Negro remains a cultural nonentity as far as books, television, movies, and Broadway are concerned. It is as if twenty million Americans did not exist; as if twenty million people were committed to oblivion. A Negro child can read at home or go to school and look into his school books, come home and watch television or maybe go to an occasional movie, and follow this routine from day to day, month to month, year to year, and hardly, if ever, see a reflection of himself in the mass-communications media. This has a tremendously negative impact on a child, who must have a sense of belonging and not of being here by toleration. A child must have a sense of selfhood, a knowledge that he is not here by sufferance, that his forebears contributed to the country and to the world down through the years.

America knows that the blood, sweat, tears, and muscles of black folk helped to build this mighty country. You wouldn't be so high and mighty if it weren't for me. You built this country on the black backs of my forefathers. Slave labor, that's what it really was, slave labor at a time when slavery was already obsolete throughout much of the earth. That's how you constructed your great temples and stored them with riches. That's how you got so far ahead of the rest of man in treasures stored up here on earth. You cruelly exploited my forebears. And now you deny my children a cultural existence. You pretend they are invisible.

I know the impact. I was a black boy once in Georgia. I remember. And I know the impact now, because I am the father of two African-Americans in New York City. I remember when my son was nine or ten years old, my great friend Langston Hughes came to dinner and brought my son a book he had written called *Famous American Negroes.* In it Langston had written, for children, stories about the Negro heroes of American history. Of Harriet Tubman, Frederick Douglass, Crispus Attucks, and Benjamin Banneker. This book opened many doors for my son, Chuck. He was so thrilled he took it to school the next day and showed it to the teacher, then asked, demanded really, that she read it to the class.

We lived at the time in the now "infamous" Bedford-Stuyvesant area in Brooklyn and the school was about fifty-fifty in its composition (meaning Negro-white, not co-educational). This was just before the great white exodus from the community had developed into full-scale, panic-stricken, disorderly retreat.

The teacher read passages of the book to my son's class and that night at the dinner table I asked him how it had gone.

"It was wonderful, Daddy! Everybody enjoyed the book." Then Chuck frowned and said, "But you know, Daddy, nobody at that school knows anything about Negro culture or Negro history."

"I suppose it's understandable that the white children don't know," I said.

"Oh no, Daddy, I mean the Negro children, too. Not even the teacher knows." And then he poked out his chest and said very proudly, "I'm the only one in that school that knows *anything* about Negro history or culture."

I looked at him and wanted to laugh and shout for the joy and pride he felt. At the same time I wanted to cry for all the black kids all over America caught up in what playwright Ted Ward has called the Big White Fog, never knowing that they have ever been anything and therefore never believing they'll ever amount to anything.

My daughter, Barbara, was then six years old. We lived in a brownstone on Lafayette Avenue, the parlor floor and basement. She would sit in the living room on the parlor floor and stare at the idiot box for hour upon hour. What program didn't matter, she even watched the commercials. We figured this was rather precocious for one of her tender age, for some of the commercials were better than the programs. Ultimately the fog lifted (for us, I mean), and we realized that our daughter was watching to see herself reflected on the television screen, a black man or woman presented with dignity, for she already knew the difference between dignity and *Amos 'n' Andy*. When once or twice during a long and arduous vigil she saw a black face on the white screen, she would run downstairs where we usually were, shouting, "Daddy! Mommy! Negro on TV!" But by the time we got upstairs he or she would be gone.

When we first moved to the neighborhood where we now live, Barbara was the only Negro in her class. She came home from school one day in tears. The history teacher had told the class that the Civil War was fought too soon, that the slaves weren't ready for freedom, and were happy and contented on the old plantation. Barbara took on the entire class and the teacher. "I don't know if I said the right things, Daddy. But I knew that what that teacher was saying didn't sound like anything I'd heard at home."

She burst into tears again as if her heart would surely break. Barbara was a happy girl most of the time. She rarely cried. She ran headlong into life, smiling, laughing, tripping, falling, getting up and running smack dab into life again, with hardly ever a thought about the very high cost of living. How could a teacher be so vicious to such a tender-hearted child? Or was the lady just plain ignorant?

I know a young black artist whose art is a monument to black life in America. He renders a toast to life in every stroke of his talented brush. Yet when I saw Tom Feelings at a meeting a few months ago, he was disheartened and told me he was leaving America. He had been going to the public schools of Bedford-Stuyvesant and giving chalk talks to black children on Negro and African history. But he explained that he could no longer do so because he realized more and more that the Negro kids thought themselves ugly. Because they were black. He said it was just too much for him. He thought they were beautiful; they thought they were ugly. Obviously their parents agreed with them. How else can one interpret stocking caps and straightening combs and bleaching cream?

"John, I've got to get to Africa. I've got to go to a place where black children know who they are and what they are and know that they're beautiful and that they are somebody. I've got to go some damn place where black folk don't think of themselves as 'niggers.'"

He was almost in tears. I knew the desperate feeling. From generation to generation the "nigger" feeling is handed down from parent to child. The feeling that what is white is right, and what is black is wrong. White is the symbol of purity and virginity and everything else that is good and powerful and

eternal. Oh, how many times in the days of my youth did
I sit in the humble pews of black churches and hear the
wonderful, soulful, beautiful, hard-working black sisters, young
and old, shout supplications of utter futility: "Wash me, Heavenly Father, And I will be as white as snow!"

The Western world deliberately made black the symbol of
all that was evil and ugly. Black Friday, blacklist, Black Plague,
black look, blackmail. Oh, the way the white Establishment
made us hate ourselves. "A nigger ain't shit!" is a black pass-
word, a common utterance of black folks. You took a great
people from a great continent and turned them into "niggers."
That is the job you accomplished in the name of "civilizing the
natives" and "Christianizing the pagans." That is the essence
of what America is, from the black man's point of view. The
land of the "niggermakers."

This distorted image of the Negro has its negative effect
on your children too. It gives them a distorted picture of this
earth and of human potential and ill-equips them to live in a
world, three-quarters of which is colored and fast becoming free
and independent.

That is why my friends from the African embassies run into
difficulties "Down South" in Atlanta and New Orleans and
even "Up South" in New York City. To the average American,
they are simply "niggers." In a way, I cannot truthfully say
that I am sorry. As long as indignities are commonplace for
black Americans, it is all to the good for black brothers from
across the seas to labor under no illusions as to the (universal)
American attitude toward men and women of color. I am not
sadistic. Neither am I masochistic. I just don't want America
to hoodwink black folk throughout the world. Let us set things
straight at home first.

Along with the fight to desegregate the schools, we must
desegregate the entire cultural statement of America; we must
desegregate the minds of the American people. If we merely
succeed in desegregating the school buildings, we may very well
find that we have won the battle and lost the war. Integration

begins the day after the minds of the American people are desegregated. This is the great challenge to all American writers, but especially to the black writer. Who will tell the real story of America if the black writer doesn't? Certainly not the gentlemen of the "mainstream" who still believe in Gunga Din and Uncle Tom and Aunt Jemima, or the "avant-garde," the rebels who are really anti-revolutionary. Jean Genet and his genre, the "theater of the absurd," the "beatnik," the "new wave," would appear to be merely Johnny-come-lately Kiplings. Apologists for white supremacy die hard and recur in varying disguises.

Behind the "avant-garde's" beards and dark glasses, they rationalize, apologize, as they strut and posture. The underlying statements of *The Blacks* and *The Balcony* are the same, that all civilization stinks, *period*. "When the *have-nots* overthrow the *haves*, nothing will really change except the relative positions of the adversaries. It will be the same thing all over again. There is no revolution ever. It's the same merry-go-round, so stop the world, I want to get off." Well, pardon me, fellows, I don't want to get off. The world never looked so good to me before.

"Sure—don't worry how you treat the *blacks*. The blacks will do the same to you when they seize power." This is Genêt's message, as far as I'm concerned. *The Blacks* was excellent therapy for many guilt-ridden white folk, which probably explains the long New York run it enjoyed, so much so that many whites went back to see it time and time again. Actually, the so-called "avant-garde" is really a rear-guard action in disguise. It is neither revolutionary, anti-bourgeois, as it sometimes makes pretensions of being, nor anti-white supremacy; it is not even anti-Establishment. It is essentially anti-people. "The West is humanity, humanity is the West, we're all sick to the guts, so let's, man, like all of us get into this here Western style pigsty, and have one final everlasting orgy."

There seems to be a growing tendency in the literature about black and white relationships to give the impression that everything could be solved on the analytical couch. I imagine this approach is a part of the so-called "sexual revolution." The whole "color" thing is merely a deeply rooted psychological sexual complexity and if we could only gather together 190 million black and white Americans into one gargantuan orgiastic group therapy, or perhaps one gigantic therapeutic orgy, all the problems would be solved. I submit that though we might have a ball, after the smoke and funk cleared away, the Great American Problem would still be with us; the Black Man's Burden would not have disappeared. Because the Problem and the Burden are historical, economic, cultural, and social, as well as psychological and sexual. The root of the problem is the Negro Invention.

So now comes the question: Who will uninvent the Negro? For nearly four hundred years the black man's personality has been under attack, his selfhood devastated. Ever since he was brought to this country in chains he has constantly been given the ultimatum: "Deny your humanity or perish!" Where are the artists and prophets who will undo this white destruction? Who will write the songs for us to sing of our black heroes? Who will tell our children of valiant Chalka? Who will re-create the ancient glory that was Timbuktu and Kush and Ghana and Songhay? It is important for us to know that our history on this earth did not begin with slavery's scars.

In order for a people to develop a highly political and revolutionary consciousness, they must hold a high regard for themselves. They must know that they came from *somewhere*, in order to believe themselves capable of going somewhere; they must have a past before they can create a future for themselves. A people needs legends, heroes, myths. Deny them these and you have won half the battle against them.

The French needed legendary figures like Joan of Arc in order to develop a national consciousness, without which any revolution is impossible. So we black folk need Saint Harriet of the Eastern Shore. We must build a literature of heroes, myths, and legends. The lives of Harriet Tubman, Frederick Douglass, Nat Turner, Sojourner Truth, are as formidable as

George Washington's, and are based on a much more substantial reality. Our people, young and old, need such heroes desperately. Slavemasters Washington and Jefferson do not belong to *our* children. We need our own myths and legends to regain our lost self-esteem, our regard for each other as a people capable of working together to move the mountains that stand before us. We need such a heritage in order to really believe that we shall prevail.

I'm reminded of a story. A little boy had read numerous stories in his children's books about various life-and-death struggles between a man and lion. But no matter how ferociously the lion fought, each time the man emerged victorious. This puzzled the boy, so he asked his father, "Why is it, Daddy, that in all these stories the man always beats the lion, when everybody knows that the lion is the toughest cat in all the jungle?"

The father answered, "Son, those stories will always end like that until the lion learns how to write."

Few white American writers care enough about the country to criticize it fundamentally. Compared with the ambivalent lot who clutter up the mainstream, they make up a pitifully small pool of courageous talent. Mention James Jones, Norman Mailer, Warren Miller, Lillian Smith, Arthur Miller, Harvey Swados, Ginzburg, Buckmaster, Rosten, Williams, and you have very nearly run out of names. Regardless of how one feels about their views of this society, one must concede that they are writers who care about things deeply. One hopes that one day at least one of them will care deeply enough to dramatize or novelize the white folk who are completely taken in by the "righteous" cause of white supremacy, explain them to us and particularly to themselves in all their myriad contradictions. What is the metamorphosis of a racial bigot? Are they born retarded? Is it fed to them with their mother's milk? The public schools? The press? The church? The mass-communications media? How? Why? When? Where?

America needs to understand what goes into the making

of a man who will go out on a Sunday morning in Birmingham, Alabama, and participate in the strange ritual of throwing bombs into a church and killing innocent little Negro children as they are being taught about Jesus, the same Jesus of Nazareth whom the killers profess to worship. And what about the sickness of men who will stand on the sidelines and watch such bloody rituals enacted, without daring to speak? What sort of unspeakable fear has locked their jaws? What is the true anatomy of racial prejudice? Here is a challenge for some writer who cares.

What happens to the dream too long deferred? What white writer will ask America Langston Hughes's question, and come up with some answers? For the dream has been deferred for all the country, black and white. But who will help convince white America that the dream is important to them also? Or have you, too, stopped dreaming? Come on, white brothers. Or don't you really give a damn?

Historically, white America put words in the black man's mouth and bade him sing improbable lyrics like:

> *All the darkies am a-weepin'*
> *Massa's in de cold, cold ground.*

But my great-grandmother told me differently. "We wept all right, honey! Great God A'mighty! We cried for joy and shouted halleluyah!"

Even long after slavery, white America continued the black man singing such banalities as:

> *I got plenty of nuthin'*
> *And nuthin's plenty fo' me.*
>
> or
>
> *Summertime and the livin' is easy.*

Certainly the American Negro knows, more profoundly than anyone else, that the living is *never* easy.

Even a short while ago, you had us singing:

> *It ain't no sin to dance and grin*
> *That's why darkies were born.*

Yet a black poet once wrote:

> *Carry me back to ol' Virginia—*
> *That's the only way you'll get me there.*

And in our own songs we sang:

> *Sometimes I feel like a motherless child,*
> *A long ways from home.*

We sang:

> *Nobody knows the trouble I see.*

Happy, contented people, we sang:

> *Before I be a slave*
> *I'll be buried in my grave*
> *And go home to my Lord*
> *And be free.*

How did all this begin, this billion-dollar misunderstanding? It started with your determination to have my labor without pay.

In order to justify slavery in a courageous New World spouting slogans of freedom and equality and brotherhood, the enslavers had to create the fiction that the enslaved were subhuman and undeserving of human rights and sympathies. The first job was to convince the outside world of the inherent inferiority of the enslaved. The second job was to convince the American people. And the third job, which was the cruelest hoax of all, was to convince the slaves themselves that they deserved to be the slaves. The propagandists for American slavery (the "creative writers" of that time) tackled their tasks with alacrity and a great measure of success, the effects of which still remain with us today, a hundred years after the Emancipation Proclamation, almost two hundred years after the Declaration of Independence. Thus was the Negro invented and the American Revolution thwarted. To this day, supposedly born in revolution, America is embarrassed by that word. Americans shy away from the word "revolution" like the plague, as if the American Revolution had never happened. Well, did it happen? Knock on any door in Harlem; in all the Harlems of the U.S.A. Ask any black man or woman in Alabama or Mississippi: Was 1776 for real? We black folk are the living proof of whether your revolution was a fake or not.

I attended a party some years ago near the Northwestern University campus, given by some university instructors to celebrate the publication of my first novel, *Youngblood*. One of them told me how much she had enjoyed *Youngblood*, but then asked, "Mr. Killens, do you think you could ever write about people, I mean, not just about Negroes? I mean about people." The nice lady was a trifle flustered.

"You mean, white people, don't you?"

She answered, "Well—yes. I suppose that is what I mean."

"Yes, I believe I could if I wanted to. In fact there are white folk in *Youngblood*. Actually, I believe that a black writer would find it easier writing about white folk than the white writer writing about black folk. The black man has had to know you in order to live in *your* world. I had to know what questions you were going to ask before you asked them, and I had to have the answers ready. But you've always taken me for granted. You come to me with all kinds of preconceptions about my innate inferiority. You never get past the myth to the real me."

My rejection slips reveal so much. I've gotten many a "Dear John" in my day, and I still get them.

Dear John:

Thank you for submitting your story to us. It is a powerful and beautiful job. Unfortunately the subject matter is not for us. Frankly, we are not a controversial house.

However, do keep us in mind when you write something else, especially if it has no racial overtones.

Sincerely,

Meaning of course: "John, why do you insist on writing about Negroes? Why don't you write about people?" Why this pressure on the Negro writer to deny his roots? Because the Negro experience in this country is the most fundamental criticism of the American way of life. This reality America has refused to face. It always was and always will be, so long as black remains the symbol of human dispossession. As long as we black folk are D.P.'s in our native land, the controversy will continue to rage. It will always remain a stumbling block in our attempts to win friends and influence people among the African and Asian populations. Africans are concerned with the welfare of their American brothers, and the American brother is becoming more and more concerned with Mother Africa.

Don't write about the Negro, write about Americans. But surely the American Negro is the most uniquely American of all Americans, because he was created *here*, in this place, physically, psychologically, sociologically, culturally, economically. He is an American product. The Negro, in his black presence, is the barometer of this nation's Constitution, and all its democratic traditions yet unrealized. Still deferred. The black man's sojourn in this country is the universal story of man's inhumanity to man, capable of being understood in any language in any nation on the earth. Here is the place for the literary prophets! But maybe Western man is right. "Everything to be said has already been said by Western man." I mean, it may be true that Western man has said all he has to say. It may be that he has run out of meaningful dialogue. God knows, he has talked long enough.

But colored people throughout the world have been sentenced by Western man to centuries of silence. And now in the middle of the twentieth century, it is time for them to speak. Western man wrote his own history as if it were the history of the entire human race. I hope that colored men have watched Western men too long to commit the fatal folly of writing history with a "colored" pencil. For there is a great wisdom in the old Ghana proverb that says: "No one rules forever on the throne of time." Notwithstanding, in this cultural revolution, we must reconstruct the history of the last four hundred years and this time tell *How the West Was Really Won.*

There is much inhumanity, violence, and brutality in our country's history. We must face that. For neither a people nor a nation can free itself from its past by denying or distorting it. White Americans have been sheltered from their history. History is a people's memory, and people have a habit of remembering the very best about themselves. It is an all too human trait. But in the final analysis, a people must face its history squarely in order to transcend it.

SOME OBSERVATIONS ON A BLACK AESTHETIC
Adam David Miller

Just as for the past hundred years blacks have provided the
most creative force for dance and music in this country, that
is, as the senses of sound and movement in this country have
been the creation of Afros, many now feel, I among them,
that the seventies will see this Afro creative force ascendant
in the other arts. Few can ignore the effects of the cake walk,
fox trot, lindy hop, the twist on the movement habits of people
in the States. Few, except the issuers of Pulitzer prizes, will
doubt that the American sense of music is of Afro origin.
A catalogue of names would overrun the page. Today we
are seeing fine black filmmakers, painters, sculptors, graphic
artists, and craftsmen. And in all fields of literature, the
writing aimed at the heart and life of the country is coming
increasingly from Afros.

I would like to think of aesthetics as *a way of viewing
and sensing and the results of what is viewed and sensed.*
Through such thinking, I would like to move the question
of aesthetics from "the contemplation of the beautiful" to that
of knowing, perception, and feeling. If we take this working
definition and apply it to U.S. blacks, we will have to ask how

have we blacks seen ourselves, through whose eyes, how do we
see ourselves now, and how may we see ourselves? By so doing,
we may at least put the question of a black aesthetic in some
perspective.

To examine the question of how we have seen ourselves, it
would be useful to be reminded of the definitions our former
legal slavemasters made of us and some of our early responses
to them. As early as 1847, Alexis de Tocqueville noted in
Democracy in America: "To induce the whites to abandon the
opinion they have of the moral and intellectual inferiority of
their former slaves, the negroes must change, but as long as
this opinion subsists, to change is impossible." Note that De
Tocqueville states that a change in blacks, not whites, is needed.
Being European, De Tocqueville could not see that the masters
had no way into the minds of their slaves. The slaves had
not only a different language from that of their masters, but
also an entirely different view of the world. Thus, having
no tools to measure their intellect, most masters found it both
convenient and profitable to suppose they had none. Having
made this supposition, they proceeded to set up and enforce
systems of denial and restriction that had the effect of sup-
pressing the slaves' intellect and directing it so that it was
hidden from the masters. And again, as a European, De
Tocqueville himself was of such a limited moral sense that he
could not understand how preposterous it was that the master
should presume to judge the moral condition of his enslaved.

Lawrence Gellert summed it up this way:

> Me an my captain don't agree,
> But he don't know, 'cause he don't ask me;
> He don't know, he don't know my mind,
> When he see me laughing
> Just laughing to keep from crying.

> Got one mind for white folks to see,
> 'Nother for what I know is me; . . .

For generations, then, as slaves and former slaves in this country, we were thought to be morally and intellectually inferior beings. As writers, our responses varied. There was often a discrepancy between what we argued ourselves to be and how we characterized ourselves. For example, see Leon R. Harris:

> . . . When everything's put to the test,
> In spite of our color and features,
> The Negro's the same as the rest.

Meanwhile, Afro writers often used the same stereotypes as white writers when portraying Afros.

What had happened was that the job of conditioning had been so thorough, the intimidation, forced breeding, dispersal, warping, brutalization, so complete, that the values of our former legal owners had become our own, so complete that we saw ourselves as our "masters" saw us; so that while the logic of our lives was clear, the sense of it was not; so that while we could say we were men and equals, we could not imagine ourselves as such. Forced to accept an alien language, alien and hostile gods, and an alien view of the world, our imaginations were shackled to those of our rulers, with the result that we continued for a considerable time the work they had begun in their manner.

Partly because our early writers thought of themselves as spokesmen for the race to outsiders rather than spokesmen to the race, they allowed themselves to use the language of outsiders instead of their own. They felt that if they accepted the standards of white writing, its conventions of language and correctness, its decorum, they and their race would be presented in a better light. With these early writers, language had to be correct, even to the point of stiffness and woodenness; they eschewed "barbarisms," meaning certain characteristic Afro images and usages. Because their speech was "purified," many slave narratives sound as though they could have been written by anyone.

When black writers tried to use dialect to reproduce sounds characteristic of our people, they were told that the only emotions dialect could convey were humor and pathos. We can either laugh at you or be maudlin over you. Our early writers accepted this two-valued orientation, apparently not realizing that this judgment on the possible uses of dialect had nothing to do with dialect, but rather with the only two feelings the arbiters of culture were willing either to show toward us themselves or to allow us to show.

Some writers of the twenties, especially those spoksmen for the "New Negro," attempted to stake out a space for black writing, where black art and culture could flower. In a foreward to his 1925 anthology *The New Negro*, Alain Locke states: "Negro life is not only establishing new centers, it is finding a new soul. There is fresh spiritual and cultural focusing. We have, as the heralding sign, an unusual outburst of creative expression. There is a renewed race-spirit that consciously and proudly sets itself apart."

Out of this "renewed race-spirit" some of the young writers began to present black life as it was lived by the majority of blacks—its vitality, its inventiveness, its strength, its fun, but also its poverty, its bitterness, its squalor. They were misread by both whites and blacks; praised by whites, who hailed them for presenting a new "primitive," and reviled by blacks for presenting "bad" things. Anticipating what was to follow and attempting to prepare the way for it, Langston Hughes issued a manifesto, a declaration of freedom, in "The Negro Artist and the Racial Mountain." He declared himself to be free to write as he chose, for whoever cared to read him. As a writer, he was going to be true to what he saw instead of to some imagined something he ought to see.

Hughes, Wallace Thurman, and others found themselves castigated by that minuscule body of blacks who had successfully copied what they thought were white manners and habits and did not wish their shaky middle place to be disturbed by an awareness of those blacks they knew were "beneath" them. They were so put off by surfaces, that a few years later they were to reject Zora Neale Hurston's *Their Eyes Were Watching God* as a story of black migrant workers, when what Miss Hurston was doing was presenting at eye level two lovers who dared to be happy in a society where happiness was sinful, where work was a duty not a pleasure, and pleasure something other.

Fortunately for us, Hughes, Miss Hurston, and Arna Bontemps (*Black Thunder*) were not dissuaded by indifferent or negative receptions, and as a result we have several works by writers who took the lives of their characters seriously, and rendered them with integrity, clarity, and precision.

In looking at our early writers, we can first see them attempting to shake off the stultifying yoke imposed by their legal masters, then writing in the manner of their masters for a time, hoping thereby to please the more book-educated blacks and not offend whites, and a few of the more courageous seeking to promote a race spirit and to recreate this spirit for their fellows. The writers of the twenties began to feel they should write for black audiences, even with the limitations this task imposed. Many of their readers were still seeing art as "universal," as some of the writers themselves did, and alas still do.

I would like to see the idea of "universal" laid to rest, along with such outmoded usages as *civilization,* as applied to the West; *social protest,* as applied to Afro literature; *pagan* and *fetish,* when applied to non-Christian religions; *primitive,* *barbarian,* and *folk,* as applied to life-styles or as judgments of culture; and *jungle,* as applied to African space. These terms are too-heavily weighted European culture judgments to be of much use.

James Weldon Johnson, writing in 1928 on what was more a dilemma for black writers then than now, that of the double audience—one white, the other black—saw a way out of that dilemma if the black author could make one audience out of what had been formerly two. He said: "The equipped Negro author working at his best in his best-known material can achieve this end; but, standing on his racial foundation, he must fashion something that *rises above race,* and reaches out to the *universal* in *truth* and *beauty"* (emphasis mine), ("The Dilemma of the Negro Author," *The American Mercury,* December 1928). When Johnson says the Afro writer's work must "rise above race" to be important, he anticipates the attempted putdown of Gwendolyn Brooks's work by a white poet: "I am not sure it is possible for a Negro to write well without making us aware he is a Negro; on the other hand, if being a Negro is the only subject, the writing is not important." Something is wrong with being *only* Negro?

Were someone to say to Johnson, "A nigger is a nigger is a nigger," he would probably be questioned about his sanity. But this same man could say, "'Beauty is truth, truth beauty, —that is all/Ye know on earth, and all ye need to know,'" and Johnson would probably say, "How profound!" Now neither statement says any more about experience than the other, yet because of his cultural conditioning, Johnson imagines "universal in truth and beauty" says something about a standard of aesthetics, when in reality he is talking about cultural judgments, and ultimately the way power is exercised in our society.

Johnson said that we should not ignore whites, because they made up 90 per cent of the population and we were surrounded by them. He might have added, had he dared, that they also control publishing, film, and broadcasting, and make up the largest share of the market for our wares.

Clearly, much of the koash-koash hinges on *universal,* and the value some of us give to it as opposed to the idea of black. Some of us keep feeling that to be black is not to be universal, and to be black is to be limited. Why is black such a limiting idea? Underlying much of the clever words and prolonged agonies is the simple refusal, no matter how sophisticated and learned the attempt at concealment, no matter how much "evidence" is presented for the evasions, the by now complex refusal, to accept the validity of our experience and to give that experience the same credence as any other.

LeRoi Jones said that a man once said to him: "But your experience is weird." Jones replied: "Yes, it *is* weird. Which means it's a weird place we live in." Al Young, black poet and college professor, whites in *Dancing:* "Life *is* more than fun & games/The thought/after all/that either of us is capable of being assassinated/at any moment/for absolutely nothing/& relatively little/is of course unnerving."

At one point in our history, many U.S. writers made a conscious effort to break with the literatures of Europe. To the extent of taking many of their themes from mainland North America and developing local language, the language founded by Mark Twain, they were successful. There were not successful, though, in eliminating a vertical structure for society, the two-valued orientation, the Platonic ideal, monotheism, and finance capitalism. These were as thoroughly ingrained in the new literature as in the old. What was omitted by the new literature was an attempt to get inside the slave or freedman and inquire: What is it like for *me* in this alien place? Because of this omission, Hughes was prompted to say: "If anybody's gonna write about me, I reckon it'll be/Me myself!"

The black story has not been told. We have written about ourselves neither enough nor well enough. Today's young writers are again attempting to continue the work begun in the twenties, that is, to write out of a central experience of black life in the United States and show that life from their particular racial foundations. That the objections to such a path by our book-educated have not changed much from the earlier time, may be suggested by some reactions to the idea of a black aesthetic.

In a questionnaire to black writers on writers and literary values, Hoyt W. Fuller asked in the January 1969 *Negro Digest* (now *Black World*): "Do you see any future at all for the school of black writers which seeks to establish 'a black aesthetic'?" This question, partly because of the anxieties it raised, drew some put-offs, some guffaws, and some considered replies. Despite its form, Mr. Fuller has not asked an easy question, as, I think, what follows will amply demonstrate.

Saunders Redding answered: "No. Not in America. Besides, aesthetics has no racial, national, or geographical boundaries. Beauty and truth, the principal components of aesthetics, are universal." Robert Hayden, through implication, shares a point with Redding and asks a question of his own: "It seems to me that a 'black aesthetic' would only be possible in a pre-dominately black culture. Yet not even black African writers subscribe to such an aesthetic. And isn't the so-called 'black aesthetic' simply protest and racist progaganda in a new guise?" An answer with very different implications was Addison Gayle, Jr.'s: "The 'black aesthetic' has always been a part of the lives of black people. To investigate these lives, and the conditions surrounding them, is to reveal an aesthetic inherent in the soul of black people."

What I have been saying is more closely in keeping with Professor Gayle's views. It may be that a black aesthetic is inherent in the black experience, and is rendered when we honestly recreate that experience. No writer "tells it like it is." If he did, we'd probably be bored to sleep. What a writer tells is "it like he needs it to be," in order to make sense out of his experience and the experiences of those whose world he recreates. When we write about ourselves from a point of view that takes black life seriously, that views it in scale, with human dimensions, then we are creating a black aesthetic.

CAN A METRONOME KNOW THE THUNDER OR SUMMON A GOD?
Ishmael Reed

The New Literary Neo-HooDooism

Dance and Drums preceded the word. Thousands of years
before the invention of the "Novel" or the "Short Story," Thoth,
the black Birdman of Egypt, "invented letters" and "gave names
to things." Magic/Religion came before "criticism," and words
(nommos) were the rappings of not one but thousands of
Spirits. Centuries before the "literary capitals" of London, Paris,
and New York, Ife, in Nigeria, was the home of the Necromancers, heavier than Solomon, conjurers of dread and joy.

Kidnapped by bandits to North America, they became Hoo-
Doo men, maintaining the faith of the old religion. A slave
told a whopper about a hurricane that "went on about its
nevermind" long before James Joyce thought of punning Homer.
The words, drums, and wood sculpture mystified and frightened
the bandit who punished those slaves using them. The void
was filled by Christianity, whose "straight" mythological system
patrolled the drums of passion. Witness "spirituals," in which
often the slave became his own enemy, or the hard time
black Pharaohs and Babylonians receive in D' Good Book. But
fragments of the old religion remained intact. The subversive

music of New Orleans Jazz, in which instruments substituted for voices as vessels of the Loa (Spirits) and the blues ("Somebody done HooDooed the HooDoo man"—Junior Wells).

Some slaves excelled at "Sonnets," "Odes," and "Couplets," the feeble pluckings of musky Gentlemen and slaves of the metronome. Others became polemicists/spokesmen, writing narratives in which traces of the old faith—"Africanisms," as they were called—were deleted by Christian abolitionist editors. But there were always the prophets—necromancers whose folk tales and sermons defied the conventions of plot, conflict, causality, and motivation—not elements of "art forms" as much as mere habits chained to a Western way of seeing things, and thus not "universal." (Note the Western literary term "epiphany." Isn't that some kind of Christian rite?)

It all comes down to this: can a metronome know the thunder or summon a God?

Milo Rigaud writes of the old religion: "Unlike other established religions, there is no hierarchy of bishops, archbishops, cardinals, or a pope in Voodoo. Each oum'phor is a law unto itself, following the traditions of Voodoo but modifying and changing the ceremonies and rituals in various ways. This is because the religious leaders of the oum'phor speak directly with the gods of Voodoo, and are not obliged to answer to anyone else to interpret what the gods tell them."

Similarly, this individualism holds true for the writers in *19 Necromancers from Now* (Doubleday, August 1970). Nineteen Necromancers of two worlds do a "speaking in tongues." From the interplanetary "way-out" to a supranaturalism so precise and fine that we know the brand of lipstick on the filter-tipped cigarette dangling there from the blue triangular ashtray. The poetypographer does his rappings along with the writer for whom "meaning" is all.

19 Necromancers from Now. The new Literary Neo-Hoo-Dooism. Some plant their flags on things; we plant our flags on the seventies.

THE FUNCTION OF BLACK LITERATURE AT
THE PRESENT TIME
Addison Gayle, Jr.

"One of the most promising of the young Negro poets once said to me," Langston Hughes related in "The Negro Artist and the Racial Mountain," "I want to be a poet—not a Negro poet, meaning, I believe, I want to write like a white poet; meaning subconsciously, I would like to be a white poet; meaning behind that, I would like to be white. . . . This is the mountain standing in the way of any true Negro art in America— this urge within the race toward whiteness, the desire to pour racial individuality into the mold of American standardization, and to be as little Negro and as much American as possible."

We, too, have our literary assimilationists in the 1970s. More sophisticated than their counterparts of yesteryear, they declaim in the language of the academic scholars. The black writer, they argue, must "join the American mainstream"; he must "make his work more universal," and, instead of "writing about Negroes all the time, he must write about people." "Your book" (*The Black Situation*), remarked a black colleague, "is interesting; but you should've included more universal experiences."

"Black-Writing—The Other Side" (*Dissent*, May-June 1968),

by Jervis Anderson, is a case in point. One supposes that Anderson is an honest man and should not be held accountable for the unsavory company he keeps. Afro-Americans, however, do not publish in *Dissent*, edited by Irving Howe—a racist *par excellence*—unless they are content to play the role of Friday to Irving Howe's Crusoe.

Apparently, Anderson has few compunctions about playing such a role. As a prelude to his major thesis, he quotes William Melvin Kelley: "There's no basic reason why we should talk to white people. Dostoyevsky did not talk to the Germans but to the Russians. . . . And we have to talk to our own people." The voice of the rebuttal is that of Anderson; the theme, tone, and contempt belong to "Father" Howe, who, one supposes, smiles approvingly over the shoulder of his young protégé: "Dostoyevsky's importance in the tradition of Western writing rests as much on the fact that he made a *great and universal art* (italics mine) out of Russian experiences as on the fact that diverse peoples of diverse life styles were able to find in his work images of their own situation. Obviously, black separatist writing has not left itself open to such accomplishments."

The "urge . . . toward whiteness" in the race, as evidenced by Fridays, past and present, has prevented the creation of a nationalistic art. Moreover, because of it, black writers have postulated an imaginary dichotomy between art and function that has made much of the writing of black authors irrelevant to the lives of black people. In an attempt to curry favor with the Crusoes of America, such writers, like Anderson, negate the idea of a unique group experience, and deny that black people, but for the accident of history and geography, would constitute a separate nation.

When put forward by black people, the thesis of a separate nation is dismissed as an absurdity. Yet, the same thesis, argued by white men of the nineteenth century, is catalogued in American history texts as "sound, patriotic, idealism." The poet Philip Freneau was one of the most vociferous advocates of a break with the cultural traditions of Europe—he was only slightly more militant than his contemporaries Ralph Waldo Emerson, John Trumbull, and Noah Webster.

Another of his contemporaries was the black poetess Phillis Wheatley. Like Freneau, she borrowed extensively from the poetical forms of the English neoclassicists. However, unlike Freneau, she failed to use these forms to call a new nation into being. Oblivious of the lot of her fellow blacks, she sang not of a separate nation, but of a Christian Eden. She wrote, as Richard Wright so aptly put it, "as a Negro reacting not as a Negro."

In the main, black writers have traveled the road of Phillis Wheatley. They have negated or falsified their racial experiences in an attempt to transform the pragmatics of their everyday lives into abstract formulas and theorems. They believe, with Margaret Just Butcher and Hugh Gloster, that there is a universal condition that transcends race and nationality, and that this condition is relevant to men of all colors. In this analysis, the function of the artist is to depict the unique manner in which each man reacts to his condition. Therefore, Eric Jones, of *Another Country*, is a more universal character than Rufus Scott, because he copes with his condition (homosexuality) in a way in which Rufus cannot cope with his (blackness).

The degree of similarity between the conditions under which blacks and whites live has been exaggerated. This exaggeration results from the tendency to regard American slavery as an economical, political, and legal institution, capable of being legislated out of existence by the thirteenth, fourteenth, and fifteenth amendments. However, under the creative aegis of the Americans, slavery assumed a uniqueness heretofore unsurpassed in the annals of slave institutions. Men were separated, not only in terms of laws and economics, but also in terms of basic human qualities. For Quaker and southern plantation owner alike, the black man was a subhuman being whose condition could be alleviated—if at all—only by divine intervention. He was not an American, nor was his condition analogous to that of Americans. To be an American was not to be censured with Benedict Spinoza: "Let him be accursed by day, and accursed by night; let him be accursed in his lying down, and accursed in his rising up; accursed in going out and accursed in coming in. May the lord never more pardon or acknowledge him; may the wrath and displeasure of the lord burn henceforth against this man, load him with all the curses written in the book of the law, and blot his name from under the sky. . . ." The criteria for defining an American went beyond accidents of birth, acts of immigration, or legal statutes erected during periods of national frenzy.

Nevertheless, with more zeal than whites, Blacks continue to flaunt their Americanism. Like Don Quixote, they insist that this earthly hell can be transformed into a heavenly paradise through the sheer effort of will power. No one is more culpable in this respect than the black writer. He attempts to gain recognition as an American by arguing that there are no separate cultural streams dividing the two races. There is, he supposes, only one giant cultural ocean, in which white and black experiences have been churned into one. The result of such assimilationism is the transformation of black men into carbon copies of white men.

Nowhere is this attempt at cultural assimilation more readily apparent than in the Afro-American novel, of which the works of William Wells Brown are early examples. The first Afro-American novelist and playwright as well as one of the first historians, Brown was also an eloquent speaker, ranking—with Frederick Douglass, Charles Remond, and Henry Highland Garnet—among the giants of the Afro-American oratorical tradition. Yet, Brown the abolitionist orator differs noticeably from Brown the novelist.

The orator dealt with the American society in uncompromising terms, pointing out, in the vein of Douglass, the manifest differences in a nation composed of masters and slaves. However, in his novels—and the second, *Miralda; or The Beautiful Quadroon,* is a better example than the first, *Clotel, or The*

President's Daughter—he attempted to convince his white reading audience that Blacks and whites, with few exceptions, were indistinguishable in terms of cultural artifacts. *Miralda* was written to prove that Blacks were willing to deal with their experience in terms of the American experience.

The function of the novel as delineated by Brown has survived the years. His ideas of cultural assimilation have been adopted and refined by writers more sophisticated—if not more talented—than he, and his thesis is restated in the twentieth century in three works that are considered among the best literary efforts by Afro-Americans: *The Autobiography of an Ex-Coloured Man*, by James Weldon Johnson; *Go Tell It on the Mountain*, by James Baldwin; and *Invisible Man*, by Ralph Ellison.

The Autobiography of an Ex-Coloured Man presents a portrait of the Afro-American artist as a young man. The child of a white father and a black mother, the protagonist is forced to choose between two worlds—one black, the other white. A man with no ethnic ties, he symbolizes what James Baldwin has called the "blood relationship" that exists between Blacks and whites in the American society.

The world of art is also delineated in terms of black and white. Black art is to be found in the spirituals, in the surviving African cultural artifacts, and in jazz. White art is depicted in Bach and Beethoven, the paintings of Michelangelo, and the Chartres Cathedral. The protagonist, a concert pianist, makes a pilgrimage to Europe, where he plays the works of European composers.

His objective is to merge the two worlds into one, to saturate the white artistic world with the black idiom. Like Dvořák, who synthesized symphonic music, spirituals, and jazz in the *New World Symphony*, the narrator will also attempt to assimilate the two in the hope of producing a new American product. How far we are from Stephen in Joyce's *Portrait of the Artist as a Young Man!* Stephen wanted to cultivate and hold on to the artifacts of his Irish heritage; Johnson's narrator wants to debase his by fusing it with another. After spending time in both worlds, the protagonist finds his identity in the white world. In so doing, he fails as artist and as man; for although he realizes the richness of his African heritage, he cannot allow himself to think of his culture as unique and distinct—he can accept it only as a submerged entity within a larger cultural sphere.

The theme of identity, so prevalent in the works of Brown, Baldwin, and Ellison, is presented in *The Autobiography of an Ex-Coloured Man* in terms of its varied dimensions. Forced to choose between a white world and a black world, between a white culture and a black culture, the narrator opts for the former. With the exception of Ellison's protagonist, who, by the end of the novel, is content to remain faceless, formless, and rootless as he hangs midway between heaven and hell, each protagonist chooses cultural sameness instead of cultural diversity, and surrenders his racial identity to the American Mephistopheles for a pittance that Faust would have labeled demeaning.

"One writes out of one thing only—one's own experiences," notes James Baldwin in *Notes of a Native Son*. For the serious black writer, this means writing from a group experience, for, in the American society, the individual experiences of the Afro-American, unless he is quite fair or quite lucky, is indistinguishable from that of the group.

John Grimes of *Go Tell It on the Mountain*, however, is ashamed of his group (read racial) experiences and attempts to transcend them by negating his racial identity. On two occasions in the novel, he is confronted with the problem of choosing between the two worlds offered him by his creator.

The initial, and most important, confrontation takes place on the mountaintop—a hill in Central Park overlooking New York City. Young Grimes is tempted by Satan, who offers him "the pottage" of the world in exchange for his birthright: ". . . the gigantic towers, the people in their dark grey clothes: and Broadway. The way that led to death was broad, and many could be found thereon; but narrow was the way that led to life eternal; and few there were who found it."

There is this difference between the worlds: the white leads to death and decay; the black, to life and vitality. Nevertheless, Grimes ". . . did not long for the narrow way, where all his people walked; where the houses did not rise, piercing, as it seemed, the unchanging clouds, . . . where the streets and the hallways and rooms were dark."

Baldwin prefers light to darkness, life to death. The dilemma confronting his protagonist is the same as that confronting Johnson's: to what world am I morally and culturally bound? Like Johnson's narrator, John Grimes has also "been down to the valley" and received the message of the anointed: ". . . they move with an authority which I shall never have; . . . they have made the modern world, in effect, even if they do not know it. The most illiterate among them is related in a way that I am not to Dante, Shakespeare, Michaelangelo, Aeschylus, Da Vinci, Rembrandt and Racine. . . . Out of their hymns and dances come Beethoven and Bach. Go back a few centuries and they are in their full glory—but I am in Africa, watching the conquerors arrive."

These are the words of John's creator in the essay "Stranger in the Village." The tone of assimilation, the obsession with fusing the black and white cultures—even at the risk of destroying the black—is as pervasive in the novel as it is in the essay. At the outset, John will settle for nothing less than a colorless world. Unable to bring this about, eventually he will sell "his birthright for a mess of pottage."

On the first reading, *Invisible Man*, by Ralph Ellison, does not appear to be a novel in the assimilationist tradition. Ellison is a student of black literature and history, and his novel illustrates a remarkable grasp of the Afro-American's historical past. No other writer has presented so well, in fiction, the vicissitudes of "The Age of Booker T. Washington"—an age that is fundamental to an understanding of black nationalism. Ellison's knowledge of black culture might have enabled him, with Joyce, to "forge in the smithy of [his] soul the uncreated conscious of [his] race." However, the assimilationist aspirations are as strong in Ralph Ellison as in black writers of the past: "When I began writing in earnest," he relates in *Shadow and Act*, "I was forced, thus, to relate myself consciously and imaginatively to my mixed background as American, as Negro American, and as Negro from what in its own belated way was a pioneer background." In addition, there was "the necessity of determining my true relationship to that body of American literature to which I was most attracted and through which, aided by what I could learn from the literatures of Europe, I would find my own voice, and to which I was challenged by way of achieving, myself, to make some small contribution, and to whose composite picture of reality I was obliged to offer some necessary modification."

We are again with James Baldwin, and the Chartres Cathedral stands before us, dazzling in its ancient beauty, striking in its reminder of the genius, mastery, and artistic superiority of white, Western man. Although Ellison's journey was only spiritual, like Baldwin, after the pilgrimage to Gethsemane, he, too, was able to stare "down the deadly and hypnotic temptation to interpret the world and all its devices in terms of race."

"It is quite possible," he writes after the baptism, "that much potential fiction by Negro Americans fails precisely at this point: through the writers' refusal (often through provincialism or lack of courage or opportunism) to achieve a vision of life and a resourcefulness of craft commensurate with the complexity of their actual situation. Too often they fear to leave the uneasy sanctuary of race to take their chances in the world of art."

Such statements do little justice to Brown, Johnson, and Baldwin, who, like Ellison, have not only refused to use race as a sanctuary, but instead have attempted to negate race either by integrating the racial idiom with that of whites, or by obliterating racial characteristics altogether. The narrator of *Invisible Man* is a good example. He is—to be sure—a Rinehart, the identity he assumes near the end of the novel. A man without a distinctive identity, he is all things to all men, and after the excursion through the black world, he retreats to his dungeon to await the coming millennium, when race will have become irrelevant.

"Dr. Johnson," T. S. Eliot wrote of Samuel Johnson, "is a dangerous man to disagree with." The same may be said of Ralph Ellison. For this reason, among others, academic critics have been reluctant to meet the author of *Invisible Man* on his own terms. Ellison traces his literary lineage to the "comic tradition inherent in American literature"—one critic has called him "the Negro Mark Twain"—irrespective of the fact that there is no comic tradition in American literature. There is what can be labeled, at best, a tradition of minstrelsy, slapstick, and buffoonery. In terms of the comic tradition, therefore, it is in Europe, not in America, that Ellison's predecessors must be found; and *Invisible Man*, to get a fair hearing in the court of "mainstream criticism," must be evaluated in light of the comic tradition handed down from Aristophanes through Cervantes to Fielding, Thackery, Dickens, and Meredith.

Dickens, Thackery, and Meredith, England's nineteenth-century masters of the comic tradition, postulated no dichotomy between art and fiction. The Preface to *Joseph Andrews*, by Henry Fielding, is as nationalistic a tract as there is to be found in literature, surpassed, perhaps, only by sections of *The Republic*, and the Preface to *Lyrical Ballads*. The English novelists did not use the novel form to negate their identity as Englishmen. The pride in English cities, churches, and towns, the love for England's cultural past, and the sense of the Englishman as different from other Europeans led Dickens to create his people and his cities.

As a result of English nationalism, a comic tradition was continued and a comic theory was enunciated—a theory to which American writers have only in part been attuned. "Comedy," writes George Meredith, "is an interpretation of the general mind. . . . The comic poet is in the narrow field, or enclosed square of the society he depicts; and he addresses the still narrow enclosure of man's intellect, with references to the operation of the social world upon their characters. . . . To understand his work and value it, you must have a sober liking of your kind, and a sober estimate of our civilized qualities."

The function of comedy—"the perceptive or governing spirit" —is to awaken and give "aim to the powers of laughter." Laughter is, then, the cathartic instrument, capable of deflating egos, of forcing the individual to laugh at himself, and by so doing, force him to relate to others. On this level, comedy is the saving grace—the *deus ex machina* for man and society alike. Instead of laughing themselves to death, men will laugh themselves into greater unity with their fellows.

Meredith, the Englishman, spoke to other Englishmen. His faith in his countrymen led him to believe that they were endowed with that "sensitiveness to the comic laugh [which] is a step in civilization. . . . "We know," he argues at one point, "the degree of refinement in men by the matter they will laugh at; but we know likewise that the larger natures are distinguished by the breadth of their laughter. . . ." Such statements have little relevance in America, where historical racism occasions—in the majority group—contempt instead of understanding, barbarity instead of refinement, and an animosity toward the minority group that renders the term "civilized" obscure and irrelevant.

The lack of an American comic tradition "which feeds upon civilized and sensitive natures" makes Bret Harte so unreadable, Joel Chandler Harris so contemptible, and Mark Twain such a sentimentalist and buffoon. America is the last place to which one would go to find laughter. For instead of being transformed by the comic spirit, Americans, when gazing at the reflection of their egotistical selves, are more likely to be inflated than deflated. Richard Wright knew this very well, and thus there is no laughter in his fiction.

"If my work fails," writes Ellison, "it fails on artistic grounds alone." When *Invisible Man*, like its American mainstream predecessors, is evaluated by the criteria established by England's comic artists, the verdict that Ellison demands can then be rendered. There is, however, an Afro-American comic tradition, as manifested in the works of George Moses Horton, the best of Paul Laurence Dunbar, Langston Hughes, George Schuyler, Wallace Thurman, and Ishmael Reed. In this tradition, despite its assimilationist denouncement, *Invisible Man* ranks high indeed. This will bring little satisfaction to Ellison, who, like Brown, Johnson, and Baldwin, remains wedded to the concept of assimilation at a time when such a concept has ceased to be the preoccupation of the black writer.

"Season it as you will," writes Saunders Redding, "the thought that the Negro American is different from other Americans is still unpalatable to most Negroes. Nevertheless, the Negro is different. An iron ring of historical circumstance has made him so." This difference is manifested in our cultural and social institutions. Although most black institutions are photographic copies of white ones, each has its own uniqueness—white form with black content. An example is the Afro-American church, which though white in form—Methodist, Episcopalian, Baptist—differs in ritual and message.

Black artists of the past expropriated and remodeled the forms of white America to fit the needs of black people. Nowhere is this more evident than in the letters, speeches, and essays of David Walker, Henry Highland Garnet, Charles Remond, and Frederick Douglass. But not all was expropriation! The earliest Afro-American artists—the creators of the spirituals—constructed new forms with which to deal with their racial experiences. Not having been seduced by the scholastic Merlins, they were free from the myth that black manhood was attainable only if one transcended his race and group experiences. ". . . the nationalistic character of the Negro people," wrote Richard Wright, in 1937, "is unmistakable. Psychologically, this nationalism is reflected in the whole of Negro culture, and especially in folklore. Let those who shy at the nationalistic implications of Negro life look at this body of folklore, living and powerful, which rose out of a unified sense of common life and a common fate."

The black writer at the present time must forgo the assimilationist tradition and redirect his art to the strivings within the race—those strivings that have become so pronounced, here, in the latter half of the twentieth century. To do so, he must write for and speak to the majority of black people; not to a sophisticated elite fashioned out of the programmed computers of America's largest universities.

For here we stand, acknowledging those truths we would not admit at the beginning of the twentieth century: that the problem of the color line is insoluble, that the idea of an egalitarian America belongs to the trash basket of history, and that the concept of an American melting pot is one to which sane men no longer adhere. In light of such realities, the literature of assimilationism belongs to the period of the dinosaur and the mastodon.

To return to Richard Wright: "The Negro writer who seeks to function within his race as a purposeful agent has a serious responsibility. In order to do justice to his subject matter, in order to depict Negro life in all of its manifold and intricate relationships, a deep, informed, and complex consciousness is necessary; a consciousness which draws for its strength upon the fluid lore of a great people, and moulds this lore with the concepts that move and direct the forces of history today; . . . a new role is devolving upon the Negro writer. He is being called upon to do no less than create values by which his race is to struggle, live and die. . . ." This is no easy task. To create such values, the writer must undergo a baptism in thought and spirit. He must descend into the pit of the mountain and rise to the top with a clearer vision than before; he must have a greater understanding of the task that lies before him; and above all, if he is to function effectively as a black writer, he must believe with Don L. Lee: "Black! Poet. Black poet am I. This should leave little doubt in the minds of anyone as to which is first. Black art will elevate and enlighten our people and lead them towards an awareness of self, i.e., their blackness. It will show them mirrors. Beautiful symbols. And will aid in the destruction of anything nasty and detrimental to our advancement as a people."

BIOGRAPHIES

WILLIAM E. BURGHARDT DUBOIS (1868–1963) was born in Great Barrington, Massachusetts. He attended Fisk University, Harvard, and the University of Berlin. He received a Ph.D. from Harvard. One of the founders of the NAACP, his long list of accomplishments and publications span over half a century. Among his works are: *The Souls of Black Folk* (1903), *John Brown* (1909), *Darkwater* (1920), *Dusk of Dawn* (1940), and *The World and Africa* (1947).

JAMES A. EMANUEL (1921–   ) was born in Alliance, Nebraska, and educated in the public schools. He received an M.A. from Northwestern University and a Ph.D. from Columbia University. An Associate Professor at the City College of New York, he has written for a number of periodicals and magazines. He is author of *Langston Hughes* (1967) and *The Tree House and Other Poems* (1968), and coeditor of the anthology *Dark Symphony: The Development of Negro Literature in America* (1968).

SARAH WEBSTER FABIO (1928–   ) was born in Nashville, Tennessee. She received her B.A. from Fisk University and her M.A. from San Francisco State. Presently professor of Afro-American Literature at the University of California at Berkeley, she has been widely published in magazines and anthologies. She is currently working on a dictionary of Black language.

HOYT W. FULLER (1927–   ) was born in Atlanta, Georgia. He studied at Wayne University and the University of Florence. Managing editor of *Black World,* he has been published in many journals and periodicals. He is one of the leading voices in the new black literary movement.

ADDISON GAYLE, JR. (1932–   ) was born in Newport News, Virginia, and educated in the public schools. He attended the City College of New York and the University of California. An Assistant Professor of English at the Bernard M. Baruch College, he has written for magazines and periodicals. He is editor of: *Black Expression: Essays by and About Black Americans in the Creative Arts* (1969) and *Bondage, Freedom and Beyond: The Prose of Black America* (1970), and is author of *The Black Situation* (1970).

CAROLYN F. GERALD was born in Lafayette, Louisiana, and educated in the public schools in California. She attended the University of California at Berkeley, where she received a B.A. and an M.A. Her critical essays have appeared in a number of journals.

LANGSTON HUGHES (1902–1967) was born in Joplin, Missouri. He attended Columbia College and Lincoln University. A prolific writer, among his books are: *Not Without Laughter* (1930), *The Big Sea* (1940), *The Dream Keeper* (1932), and *One-Way Ticket* (1947).

LEROI JONES (Ameer Baraka) (1934–   ) was born in Newark, New Jersey, and educated in the public schools. He received B.A. and M.A. degrees from Howard University. One of the most respected black writers, he has written widely in all genres. Among his works are: *Blues People* (1963), *The Dead Lecturer* (1964), *The System of Dante's Hell* (1966), and *Black Revolutionary Drama* (1970).

RON KARENGA is a black nationalist and founder of the militant organization U.S.

W. KEORAPETSE KGOSITSILE is in exile from Johannesburg, South Africa, where he was born. Winner of the Conrad Kent Rivers Memorial Award, his poems and essays have appeared in various journals. He is the author of a collection of poems, *Spirits Unchained* (1970).

JOHN OLIVER KILLENS (1916–   ) was born in Macon, Georgia. He studied law at Columbia University and New York University, in addition to serving in the Armed Forces and working with the National Labor Relations Board in Washington, D.C. A prolific writer, Mr. Killens has written novels, among which are *And Then We Heard the Thunder* (1963) and *Youngblood* (1966); a collection of essays, *Black Man's Burden* (1965); and the movie script for the film *Odds Against Tomorrow* (1959).

DON L. LEE was "born into slavery in 1942." Poet, essayist, and critic, he has been visiting lecturer and writer in residence at Cornell University and Northeastern Illinois State College in Chicago. He has written essays and poems for magazines and periodicals. Among his books are: *Think Black* (1969), *Black Pride* (1968), and *Don't Cry, Scream* (1969).

ALAIN LOCKE (1886–1954) was born in Philadelphia, Pennsylvania, and educated in the public schools. A Rhodes scholar, he attended Harvard College, Oxford University, and the University of Berlin. He received a Ph.D. from Harvard. Professor of Philosophy at Howard University from 1912 to 1925, he was one of the leading intellectuals of the Harlem Renaissance. He is best known as editor of the anthology *The New Negro* (1925).

JULIAN MAYFIELD (1928–   ) was born in Greer, South Carolina, and educated in the public schools. In addition to publishing numerous articles, teaching, and serving on the staffs of two journals, he is author of three novels: *The Hit* (1957), *The Long Night* (1958), and *The Grand Parade* (1961).

ADAM DAVID MILLER was born in Orangeburg, South Carolina, and educated in the public schools. He received an M.A. from the University of California at Berkeley. A lecturer on Afro-American drama and literature, he has been instrumental in founding several black theater groups, among which The Aldridge Players are the best-known. He has written widely for periodicals and magazines.

RONALD MILNER (1938–   ) was born in Detroit, Michigan, educated in the public schools, and attended "nearly every college in the Detroit area . . . without graduating anywhere." He has received grants from the Rockefeller and Whitney foundations, taught at various colleges, and, at present, directs The Spirit of Shango Theatre Co. in Detroit. His best-known plays are: *Who's Got His Own* (1966) and *The Warning—A Theme for Linda*.

LOFTEN MITCHELL was born in Harlem and educated in the public schools. He attended CCNY and Talladega College in Alabama. The author of a history of the theater, *Black Drama* (1967), he is best known as a playwright. Among his productions are: *A Land Beyond the River* (1956) and *The Ballad of the White Soldiers*.

LARRY NEAL (1937–) was born in Atlanta, Georgia. A graduate of Lincoln University, he received an M.A. from the University of Pennsylvania. Poet, critic, and essayist, he has been represented in anthologies as well as periodicals. He is coeditor of *Black Fire* (1969).

JOHN O'NEAL (1940–) was born in Mound City, Illinois, where he attended the public schools. He received a B.A. degree from Southern Illinois University. In addition to working with SNCC, he has published widely in such periodicals as *Negro Digest, American Dialogue,* and *Cavalier*. He is author of the forthcoming book about SNCC *Will the Circle Be Broken?*

DUDLEY RANDALL (1914–) was born in Washington, D.C. He received a B.A. from Wayne University and an M.A. from the University of Michigan. His poems and critical essays have appeared in anthologies and journals. He is editor and publisher of the influential Broadside Press, in Detroit, Michigan.

ISHMAEL REED (1938–) was born in Chattanooga, Tennessee, and educated in the public schools. He attended the University of Buffalo. Poet, novelist, and anthologist, he is the author of: *The Free-Lance Pallbearers* (1967) and *Yellow Back Radio Broke-Down* (1969).

CLAYTON RILEY (1935–) was born in New York City. He was educated in the public schools and graduated from Iona College. Drama critic for *Liberator* magazine, he has also written criticism for various newspapers and journals, including the New York *Times*. He is the author of two television plays: *The Basis of Need* and *The Record Is Twenty-one Minutes*.

J. A. ROGERS (1880–1966) was born in Jamaica, West Indies. He became an American citizen in 1917. In addition to being a war correspondent and a member of the Academy of Political Sciences, he wrote articles for newspapers and magazines. Among his books are: *From Superman to Man* (1917), *World's Greatest Men of African Descent* (1931), and *Sex and Race* (1940–44).

LESLIE B. ROUT, JR. (1936–   ) was born in Chicago, Illinois, and attended the public schools. He received his bachelor's degree from Loyola, M.A. from the University of Chicago, and Ph.D. from the University of Minnesota. A Professor of Latin American History, he is author of *The Politics of the Chaco Peace* (1935–39).

JIMMY STEWART is a poet, musician, and writer who makes his home in Philadelphia, Pennsylvania. Besides the involvement with his musical group, The Kuntu Quintet, he has published widely in a number of periodicals and magazines. Among his articles are: "Revolutionary Nationalism and the Black Artist," *Black Dialogue Magazine* (Winter 1966), and "The Development of the Black Revolutionary Artist," *Black Fire* (1969). He is also contributing editor to *The Cricket* magazine.

DARWIN T. TURNER (1931–   ) was born in Cincinnati, Ohio. He received a B.A. and an M.A. from the University of Connecticut and a Ph.D. from the University of Chicago. He is editor of *Black American Literature—Fiction* (1969) and *Black American Literature—Poetry* (1969).

ORTIZ M. WALTON is currently completing work on a Ph.D. in sociology at the University of California at Berkeley. A teacher of music, he has also played with the Boston Symphony and the Buffalo Philharmonic, and was principal bassist with the Cairo (U.A.R.) Symphony.

RONALD WELLBURN (1944–   ) was born in Bryn Mawr, Pennsylvania. He received a B.A. from Lincoln University and is currently working on a Ph.D. He has written for a number of periodicals and magazines.

RICHARD WRIGHT (1908–1960) was born in Natchez, Mississippi. The best-known black writer, he wrote in all genres. In 1947, he began a self-imposed exile in France. Among his best-known works are: *Native Son* (1940), *Black Boy* (1942), *The Outsider* (1953), and *The Long Dream* (1958).

INDEX